Phillip Noyce

Backroads to Hollywood

Phillip Noyce

Backroads to Hollywood

INGO PETZKE

To Dicken,
Hopefully you'll
be in one of my
movies.
Phillip Noyce.

MACMILLAN
Pan Macmillan Australia

Extracts taken from *Harrison Ford: Imperfect Hero* by Garry Jenkins © 1997 by
Garry Jenkins reprinted by kind permission of Simon and Schuster UK Ltd

First published 2004 in Macmillan by Pan Macmillan Australia Pty Limited
St Martins Tower, 31 Market Street, Sydney

Copyright © Ingo Petzke 2004

National Library of Australia
Cataloguing-in-Publication data:

Petzke, Ingo, 1947– .
Phillip Noyce: backroads to Hollywood.

Includes index.
ISBN 1 4050 3595 1.

1. Noyce, Phillip, 1950– . 2. Motion picture directors and
producers – Australia – Biography. I. Title.

791.430233092

Typeset in 12/15pt Sabon by Post Pre-press Group
Printed in Australia by McPherson's Printing Group

In memoriam

IAN STOCKS
(1942–2002)

**whose idea it was
and
in loving memory of**
PHILIPPA NOYCE
(who started it all)

Contents

INTRODUCTION

It is a strange phenomenon indeed: when you ask someone about director Phillip Noyce, chances are people won't know him. But when you start listing his films they will look awed and say of each, 'Oh, sure, I know that one. Great movie!' In fact, his films are so popular, most of his Hollywood productions have grossed more than US$100 million. An impressive collection of distributors' posters on the walls of his LA office attests to the commercial success of his films. Among them is even a platinum record for the soundtrack of his film *Sliver*. There is no doubt about it: Noyce is one of the masters of mainstream Hollywood movies, particularly in the action genre.

It would be wildly unfair, however, to dismiss Noyce's films as just being 'popular'. The majority of critics, deceived by his mass appeal, seem to have lost track of his achievements and intentions, although a closer view reveals certain notable undercurrents. In his Australian films, for example, Noyce is often at the political edge, particularly concerned with the issues of his home country. Old versus new, gentrification and Americanisation, acknowledgment of the Aborigines, the change of role models, and so on. In his American films, on the other hand, he seems to be nearly obsessed with high-tech equipment, particularly surveillance technology in all its forms. This is most obvious in his Jack Ryan films, *Patriot Games* and *Clear and Present Danger*, but can be found in many others as well. Also typical is his thorough researching of the subject matter of his potential films.

But whatever may be behind his films, Noyce makes no attempt to lecture his audience. He is not a political poster boy. He wants to create entertainment – good, thrilling entertainment. With him we usually see a style that is in love with the power of the film image, and the use of large forces to tell stories for a mass audience. He works with skill and commitment to get the best out of any film project – with sensitive interpretation of the actors' performances and mastery of image composition and *mise en scène*. Noyce has worked with the best actors Hollywood can offer – and quite often has contributed profoundly to their stardom.

All this, and much more, is surely worth a second look. And this is exactly what the following pages are all about: a closer look at the often surprising stories behind these popular films – and at the man who created them but remains somewhat in their shadow. This book is based on extensive interviews conducted with Noyce in Los Angeles and in Australia between 2000 and 2004. Some use is also made of interviews conducted with other film people in his orbit. Written sources have been used only sparingly. Far from attempting to produce a scholarly work on Noyce, the aim was to write as much oral film history as possible. Phillip Noyce lives and breathes film. 'I *am* my films,' he admits frankly.

This book had its beginnings back in January 1999. The small but high-profile Würzburg International Film Weekend, held each year in Germany, had for some years made its special focus Australian and New Zealand films. That year we were successful in staging the first-ever retrospective of Noyce's films. And Ian Stocks, my Australian friend and colleague, who knew Noyce from the days of the Sydney Filmmakers Cooperative, had persuaded the master to come along and present his films in person – easily accessible as Australian directors are. Additionally, I managed to get Noyce interested in talking to my film students at the university. It was a lively affair, quite obviously thoroughly enjoyed by the students and Noyce alike. Ian recorded Noyce's lecture and the subsequent question and answer time on his MiniDV Camcorder. Noyce obviously had a lot to talk about and is a skilled raconteur, and so we were at a loss to understand why no one had yet written at length about this major director.

That evening over a beer, Phillip Noyce, Ian Stocks and I drafted and signed a memorandum of understanding – on a napkin, which is not an easy thing to find in a German pub – outlining Noyce's agreement to let us write this book and granting virtually unlimited access to his archives. Since then, his support has been unfaltering despite the many delays caused by my relocation to Australia, and Ian's marriage breakdown, illness and subsequent death.

It became clear from the outset that this publication would have to be different from any other Australian film book. Some examples of the genre boast fancy covers but are devoid of any substantial content. Others offer analysis of each frame of a film and of each word that is uttered, severely clouding the joy of film perception. Usually, scant attention is paid to the production background, though often this is like a movie in itself, as the following pages will reveal. Despite objections from some academic colleagues who were unable to see what light the director might cast on his own films, we eventually settled on writing a good old-fashioned oral history.

Noyce's commentary is set in bold and constitutes the major body of this publication; this material is composed of answers to questions I have put to him. No particular date is assigned to his remarks. Where his comments were taken from a source other than our interviews, they appear in quotation marks. Wherever possible, additional interviews were conducted with persons who at different stages have played a role in Noyce's professional life. Quotations from other publications and reflections of this author play a secondary role.

Every reasonable effort has been made to check – and double-check – the available information. I hope this book will in future become the benchmark for all factual information regarding Noyce's films and may lead to a new, or at least better, understanding of the man and his work. In outlining the life of an extraordinary person and gifted filmmaker through telling the stories of his films, this book aims to provide enjoyable reading for general audiences, film buffs and serious scholars alike.

The latter groups are catered for with an additional CD-ROM. It contains hundreds of pages of storyboards, a wealth of photographs, the most complete filmography available, and a bibliography listing 1200-plus items. Additionally, it features a chapter on Noyce's work for US television, a couple of remarks about uncompleted projects and a longer version of Chapter 17.

Numerous people helped to make this book possible. Phillip Adams, Shirley Bates, Eric Black, Kirsten Bodenstedt, Babette Büttner, Joseph Buttigieg, Karen Colston, Emma Cooper, Gulcin Cribb, Tom Cowan, Kathy Day, Natalia Gloduniok, Steve Guttormsen, Enno Hermann, Ross Hamilton, Richard Keys, Sergij Kochurin, Marcus Krauss, Kelli Mark, Catherine McGuire, Bruce Molloy, Peter Mudie, Robyn Murray, James Nicholas, Alan Nierob, Anna Nolan, Ben Paterson, David Perry, Jesper Petzke, Karen Rudolph, Margaret Sparks, David Stratton, Jennifer Thompson, Albie Thoms, Ralph Tyrell, Denzel Washington, Rod Webb, Georg Wiesmüller, Sharon Williams, Tim Winton and any I have inadvertently forgotten to list here – as diverse as their contributions may have been: thank you all!

What would this book be without the gallant people who volunteered to be interviewed – sometimes at strange times of the day, in a cab on the way to somewhere else or even on a plane? Gillian Armstrong, Jan Chapman, John Cox, Robert Defoe, Gregor Jordan, Tom Manefield, George Miller, Sam Neill, Mace Neufeld, Philippa Noyce, Tatiana Petrenko, Marc Rosenberg, Jan Sharp, Billy Zane. Bless you!

Noyce's assistants have been invaluable in helping me to come to grips with the nitty-gritty of this publication – even though this seemed to be piled mountain-high over long stretches of time. I am indebted to Laura Burrows, Miranda Culley, Cory McCall and Beatriz Sequeira. Amanda Ladds, my research assistant for too short a time, deserves high praise for her never-faltering enthusiasm and invaluable skill in unearthing material on Noyce.

Trish Lake, my agent, and Tom Gilliatt, my publisher, believed in this project even during the occasional lows, and remained patient when progress was slow. Dubravka Križnjak-Petzke, my beloved wife, succeeded in keeping me focused on this book – not a minor achievement.

But above all I will forever be indebted to Phillip Noyce; a person more humble and professional would be hard to find. What started out as an exuberant idea over some beers in a German pub turned into a serious undertaking because of his willingness to commit. He granted literally unconditional access to his private and professional archives, and provided many important contacts. But he never intervened in any way in the outcome of our research. Forever patient in the face of our sometimes silly, sometimes intrusive and sometimes simply repetitive questions, he gave generously of his time both in front of our mikes and in checking facts and transcripts, while also permitting us to spend time observing him at his work. I feel sure that, like me, he is relieved the ordeal is over.

PHILLIP NOYCE
– THE MAN

Blowing up people ... that's all they want me to do.

'Phillip Noyce is a bear of a man in person – 6'4", with a frame that would make most NFL linebackers cringe.'[1]

An impressive appearance, indeed. Does this mean he is 'larger than life'? As a director in the Hollywood A league: yes, positively. As an individual, however, he is down-to-earth, modest, even 'normal'. He doesn't hide behind agents and assistants; he isn't eccentric or formal in his dress or manner, favouring casual wear even at premiere screenings of his films, and an unobtrusive Lexus over the more flamboyant vehicles usually preferred by his Hollywood peers.

This kind of modesty spills over into his professional life. When watching a film he's made, you won't find fancy opening credits on the screen declaiming 'A Phillip Noyce Film'. Instead he feels that *'directed by* is an ample description'[2] of his achievements. During the many hours of interviews conducted for this book, he would rarely claim sole ownership of his films, preferring to use the plural pronouns 'we' and 'our' over 'me' and 'my'. This is in no way *pluralis majestatis* but rather an acknowledgment of the contribution his team and the crew make to the final product. He is quite adamant that the director cannot take sole responsibility for a film:

A director is totally dependent on their crew. We might wish it were otherwise, but we can't make movies by ourselves. It's true that the dynamic that results from the interaction of the director with the other crewmembers is what makes a great movie, and that the director chooses the cast and crew. But you're nothing without the enormous contribution of everyone else who works on the movie.

While in Los Angeles to interview Noyce I picked up a video cassette in the video store around the corner from the offices of Rumbalara, Noyce's company. Though Rumbalara (named after an Aboriginal word for 'rainbow') keeps an account with the store – as Phillip watches films all the time – the guy at the counter wasn't familiar with the name 'Noyce'. Not once during my stay did I see anyone approach Noyce for an autograph or to have their photo taken with him. Either people don't recognise him, or they are so used to seeing celebrities they just don't bother anymore.

In fact, he turns our idea of the Hollywood lifestyle on its head. It's not about partying until the wee hours of the morning, as the gossipy glamour magazines would have us believe. 'That may partly be true for the actors and is part of their image,' he says. 'But the directors and producers are hardworking businesspeople who can't afford such excesses.' Parties tend to be held during the afternoon or early in the evening, and are over by ten o'clock. These people tend to get up at 5 am and start the day with their personal physical trainer, a tennis match, a few laps in the pool. Over breakfast, they scrutinise a (hopefully) promising script before they head off to the office. During my visit, Noyce never arrived at his Rumbalara office later than 8 am.

Things get even stricter once shooting approaches. 'Preparing to shoot a film is like training to run a marathon,' he explains. Even before he knew what his next project would be, he prepared himself physically. In Los Angeles, he worked out three times a week at the Paramount gym, tried to maintain his optimum weight with a high-protein diet, and saw a nutritionist regularly. He had given up his habit of taking a short afternoon nap and used nicotine chewing gum to try to overcome his three-pack-a-day smoking habit, with limited success.

Staying in good physical condition isn't just a personal choice for Noyce; these days, investors won't entrust big money to a director who hasn't passed a thorough health screening.

In his approach to work, Noyce is incredibly professional – and frankly admits to being a perfectionist, 'unfortunately'. He can spend hours, in deep concentration, developing a script. I was privileged to be present while he worked with the crème de la crème of Hollywood scriptwriters, analysing and developing characters and their motivations in great detail, and constructing or reconstructing plots and subplots. Noyce is always in complete control. He knows every detail of a plot and constantly asks questions that drive both action and characterisation forward. 'Although he doesn't write a word, you can't shut him up about the script,' says scriptwriter Terry Hayes.[3] Noyce's mind is always ticking over. Even when he appears to have finished making a statement, he is likely to interrupt someone else moments later to add something further.

In the interview sessions conducted with Noyce for this book it became obvious that he is a born raconteur, a talented storyteller who knows what he is talking about. And he is gifted with a phenomenal memory. He was quick to see where my queries were leading and to provide answers before I had asked the question. He chose his words carefully, sometimes pausing for several minutes to formulate a response that satisfied him. His concern with explaining himself accurately and fully was shown by the very disciplined approach he took to the interviews; he took no calls, tolerated no interruptions. Whenever aspects of his work came up which he hadn't thought about before, he took his time in answering. In the few instances when he didn't want to answer a question, for whatever reason, he simply chose not to understand it. He is not one to dwell on the past. 'He is the least retrospective person I know,' his wife, Jan Sharp, remarked.[4] He is always looking forward to new projects, reaching towards new shores. Even when he is excited about a new project, he comes across as being self-contained and quite reserved.

Noyce doesn't appear to make enemies. Not once during the preparation of this book did anyone have anything bad to say about him. Director Gillian Armstrong said of him: 'I think that from those rough-and-ready experimental days at the filmmakers co-op he has developed into one of our generation's most sophisticated filmmakers. He did get up there and play at the top of the hill with the big boys, and meet them and beat them. I felt proud that he had got there and done it. Phil was always a great leader, very passionate with a strong sense of humour.'[5]

People who have worked with Noyce, his peers, have only the highest praise for him, while his minders simply adore him. His seemingly unlimited reserves of energy make him radiant. 'He seemed like a magician with his amazing energy which cut through the terrible cold, energising everybody and making it happen,' recalls Rade Šerbedžija[6] of the nightly shots in Moscow for *The Saint*.[7] People who have worked with Noyce on his other films recount similar experiences.

But the characteristic most commonly attributed to Phillip Noyce is generosity. Since his early days of filmmaking he has helped other people to develop and make their films, opening doors for them, acknowledging their contributions to his work. In an era of greed and artistic megalomaniacs, this generosity of spirit shouldn't be taken lightly. 'Whenever I am in Los Angeles we have caught up with each other and he's been very supportive. I've always used him as a resource to check crew or cast or studios that I might have been dealing with,' says Gillian Armstrong.[8]

His even-tempered nature may be another reason for the high regard in which he is held by his peers and employees. Noyce is highly demanding in his professional approach. But it is rare to see him angry over something. Even when he is dissatisfied with a particular performance, he doesn't lose his temper. He is more likely to nudge someone along good-humouredly than resort to confrontation to achieve what he is looking for.

But make no mistake: Noyce is obsessive. 'Phil was always working on something, always editing something. He was very obsessive about film, very engaging and inspiring about it, too. Since the age of eighteen, film has been his intimate way of expressing himself, like breathing,' recalls producer Jan Chapman, Noyce's first wife.[9] And this obsession can pop up in the most unlikely places. 'When I had my first baby,' says Gillian Armstrong, 'he came to visit me in the hospital. My baby was three days old and he brought his daughter, Lucia, who was only about three. I was completely out of it and hadn't been sleeping. He came to see me to talk about some deal. He had this great idea that we could set up a company, he and I and a couple of other filmmakers. And I just didn't know how to get rid of him [*laughs*]. His enthusiasm for this idea and my lack of ability at the time to think about anything but the miracle of my baby was something I remember fondly as being so Phil. He was absolutely swept up in a concept, bubbling with ideas and passion, with blinkers on about anything else. His joy for life and people and film is so contagious, even if sometimes he is like a bull in a china shop. We love him for it.'[10]

It is possible that his trademark energy, enthusiasm and obsessiveness are rooted in his rural upbringing. The world of arts and entertainment is full of individuals who moved from the country to the cities during their early years, only to take the scene by storm. In Noyce's direct professional neighbourhood, Bob Ellis, Don McAlpine and Dean Semler are other examples.

As far as we know, Noyce was only once[11] prepared to try his luck on a comedy: in 1990, he worked on developing the script of a project that would eventually be named *The Adventures of Pluto Nash* and star Eddie Murphy. (Directed by Ron Underwood, it was one of the biggest flops of the year when it was eventually released in 2002.) If there is one genre Noyce isn't too interested in, it's comedy. Yet, that doesn't mean he lacks a sense of humour. He often laughs, though you probably won't catch him cracking jokes. He likes to make puns and has a very fine sense of situational comedy. During our first extended interview session in April 2000, the Nasdaq high-tech stock index dived for five consecutive days, providing a first glimpse of the soon-to-burst tech stock bubble. Each morning upon arrival in his office at around eight o'clock he would grab his iBook and log on, eager to find out what the New York Stock Exchange was up to. We would then discuss our respective share portfolios. One day Noyce suddenly burst out laughing. 'Can you believe this? Here we are, two old hippies, dealing on the stock market!'

Noyce married Jan Chapman in December 1971 and then tied the knot with Jan Sharp in February 1982 after some years spent living together. Noyce is a proud father, frequently mentioning his daughter, Lucia, during our talks. Lucia has followed in her parents' filmmaker footsteps – she was responsible for the 'Making of . . .' documentary for *Rabbit-Proof Fence*. In December 2003 she started working with Amnesty International in Dublin. Stepdaughter Alice works as a props-maker in movies, most recently in P.J. Hogan's *Peter Pan*. For Noyce, 'home' is not a readily accessible concept.

The wonderful thing about making movies is that once you reach a certain level of visibility it doesn't really matter where you live, because as a director you're always going to be shooting somewhere else. And working in foreign countries is one of the gifts.

My family used to come on location as much as possible, because in this business, particularly with the kind of films I was shooting in Hollywood, unless you take them it's no use having a family, as I can be away for a year with pre-production and so on.

On *Dead Calm*, Jan [Sharp] and Lucia lived on tiny Hamilton Island in the Whitsunday Passage of the Great Barrier Reef, off the northeastern coast of Australia. For *The Saint* I rented a house in London and Lucia went to school in England, and eventually we stayed for three years until she finished high school. For the Mexico shooting of *Clear and Present Danger*, we rented John Huston's former house in Cuernavaca outside Mexico City and all lived there.

His Los Angeles home is located right in the centre of old Hollywood and seems to cascade down the slope it's on.

Different buildings and wings house different people – family, friends, visitors. Comfortably stretched out in the guesthouse's bathtub you look straight at the near-mythical Hollywood sign on the opposite hill. Of course, the view of that iconic land-mark is even better from one of the living rooms or most of the terraces and balconies. One of the big rooms is dimly lit and houses only a sofa, from which you can operate the control panel for a stunning video projection system. Like many homes in Hollywood, this one has a pedigree — most prominent of its former owners is the veteran actress Barbara Stanwyck. And the neighbourhood boasts some of the Coppola clan and the director Wim Wenders.

I like the romance of living in the Whitley Heights area of old Hollywood here in Los Angeles, and also that it's a socioeconomic and ethnic mix with rich and poor butting up against each other. So much of the Hollywood movie industry and the city of Los Angeles is very, very segregated.

Unexpectedly, perhaps, there are no maids, cooks or other domestic servants. Instead, we often sat at a small table in the kitchen and ate food Jan had prepared. Afterwards, Phil would wash the dishes. The routine is the same even when more illustrious guests than this author are invited to dinner. Unless it's a barbecue, of course. Then, Phillip, the true-blue Aussie, will take over the cooking and throw another steak on the barbie.

The last three minutes of *Dead Calm* may show the impos-sible resurrection of Hughie Warriner and his second death, but the soundtrack is all food talk. Here we have arguably one of the most sensual food scenes in film history. Nicole Kidman, all wet after a dip in the sea, and sparsely clad in a swimsuit, sits on a chair, head bent backwards with shampooed hair dangling, and her eyes closed in semi-erotic anticipation – the quintes-sential sacrificial lamb. While Billy Zane appears from behind to strangle her, she continues where she had left off when Sam

Neill went to fetch her sumptuous continental breakfast. 'You know what I'd like for lunch? Fresh asparagus. Then, hmm, pasta, angel hair pasta – with heaps of basil, garlic and olive oil. And, hmm, apple pie.'

But Noyce strongly denies being a gourmet. Maybe it is an inadvertent result of his childhood in rural Griffith with its many Italian settlers (even though 'inadvertent' seems an altogether outlandish concept, considering Noyce's concentrated working style). If he were stranded on an isolated island for weeks, the food he would most want to eat upon his return to civilisation would be one of his own barbecued steaks. But as a true wanderer of the world, his tastes aren't confined to homemade delicacies. Noyce particularly likes tasty Asian food – mostly Thai and Indian – but is open to other cuisines as well. He is a regular customer of cheap little restaurants as well as fancy ones. During working hours, there seems to be a certain pattern: he only goes out to eat for a business lunch. Otherwise he prefers to have simple food on the premises, like everyone else at Rumbalara – though they never seem to take their lunch together.

With wine, however, it is a different story. Noyce is known in the industry as a true connoisseur and he prefers a good bottle of Australian wine to all others. During my stay, we had some palate-tickling encounters with wines I'll probably never be able to afford – but maybe that is one of the perks of being a Phillip Noyce biographer. He has built a wine cellar in his Los Angeles office, though this idea met with some initial ridicule from family and friends. The year 2004 will see the first vintage of the Australian Old Byora Vineyard he runs with his two brothers.

To finish off the menu, Noyce likes good Italian coffee. The authentic three-tiered macchiato is his favourite.

Obviously, Noyce watches a lot of movies. He is constantly on the lookout for promising, talented actors, but is also interested to see what the current trends in the industry are and where the cutting edge of creativity and storytelling is. Like everyone else, he has personal favourites – *Apocalypse Now* by

Francis Ford Coppola (but he considers the *Redux* version a waste of energy); *Il Conformista* by Bernardo Bertolucci; and *Salvador* by Oliver Stone – though, like any list, it is subject to change. In their private life the Noyces keep a certain distance from 'showbiz' people and prefer to make friends in the 'real' arts world. Among this illustrious bunch is J.G. Ballard, the English science-fiction novelist of the New Wave era, and the recently deceased photographer Helmut Newton, who for some time was their neighbour when they originally lived at the Chateau Marmont hotel in Los Angeles.

Noyce's second love in the creative arts, however, is music. He has been awarded a platinum record from Virgin Music for sales of more than one million copies of the soundtrack of *Sliver*, which contained four number 1 hits. Once in a while he gets invited on radio shows such as *Castaway's Choice* or *soundbreak.com*, for which he has to choose ten songs to be played in between interviews. Some choices seem typical of a man of his generation, such as the 1965 hit 'Eve of Destruction' sung by Barry McGuire; others are more unexpected, such as Frank Sinatra's 'High Hopes'. He always seems to choose some Ryuichi Sakamoto or something completely unusual, such as Javanese gamelan music. The last item on his list, Cheb Mani's 'H'bai', proved a hard nut to crack for one station. Though they finally got hold of it, Phil brought his own copy of the CD along – just in case. In general, the lists show he is very into music right to this day: 'It keeps me young,' he says.

With his hectic schedule, time for other kinds of intellectual stimuli is usually scarce. Time permitting – as a castaway, perhaps – he would be curious to explore Buddhism 'just to see what all the fuss is about' or to re-read *Great Expectations*, ''cause it's such an emotional adventure story'.

Noyce's career has taken him around the world – he has lived in glitzy Los Angeles, cosmopolitan New York and cultural motherland London. Still, he has managed to remain, in many respects, an Aussie. Maybe that is where his egalitarianism stems from. His New York apartment doesn't overlook Central Park, but is located in bustling SoHo in lower Manhattan. (In fact, the view from the apartment looks pretty much like that from Lincoln Rhyme's room in *The Bone Collector*.) During a visit to his Rumbalara offices in LA, I noticed two vagrants had taken up 24/7 residence on the grass under a nearby shady tree. I never saw Noyce enter or leave the premises without at least giving them a wave, exchanging a couple of friendly words or slipping them some coins. Two outcasts of an affluent society, acting kind of as true guardians of the compound.

Overseas for the first time back in the seventies and meeting so many Europeans, I felt they were almost straightjacketed, gagged by all the great artists over all of the centuries of European civilisation that had come before, compared to we Australians who had just been born, whose eyes had just been opened. We were free to do anything because there was no tradition to hold us back. We didn't have Manet, Monet, Rousseau and so on, looking over our shoulders. I think the reason the new wave of Australian films in the early 1970s were distinctive was because they followed their own rules and there was a real freedom about the way in which they made movies. I don't mean technical freedom; I just mean that we were not constipated.

This freedom also came from growing up in a country without a continuous movie-making tradition, with no expectation of a career in the cinema. Therefore, everything that happened and every movie that generation ever made was a gift – you are winning a prize, which is the ability to work in cinema. This was a dream, a stupid, impossible dream for an eighteen-year-old Australian in 1968. So, when I'm making a film costing US$70 million, I don't have nightmares or think about money or anything like that. It's just the same as when we were back there in the film co-op in the early seventies shooting a little movie on the weekend to screen on Sunday. Perhaps someone from a different culture may have grown up with a different set of expectations about a career in the cinema, and a different set of responsibilities towards the money they are given to make movies with. But for me, it's all been a gift.

A tyranny of distance existed before the advent of fax machines, satellite communication and the Internet, and it came from being way down there at the bottom of the world. But I still feel we suffer from that tyranny, which in the case of cinema is not a tyranny but a freedom, because we look at everything through the filter of South Pacific sunglasses. Our interpretation of characters and situations on the screen is different. There is also a strong tradition of humanism in Australia, and a strong concept of egalitarianism. When I went to Hollywood the strangest thing on set was called a director's chair. You know, those chairs that directors sit on. I realised there was a guy whose job it was just to move my chair. In Australia we never had a chair – we used to sit on a box, begged from the grip department and loaned begrudgingly.

Regarding other aspects of being Australian, Noyce isn't so sure. How does it feel, I ask him, to be in his homeland again after so many years in Hollywood, being embraced as a kind of lost son who has come back with all the credentials, and suddenly being a major figure in Australian cultural life?

It's gratifying after being a sideshow in America, where you're making films that entertain a lot of people but are not really taken seriously as art or history. In some ways I feel connected back here in Australia, but in other ways not.

'Connected' in as much as I understand the values. But disconnected because those values can sometimes seem rather parochial. People looking at the world with blinkers on, and not able to take a wider view. That's not a bad thing, it's just that in some ways I left to escape that, feeling I understood the culture and what it had to offer – and it was time to charge up the batteries. Coming back to Australia, in turn, has been a recharging as I've had the pleasure of reconnecting with my beloved homeland as if falling in love for the first time. But occasionally I feel depressed here in Australia [laughs]. Depressed just by the thought, 'Is that all there is?' [laughs]. Whereas when you're in America you may not be any closer to reality but you never say, 'Is that all there is?' [laughs]. It's such a dynamic and impossibly fucked-up, complicated culture.

The film industry exists in its own tiny fishbowl in Australia, like a dysfunctional family who spend as much time fighting each other as the real enemy. Whereas in America – and Britain to a lesser degree, but certainly more than here – there is enough diversity of opportunity so that people are constantly fixed on the real target of their relationship with the audience. Here, everyone seems in competition with everyone else. Getting out of that dog-eat-dog arena into a meritocracy was certainly a relief.

During their ten years in the United States, Phil's wife, Jan Sharp, was frequently asked by Australians when Phil would finally start making the films he really wanted to make (meaning the generally more personal films Noyce had made earlier in his career in Australia). She would always reply that high-tech spy films *were* what he really liked to make – and was good at making. Still, there was a barely discernible but growing discomfort with the formula, which saw Noyce move to Universal after declining a contract with Paramount, and drop out of *The Sum of All Fears* to instead take up *Rabbit-Proof Fence* and, subsequently, *The Quiet American*. These decisions must have cost Noyce millions of dollars in the short term, but they restored some personal freedom and made a statement about his artistic integrity, which may ultimately prove even more financially beneficial.

Blowing up people and spying on people: that's all they want me to do – but I'm a bit tired of that. I'd like now to move freely between two types of movie and both countries, enjoying the best of Australia and the US. I don't know if dropping out of *The Sum of All Fears* will affect my relationship with the studios. I mean, I did my dues in that system. I had a great time making all those movies, being on the inside, not an outsider – exposed first-hand to the way the Hollywood factory operates at every level – and, you know, that was fascinating.

In theory, for a few years at least, I can go back. I fell into that Hollywood career, into those big-budget projects, but you don't want to be captive to that world and its values. I'm no longer in prison.

Hopefully, because I served my sentence, I've been let out for good behaviour.

Noyce is no political animal, at least not in terms of prevailing party politics in Australia. But he can't remain uninvolved, as the usually ill-grounded assaults of writers Phillip Adams has labelled 'right-wing *agents provocateurs*'[12] – Akerman, Bolt and co. – in several newspapers show. Also, it is no secret that he is less than happy with John Howard's government – given his battle-cry of 'Hands off our film industry'.[13] But Noyce's political stances are essentially ethical ones and could be labelled truly liberal – not in the sense of the term that has been usurped by the conservatives in Australia. The latest indicator of his sensibility was his involvement in the dismal *Ken Park* censorship case.[14]

His political attitudes were widely acknowledged when Noyce was nominated as 'Australian of the Year' in *The Australian* newspaper. Parts of the nomination letter of 26 December 2002 read: 'In his determination to get the films made (particularly *Rabbit-Proof Fence*) and his struggle to get them released (particularly *The Quiet American*) Noyce displayed virtues which until recently have been acknowledged as typically Australian: open-mindedness and a deeply humanitarian approach; compassion for the oppressed and disadvantaged; resisting political authorities here and abroad; battling for historical facts in the face of right-wing whingeing and political jingoism.' As *The Australian* put it, 'By way of these two films Noyce has not only resurrected his artistic integrity but he also transformed into an Australian icon – both at home and abroad.'[15]

Even though the looming shadows of the 2002 Bali bombings prevented serious consideration of his nomination, it illustrates what a long way Noyce had come in a short time to become, as he had been before his departure for Hollywood in 1990, an integral part of the Australian collective consciousness. It is little wonder that by the end of 2002 Noyce was considered, by far, the single most influential individual in the

Australian film industry, and number thirteen among an impressive list of 'Australia's most influential entertainers'.[16]

On 11 May 2002 *The Australian*[17] newspaper reported Rumbalara's official announcement that Tim Winton's *Dirt Music* would be one of Noyce's next projects. 'Set in the wild landscape of Western Australia, this is a novel about the odds of breaking with the past, a love story about people stifled by grief or regret, whose dreams are lost, whose hopes have dried up. It's a journey across landscapes within and without, about the music that sometimes arises from the dust', the book's dust jacket tells us. It sounds inviting, but definitely unlike anything Noyce has tackled so far. So why is he determined to make this film?

Well, it's a love story; that's what I like about it. Also, I like Western Australia. I think it is a new frontier. I like the way in which the story reflects parts of vanishing Australia, the wilderness areas. And I think the female character in the story [Georgie Jutland] is very interesting – independent, self-determined, searching. You know, I recognise her; I've seen her in real life. A woman who is almost 40 but who still hasn't been able to satisfy herself, caught between settling down and searching. Not content to accept the traditional female roles.

All this sounds challenging, indeed. In fact, the character of Georgie Jutland so dominates the novel, it would seem impossible that she won't be the first real heroine in any Noyce film – despite his repeated efforts to label most of his films as 'love stories'.

Winton is 'delighted Noyce wants to do *Dirt Music*. I like his early films and think he's a real talent. Only met him once but was amazed by his energy and his generosity and sensitivity during the release of *Rabbit-Proof Fence*. He strikes me as a pro, which is a relief in an industry that's 90% bullshit and 10% insurance (in Australia 50% subsidy and 50% PR).'[18]

But the dust jacket of the novel continues: '*Dirt Music*

confirms Tim Winton's status as the pre-eminent Australian novelist of his generation.'[19] And I am tempted to believe this is what Phillip Noyce is ultimately up to: becoming the pre-eminent Australian film director of his generation, Australian and cosmopolitan, versed in low-budget and monster-budget films alike, successful with escapist entertainment as well as films dealing with social issues. A suave A league citizen of planet Hollywood who domestically acts as a voice in the wilderness. But, in any case, a respected Australian voice to the world – an Australian icon.

The odds of his achieving this goal aren't too bad at all.

---

[1] Alex Simon, 'The art of Noyce', *Venice*, November 1999.

[2] Email dated 16 June 2003.

[3] Quoted in Scott Murray (ed.), *Back of Beyond: Discovering Australian Film and Television* (Sydney: Australian Film Commission, 1988), p. 47.

[4] Jan Sharp interview.

[5] Gillian Armstrong interview.

[6] He anglicised his name to 'Sherbedgia' after leaving his native Zagreb for good.

[7] *The Saint* press kit, p. 7.

[8] Gillian Armstrong interview.

[9] Jan Chapman interview.

[10] Gillian Armstrong interview.

[11] Noyce considers even *Blind Fury* to be a comedy–action film.

[12] D.D. McNicoll and Emma-Kate Symons, 'Barns makes bolt for ABC', *The Australian*, 9 December 2002.

[13] Lynden Barber and Sophie Tedmanson, 'Noyce to PM: Hands off our film industry', *The Australian*, 7 December 2002.

[14] Dated 4 July 2003, Lynden Barber in *The Australian* quoted Noyce as being 'shocked' by the banning of the film at the Sydney Film Festival. The film had been shown at two festivals in North America in 2002, where Noyce didn't watch it. '[But] this was my choice, and one that all Australians should be able to make for themselves.'

[15] Ian Gerard, 'A movie director of artistic integrity', *The Australian*, 28 December 2002.

[16] 'Who's Weekly', *Gold Coast Bulletin*, 13 December 2002.

[17] Layla Tucak, 'Noyce to put *Music* on film', *The Australian*, 11 May 2002.

[18] Letter to the author dated 29 January 2003.

[19] Tim Winton, *Dirt Music* (Sydney: Picador, 2001).

Part I

AUSTRALIA
(1950–1989)

Capturing images of our own life

Chapter 1
THE EARLY YEARS

*I grew up almost never hearing an Australian voice
on the cinema screen.*

Phillip Roger Noyce was born a fourth-generation Australian
on 29 April 1950 in Griffith, in the Riverina district of New
South Wales.

On my father's side the family is part-German, part-Irish. The
Germans and the Irish both arrived in Australia in the mid-
nineteenth century. My great-grandfather, Georg Neuss, came from
Wetterfeld near Oberhausen in northern Germany. He arrived in
Melbourne in 1863, supposedly both to escape the military draft
and to join the gold rush at Ballarat in Victoria. But the gold had
been worked out by then, so he continued his trade as a wheel-
wright and married Mary Ann McKendrey in 1871. On my
mother's side it's a combination of English, French and other parts
of the United Kingdom. Her mum's family came from the UK in the
early part of the nineteenth century and took up land-holdings in
the Hunter Valley of New South Wales and the north of Queensland, and they were part of the famous Wright family. The most
well-known member is Judith Wright, the Australian poet, a distant
relative, who retells the early family history in her 'faction' novel
The Generations of Men [1959]. My maternal grandfather was a
minister of the Church of England who came to Australia to spread
the gospel in the early part of the twentieth century and then
married one of the Wright girls.

My father was born on a farm, and I grew up on one. He met my
mother literally on the eve of going to war in 1940, after volunteering

for the Australian infantry forces serving overseas. She was training as a nurse and living in a bedsit, sharing a one-roomed apartment in Kings Cross, Sydney, with my father's sister, who was also a nurse. So the two nurses would work alternate shifts – twelve hours on, twelve hours off – and share the one bed. One particular night my mother came home and found a very large man lying on that bed. They both knew who the other was from the sister and the friend. And it was decided that ownership of the bed for the evening should be settled by the toss of a penny. He won and two days later left on the *Queen Mary* for the Middle East and the war against Germany. They were engaged to be married an hour before he sailed. He didn't return for two-and-a-half years, and then only for a few weeks, but during that time they married. Then he shipped out again to fight the Japanese in New Guinea and eventually returned to his family and young son, my older brother, Michael. He became a lawyer and chose to live in the country town of Griffith. My mother was a housewife and later in life she became a make-up artist in film and television. When I started making films she decided that she would join me and she in fact did the make-up for *Heatwave* and *Backroads*.

'Griffith is a small town in the southwest of New South Wales. It is surrounded by a desert but due to the marvel of irrigation is actually an oasis of citrus growing. It is unusual for an Australian country town because half of the population, in fact more, are of Italian origin and . . . the farms around the town are not thousands of acres like most Australian properties, but 20 acres. So I grew up on a farm; my father was a lawyer, although he had a thousand chickens and 600 orange trees, because he was a farmer who became a lawyer but couldn't quite give up farming . . . [As] a lawyer to so many of the new arrivals from Italy, we were often paid in produce, so it was a marvellous existence as a child . . . eating this lovely salami, and even drinking the great wines they made for us, and the fresh bread that came over from the adjoining farm every morning.

'We were three boys. One is now an ear, nose and throat specialist, which comes in handy, and it will do when I finally get throat cancer. The other one is a lawyer, which also comes in handy, as I've been divorced and so on.'[1]

The best day of the week was Saturday 'cause you got to play football in the morning and go to the cinema in the afternoon. I went to the Lyceum Theatre most Saturday afternoons. I loved movies because I could escape into the stories. And it wasn't just about watching the movies; it was also a chance to swap comic books. Everyone would collect comics in those days, and before the show, during interval and afterwards we would swap them.

I saw three films set in Australia that I particularly remember: *Smiley* and *Smiley Gets a Gun*, and another one in the late fifties called *Robbery Under Arms*. All three films were actually made by English directors. *Robbery Under Arms* I can still remember being startled by, because it was an Australian setting with Australian voices – but also Australian bird life. It was unusual to hear the sound of the kookaburra and the galah up on the silver screen.

The three-day agricultural show was the biggest event of the year. My parents used to give us one pound – most of the tent shows cost two shillings. Together with a battered sav – a frankfurter on a stick in batter – and a drink and so on, it would cost four shillings. And the boxing, which you *had* to see, Jimmy Sharman's troupe, was four shillings as well. So you could go to six or seven shows before you ran out of money. After that, the only way into other shows was either to sneak under the tent, which sometimes you were lucky enough to do, or to offer yourself as a stooge. A stooge was a local lad who would be used for what was often the best show, the show outside the tent where the spruiker would try to drum up some business to get people inside. And I always used to offer to be a part of that.

I remember this man and woman running a show called 'The Roaring Twenties'. She wasn't very tall and she had this great big sword. The guy says to me, 'Stick your tongue out.' He takes a bit of paper an inch long and puts it on the end of my tongue. The woman raises up this big sword, brings it down and cuts the paper in half. The audience goes, 'Uuuhhhh!' – you know, everyone screamed. And, of course, all I could think was, 'Wow, that's great!' I wasn't worried about my tongue, which I should have been; all I could think was, 'Wow, the audience are all involved in that moment.' In the months until the next agricultural show I would put on my own tent shows. I would make a ghost train, and get the local kids to come around.

The other major events were the Bullen's and Wirth's circuses. The famous Wirth's Circus arrived in town on a train. Griffith was the end of the line. The Wirth family had their own wonderful carriages, with bedrooms and dining rooms. And then they would set up a tent beside the railway line. I would go down there and look in those carriages. I wanted to run away with them, get on that train, travel around, put on a show.

When I earned my entry to the 'Roaring Twenties' tent show, they had this act with a young girl. A guy took a .22 rifle and had some local in the crowd load the gun with live bullets, and then he fired at the young girl. A mirror behind her cracked and she collapsed, revealing a thick pad in front of her stomach. The trick was intended to convince the audience that the bullet had passed through her body, whereas unbeknown to them it was meant to be caught in the pad. She was fifteen years old. She had run away with the circus from the nearby town of Leeton, got 37 miles and ended up in hospital, with a .22 bullet lodged in her tummy.

All of that stuff was the inspiration for my film school short *That's Show Biz*. But it was also inspiration for a life in the circus, which is all that we do, really. We are just circus people. To a certain degree in this business you can just continue being kids. You know, make-believe, dressing up people and putting on a show; in a sense, each cinema becomes a tent.

'I went to primary school in Griffith up to twelve years of age and then my family moved to Sydney . . . I went to an all-boys Church of England, or Episcopalian, school called Barker College on the outskirts of Sydney. My father bought a small farm about 80 miles away,[2] so my mother and father were now equidistant from their hearts. My mother's heart was . . . in the middle of the city where she had grown up and my father's heart was an hour and a half the other way, north, on his little farm . . . [He] now has 200 beef cattle and a 10-acre winery and he still hasn't quite cleared the farm of trees. I think that is going to be a life-long project.

'Sure, you get a kick out of big city life . . . I think that city people often are too cynical, too suspicious, not open enough, whereas country people – because of the nature of the place – we never locked a door, you never denied a stranger help. It was a different code of ethics in your dealings with people, and that is not appropriate to living in many cities of the world, including Sydney, but nevertheless some of those country attitudes are helpful in life in general. To have perhaps a more laidback attitude.

'. . . I was happy to be in the city because the alternative was that I would have been in the city anyway, but I would have been a boarder living in a dormitory . . . and probably I would have suffered some of the same anxieties that my brother described in the pitiful letters he sent home to us through his four years of incarceration in this boys' boarding school . . . Every night we would wait for the . . . latest letter from my brother describing his mournful experiences, and how he just lay in his bed with the blankets covering him and cried himself to sleep because he was locked up in this dreadful prison.'[3]

After we moved to Sydney we often went to the drive-in cinema. I remember seeing Hayley Mills films – and, in particular, a marvellous adventure story called *Elephant Walk* – but the biggest impression was left by *Psycho*. That was a very scary film for a young teenager in the early sixties, 'cause the movie had been preceded by an inflammatory advertising campaign with lines like 'Nobody will be admitted after the first 15 minutes.' You were led to believe that you would be lucky to survive the screening – so terrifying was the experience that was promised.

I didn't know it then, but I was already interested in the thriller genre. The Hitchcock films were an event, each one of them, that you remembered because they affected you so greatly when you watched the films. They were working on deep psychological levels to disturb you.

I was mainly watching American and British films because, even though we had enjoyed a thriving domestic film industry through to the late 1930s, now there was almost no film industry in Australia. The theatres and means of distribution were all foreign-owned, principally by American companies showing their own product, and it became a chicken-or-egg situation. The distributors would say that no one wanted to see Australian movies, and the would-be film-makers would say, 'You don't *let* them see Australian movies!' Occasionally a French film turned up at the art-house Savoy Theatre, or a Russian movie, thanks to Soviet sponsorship. But I grew up almost never hearing an Australian voice on the cinema screen.

There has always been a strong sense of Australian nationalism. We have always felt very, very different to everyone else in the world, probably because we are an island at the bottom of the world and your sense of identity is increased by that isolation. I think Australia, until quite recently, has always suffered from what we call 'the tyranny of distance' – we're separated from each other, from the mother country of England and from the cultural mother country of America. English newspapers and American magazines were very coveted objects when I grew up; even if we didn't receive them until months after publication, they were still very precious.

I started to become interested in theatre while I was at high school in Hornsby and I acted in a number of plays. Then, in my last year, I adapted a couple of novels for the stage and we performed these at lunchtime in front of the other kids. We did an adaptation of Arthur Conan Doyle's *The White Company* but it didn't go over well. The other kids just laughed at us up there in tights. But I did like being up on the stage.

Contrary to claims in some publications,[4] Noyce in his youth never shot films in 8-millimetre, let alone owned such a camera.[5] In fact, unlike many other directors-to-be, he didn't slip gradually into the world of film. His interest was awoken by an experience that would change his life forever.

In August 1968, a few months before I was due to graduate from high school, I ventured into the inner-city area from my middle-class suburb of Wahroonga. I saw a poster on a telegraph pole advertising American 'underground' movies. There was a mesmerising, beautiful blue-coloured drawing on the poster that I later discovered had been designed by an Australian filmmaker called David Perry. The word 'underground' conjured up all sorts of delights to an eighteen-year-old in the late sixties: in an era of censorship it promised erotica, perhaps; in an era of drug-taking it promised some clandestine place where marijuana, or even something stronger, might be consumed; in an era of confrontation between conservative parents and their affluent post-war baby boomer children, it promised a place where one could get together with other like-minded youth and plan to undermine the establishment, which at that time seemed to be the aim of just about everyone aged under 30.

My parents grew up in the Depression followed by the Second World War and all their generation wanted to do after that was buy a house, have three children and live very quietly. And so all *their* children wanted to do was *not* live in a house in the suburbs, *not* live quietly. Those conservative values had to be completely rejected.

'[So] in early September 1968 I joined a sold-out crowd at the Union Theatre and there I saw seventeen short films assembled by Ubu [Films]. And on that night I guess my whole attitude to art, my whole attitude to movies – in fact, my whole life – changed.'[6]

I went there for vicarious thrills and watched these seventeen movies[7] and then listened afterwards in the foyer to the guys promoting the screening. And I left the cinema that night thinking, 'I'm gonna make movies like that. I can do it.' Here was a style of cinema that seemed to speak to me. It was immediate, it was direct, it was personal, and it wasn't industrial. It was executed for personal expression, not for profit; it was individual as opposed to corporate, it was stylistically free, it seemed to require very little expenditure, innovation being the key note. It was a completely un-Hollywood-like aesthetic; it was operating on a visceral level that was often non-linear and was akin to the psychedelic images that were in vogue at the time – whether it was in music, in art or just in the patterns on your multicoloured shirt. These movies spoke to me.

The term 'underground movies' came from a *Time* magazine article published in 1968 entitled 'Up from the Underground'. This was an anti-Hollywood movement relying on the advent of portable cameras, which could be hand-held, as opposed to the great big machines needed for Hollywood films, and also relying on fast film stock like Kodak 4X film, which eliminated the need for expensive artificial lighting.

In America, in particular, a group of filmmakers emerged in the 1950s and flourished in the 1960s who weren't making films to feed a distribution network, but just for personal expression. And they formed cooperatives to distribute these movies. In New York, Jonas Mekas, who made *The Brig*, and his brother, Adolphus Mekas, started the New York Film Makers' Co-operative, and then there was a cooperative in San Francisco, the Canyon Film Makers' Co-operative.

What I saw was a group of films made frequently for next to nothing. I think the cheapest one cost ten dollars. None of them featured anything that you would associate with Hollywood production standards, and they weren't the product of some Los Angeles sausage factory churning them out for hungry consumers all around the world.

I could also see immediately from the packed cinema that Ubu Films were promoting a certain type of movie to a certain subculture of artsy-fartsy people. It seemed that you could get anyone to pay money even for extreme entertainment, as long as you advertised it in the right way.

'... I hung around the Union Theatre for several nights and I picked up a lot of literature, leaflets and newspapers, and various things that had been left there by the guys from Ubu. And I worked out that the leading lights in this Ubu Films seemed to be three guys – Aggy Read, Albie Thoms and David Perry ... [They] all had beards and ... seemed to come from the basement of a terrace house in Redfern. Watching those movies that night, picking up all this information, I was immediately seized by three great ambitions. First of all, I wanted to grow a beard; secondly, I wanted to live in a terrace house in the inner city; and thirdly, I wanted to be a filmmaker.'[8]

In the determined fashion so typical of Noyce, after his epiphany he immediately made contact with 'the guys from Ubu', the acknowledged gurus of underground film in Australia. Remembers Thoms: 'He visited our office in Redfern to arrange a screening of my films at Barker College, his school. I remember him coming into the office in his school uniform and banging his head on the stairwell because of his height, dislodging his straw hat. It is notable that the school film screening was to raise funds for an Aboriginal kindergarten, and that the school censored some of the films.'[9] Noyce would from then on regularly attend the weekly meetings organised by the young filmmakers.

I discovered there were a lot of people like me who wanted to make short films, for personal expression, but also as a form of nationalism. We wanted to capture images of our own life, Australian images. We wanted to make Australian movies. Aggy, Albie and David encouraged everyone to go and make a film for themselves.

Five months later, during the holidays between graduating from high school and entering university, I got a job digging sewerage ditches for the Water Board in Sydney. The job allowed me to save money to make a short film. During those holidays I went to other screenings and sort of started working with those guys. They also had a company who put on light shows.

They started printing an alternative-culture newspaper called *Ubu News*. Another way I financed my first film was by selling that newspaper, and I was sort of the best *Ubu News* salesman. In fact, I got arrested for selling it. There was an ad in one of the issues for Levi's jeans, and it showed a guy trying to put his Levis on his head, so his penis was showing, and that was judged by the police to be obscene. I was found guilty and given a suspended sentence, a bond for a year or something, for publishing an indecent publication. In his address to the magistrate, the prosecutor even mentioned *Phil's Pill*.

This was my own newspaper. For a few months I was speaking in the Domain. The Domain is like Speakers' Corner in London. On Sundays a number of speakers would go to the area in front of the Art Gallery of New South Wales and set up their boxes or step-ladders and just speak on any topic. It was a great Sunday afternoon entertainment to go down and debate with them. There was one guy called Webster, who was quite famous because he was a great raconteur; he also sold a newspaper each Sunday. I saw how many newspapers he was selling, and thought, 'Well, this is a good idea. I'll have my own newspaper.' So I started to publish *Phil's Pill*. The idea was that you would speak for a couple of hours, but what you really wanted to do was sell your paper, which cost a cent each to produce but you would sell them for twenty cents. And you could sell 500 of them. It was quite a good business. So, every Sunday for a couple of months, we would do that.

I realised that the people who attended were there to be entertained as well. The second Sunday I went back, I noticed that people were sitting where I had spoken the week before and were waiting for me. I thought, 'This is amazing – people will listen to anything.' Basically, the philosophy I was espousing was one that was partly true passion – such as anti-police and anti-censorship statements – and partly invented for effect. It was made up in order to offend people, because that was the way you could sell newspapers. If you could upset someone in the audience, then you could get a debate going and also fill in maybe half an hour while your sellers peddled some more newspapers. For example, one tactic that I found was very, very good for business was to advocate that anyone aged over 60 who wasn't productive should be executed. Of course, all the old people would get up and start yelling and screaming. And we'd sell even more papers.

I had to give it up because the police came to arrest me after I published some erotic poems that I'd taken from the *Penguin Collection of Erotic Poetry*. I had heard on one of the talkback radio shows some parents complaining about my newspaper, which their kids had bought. I knew my time was up when I heard that. So, the next Sunday I didn't turn up and, sure enough, the cops were there in force. Still, I managed to publish six or eight issues, and to avoid being arrested again.

Noyce is here referring to his earlier arrest in November 1969 'for selling "an indecent item"' (a copy of *Ubu News* No. 12) at an inner city railway station as Mudie[10] records. According to Noyce, however, this happened outside a suburban dance hall.

He was found guilty and released on a good behaviour bond without a conviction being recorded.

In the meantime I had approached some friends and told them that if they invested in my film, they could have an acting role. Unfortunately, the guy whose dad had the most money – he was a doctor's son – was also maybe the worst actor that was ever put in front of a camera. But he had invested 400 dollars, so I had to give him the lead. Strangely enough, he was called David Frost, but was no relation to David Frost the English interviewer and raconteur. The title of my film was *Better to Reign in Hell*, taken from Milton's *Paradise Lost* ('Better to reign in hell than serve in heaven'). Essentially the film was the story of a young man's obsession with a woman who he sees repeatedly in advertising and the hallucinogenic dreams he has about her, which may or may not be real. It was a film very much inspired by the images, the montage and narrative techniques of the underground movies that I'd seen at the Ubu screenings.

I had decided that I couldn't shoot the film because I didn't know how to use a camera. (I realised later that there's not a lot to loading the camera and exposing film.) I hired David Perry, who had photo-graphed a lot of Albie Thoms's films, as my cameraman and paid him 25 dollars a day for the three-day shoot. I also hired Clemency Weight, who had appeared in Albie Thoms's movies, to play the woman of the hero's obsessions and to run naked along a beach.[11]

The film cost about 600 dollars to make and was shot in 16-millimetre black and white.

Despite its later reputation, the film was relatively mundane. Being shot in black and white, it lacks the typical psychedelic ingredients of the time and is reminiscent of the surrealistic pre-decessors to underground film. Some contempt for the prevailing consumer society is thrown in for good measure. 'A youth is per-secuted by the haunting reappearance of a girl's image in various commercial outlets. He finds escape from this commercial brain-washing only in his own confused sexual hallucinations.'[12] *Honi Soit*, Sydney University's undergraduate student newspaper, assists: 'A penetration into the paranoia developing in the hum [sic!] subconscious as a result of utter obsession with image, forcibly intensified by the medium of advertising.'[13] But except for the excellent advertising that so convincingly captures the 'hint! hint!' mood of the time, Noyce's first film isn't really outstanding even in terms of experimental film.

'I was able to show it in Australia, but unfortunately it was banned from export. Well, up until the election of the Labor Socialist Government in 1972 . . . Australia was ruled by one party for 23 years and by one man for sixteen of those 23. The party was the Liberal Party, and they weren't liberal, I can tell you. The equivalent, I guess, of the Republican Party in America, and the man was Sir Robert Menzies, a royalist through and through. We suffered the worst censorship of almost any Western country in the world, even worse than South Africa. Books would be seized by customs officers at the airports and when ships docked. Customs would be looking for *Lady Chatterley's Lover*. We were very censored in literature and films and plays, and my film was banned from export. I tried to send it to a film festival in Holland and it was denied an export permit [by the Australian censors, who checked films entering and leaving the country. However,] because it had been shot in Australia . . . until someone in the audience complained, it could still be screened locally [without being subject to censorship].'[14]

I was studying law at Sydney University, but I was more interested in being on the main campus near inner-city Glebe than at the high-rise law school, which was located downtown adjacent to the law courts on Phillip Street.

I continued to make other short experimental films. There was no story in any of them, not even the pretence of a story. I was just experimenting with my gear and finding my own way to use the techniques of the underground cinema.

Megan[15] was made at Sydney University Law School to be projected as part of the law students' revue. It was a three-minute silent film that featured a woman called Megan, who I had a crush on.

Intersection was 2 minutes 44 seconds in length and shot on 16-millimetre black and white in the middle of a five-way or four-way intersection in North Sydney. I walked into the intersection and spun around in a continuous circle from the beginning of the roll of film to the end. It was an experiment with disorientation and, I guess, a comment about urban development.

Adds *Cantrill's Filmnotes*: 'The sound is an incessantly repeated car horn at very high pitch.'[16]

Memories was a seven-minute short in colour about childhood and the bush. It was accompanied by a smell track, which I created in the cinema by burning eucalyptus leaves, so that the smoke filled the cinema and the audience could smell the burning leaves. It was inspired by my father, who always used to burn off the leaves. A wonderful smell. I guess I should call it 'aromatherapy'.

Sun was 90 seconds in colour and examined the pulsating winter sun by way of 100 single-frame shots.

To round out the list of short experimental films Noyce made before he entered film school, *Home* was a one-and-a-half-minute single-frame camera exploration of the filmmaker's home, inside and out, including its inhabitants and pets.

'I thought Phil had a great career ahead of him as an experimental filmmaker,' says Albie Thoms.[17] As a true experimental filmmaker, he had a deep interest in technical aspects. It was recommended *Sun* 'be projected through a special five image lens',[18] *Memories* and *Intersection* with 'an anamorphic lens'.[19] The preferred[20] double-projection for his film *Better to Reign in Hell* and the two screens required for *Good Afternoon*, as well as the addition of the smell of burning leaves in *Memories*, were inroads into the subgenre of so-called Expanded Cinema.

But already, though totally absorbed by the concept of experimental films, Noyce had his potential audience in mind – a relic from his love of the old travelling shows, that would eventually surface dominantly in his mainstream films.

It was from Read, Thoms and Perry that I learned about promotion, that there's no use just placing an ad; you had to create a vibe about something, that was the key to it. Create magic and they will all come.

You can put up a sign, but nothing will happen unless you work deeper than that, below the surface, trying to tap into the collective unconscious desire. The key thing is to find out what that desire is, and then tell the potential audience that you can maybe satisfy it.

I never made my little experimental films without some audience in mind, always being excited by the idea of getting a response. I wanted to feel, in an old-fashioned showman's way, that the audience had got their money's worth. And that comes from being inspired in the first place, not by the movies, but by vaudeville, by the travelling shows that regularly came to Griffith in the days before television.

Gillian Armstrong says of the experimental film scene in Sydney at this time: 'Ubu film screenings were like hippie "happenings". You went to the films and there were bands and things. I suppose now you would call it marketing, but nobody had ever heard of that word at that time. They turned them into an event. And Phil took that up; he's always been a showman. He always had an instinct about selling and making events, right from the beginning.'[21]

During the Christmas of 1969–1970, at the end of my first year at university, I worked at Film Australia for about three months. Renowned director Cecil Holmes was making a film called *Styles of Champions*, shot by Mike Edols and starring Australian swimming champion John Konrad. Cec took me on as his assistant, which meant that the first job of the day was going to his hotel in Surry Hills and getting him out of bed. He had come down from the Northern Territory, where he had been living and working with his wife, Rhonda. I didn't know who he was at the time, but when I started to work on the film they were all treating him with great reverence, and then I realised the reason was that he had directed a feature, which made him an unusual animal in Australia. His film, *Three In One*, had screened at the Moscow Film Festival. Cec would tell me stuff like: 'Every scene I am going to do now is going to have a Jean-Luc Godard cut.' I'd say, 'What's a Jean-Luc Godard cut?' He would explain: 'Well, Konrad is going to be swimming, and then he will be somewhere else doing something else. Technically, he should leave the first frame going in a certain direction and then enter the next frame travelling in the same direction. But in this case, we are going to do a jump cut and he will be somewhere else and it will only be linked by the fact that it is the same person, but he will be dressed differently, with different actions and even going in a different direction. And that is a Jean-Luc Godard cut, son.' And so he would go on, often as I drove him from location to location or back home again.

I worked out that the very best way to learn was to watch rushes. Every morning at Film Australia they would screen all the footage from the previous day's shooting in the theatre and all the producers would watch, along with the head of the place, Stanley Hawes. So I would wait until they were all in [the theatre] and then, when the lights went out, I'd come in and sit down at the back and watch. They were shooting a three-part feature, *Three To Go*. Peter Weir was doing this 30-minute story, *Michael*, and Brian Hannant and Oliver Howes were also making 30-minute dramas as part of the feature. And there was another bloke called Antonio Colacino, an Italian, who used to direct really great montage sequences in a totally different style to the other directors. It was a great film school. There was no other place in Australia where any of this stuff was being done, and I would try to get in there every single day I could – if I wasn't working with Cecil. I realised that that's the place to learn, because you could see how directors are putting together their sequences, and you could hear the producers debating the merits of each director's work.

Eventually, I got fired from there. I had been given a float of money to pay for everything – taxis, food, all of the incidental expenses – and I was meant to turn in receipts. Well, at the end of the month, I realised that not only had I spent however many hundreds of dollars it was, but all of my own savings as well. And I sat there with my receipts trying to work out if I could reconcile them. I found out later from old hands that the way to do it is to get someone to sign a new receipt for you. But instead, I went through all the receipts changing a '1' to a '4' here or a '1' to a '9' there, to try to build up the expenses. So, of course, because the receipts had been tampered with, they called me in. I was asked to resign because I was guilty of 'forgery with an attempt to defraud the Commonwealth of Australia.'

Back at university after the summer holidays, Noyce decided to give up law and transferred to arts instead. He studied fine arts, English and history for the next three years, 1970–1972, and finished his arts degree in 1972. But more important were the developments on a different front.

In 1969 Ubu Films went out of business after the relative lack of acceptance of Albie's experimental feature film *Marinetti*. And floating in a no-man's land was the vast collection of Australian and overseas films that Ubu had been distributing. So, in 1970, Aggy Read, who had been the full-time manager, proposed that Ubu be reinvented as a cooperative, registered under the NSW Co-operatives Act, whatever that meant – tax-free, or some form of charity status or something. So, we needed a part-time manager. I volunteered [to stand for election].

At the first general meeting of the co-op on 28 May 1970 I was somehow elected by the seven or eight people attending. (I don't think there were many applicants.) The cooperative had inherited 250 films and now I had to look after these films, which I kept in my bedroom at my parents' house in Fox Valley Road, Wahroonga, where I was still living. And I used to sit there day after day just screening those movies for myself. My pay at the cooperative was to be one-eighth of the rentals that I generated, 25 per cent was kept to run the co-op, while the rest went back to the filmmakers. Some of those films actually turned a profit, as they were made for 400 or 500 dollars. So we published a catalogue and sent it out and advertised ourselves, and people would write or ring and rent movies. I would sometimes make extra money by taking a movie projector and screening the programs at schools or wherever.

Noyce concedes that taking on an arts degree at Sydney University was really just an excuse to get hold of the film equipment that was owned by the university's film society.

I discovered that the Sydney University Film Society, which screened feature films to students at lunchtimes, had money and equipment – money that no one was spending and equipment no one was using. Somewhere along the line they had purchased a Bolex camera and rudimentary editing equipment, and stuff like that. So I thought, 'This is great. I'll use this equipment.'

In the meantime, I had finished *Better to Reign in Hell*. I had added a soundtrack of found music and radio commercials. I would rent the cinema at Sydney University, which held 600 people, and at lunchtimes I would often screen the shorts that I'd made, together with some other shorts from the cooperative's library. We would charge 50 cents. If I handed out the leaflets in the mornings, particularly concentrating on the fact that these films were uncensored and a little risqué, then usually there would be 600 people in that cinema, and as it didn't cost much to rent, it would be a good profit. One or two screenings per semester would usually give me all the pocket money I needed to live.

He discovered on the premiere night of *Marinetti* that there was even more money to be made when 'the box office was full of money as Aggy Read struggled to deal with the turn-away crowd, and Phil was at his feet putting it into a plastic garbage bag!'[22] Noyce was also involved in Ubu's Underground Festival, held in August, as well as other activities of the time – in particular, anti-war protests.

He published some articles on film in both *Honi Soit* and *National U*, the Canberra University undergraduate student newsletter. Although not particularly sophisticated or analytical, they were at least opinionated. In one such article, he lamented: 'With all the publicity over the present Sydney Film Festival, our mass media has rather neglected a far more important cinematic assent: the world premiere of Albie Thoms' 90-minute colour feature *Marinetti*.'[23] In an article on *Easy Rider* he concluded: '[What] emerges from the film is despair with society, both the establishment and the breakaway elements.'[24] He also revealed that 'David [Perry] has just completed filming *Better to Reign in Hell*, a sex-fantasy film which includes a daring rape scene and was produced and directed by a group of Sydney University students.'[25] With announcements like this it is hardly surprising that Noyce had yet another brush with the law, after showing the 'pornographic film' *Better to Reign in Hell* at the Newcastle Law Students Ball.[26]

Jan Chapman was one of the students that I met in my frequent visits to the main campus in my escapes from the high-rise law school in 1969. Jan was also interested in movies and so we became friends.

'I met him on the night of a law school revue. I was just going to this party with some other people, you know, it was just a social event. Or maybe he was screening a film and I went there and we met – I'm not sure exactly. I remember that Phillip was very tall and that he used to drive a Mini Minor, you know those very small cars? Anyway, I remember just meeting him and then just keeping on knowing him – we kind of became involved fairly soon after that. Actually, what I remember is that everything to do with Phillip was associated with film – the two things were completely inseparable. He was absolutely passionate about films, he had already made his first film and he'd had Albie and Aggy up to Barker College to talk to the schoolboys. So what I was meeting wasn't just a person who was larger than life, both literally and imaginatively and in every kind of way, but I was introduced to the idea that your imagination could take the form of making film[s] and that anyone could make films and could make them about anything you liked. So it was an amazingly exciting time.'[27]

We worked together on short films that she directed and produced, and I edited or photographed, like her first film *Just a Little Note*. It was essentially a documentary about a guerrilla theatre group run by a friend of ours, George Shevtsov, a Russian–Australian actor that we went to university with. George went on to play the lead in one of her films, the one directed by Shirley Barrett, *Love Serenade* – he was the radio announcer. He also played the Russian interpreter to the Japanese prisoners in my miniseries *Cowra Breakout,* and was the doctor in the opening sequence of *Dead Calm.*

Jan Chapman: '[Phil] was very encouraging about my making films. There were two. One was called *Just a Little Note,* which was a record of a moratorium march and of the theatre group that George Shevtsov was involved in. *I Happened to be a Girl* was more of a documentary kind of film about four women friends of mine and their aspirations in life, and there were some more experimental kinds of dramatisations of their imaginings of what they would do. But, I guess, what I think was interesting about [Phil] was that as well as being very obsessed with his own films and his own ideas, he did really try to encourage me and other people with their own ideas. He was very happy to talk about your ideas. He seemed to have an endless appetite or time to talk about films or work on films; he would sit up all night editing, he was sort of tireless and very obsessive – it was a kind of world you got caught up in, really. He was really intent upon every individual, including me, finding their own voice. That was one of the charming things about him, actually. He had incredible generosity to anyone who had an idea, to try to help them to find their way of doing it. It is amazing that that was the way it was, but that was the philosophy at the time – it wasn't about people trying to force their own voices; it was about encouraging personal expression if anyone had something to say.'[28]

In December 1971 Jan Chapman and Phillip Noyce married. They were both 21 years old. 'When we got married we moved all the films to our house in Annandale,' Jan explains. 'So one of the rooms upstairs in this terrace house was full of a library of films. And once again, our life was people coming and there being screenings, and there always being projectors in the back of cars and film cans everywhere. Phil was always working on something, always editing something; he was very obsessive about film, very engaging and inspiring about it, too.

We were both members of the Sydney Filmmakers Co-op and we'd have meetings into the middle of the night – just the idea that you could make your films, and you could distribute and exhibit them, was what was behind it; that [you] could some-how control the means of exhibition and distribution and, by doing that, you could make a more radical kind of film [and] could kind of educate people's taste, I suppose.'[29]

In 1972, while I was still completing my arts degree, Jan started work as a secondary-school English teacher, a job she stayed with until 1974, when we went overseas together for six months. And I was very lucky because she was the major breadwinner of the family in the first two years of our marriage. She had a full-time job and I had a part-time job as the manager of the film co-op. And a non-paying job as a fledgling filmmaker.

But she was there in all those early years and during all the early events. We were both Sydney Filmmakers Co-op members and both worked at the Filmmakers' Cinema. We were very much a team, work-ing the projectors, collecting the money and advertising the screenings together. Filmmaking was a hobby, a part-time job and a religion for us.

Noyce was on the organising committee of the 1st Australian Filmmakers' Festival in August 1971. He performed more or less regularly in an agit-prop acting troupe (later depicted in *Renegades*) that featured prominently at a Sydney rock festival that year, and shot *Good Afternoon* at the Aquarius Festival in May. In 1972 he participated in cataloguing all the films dis-tributed by the co-op together with Thoms, Read and Ian Stocks. With his many additional activities, one wonders how Noyce managed to combine university studies, family life and an emerging filmmaking career. His still-inexhaustible energy and stamina must have helped, along with his obsession with film. But there was another factor:

It was no coincidence that all this was going on at the same time. The first factor was the new nationalism emerging in the late 1960s and early 1970s in Australia, which peaked after the election of the Labor socialist government in December 1972. Making and screening Australian film was a declaration of our cultural independence from the US and UK. Second, there was the maturing of the baby boomer generation with the economic mobility earned by our parents, who were very, very anxious that their children should have more opportunities than they had had during their own war- and Depression-interrupted youth. There was also a new economic prosperity in Australia, which lasted until the recession after Australia pulled out of the Vietnam War. And there was, among the baby boomers, very much a feeling of wishing to conquer the 'disease' that had infected everyone previously – the dreaded 'cultural cringe'. The cultural cringe told Australians that they needn't bother with artistic pursuits because we could more cheaply import better films and plays and books from overseas. On top of this was the whole underground film movement which was gaining vogue in Australia. All of these elements coalesced in Australia with the introduction of the government-sponsored Experimental Film Fund in 1970. With this new fund there was suddenly an even larger number of short films being made and a resulting need for exhibition. Initially, the film co-op had to round up films; but with the sudden production boom, it seemed that people were just coming out of the woodwork with movies.

Noyce ran the Law School Film Society as well as being heavily engaged in the Filmmakers' Cinema at Sydney University. As demand for independent screenings increased still further, Albie Thoms started a forum for them in the Yellow House[30] in Kings Cross in May 1970. But still more was to come:

The screenings were initially held at Sydney University in the union rooms next to the Union Theatre. We would just grab hold of the university's projector and a different filmmaker would come in each month, show some films, discuss his or her work, and then we would have a co-op meeting.

In 1971 Tom Cowan was instrumental in advocating that we start a cinema in the city. After a few screenings at a restaurant in Glebe, we took over a space above a socialist bookshop next to Chinatown, called the Third World Bookshop, in Goulburn Street. The owner, Bob Gould, figured that if he gave us the top floor we could turn that into a cinema and that our audience would be his customers, and as Sunday night was pretty dead for him our cinemagoers would all come through his bookshop on the first two floors, buy his books and then go up to see our movies. But it was a firetrap. I mean, if there had been a fire in that building we all would have been killed. We built a little projection booth, and, with a 16-millimetre projector, started screenings. We would collect together one person's films, or films on a theme, and advertise in Saturday's *Sydney Morning Herald* as the Filmmakers' Cinema. It became a very chic thing to go to, with a lot of the audience being fledgling filmmakers themselves, so it was sort of like a film school, in a funny way.

The idea of screening movies in an unregistered theatre, in a socialist bookshop on the edge of Chinatown, was irresistible and the audience were also increasingly fascinated by the images of themselves they could see on that screen, when there was as yet almost no Australian film industry.

During this time I continued making short experimental films. *Camera Class* was made in 1971 with footage shot for the longer documentary *Good Afternoon*. As a group of students were taught how to use a movie camera, the camera was rolling footage. It was an exercise in subjective camera, where the camera itself is the character whose point of view you're being introduced to.

ScreenSound seemed a bit lost in its description of this film: '[It] begins with various scenes of people with cameras; a clapperboard reading "Students Roll, 36"; continues with various scenes of a number of young men in various states of undress sitting on pit toilets in a tentlike temporary toilet block. There is a break at about 48'. The second portion of film, about 10', shows a naked man chasing a naked woman along a beach, he catches her and finds he is looking at a human skull, they roll on the beach, then there is a metronome ticking. The film is obviously incomplete.'[31] But, in fact, it is not. What Screen-Sound is describing here is not a finished film, but some material from both *Better to Reign in Hell* and *Renegades* that accidentally ended up at the archive.

I started a newsreel, screening footage at the Filmmakers' Cinema with a live commentary. I would shoot events in Sydney, such as protest meetings and so on. One in 1971 was called *Springboks Protest*, footage of the demonstration at Sydney Cricket Ground against the South African rugby tour. There were probably two or three more, but I can't remember.

'Well, we were involved in the Vietnam War up to the night of the election of the Labor socialist government in December 1972. On that evening the new prime minister, Gough Whitlam, formed a two-men cabinet with his deputy, Lance Barnard, and they enacted legislation even before midnight. The first piece of legislation enacted was that all of the draft dodgers would be freed from prisons around the country, and they announced the total withdrawal of all Australian troops who were still supporting the Americans and their allies in Vietnam.

'We had a similar sort of draft that you had here [in the United States]. In Australia it was a lottery system. I watched as my two brothers' birthdays didn't come up and sure enough mine didn't either, so I escaped the draft, escaped going to Vietnam or becoming a conscientious objector or going to prison or whatever would have happened. I escaped having to make a decision. Peace marches were exactly the same as here, exactly the same, just a little bit later.

'As a fledgling filmmaker, I made a number of films about the protest movement. [One] was called *Renegades*, which was – I guess it was like a chronicle of the times. It was a poem but it also owed a lot to the American newsreel movement of the late '60s and early '70s. It was a combination of poetic images and reportage on the street demonstrations. The feeling of siege that everyone who was opposed to the war felt all over the world, which I suppose in another way, was a confrontation of two generations.'[32]

Renegades was a sort of a diary film funded by the Experimental Film Fund. It included footage of the street theatre group that I was a part of, with George Shevtsov and Jan Chapman. It wasn't released until 1974, but it was being shot throughout this time.

The audience at the Filmmakers' Cinema were mightily enthusiastic about seeing themselves up on the screen. And there was always a great discussion. So, generally the screenings were a huge success, with many full houses. The screenings grew from once a week, to three times on each Sunday, to all weekend, and then seven days a week at several locations. One program could play in three different illegal cinemas around the city.

With the new nationalism in the air, there was a shift in interest from risqué underground films to the concept of Australian cinema. The audience were suddenly coming for a dose of Australian culture and also because the films themselves were becoming much more sophisticated. Among the people who showed their films were Bruce Petty, George Miller, Gillian Armstrong, Bruce Beresford, myself, Peter Weir, Arthur and Corrine Cantrill, Paul Cox and Nigel Buesst from Melbourne.

In fact, I remember Gillian Armstrong coming up the stairs one Sunday afternoon in 1971 with a little film called *The Roof Needs Mowing* that she had made at Swinburne Tech. I was the projectionist as well, and she said, 'Do you screen movies here?' I said, 'Yes, have you got one? We need another film for tonight.' And we immediately added her movie to that night's program. It was a very exciting time.

Gillian Armstrong recalls: 'In my second or third year of film and television at Swinburne College of the Arts in Melbourne they brought in a new film lecturer named Nigel Buesst, to have someone who was a real practitioner. Nigel made the film *Come Out Fighting*. As our lecturer he felt that we should all learn about distribution, something [none] of us had ever thought about. He set out an assignment where we had to find out about various avenues of distribution. I had to find out about the independent film market and, as part of that,

I tracked down that there was an association called the Sydney Filmmakers Co-op and I wrote a letter to [its] president. I can remember addressing the letter to a Mr Phillip Noyce. His address was in Wahroonga, so he was obviously still living at home with his parents. And he answered my letter very politely, sent to my address in the suburb of Mitchum, where I was still living with my parents, and gave me some information about the co-op, which I fed into my essay.

'And then the following year after I graduated, I was in Sydney and I thought I might track down this cooperative that I was forced to learn about. I was actually very pleased later that Nigel made us learn about the practical side. So I turned up with my graduation 16-millimetre ten-minute film *The Roof Needs Mowing* under my arm and went in. It was up a steep staircase and there were these wild revolutionary posters all over the wall. I [said] that I'd heard that part of this cooperative was that you could just arrive with your film and [asked] if it was possible to run mine. And they said yes. I did run my film that night and I remember that Albie Thoms and Jane Oehr were sitting in front. I was actually very nervous about running my film in front of all these very serious Sydney independent filmmakers. After the film, Albie turned around, and he and Jane Oehr said something complimentary about my film. I remember that moment quite vividly.'[33]

The idea was that you never wasted a weekend. Whenever you could get a roll of film you would shoot, and if you only had one roll then that's all you needed because 2 mins 40 secs was enough to do a very intense movie. You only needed a Bolex and you could do animation, with single-frame images if you wanted to. Inspired by Arthur Cantrill and Albie Thoms, we had a whole movement of direct animation. Find exposed film that had been thrown away, start to scratch, paint the scratches with Texta colour, put it straight on the projector – and you had a movie. You could have no movie on Friday and yet you could have a movie ready for screening by Sunday night if you stayed up the whole weekend.

For the latter part of 1971 and early 1972 I had been working on *Good Afternoon*. The cultural arm of the Australian Union of Students, the Aquarius Foundation, had contracted me to make a documentary about the Combined Universities' Art Festival in Canberra in 1971.[34] This became a two-screen movie à la *Woodstock*. The Hokushin projectors used to screen it were sponsored by Pepsi-Cola, and a friend worked out how to connect them through the inching knobs so that the two projectors would stay in sync. The projectors had their own case and we would ship the movie with the projectors around the country – all the way, even, to Perth.

Noyce's earlier experimental films had been met with a lot of goodwill and sympathy in the – rather limited – publications that reviewed this genre of films. *Good Afternoon*, however, reached out to a wider audience, encompassing even the undogmatic left, cultural elites and hard-core documentarists. Accordingly, reactions were split for the first time. Julie Clark praised its juxtaposition of 'the sterility of Our Capital and the richness and vitality of the arts festival',[35] but Sylvia Lawson was more ambivalent: 'It works as an exploration of a complicated, clamorous event' but observes likewise that it 'communicates most effectively where it's least impressionistic and most intently a confrontation of people and happening'.[36]

P.P. McGuinness discounted the film as 'unsuccessful': 'sympathetic, but otherwise undistinguished'.[37]

A filmmakers' cinema also started in Melbourne, and Melbourne directors would come to Sydney to present their programs and vice versa. Eventually the film co-op was given a grant and in 1973 – while I was already at film school – we moved to St Peters Lane in Darlinghurst to set up a really good licensed cinema, running seven days a week.

Inevitably three aspects of the co-op are remembered vividly, whoever one talks to: the grass-roots democratic structure, the fact that you had to help out with everything, and Noyce being the driving force behind it. Jan Chapman recalls: 'Upstairs there were offices and downstairs there was a cinema. He and I were very much involved. I remember getting that cinema together. I mean, I remember making curtains for the cinema, I remember going to meetings there endlessly because as a co-op everyone would have an opinion about how the place should be run. So a lot of his time was spent still involved with that cooperative, even when he started to go to film school.'[38]

Gillian Armstrong joined the co-op and went regularly to their screenings. 'Phil was always a great leader, very passionate with a strong sense of humour. His personality was obviously the key in keeping that co-op alive because it was such a mixed bunch at the time – people of all political persuasions. The whole thing was terribly political and nothing was to have a hierarchical system. So there were these endless meetings where everyone had a vote and it went on all night with heated arguments about those things that had to be a group decision – whether it was important or not. Whether it was about tickets, or whether the walls had to be painted or something. We all ended up doing things to help the cooperative. I remember I helped [to paint] one wall white over one weekend with Martha Ansara and Chris Tillam and a number of the other filmmakers. So it's wonderful that he's taken that out into film. But you wouldn't have thought he was going to be a feature film director. I wouldn't have thought that from his early films.'[39]

The move to St Peters Lane was sort of the end of an era, because initially the cinema was self-funded, but once it became government-sponsored everything changed. And then, of course, the women took over, as they had the strongest voice at the time, with the most urgent need to be heard and express themselves. The men just wanted to make movies, but for the women it was sexual politics as well as cultural politics. For us it was just cultural politics; for them it was both.

Gillian Armstrong recalls: 'At the time, Australia had [strict] censorship and it was very hard to see independent films. There were also anti–Vietnam War films and then it moved into a number of the feminist films that all came out of America, and we saw them all at the co-op. There was nowhere else they would have been shown. The Sydney Film Festival had been going for many years, but it showed much more sort of classic cinema.'[40]

The next logical step in developing an alternative film economy was never fully taken. In 1973 Tom Cowan – while returning from the Moscow Film Festival – made a lengthy stop in Munich and there became acquainted with the recently founded 'Filmverlag der Autoren'. Based on the idea of a co-op, it was a combination of production and distribution company, owned and operated by many of Germany's brightest young feature film directors. Cowan tried to introduce these ideas into Australia, but in vain. Some of the major directors-to-be had already embarked on their own individual professional career paths, with others to follow suit.

The late 1960s and early 1970s were a turbulent time in Sydney's artistic circles, as they were elsewhere in the world. So many things happened simultaneously and with the same people involved that a strict chronology of events is near impossible to relate. It is obvious that Noyce entered the scene with a voracious appetite for his new discovery, the experimental film, but that his passion wasn't simply for making films, but for distributing and exhibiting them as well. But his activities – which often seemed to border on the obsessive – weren't confined to film alone. With the curiosity of a youngster stepping into the world of adulthood, he embarked on a journey through the world of the counter-culture that was opening up all around him – film, theatre, rallies, music, art, and politics in general. He was a frequent participant in all these activities, as his cameo appearances show.[41] In the best spirit of the times, he followed Jerry Rubin's adage, 'Do it!'[42] – and supported (and sometimes even pushed) others to get involved as well. But so untamed was his hunger for the new, so high were his personal levels of energy, that it must have been clear his aspirations couldn't possibly end here. Unlike others, he didn't linger on once the alternative thing started fading away. He was available at the right moment when something important happened.

---

[1] *Castaway's Choice*, radio broadcast by KCYTW, 1990.

[2] Noyce has invested in the farm, which since 2003 has cultivated wine grapes.

[3] *Castaway's Choice.*

[4] For example, David White, *Australian Movies to the World – The International Success of Australian Films since 1970* (Sydney: Fontana, 1984), p. 60.

[5] Phillip Noyce, email dated 24 June 2003.

[6] Unreleased five-minute video for the promotion of the Peter Mudie book *Ubu Films: Sydney Underground Movies 1965–1970* (Sydney: UNSW Press, 1997).

[7] One of the shorts shown was Peter Weir's first film, *Count Vim's Last Exercise.*

[8] Unreleased five-minute video for the promotion of Peter Mudie's *Ubu Films.*

[9] Email dated 9 June 2003. Details of the screening on 27 September 1968 can be found in Peter Mudie's *Ubu Films.*

[10] Mudie, *Ubu Films*, p. 19.

[11] She was Albie Thoms's partner at the time.

[12] A. Thoms, I. Stocks, A. Read, and P. Noyce (eds), *Film Catalogue* (Sydney: Sydney Filmmakers Co-op, 1972), p. 52.

[13] *Honi Soit*, cited in Thoms et al., *Film Catalogue.*

[14] *Castaway's Choice.*

[15] This film is not listed in Thoms et al., *Film Catalogue.*

[16] *Cantrill's Filmnotes*, no. 5, August 1971; cited in Thoms et al., *Film Catalogue*, p. 53.

[17] Email dated 9 June 2003.

[18] Thoms et al., *Film Catalogue*, p. 52.

[19] Ibid, p. 53.

[20] As stated in Thoms et al., *Film Catalogue*. Noyce insists it was never intended to be screened like that.

[21] Gillian Armstrong interview.

[22] Email dated 9 June 2003.

[23] Phillip Noyce, 'And after the film festival!', *Honi Soit*, June 1969.

[24] Phillip Noyce, 'Two views of *Easy Rider*', *Honi Soit*, March 1970.

[25] Ibid.

[26] David Stratton, *The Last New Wave – The Australian Film Revival* (Sydney: Angus & Robertson, 1980), p. 202.

[27] Jan Chapman interview.

[28] Jan Chapman interview.

[29] Jan Chapman interview.

[30] The house at 59 Macleay Street, Potts Point – built in the late 1890s – became an artistic hub in 1959 when owner Frank Clune opened the Terry Clune Galleries.

In 1969, Martin Sharp, newly returned from 'Swinging London', coined the name and used the premises from May 1970 as an innovative multimedia space that housed artistic exhibitions and colourful events. It had closed down by the end of 1971.

In many ways the Yellow House was the culmination of the 'underground' in Australia, recognised by a retrospective exhibition at the Art Gallery of New South Wales in 1990. A short comprehensive history can be found at www.milesago.com/features/yellowhouse.htm, an excellent website dedicated to the history of Australian popular culture.

31 Cited at www.milesago.com/visual/cameraclass.htm. It looks as if an excerpt from this film can be seen in Episode 3 ('Billy Killed the Fish, 1986–73') of the ABC-TV documentary series *Long Way to the Top*.

32 *Castaway's Choice*.

33 Gillian Armstrong interview.

34 Recent publications (*The Courier-Mail*, *The Weekend Australian*) claiming that the Aquarius Festival series started in 1973 in Nimbin 'as a victory celebration for the withdrawal of Australian support for the Vietnam War' are obviously wrong.

35 Julie Clark, 'Local film making gets a shot in the projector', ca. 1972.

36 Sylvia Lawson, 'Films', ca. 1972.

37 P.P. McGuinness, *National Times*, ca. 1972.

38 Jan Chapman interview.

39 Gillian Armstrong interview.

40 Gillian Armstrong interview.

41 For example, in his own *Renegades* or in . . . *Or Forever Hold Your Peace*.

42 Jerry Rubin, *Do It!* (New York: Simon & Schuster, 1970).

Chapter 2
FILM SCHOOL AND OTHER SHORT MATTERS

*The idea was that you immersed yourself
in filmmaking.*

'In 1969 some dreamers conceived a grandiose idea that it would be a good idea to have an Australian film industry and the way to do this was to pump a lot of money around the country and pretty soon there would be a film industry. It sounds fantastic, but it actually came true.[1]

Two of the planners [Phillip Adams and Barry Jones] came up with a three-tier system with an experimental film fund, another fund supposedly for commercial feature films, and a film and television school.

By that time I was earning a little bit of money as manager of the film co-op, something like twenty dollars a week. But I had also signed up to become a teacher. A really smart high school graduate could earn a Commonwealth Scholarship, which meant the federal government paid your university tuition plus a small stipend. But the next best thing was a teachers' college scholarship, where the NSW Education Department paid your university fees and gave you about 30 dollars a week to live on. But in return, unless you could repay the government, you were indentured to them for several years after graduation and forced to teach, initially most often in a rural location. So I guess, if it wasn't for the film school, I would probably have become a teacher. That was about the only paid employment I could look forward to. But for most of the time, Jan Chapman was the breadwinner in the family.

'I had forgotten that but I suppose that's true. I just happened to start earning money before [Phil] did. I taught English and art, but I also taught film. [Phil] was at film school, I guess, in the first year, and it must have been a while before he started earning money, but it wasn't an issue that I remember feeling anything about. It was more that I happened to be able to earn money and he wasn't quite there, I suppose. It was an incredibly exciting time.'[2]

In 1972 it was decided to start the Interim Australian Film and Television School and they wanted to get it going really quickly because of fear that if the government changed, or even if the government didn't change, a new regime might destroy the embryonic structure that had been set up. Jerzy Toeplitz was employed from the Lodz Film School in Poland to lead the place and it was decided that the school would start in 1973. I applied while in my last year at university and was one of twelve accepted. This meant that I was now paid 50 dollars a week, or it might even have been 100 dollars – it was something amazing in those days. So you didn't need to seek additional work to support yourself. The idea was that you immersed yourself in filmmaking for that year, spent in makeshift premises on the sixth floor of an office building in Chatswood, a northern Sydney suburb.

Gillian Armstrong was a fellow student at the film school: 'We were all in the co-op together, but Phil and I were the only two that got into the first intake of the Film and Television School. Others, like Martha Ansara, came in the second year. So Phil and I had a little bit of a friendship and we always got along very well. It's been a little bit of a bond [between us].'[3]

Applicants had to be above 21 years of age, but below 25 – later they relaxed that – and you needed to have made a film already, and preferably the school was some sort of postgraduate course for the chosen ones. In that year also were Gillian Armstrong, who later directed *My Brilliant Career* and many other wonderful films, and Chris Noonan, of *Babe* fame.

The school was a one-year course in directing, with very little formal instruction, beyond a six-week course in live TV direction at the end of which each of us made a short live-television drama. Then, for the next ten months, we were set the task of making three films: a drama, a documentary and, finally, a genre of your choice. We were given set budgets for each film, but you could raise additional money if you wanted to. We were told that crew and cast had to be paid professionals, unless we could make a case to our producer that someone who was a non-professional could be considered. We had to direct each project, which we could also write, but if we wanted to perform any other function ourselves we had to get permission.

The purpose of this course structure was to force the twelve would-be directors into an accelerated pragmatism. We had to learn to choose crew and get the most out of a set budget – if you went over budget you just didn't finish. That was it. We had to be manipulative in terms of how we got our material, how much we paid for it, the crew we hired, and our shooting methods. The big, big, *big* proviso was that once we finished the movies we owned the finished product, so we could exploit them any way we could devise. This really was an accelerated course in the realities of filmmaking. There were a small number of professionals working in the industry, and we had to go to that professional talent pool and choose a cinematographer, sound recordist, editor, and so on, and negotiate how much we paid them. The only thing lacking was that we didn't receive a really firm grounding in film history. John Flaus [a noted left-wing cinema lover] would come in once a week, on Fridays, and show a movie and talk [as lecturer in film history]. That was it.

For the first short film project we had a number of different producers assigned to work with us, drawn from among the newly established filmmakers like Peter Weir and Fred Schepisi. Fred taught me to approach film like an architect, to plan, though perhaps not as extremely as Alfred Hitchcock. Under his guidance I started to formulate this idea, which was exacerbated by working with George Miller, of storyboarding, of planning things out, of trying to look at the whole thing as a piece of architecture. There may be abstract expressionism within a particular room, but basically you're trying to look at the whole and see its overall design and how it will be utilised by the people who live in that 'building', the building being the film. The other producer I had was Tom Manefield, for the documentary segment, and then they brought in Joseph Strick, the American director of *Ulysses*, for the last film.

Tom Cowan and Russell Boyd both worked there as directors of photography [DoPs] and they were probably the first true film teachers, because the cinematographers had a little bit more experience than the emerging directors who were producing our films.

With regard to acting, there was no formal instruction, although there was a strong ethos at the time towards naturalism. You've got to remember that this is a period of nationalism in Australia, where a generation of maturing baby boomers were anxious to express themselves personally and culturally to define the Australian identity. And the country is in rebellion against its old cultural, economic and political masters, England and America; we're trying to find an Australian idiom, a way of speaking, a way of expressing ourselves, a way of expressing our lifestyle in art, in literature, in cinema and in theatre.

My first film-school short, with a budget of 3000 dollars, was called *Caravan Park*. It was a largely improvised drama based on a short story by South Australian writer John Emery. I had written the script inspired by the story. What I didn't like about Australian films and TV at the time was the formality of the language, which was very stilted. There seemed to be a big difference between the language we were seeing on the screen and spoken Australian. It was starting to change, of course, with *Barry McKenzie*, which came out around the same time, and *Stork*, and in the work of David Williamson and Alex Buzo and other playwrights. My approach to acting in *Caravan Park* was, first, to cast people that looked real, and secondly, not to give them formal dialogue, but rather to force them to search for ways of telling a story in their own words, which would force them to use their own vocabulary, their own syntax, their own construction, their own meter. You then find yourself exposed to a way of speaking which maybe you haven't seen on the screen before that time in Australian cinema. That was my own particular obsession in the first film that I made there.

'We had to be PA [production assistant] on each other's films. I'm sure I'm on the credits [for *Caravan Park*],' Gillian Armstrong recalls. 'Basically all I had to do was babysit the little boy, Martha Ansara's son, in between takes and play games with him to keep him amused when he wasn't shooting for Phil. Babysitting wasn't really my idea of working on a production with this young, ambitious filmmaker.'[4]

For the second film-school project we had to make a documentary on a subject of our choice. At the time I was living in a little terrace house in inner-city Annandale. Some people were coming over for a Sunday afternoon party, and I noticed there were extra guests who I didn't really know. Gillian Armstrong and a few others had arrived at the same time, and I thought the unfamiliar guests must be with one of the new arrivals. And then after a while, Jan Chapman, my wife at the time, came and asked whether I knew these people, because no one else did. Then there seemed to be more and more of them and when we ran out of grog, one of the strangers introduced himself and said not to worry because they would arrange to open up the local pub. And that was when I realised our party had been taken over by our neighbours. We were living between two groups of notorious bikers, the Finks motorcycle gang. There was no choice but to more or less co-opt them into your life because you couldn't escape these guys – we had to make friends with them. At the time, they were in a murderous feud with another gang called the Gypsy Jokers and had already assassinated a couple of Joker members. I thought the only way of turning this nightmare into a positive situation was to exploit them as subjects for a movie. (During the filming there was a reverse assassination attempt, with the Gypsy Jokers trying to kill one of the Finks.) I had immediate access to them at all times, even when I didn't want it. So that's how it all evolved.

The documentary was called *Castor and Pollux*, after the two Roman gods, and we were given a budget of around 3000 dollars again. It was a film about a biker called Gus and a hippie called Adrian. And it compared and contrasted the lifestyles of these two middle-aged men, both of whom were leaders in their own alternative movements. Adrian Rawlins had been a counter-cultural figure in Sydney and Melbourne for about twenty years. He was a bohemian who identified very closely with the Beat poets, an enthusiast who championed counter-cultural values. I was really attracted not so much to his values as to his personality, his free spirit, and the way in which he [interacted] with people around him – the negative and positive confrontation of his values with other people's. The interesting thing was that, as I started to put this film together, I realised that, in his supposedly free-spirited attitudes, Adrian was much more doctrinaire and steadfast than the supposedly right-wing biker, Gus. The biker was the true free spirit, totally anarchic, and in many ways he was attempting to rewrite the rulebook of life in a much more determined way than Adrian, with his hippie values, was doing.

The film ends with the bikies at their annual celebration taking part in a cannon fight. They've got small cannons on either side of a football field out in the countryside, and they've built forts out of tree stumps and branches and sandbags, and they're firing cannon balls at each other made out of beer cans filled with cement. And at one stage we ended up in the centre of that field trying for a shot that showed the relationship between the two forts, and suddenly both sides turned their cannons on us. So we found ourselves dodging truly lethal projectiles, that were whizzing past us at 80 miles an hour.

While filming, Noyce with the camera had dived for shelter in one direction, his sound recordist, Chris Tillam, in another. A halt was necessary to repair the sync cable.

Initially, Tom Cowan was shooting for me. Then Bill Constable, who was in charge of the camera department at the film school, photographed another sequence. They were both very good cinema-vérité cinematographers. I watched them shoot, saw how they were working, saw the rushes and then after a day with each of them, I thought, 'Well, I reckon I could do that', and also save the money I was paying them. So I ended up being the cinematographer, which was appropriate because I realised that the only way I could truly direct the documentary was to photograph it myself, because then I could work instinctually.

It was shot on a 16-millimetre Arriflex BL with Agfa negative stock, which has a high exposure tolerance. You could just guess the exposure. We were filming the two stories parallel to each other over a four-month period.

David Stiven was initially editing it but then the money ran out again, so I finished the cutting, but David did most of the work. He taught me so much just from watching him. For *Caravan Park* I had Tony Buckley as my editor. Buckley, of course, was the doyen of film editors in Australia, having cut *Wake in Fright* with its classic kangaroo-shoot montage.

Castor and Pollux was widely acclaimed and developed a kind of cult following. Bob Ellis called it 'one of the most savagely iconoclastic and bawdily vivacious documentaries ever made – as good as anything from Miloš Forman or Andy Warhol – an absolute must.'[5] In any case it was a 'lucid observation of Australian lifestyles'.[6] At the 1974 Sydney Film Festival, Noyce received the Rouben Mamoulian Award for the documentary. David Stratton was the film festival director and had flown to Sweden to have the award designed – or so it was rumoured – but it hadn't actually arrived. There was a pillar on stage, which Stratton told the audience was symbolic of the award, before he called on Rouben Mamoulian to give the award to Noyce.

Robert Defoe recalls: 'Basically, Phil's film was about two groups. One was a bikie gang who were tough and throwing bombs all over the place. The other was a gay character with a whole heap of disciples around him, believing in what he believed at the time. Which was a lovely free-living effort and that the whole thing was sort of a lovely lifestyle where they had lovely sex, you know, [and] so forth. Anyway, Rouben Mamoulian came on to the stage to give Phil his award. Phil was dressed in a pink suit with a tie. And Rouben Mamoulian said that it was very, very gratifying to know that a young man like Phil could make a film about all these degenerates.

'The bikie gang, who was sitting directly in front of me, went: "Whoah!" They loved being called degenerates. And the gay guy and his entourage, who were sitting in front of [the bikies], got up and walked out. I believe they put an injunction [on] that film so that it couldn't be shown for some time, because they didn't want to be considered degenerates . . . That was 1974.'[7]

In retrospect, the film is a notable example of the 'direct cinema' style of documentary made in Australia at a time when this approach was already booming overseas. 'Most Australian films have utilised low shooting ratios, with commentary and interviews supplying much of the information,' wrote Martha Ansara.[8] *Castor and Pollux* didn't escape criticism, however. The *Daily Telegraph* reached new lows by criticising it for wasting taxpayers' money: 'The film was shown yesterday at a special preview which drew an audience of one . . . The best thing about this film is that a lot of the footage was spoiled in the laboratory.'[9]

At the Film and Television School there was always something happening. 'We all edited together in one big room, and it was fascinating to watch each other's process,' remembers Noyce.[10] Activities went beyond film production studies, however, and Noyce was entangled in his own additional film work.

At night I was always in there earning extra money. I edited a film for David Ahearn, the avant-garde composer, called *Cinemusic*. I was also production assistant on *Matchless* by John Papadopoulos. There was a federal election in 1974, which the Labor Party won, and we were secretly doing a lot of free-to-air commercials for Labor out of the film school and editing them there at night.

My third and final film-school film was called *That's Show Biz*, the story of a down-on-their-luck vaudeville troupe who are getting pushed further and further into the outback with the escalating arrival of television into country areas. In order to revive the family's fortunes, their son, played by me, comes home from university and tells them to import a striptease artist called Madam Lash, played by Gretel Pinninger. Just when they eventually make it all the way back to the city, the old man runs off with Madam Lash, and his 60-year-old wife has to take her place as the show's stripper. The budget was 5000 dollars.

So I finished my film-school films and, as I had always done, immediately wanted to screen them for an audience. I was inspired by what I saw Aggy Read and Albie Thoms do back in 1968 and 1969 with the aggressive selling of any elements that they could extract from the movie, and niche marketing. Whether it was sex, violence, *Mondo Cane*–type exotica, drugs and hallucinogenic imagery – whatever it was, they were always able to find an angle and push it.

I hired Sydney University's Union Theatre, which had been the venue for my first exposure to alternative cinema back in 1968, for ten screenings, and put on *Castor and Pollux* as the main attraction. There was a very popular magazine called *The Living Daylights*, edited by Richard Neville, for which I wrote an article about the inner workings of a bikie gang. The screenings were a huge success, with about 1000 dollars profit every session. That was a lot of money in 1974, when 10,000 dollars was a reasonable year's wages. And the film school brought in a new rule that from now on they would own the proceeds from exploitation of student films. Which was really stupid, because they were ignoring the whole point that the process is only complete when the film is screened, and so anything you can do to encourage students to exploit their work is going to be a necessary part of the learning curve.

'There were [600] people every night and they were each giving me $2.50, and the films ran for eight nights [with sometimes] two sessions each night, and every night I was just surrounded by all this money. It hasn't happened to me often since that time, such a phenomenon, but I certainly began to understand what motivated filmmakers over here in Hollywood. So it was a real learning process.'[11]

I was really lucky. I left school in 1968 and started to make short films, and one year later the Experimental Film Fund started and planning commenced for the film school. So I went to the film school and then the AFC [Australian Film Commission] financed *Backroads*. After that I made the feature film *Newsfront* through the AFC and the NSW Film Corporation. So I was really in the right place at the right time to graduate from hand-painted and scratched film to dramatic feature film, all the time assisted by this fabulous system of ongoing government subsidy. We really were the lucky country.

On my graduation from film school, Professor Jerzy Toeplitz called Gillian Armstrong and myself into his office and said, 'Well, technically, you two know how to make movies. But you need to broaden your perspective on the world.' He then gave us each an around-the-world airline ticket and 2000 dollars! 'Go and travel and study people, art and culture in other countries,' he told us. 'Try not to come back too quickly. In five years' time, maybe your experiences will have percolated into something worthwhile, and you'll have something to say that's worthy of feature length. If you come back earlier than six months, I want the money back.' It was roughly five years later that I made *Newsfront* and Gillian commenced shooting *My Brilliant Career*.

Gillian Armstrong is slightly less mythical in her recollection of events. 'Well, I don't remember it [being quite] like that. We had graduated and our short films had by then been shown in various film festivals, like the Sydney Film Festival. Both were finalists in the Greater Union Awards. A couple of months after we left they said they had selected my film *Gretel* and [Phil's] *Castor and Pollux* to go to this international student film festival in Grenoble in France and they would like us to go as the school's representatives. There had never been an Australian film school, so we were the first and we were both given economy-class around-the-world tickets. Like all young Australians we always wanted to get out and see the world. As the festival was later in the year we had a few months to prepare, so Phil was working separately and I was crewing on other people's films and we saved as much money as we could. And he and his then-wife, Jan Chapman, and I agreed that we would go to the festival and then try to see how long [we could make] our money last [while we] travelled around Europe on a EuroRail ticket and saw the world. And then, of course, there were the things that simply happened that I hadn't really planned ahead for and thought about. At the festival we met a number of young film-makers from countries all over the world who then said, "Come and see us in Munich" and "Come and see us in Vienna", and so we did. And it was a fantastic life experience.'[12]

Gillian, myself and Jan Chapman went first to a student film festival in Grenoble, France, and then spent the next four or five months backpacking around Europe, the British Isles and Scandinavia, and then across America on a Greyhound bus visiting people we had met at the festival, and carrying our films in our suitcases trying to get dis-tribution for them, while also visiting the great museums of the world – the Prado, the Louvre, the Tate, the Museum of Modern Art in New York, and so on. I arranged distribution for my films through the Other Cinema in London and the Filmmakers' Co-operative in Amsterdam. On this trip, I met Emile de Antonio, who made *Year of the Pig* and *Millhouse: A White Comedy*, a documentary about Richard Nixon and D.A. Pennebaker, and in Munich, Rainer Werner Fassbinder.

Jan Chapman's *I Happened to be a Girl* was also on their program. 'He was very encouraging and made it his business to make sure that I screened my film as well – I wasn't left out.'[13]

Their long trip provided more than just professional and cultural experiences. Visits to people they had met at the Grenoble festival produced encounters of a more social nature. Gillian Armstrong recalls one such visit with a German named Gunter, in Munich. 'His parents let the three of us sleep on their floor. Then we went to see an Austrian filmmaker – I think her name was Juno – in Vienna. At that point, Prague was occupied by Russia and [Juno] had filmmaking friends there and said, "I can't see them anymore. Please, if you could go and visit with your visas . . ." So we did this whole adventure, and went into Prague and finally tracked down these filmmakers. It was a great occasion for us, because we'd never been in a socialist country, behind the Iron Curtain. We had very naïve views. We were all leftist students and now we realised – especially when being occupied – what a terrible life they had and what [a] lack of freedom. At that time the Barandov Studios in Prague were empty and nobody was working. It was a strange experience.

'While we were in Prague this young man started to chat to us. Phil has always been terribly gregarious, and is always good with locals and likes to chat to them all the time. But Jan and I started to get very suspicious, because this young man – who turned out to be in the film industry – had started to follow us in the street. So we've obviously been followed and watched. He invited us back to his apartment and kept telling us what a great life they had [in Czechoslovakia]. (Later on, when we met with these filmmakers we'd been looking for, they said: "Oh no, our life isn't great. Our father is a professor but is now sweeping the streets. Please, sneak us a newspaper." All that stuff.) It was typical of Phil – he thought it was fabulous that we had this new Czechoslovakian friend. But [Jan] and I started to get a bit suspicious, [while] Phil wanted him to come with us everywhere. We thought it was a bit much. The newfound friend was always so pro the government, it was obvious that he was some sort of government watchdog.

'Then we went [by] train all around Europe and ended up in Morocco. And there a similar thing happened. We were backpacking, following our *Europe on Ten Dollars a Day* guidebook, but were a bit nervous about Morocco, so this was the only place [where we'd decided to] stay in a real hotel – not just a *pension*. I remember Phil coming up, full of enthusiasm. "I've met this great young guy and he wants to learn English. He's willing to be our guide and he'll show us where the markets are and take us anywhere we want. He's great." This is a different situation because this was obviously a young street boy. Jan and I, after a couple of days, kept saying: "[Something's] strange. This boy is with us all day long. Surely he can't be doing this for nothing?" "No, no," Phil would say.

"He wants to learn English. Isn't that great?" When we got back to the hotel after a whole day with this boy who Phil thought was just so wonderful and generous, he pulled Phil aside. Jan and I went up to the room, but when Phillip was gone for about half an hour we finally went out to see what was going on. Phil came back [looking] as white as a sheet and said, "He wants all this money for having been our guide, and if I don't pay him I'll be stabbed" [*laughs*].

'Anyway, that was very typical of [our] travels with Phil. Let's say he's very enthusiastic and sometimes quite gullible [*laughs*]. We all really wanted to get to know [the] local people, we all felt that. It was just interesting the times that Phil actually got so enthusiastic he didn't realise sometimes that he was being taken for a bit of a ride.'[14]

After Europe, Armstrong returned home, while the Noyces continued on to the United States. Jan Chapman remembers 'catching a Greyhound bus with Phil from New York to Los Angeles, right across America, which was very exciting and strange. We were so young, we were 24 then, and it was somewhat frightening being in kind of very down-and-out hotels like the Chelsea in New York, but that's more instructive about his curiosity and interest in life, I suppose. I think we all realised on that trip that we did have the beginnings of a strong, idiosyncratic film industry in Australia, and government support for film meant that we were able to use grants to make further short films on our return.'[15]

We left in June 1974 and came back in early 1975. Jan returned to Australia with me and then went to work at the ABC before embarking on her career as a feature film producer of *The Piano* and *Lantana*, among others. But upon our return, for the first time in my lifetime, there were unemployment lines. The recession that had hit America in 1973 after the withdrawal from Vietnam finally arrived in Australia in late 1974, early 1975. Prior to that, unemployment had been running at 2 per cent. In all the time I grew up you could get a job with ease. Even during the ten-day May school holidays, you could find a week's work digging sewer trenches as there weren't enough workers, but now it had all changed. I can remember going to the unemployment office in 1975 and you had to wait hours just to be seen. Unemployment was still way below its current level, but everyone was in a state of shock, and I guess it was like 4 per cent or something, which nowadays would be called full employment. So I worked at any little film job I could get – as an editor, DoP, assistant editor, production manager on short films, before eventually joining Film Australia. I edited *A Calender of Dreaming – Aboriginal Artists of Central Australia*, which was directed by Geoff Bardon, and was assistant director on *The Golden Cage*, a feature film. It was directed by the Turkish Australian Ayten Kuyululu in 1974. I can't remember the other titles.

At this time in Noyce's life, jobs in film were scarce, and hardly anything like an Australian film industry existed. Despite his aversion to the prospect of becoming a teacher, Noyce now applied twice to become a university lecturer. 'I thought maybe I should get a job.' He applied to Flinders University in Adelaide and to the University of New South Wales in Sydney, though he doesn't recall what the positions were. His applications were rejected both times. Eventually, however, conditions turned in his favour.

While still at the Film and Television School, two of the practitioners from the industry working as lecturers had obviously observed Noyce's extraordinary talent and were now keen to get him on board.[16] Tom Manefield and Richard Mason were both now working for Film Australia, where Noyce had been temporarily employed at the end of his first year at university in 1969.

Now, in 1975, Tom Manefield, who had been the producer of my documentary at the film school, got me back into Film Australia. I signed on as a production assistant because they only had a limited number of directors' positions.

Richard Mason, who also was a producer at Film Australia, had previously been a director. He came up with this unique concept for making a film about Archie Kalokerinos, the Greek-Australian doctor who had pioneered radical vitamin C therapy for treating certain diseases among Australian Aborigines. As conceived by Richard Mason, *God Knows Why But It Works* would mix a direct cinema movie with re-enacted scenes from the doctor's early career. I can't remember who wrote it; it might have even been Anne Brooksbank, who later wrote the domestic scenes between Len and his wife for *Newsfront*.

I learned a really valuable lesson at Film Australia. They had a cameraman there, Andy Fraser, who was a really good lighting cameraman. I learned that you really have to choose the right cinematographer for each particular job. This guy was great at the older style of documentary film, where you got your subjects to act out their reality. But he wasn't suited to the new style of catch-as-catch-can filming. Direct cinema. So the documentary material never had quite the intimacy I had hoped for.

We went to Brewarrina, in western New South Wales, and spent a couple of weeks filming Archie Kalokerinos. Then, based on what he had told us, a script was written. Several actors were then cast to play Archie from childhood through to his early thirties. And then the documentary and recreated material were intercut. At the end of the film, the actor playing the doctor stormed off the set and confronted the real Dr Kalokerinos, questioning him about the anomalies in his character that the actor had found impossible to interpret because they didn't obey any dramatic or psychological logic. That part was unscripted although the situation was set up, but it wasn't really successful because, while he was a good performer, the actor couldn't really articulate the problems he was having in playing the doctor.

Because we had very little money, the recreated sequences were all shot in the studio and stylised. For example, the Greek restaurant where Archie grew up was simply represented by the counter of a restaurant floating in a black void.

All this certainly gave me confidence to later mix actuality footage with drama in *Newsfront*.

The transitions between the documentary scenes and the recreated, highly theatrically dramatised ones work seamlessly. 'The acceptance of this dual mode of representation allows the narrative to take on the authority and authenticity of documentary as well as the narrative shapeliness of fiction . . . The merging of the fictional and the real is deconstructed, and the result is a restatement of the issues involved, a dramatic challenge to white passivity over Aboriginal conditions.'[17]

Still, a certain outdated, rather stilted look lingers over parts of the film. Considering how well the combination would work for Noyce in *Newsfront*, it must in this case be attributed to the film's often existentialist-like style, which had long been out of fashion.

But there is another aspect that makes the film still impressive today. What then seems to have been overlooked completely – but is easily recognisable in hindsight – is Noyce's strong attraction to Aboriginal issues during these years. With both *Amy* and *Backroads* just ahead, *God Knows Why But It Works* quite openly is a film about the neglect of Aboriginal health issues by the authorities. As we find much later in *Rabbit-Proof Fence*, misguided paternalism is the bottom line: what is good for white society simply cannot be questioned by the blackfellas.

The perverse irony of the Kalokerinos case is that his orthodox medical colleagues in the film frequently demand scientific 'proof' and ask for large-scale research before accepting his findings about vitamin C. And yet, since the 1940s, the American physicist Dr Frederick Klenner had built up a reputation for using exactly the same kind of megadoses to cure all kinds of diseases – and his findings had frequently been published. That an obscure doctor in outback Australia wasn't aware of his predecessor – and was totally crushed when he realised that his dream of winning the Nobel Prize for his work[18] would never eventuate – seems quite normal and forgivable. That the highest echelons of Australia's medical authorities were unaware of Klenner, is not.

After that I started directing documentaries in a series called *Why Can't They Be Like We Were?* with Tom Manefield as a producer.

The series consisted of films about adolescence with a number of different directors involved. The films were used as discussion starters for secondary school students around Australia and seem to have been very successful in achieving their goal of being social catalysts.

I did three of them: *Mick*, *Amy* and *Greg*. They were about ten to fifteen minutes each.

Says Jan Sharp: '*Greg* was about a father using sibling rivalry to push his sons to excel at sports. It was very autobiographical for Phillip, and one of his best films because of that. I think that film probably is still very relevant today.'[19]

Amy was the story of a fifteen-year-old country Aboriginal girl now living in the inner city, and *Mick* was the story of a sixteen-year-old skinhead 'poofter basher', as he described himself, growing up in the working-class western Sydney suburb of Mount Druitt. They were all shot by Dean Semler and the series was co-directed by Jan Sharp,[20] who later became my second wife. That's where we met.

'Well, it wasn't as simple as that. We worked together for a couple of years before he noticed me at all,' recalls Jan Sharp. 'We'd worked about a year on that first series. Then he'd taken time off to do *Backroads* and then he'd come back again on the second series called *Growing Up*, where we were working just the two of us. This series was about adolescent sexuality. Dean Semler was our cameraman on both series. One day I had been out shooting and everything had gone wrong – it rained, the kids in the schoolyard wouldn't talk to me – you know how these things happen. There was, like, 30 feet left on the end of the roll and Dean said to me, "Why don't you do a piece to camera? Tell Tom [the producer] what went wrong and why the rushes are so bad." So I just did this stand-up piece to camera as a joke. Anyway, Phillip and I were watching each other's rushes because we were working on the series together. It was so funny, the atmosphere in the editing room just became electric – changed in the most palpable way because when Phillip saw me on the screen, suddenly I was this kind of totally irresistible person. From that moment on he was totally mad about me. He was calling me twenty times a day. I'd open my door [and] he was sitting on my doorstep. But it hadn't been until he saw me on the screen that I was real. I think a lot of filmmakers are like this. There was always this joke of mine that if I wanted to tell him something I'd need to record it on film and say it to him. Anyway, he had been working with me for about a year and a half before he noticed me. Being on the big screen – that did it.'[21]

In 1976, after just five years of marriage, Jan Chapman and I separated and, taking advantage of the new no-fault divorce laws introduced by the Whitlam government, were divorced in 1977. We'd married too young, both of us having been 21. In only another half decade, we'd have followed the trend and lived together first. But in a way, the marriage would survive for decades, because together we married film as much as each other.

In the *Growing Up* series Noyce did two shorts, which were a combination of interview, voice-over and direct cinema material. In *Brad,* the subject 'identifies himself as a homosexual. The film examines his reaction to homosexuality and the importance of his relationships with other males. His mother expresses her feelings about Brad's sexuality; he is shown in his employment and enjoying himself socially.'[22] *Disco* was about dating and 'considers the social and sexual expectations and attitudes of teenagers attending a disco. Their perceptions of male and female roles, the similarities and differences, are portrayed through their behaviour, conversation and dress.'[23]

The *Growing Up* series was made in consultation with the personal development section of the NSW Department of Education, the Federal Department of Health and the Family Planning Association. Again, the films were designed for educational use only and not intended for TV broadcast. They were used as discussion starters about adolescent sexuality in Australian secondary schools and community groups. This possibly explains the lack of end credits on each episode. The series received mixed responses: indignant federal parliamentarians and church leaders questioned the 'inappropriate' subject matter, while health educators and secondary school teachers applauded the unique value of the films and the honesty of the individuals portrayed. In 1978 the series won the Australian Film Industry (AFI) award for best documentary.[24]

That series started a process that would convince me not to continue to make documentaries, both because of the intrusion into people's lives and because the subject inevitably doesn't always realise how the audience will judge their behaviour.

This series was aired on *The Mike Walsh Show*, a daytime TV discussion show, which was a perfect way of distributing the films, and I'm sure they raised important issues for a lot of kids around the country. But I went back to Mount Druitt for some other reason, and actually met one of the guys who had been in the film called *Mick*. The film was about this sixteen-year-old kid who I had found at a tattoo parlour in Mount Druitt. As it turned out, he was part of a gang that would travel into the inner city in order to bash homosexuals. Dean [Semler] and I travelled in their Holden sedan, along Parramatta Road on a Saturday night, filming them as they planned one of these escapades. It was then screened on television. And now, a year later, I met one of these kids. And he said that he had had to leave Sydney and move to Newcastle, and that the film had sort of destroyed his life. Of course, he made no apologies for bashing homosexuals. But, on the other hand, I guess he didn't expect anything like this to happen because he didn't understand the process he was about to participate in when he indicted himself in front of my camera.

So, the experience convinced me not to make that sort of documentary. It's much better to invent the characters and their lives, and not to shoulder the burden of responsibility that as a filmmaker you are exploiting the subjects of your work.

'I couldn't escape the potentially exploitative nature of what I was doing, though there was another reason for capturing those events on the screen. I was always trying to work out whether this educational use justified the revealing way in which I presented those people . . . [The families] said they liked them, but I think the films probably unnerved them a bit. It's a jolt to the system, especially when the film is being made about your values and the way you live – not necessarily condemning your values, but just pointing them out . . . So I eventually told Film Australia that I wouldn't make any more behaviour observation-type films.'[25]

David Elfick was running a cinema called the Manly Silver Screen. He had rented some movies from the [Sydney] Filmmakers Co-op, and somehow my film *Castor and Pollux* was sent to his office by mistake. He screened [it] and liked it, so I sort of got to know him. And then when I was in London on that trip after film school in 1974 we met up again. He had a surfing film called *Crystal Voyager*, which he was screening to potential distributors. His sales technique was to hand out the best Buddha grass. I mean, I was so stoned by the time that movie came on that it was definitely the best film I had ever seen. Best grass I ever smoked, as well.

And that's when David first mentioned this project he was trying to do, part-fiction and part-documentary, called *Our Time*, which was the story of two kids growing up in post–Second World War Australia. One of them was a migrant from Southern Europe and the other an Australian, and it followed their lives in the fifties, sixties and seventies, and was going to use footage from TV shows, newsreels and rock clips.

I screened *God Knows Why But It Works* at the 1976 Sydney Film Festival. Documentaries about determined individuals seemed to hit a nerve with that particular audience and their sensibilities, and of course they loved it. And that is when David came back to me with a finished script for *Newsfront*, written by Bob Ellis.

Newsfront itself will be dealt with in a later chapter. But, as could be expected, its success sparked opportunities for Noyce. The first one, however, didn't quite deliver.

In 1979, after *Newsfront*'s release, I went to Taiwan to film a feature called *Attack Force Z* about the Z Force, the Australian Second World War commandos. I wanted to do it because my father was in the real Z Force. The commandos land on an island where a plane had crashed and try to retrieve some information that had gone down with the plane.

I worked on the script with writer Michael Cove, and took Mel Gibson, Sam Neill and Chris Haywood up to Taiwan where it was to be shot as a co-production between John McCallum Productions and the Central Motion Picture Company of Taiwan, which was essentially a government organisation similar to Film Australia, run by the ruling Nationalist Party in Taiwan.

There were two issues that caused trouble pretty quickly, and one was that the Central Motion Picture Company was concerned about the potential for the content of the movie to be misconstrued by other Taiwanese. They were always paranoid about separatist movements being given any inspiration. Of course, Taiwan was ruled by an elite that had come across from mainland China after the Communist revolution in 1949 and subjugated the Taiwanese native people. They were reading all sorts of political possibilities into the screenplay that I didn't think were there and I didn't consider needed to be changed.

Producer John McCallum had made his fame and fortune as a stage actor and from producing *Skippy*, a successful television series about an Australian kangaroo. He had a very different aesthetic to mine and we disagreed about the characters to be cast from among the Taiwanese actors. Near the beginning of the film there is a scene where the Australian soldiers meet a wizened old rice farmer. The gentleman suggested for the role by the Taiwanese co-producers looked more like a Taipei dentist than a farmer. He was a well-respected actor with ties to the production company, and I said, 'No, we're not going to have that guy in the movie. It's the wrong look, the wrong feel. It will destroy the reality of the piece.' And I had an argument with John McCallum and was told to leave if I wasn't going to toe the line. It was sort of a small issue, but we drew a line in the sand and agreed that we would use that as the test of whose will was going to prevail on the whole production.

So I left and the Melbourne director Tim Burstall took over. But I stayed on in Taiwan because I had met Chris Doyle, who at the time seemed like a typical expat Australian – the usual story of an alienated European who leaves his homeland in search of something else and finds himself in another culture and stays there. Chris was in his early twenties, but already he was fluent in both Mandarin and Cantonese, having only been in Taiwan for a couple of years, and he was on the fringes of the embryonic independent Taiwanese film industry. There were just a few independent shorts being made there. Most of the films – being government-sponsored – were quite traditional in structure and style. Chris started to photograph the first efforts of the new wave of Taiwanese directors, then went on to do the same thing in Hong Kong. He got his training on the job. Just making it up as he went along, and he still does. Without formal training, he is constantly innovating. Proof that necessity is the mother of invention.

But this ill-fated project started another important professional friendship as well – with Sam Neill: 'My association with Phillip starts in 1979. He was going to direct a film called, at that time, *Z Man*. I didn't like the script much, but Phil rang up and said, "We're gonna change the script. I need you in Taiwan in three weeks. It'll be fantastic, trust me. I'll look after you, you won't look silly, it'll be a really good film." So we get to Taiwan and about three days before we're due to start shooting, the stupid producers fired him because Phil wanted to change the script. Which left us in a terrible position, because he was replaced by

Tim Burstall, who is a very different sort of director. I knew Phil before, but that's how I became friends with him.'[26]

Newsfront was the first Australian film to be shown on an Australian airline, and they made a big splash about it. Qantas then approached David Elfick to shoot a documentary about Bali for inflight screening, and David arranged for me to go up to Bali, where I met a guy called Michael White, an Australian who had adopted the Balinese name of Madé Wijaya. Like Chris Doyle, he had escaped from Australia a couple of years earlier and planned to live in Bali, where at the time he was a part-time tennis coach. Already, in 1979, Madé was fluent in high and low Balinese as well as Indonesian, and was a walking encyclopedia of Balinese history and culture. Madé has since gone on to establish an incredibly successful landscape gardening company that employs over 300 Balinese all over the world. Madé took me all around Bali over a period of a couple of months and explained the history and culture of that beautiful Hindu island.

Bali – Island of the Gods had no hidden agenda. Or if there was, the agenda and the content were perfectly in sync. We were told that it was a film to be shown to Australian tourists travelling to Bali to teach them about the depth of Balinese culture. So, a few months later, we came back and Russell Boyd shot the documentary, which even went into theatrical distribution in the UK through Mainline Cinema, who had distributed *Newsfront*.

To judge by the – admittedly few – critiques, *Bali* wasn't one of Noyce's stronger documentaries. After its screening at the 1979 Sydney Film Festival, under the name *Bali – Pulau Dewata*, one critic, writing in *Film News*, 'felt indignant at being subjected to such a series of hackneyed colour-postcard images of Bali, building up the usual picture of the place as a latter-day Garden of Eden . . . In my opinion, the film should be cut down to a five minute commercial for Qantas Airways. It does not deserve to be presented as anything better . . . By submitting such a film to the Sydney Film Festival, [Elfick, Noyce and co.] have only damaged their reputation as creative film makers with some contribution to make to the Australian scene.'[27]

Qantas then thought that having made this first film successfully, we'd do the same with a second one about Java. It's just that they didn't tell me what the purpose of the film, *Java*, was. We thought it was to be shown on Qantas planes to excite tourists about some aspects of Javanese culture that maybe they would otherwise not encounter. As shot, the film followed this group of travelling entertainers around tiny villages in remote parts of Java and featured a performer who broke building bricks on his head by first of all going into a trance, and other performers who performed trance dances and pierced their faces with barbed wire. At the initial screening, Qantas revealed for the first time that the film really had an audience of one and was intended to impress President Suharto, the dictator of Indonesia, with the sensitivity of Qantas's adoration for traditional Javanese culture. You know, the kind of things you see in a tourist brochure. And because my film emphasised the bizarre, they were now concerned that the film would have the opposite effect and they'd probably lose their pending application for increased landing rights in Indonesia. So they asked us, among many requests, to try to make it appear as though Indonesia was a technologically sophisticated democracy. We did our best. But the request was truly impossible to fulfil.

Sue and Mario, the Italian Australians, shot in 1980 for Film Australia, was a ten-minute documentary about an Italian-Australian family in Griffith, the town where I grew up. The documentary was really about the unique combination of old-world extended family and new-world nuclear family that evolved in the Griffith area.

During the First World War a restriction was placed on the size of the land-holdings that each individual was able to claim in the new Murrumbidgee Irrigation Area at Griffith. So the Australian soldier settlers, mostly with no agrarian experience, were given 20-acre holdings. Originally it had been thought that with the addition of the newly tapped water from the Snowy Mountains, that would be enough to support a man, a wife and a small family, but that didn't turn out to be the case.

A lot of Italians had fled from Italy in the early part of the twenti-eth century, escaping the olive and grape blight, which often forced the second and third son to flee to America, while the fourth and fifth sons would sometimes end up in Australia. The first son would stay in Italy, but no longer could the family holdings support everybody. A lot of Italians in Australia were working either as cane cutters or, in the winter season, as silver miners at Broken Hill. They heard about these new jobs as farm labourers at Griffith in the new irrigation area and they came across to work for the Australian soldier settlers. Pretty soon the 1-acre that the Italian would rent would produce more than the 19-acres of his boss. And eventually the Italians controlled most of the land-holdings in the district, though you were still restricted to 20-acres. What would happen was that the first son would buy the 20-acres next door to the father's 20-acres, and then the second son would buy 20-acres next door to that, so they would all live in separate houses, with separate families, but they would share, as in the old world, all the equipment and marketing and the best aspects of communal living.

Survival [1982] was a 50-minute television documentary made as part of a series of films hosted by media personality Mike Willesee. In this particular show, Michael was stranded on an island off the north Queensland coast with three women: Diane Cilento; a doctor whose name I forget; and the star of Gillian Armstrong's musical *Starstruck*, Jo Kennedy, who has since gone on to become a writer/director. The film was to be a test of how the four people could survive, supposedly for seven days. On the very first day Diane Cilento found a palm tree, which, as a naturalist, she claimed would be a source of water and nutrients. So they all cut and ate it. This par-ticular tree was actually poisonous and the four of them quickly started to hallucinate and be convulsed by violent stomach pains and dehydration. So when we returned next morning, having left them overnight, those who could be found were rolling around on the sand in pain and the others, including Mike Willesee, had already taken to the bush.

They had a radio, which was to be used only for emergencies. On the previous night, within fifteen minutes of leaving them to go back to the other side of the island where the film crew were being billeted, they broke the radio seal and listened into our radio conversation with base, and from that conversation discovered that there was habitation on the island. So when they escaped from our cameras, the object was to cross the 1000-foot-high hill in the middle of the island and get to the other side. And so the film ended up being the story of a film director fighting his subjects, and also trying desperately to find them. It was very funny. Almost twenty years later the same concept would fuel the tremendously successful reality TV series called *Survivor*.

Today it seems nearly impossible to track down some of the later shorts, and Noyce has only very vague memories of them. *Three Vietnamese Stories* (1980) were some short documentaries made for SBS TV. One was about a Vietnamese Buddhist monk who had set up a temple in his apartment at Toongabbie; another was about a former Saigon newspaper reporter who had started a weekly Vietnamese language paper. While SBS can provide copies of these, they are less sure about *Fact and Fiction*, a short from the same year. It dealt with religious superstition, exorcisms and witches.

Noyce also made a music video for rock'n'roll group The Angels in 1985. The song was called 'Underground' and was the first single from their 1985 album *Two Minute Warning*. The music video was financed by MCA Universal Music in America and shot in 16-millimetre. Between 1980 and 1987, Noyce directed about half a dozen television commercials, of which he remembers spots for Diet Coke, Tooheys beer, Findus Frozen Food, radio station 2SM and Crown Corning Ware.

A look at the production years after 1980 clearly indicates that Noyce no longer needed to make shorts in order to immerse himself in filmmaking. By then he had progressed from documentaries to television doco-dramas. When he did make shorts, it was more to try something new, such as music video or television commercials, in the long intervals between his feature films.

[1] *Castaway's Choice*, radio broadcast by KCYTW, 1990.

[2] Jan Chapman interview.

[3] Gillian Armstrong interview.

[4] Gillian Armstrong interview.

[5] Bob Ellis, '*Castor and Pollux*', *Nation Review*, 26 April–2 May 1974.

[6] Graham Shirley and Brian Adams: *Australian Cinema – The First Eighty Years* (Sydney: Angus & Robertson) 1983, p. 261.

[7] Robert Defoe interview.

[8] Martha Ansara, 'The other Australian cinema', *Filmnews*, September 1978, p. 11.

[9] Justin Paine, 'The bikie and the guru . . . and a $4000 bill', *Daily Telegraph*, 18 April 1974.

[10] David Stratton, *The Last New Wave – The Australian Film Revival* (Sydney: Angus & Robertson, 1980), p. 203.

[11] *Castaway's Choice*.

[12] Gillian Armstrong interview.

[13] Jan Chapman interview.

[14] Gillian Armstrong interview.

[15] Jan Chapman interview.

[16] Tom Manefield interview.

[17] Graeme Turner, 'Mixing fact and fiction', in Scott Murray (ed.), *Back Of Beyond: Discovering Australian Film and Television* (Sydney: Australian Film Commission, 1988), p. 71.

[18] Strangely enough, though Kalokerinos laments before the running camera that he didn't receive the Nobel Prize, Film Australia advertised the film in its catalogue as follows: 'He [Kalokerinos] was eventually acknowledged for his achievements by being awarded the Nobel Prize . . .'

[19] Jan Sharp interview.

[20] Like Noyce, Sharp came to Film Australia by way of Tom Manefield. She had been on the team that made the *Chequerboard* documentary series on the ABC that ran for about five years. 'Tom Manefield had been my producer on *Chequerboard*. So when he went over to Film Australia to produce *Why Can't They Be Like We Were?* he brought me in as the researcher and director of the series, and then Phillip came in having just finished at film school.'

[21] Jan Sharp interview.

[22] Film Australia: Titles Synopsis Report.

[23] Ibid.

[24] Email to the author dated 1 August 2003 from Anna Nolan, research assistant at Film Australia.

[25] Noyce interviewed by Mary Moody: 'Phil Noyce', *Cinema Papers*, October 1977, p. 111.

[26] Sam Neill interview.

[27] Linda Connor, '*Bali – Pulau Dewata*, a travelogue', *Film News*, August 1979.

Chapter 3
BACKROADS

Once again, it was a pub that I had to turn up to.

Jack (Bill Hunter), a white vagrant, and Gary (Gary Foley), a young Aborigine, steal a car and head around outback New South Wales, picking up fellow travellers and stealing booze, guns and fancy clothes while heading towards the coast. After a drunken killing, they are hunted down by police and arrested. Gary tries to escape but is eventually shot down.

Noyce considers *Backroads* his first feature film, despite its length of just 60 minutes and the fact that it was shot on 16-millimetre film stock. It is clearly influenced by other directors' work.

Monte Hellman's *Two-Lane Blacktop* left me fascinated with American road movies when I saw it in 1974 in London, and at the 1975 Sydney Film Festival Wim Wenders' film *Kings of the Road* mesmerised with its elegance. And another influence was John Cassavetes' films, which introduced the idea of improvisation.

There may have been some other influence as well, which David Stratton noted: '. . . Noyce [had] also been impressed with the way Andy Warhol let his "personalities" improvise.'[1] But Noyce refutes this claim, hinting at the usual confusion surrounding the master of making waves: 'Well, it wasn't Andy Warhol so much as Paul Morrissey in *Heat* and *Trash*.'

John Emery, Adelaide author of the short story that my film-school short *Caravan Park* was based on, had written another story about a young Aborigine, 'The First Day of Spring'. It opened with the Aboriginal character being released from the police lock-up at dawn in some outback town. Anyway, I went over and spent some time talking to John and he wrote some sort of script, which I added to. I don't remember what the document was that I used to raise money on, because I do know that most of the film was improvised. But there must have been some scenes that were written by John Emery, as well as some written by me, in the final film. I just can't remember exactly where John stopped and I started, or which ones are improvised.

Basically, it's the story of a white drifter and a young Aborigine who together steal a car in the outback and drive across-country, heading for the coast. And that car becomes a vacuum, their own world where they are kings and free to engage in intense discussions and to develop relationships between themselves and with the people they pick up along the way.

In looking around for someone to play the young Aborigine, fellow director Ken Cameron, who also suggested the title of *Backroads*, gave me some newspaper articles about Gary Foley, who was one of Australia's young black activists at the time – a handsome firebrand with matinee idol looks. I was told to ring Gary at a pub in the Aboriginal ghetto of Redfern called the Cricketer's Arms. I rang and went over to this pub full of Aborigines and told Gary that I wanted him to be a movie star. And Gary said he didn't want any part of white man's bullshit unless he got to monitor all of the black content. So we reached this agreement that he could rewrite his dialogue whenever he thought it was bullshit; he could have a say in the movie's content.

If Noyce allowed Foley so much influence on the film's script, plot and editing, was he afraid of losing his artistic authority?

No, it was consultation – and this was well before 'cultural consultation' became an in-thing. If you're a white person trying to capture an indigenous attitude and spirit, the only way you can do that is by consulting, by listening to the indigenous point of view. Now it's become a mantra but . . . It wasn't so much about being democratic on that film as admitting that the middle-class white man was always going to be outside an indigenous mentality. The only way I could ever gain access was to listen – consult and listen. And who could better capture the spirit of Aboriginal slang than Gary himself?

The choice of Foley as lead actor was significant. In 1972, he was instrumental in setting up 'the Tent Embassy' in front of Parliament House in Canberra, which put Aboriginal affairs firmly on the agenda of the Whitlam government. One year earlier, 'he had hoaxed the *Australian* newspaper into believing there was a highly militant Black Panther chapter in Australia.'[2] In a typical seventies manner he participated in street theatre groups, made films and was active in the music scene, 'appearing as a guest singer with The Clash on their Australian tour in 1981'.[3]

Elizabeth Knight was going to be first assistant director on the movie. She had been the first assistant director on *Let the Balloon Go*, a feature film that I worked on in 1975 as second assistant director at Film Australia. I was looking for someone to play the white racist drifter, Jack. Elizabeth had worked at the ABC with a guy called Bill Hunter, and so once again, it was a pub that I had to turn up to.

It was somewhere in or around Surry Hills. I think it was the same pub on the corner of William and Riley streets where I used to have to throw stones at the window to wake up Cec Holmes, the famous director for whom I worked as a production assistant at Film Australia when I was eighteen. Anyway, Hunter came out on the footpath and I told him the story of the movie and said, 'Can you read a scene from the script?' He said, 'I'm dyslexic, can't read.' So I said, 'Oh well, here's the story of the character.' And he said, 'Okay; I'll do a few scenes for you.' He invented several long monologues on the spot and he was incredible. He *was* the character.

So I cast Gary, who was a great speaker and had already said that he wanted to monitor the black content, and Hunter who, once you gave him a couple of beers, you couldn't shut up. One thing led to another and we were suddenly improvising everything.

The most important thing about improvisation is to get the actors to understand who they are playing – the imaginary character – and then hopefully they become so involved in the character that they start to speak with the character's voice, and once you press the button they'll just start to talk and think like the character. They become scriptwriters and actors in one, within a sort of circle of creativity that the director weaves around them. Gary was completely armed and ready to start speaking with the character's voice. He knew the character better than the director, the writer – anyone. So this guy was playing a variation of himself. He had come from the country; he grew up around Aboriginal reserves. The finished film represents 100 per cent the original story, but 80 per cent of the dialogue was made up on the spot by the actors.

Initially, Gary and I went on a location survey to find a route that the film might follow through the back roads of New South Wales.

The Creative Development Branch of the Australian Film Commission had given us 20,000 dollars to make the film. I had spent 3000 dollars buying a 1962 Pontiac Parisienne, a big American car that would be one of the stars of the movie. But it broke down after about half a day, and from then on it had to be jump-started and pushed; it was a complete wreck.[4] The crew consisted of myself; Lloyd Carrick on sound; Russell Boyd (who in 2004 won the Oscar for Best Cinematography for Peter Weir's *Master and Commander*) as DoP, and his assistant, Jan Kenny; Jan Chapman, my wife, and Martha Ansara as production assistants; first assistant, Elizabeth Knight; Kevin Smith, who came along as Gary's bodyguard; and the actors, Hunter, Foley, Terry Camilleri, Zac Martin and Julie McGregor. We travelled across New South Wales in a convoy of about four vehicles out to Bourke, then through Brewarrina and back. The four-week shoot ended up at Wollombi in the Hunter Valley, three hours from Sydney, where my family owned a farm. We all lived on the farm and shot the final sequences around there.

It was complex shooting because we were improvising scenes in both the front and the back of the car that were to be intercut with each other. I hadn't yet realised you could use prop wine or beer, so the flagons of sherry and white wine and stuff that were being passed around and the beer that had been consumed were all real, so by the end of most scenes everyone was drunk. I don't know how we kept it up, actually.

It was a pretty weird experience because there was frequently a lot of tension between the white and the black members of the crew and cast, and there wasn't a lot of money. Everyone was paid the same amount, 300 dollars per week, including Russell Boyd.

Access to the Aboriginal camps was a result of being with Gary. The camp in the film was at Bourke. When you think about it, seeing all those Aborigines herded behind barbed wire is a real indictment, isn't it?

People often wonder how we did the shots inside the travelling car. Russell had done that before, and so he brought along this limpet mount that he would attach to the side of the car with the camera mounted on it. The drunken actors would drive, and I would be strapped on to the front hood of the speeding car. Lloyd Carrick was in the trunk recording sound, surrounded by exhaust fumes. It was very hairy! When I needed to speak to the actors I would shout to them.

I would start and stop the camera from the hood by pressing a remote. We would check it beforehand and afterwards to make sure it had stayed still. Great stuff. When we were filming scenes in the back seat, the camera would be hand-held in the car. Insurance could have been a problem, but there *was* no insurance. We only saw what we had been shooting once we returned to Sydney at the end of the four weeks.

All the points-of-view [POV] shots from the car I actually shot several months later. Jan Chapman's brother had moved to Perth and we agreed to drive his car over to him. So while Jan drove, I photographed out the window between Sydney and Perth. Those shots are probably overused and the film becomes a little tedious in the end with all of these POVs.

For lighting, we just had 800-watt red heads and a couple of sun guns. And some bounce boards. Maybe six lights.

During the shoot we sometimes had problems with Gary, who was suspicious of the whole enterprise. After the film came out, and all the years since then, we have been the best of friends. He is now curator of the indigenous exhibition at Melbourne's Museum Victoria and a historian. He is the fittest of any of us, which he finds remarkable because 54 is a late age for a male Aborigine, according to statistics of indigenous Australian mortality. As Gary has remarked, he has increasingly few Aboriginal friends that are still alive.

Towards the end of the shoot we ran out of money. Fortunately for me, two days' worth of rushes were destroyed by the lab. So we charged the lab full professional rates for the insurance claim they put in, which yielded sufficient money to complete shooting. If we hadn't had the good fortune to lose two days' shooting, the film may never have been finished.

But I still had to go out and earn extra money. David Huggett was the editor; Frans Vandenburg, who would later cut *Shadows of the Peacock*, was his assistant. I left Film Australia and took a job as a producer back at the film school. I was employed to mentor a group of students as they made a drama. I didn't do much mentoring because I was really there just to earn a few hundred dollars more each week so that I could keep David Huggett editing. I would leave the students on location and hurry back to the editing room.

When Gary first saw the film he made some suggestions for changes, which I adopted. We had shot a sequence with Essie Coffey, an Aboriginal female leader, talking to Julie McGregor's character on a riverbank. The original cut of the film didn't include that sequence. As it is now, in the final film, it's sort of a non sequitur. Suddenly this new character is talking to Julie McGregor about what the white man had done to the Aborigines and it sort of comes out of nowhere.

Gary thought the sequence was important as a documentary record of attitudes at a particular moment in time, and within the jagged context of the whole movie it probably contributed a lot.

I wanted the film to be this weird mixture of the formal and the anarchic in style and content. On the one hand it's a C road movie – not B, not A, but a C, like *Cannonball Express*, for example: the duel between the car and the semi-trailer. I also wanted it to be a serious A road movie, like *Kings of the Road*, with formal transition devices from silent films. And then I wanted it to be almost a direct cinema documentary – for example, the sequence where the guys are singing around the campfire in the Aboriginal reserve. Another influence was *Antonio Das Mortes*, the Brazilian film by Glauber Rocha, which was also quite stylised, yet mixed elements of theatre and B-movie exploitation cinema.

The ending of the film undoubtedly seems flawed – due to the haste caused by financial problems. But at the same time, it looks much more politically correct than was intended in the script.

'Originally, the people in the stolen car – the two Aboriginals and the white man – end up by causing a traffic jam on the approach to the [Sydney] Harbour Bridge. They abandon the car, leaving it among a mass of vehicles, and disappear into the concrete jungle. The last shot was to be three or four miles of traffic stacked up behind the car.

'We were actually going to stage a breakdown on the freeway and just film it. Gary, however, felt that politically it was a cop-out. The journey these men undertake was always seen as an allegory of the journey white men and the Aboriginals took together over the past 200 years – and that journey, as we know, has been ultimately tragic for the Aboriginals. So, Gary felt the film should end tragically and that his character should be killed. And that is the way we shot it.

'I am not really happy with the ending. We didn't have enough resources of money and manpower to do the sort of ending that we finally compromised on. Also, I had been planning the other ending for more than a year and we only changed it at the last minute.'[5]

The film premiered at the Sydney Film Festival in June 1977, and in general received a rather lukewarm response. This didn't bother Noyce too much:

It was my first long drama, so I was fine with it. What could I do? I had no expectation, really.

However, there were other reactions as the film's 'threatening attitude seemed to alarm some members of the audience not used to this kind of confronting cinema in locally-made productions', as Stratton remembered.[6] Typical of contemporary attitudes was Keith Connolly, who conceded that '*Backroads* by no means is a failure' but complained that 'its chief weakness is a want of cohesion'. He continued, 'The film falters when Noyce detours into a segment of talking-head discourse by shanty-camp blacks. This presumably is intended to background an ongoing debate between the principals, but the documentary-style sequence is such an abrupt change of pace that it blunts rather than reinforces the polemic about the plight of the Aboriginals.'[7]

But no matter how irritated the critics were – mostly, anecdotal evidence suggests, by the frequent use of the 'four-letter word', which earned the film an R rating – two aspects of the film were readily acknowledged: the 'stunning photography by Russell Boyd'[8] and its 'contemporary importance'.[9] John Pym: '*Backroads* does throw a strong light on the degradation of Aboriginal life in contemporary Australia ... The film's real strength lies in the authentic exchanges between Gary and Jack.'[10]

Significant among the contemporary critics was P.P. McGuinness in the *National Times*: '[It] is the most effective and technically accomplished dramatic film that I have seen ... on the maltreatment and hopelessness of Aborigines in our society ... Noyce manages to avoid sentimentality and cliché ... which allows him to handle the real problems of contemporary Australian society without descent into facile sentiment or tedious propaganda.'[11] A minor complaint was: 'Possibly the film errs towards melodrama at the end ... [but at least Noyce] never allows the film to stop while we are given a political lecture.'

Noyce admits that *Backroads* is 'a very difficult film to come to grips with'.

'The characters are generally unattractive and it is a film where I have sought to investigate so-called "unmotivated crime". And this makes it additionally difficult for an audience to feel sympathy for the characters. The realism and forcefulness of the characters have also tended to provoke personal prejudices in some viewers, reactions that have been confused by their attitudes to certain behaviour. You always bring your own prejudices to a film so you can't really blame critics – you just have to find a way of pointing out to them how your film might appeal.'[12]

But once the film was selected for the Berlin Film Festival in February 1978 and was consequently picked up by Scala, a small British distributor, the situation improved greatly.

It was screened at Berlin and, yes, Wim Wenders liked it and so did Werner Herzog. And then it was screened in the Market Place in Cannes, not in any official capacity. Gary and I hired a little theatre, handed out advertising leaflets and screened it. Soon afterwards, it opened in London at the Scala.

It seems that *Backroads* was understood very well in Europe, where from the outset, responses were much more positive in some ways than in Australia.

'Suddenly it all came back to me what the film was intended to be about. It was a revelation to me that somewhere in the world there were critics who loved cinema and would approach the film not looking for what was wrong with it and how it could therefore be condemned, but rather what was right with it, what its good qualities were.'[13]

Admittedly, however, not all the foreign critics were raving. *Variety*, typically for most of Noyce's career so far, dismissed the film – this time as 'a schematic look at race relations . . . too arbitrary and predictable to take on greater meaning than the incidents themselves represent'.[14] Despite, or rather because of that, it 'is regarded in Australia as an important social document'.[15]

With some distance, the importance of *Backroads* has become even more evident. It is an 'admirably angry film, a sort of *Easy Rider* accusing Australia of a deeply engrained racism'.[16] And it was the first film to do just that in a very graphic way. 'With some redirection by Gary Foley, Noyce ended up with a statement much stronger than he ever set out to make.'[17]

What naturally couldn't be seen back in 1978 becomes obvious today. *Backroads* and *Rabbit-Proof Fence* act as a kind of brackets around Noyce's Australian work. Different as they are in content and intention, they are both based on the perhaps most Australian of concepts of the self: being on the road. It is celebrated in the unofficial national anthem 'Waltzing Matilda', as well as in the high-powered *Mad Max* films. Being on the move – not arriving – is the name of the game. Gary and Jack are heading nowhere – despite their odyssey leading them from the outback to the eastern seaboard, where contact was first established between the Aborigines and the Europeans. The journey is undertaken by car, the white man's way, to stretches of land that have long since lost all traces of Aboriginal identity.

Today, the rights for *Backroads* are held by Foley – maybe a personal sign of reconciliation from Noyce's side.

After a certain point I could see that the person who had invested the most in the movie was Gary. So I said to him, 'You didn't get paid much for what you've done, so you can have the rights to the film. You could make some money out of it, because there is always some new distribution outlet invented that we didn't figure on five years ago.'

What did the film mean back then, and what does it mean to Noyce today?

It was my first attempt to make a longer dramatic film. It was finished at a time when Australian audiences were very enthusiastic about national cinema and it was very much a learning process in terms of sizing up that audience. I realised from screening the film in its limited release that a story dealing with indigenous characters and themes was attractive to audiences because of its relative uniqueness. But there was very much a limit to the Australian audience that wanted to see such stories. So, in a way, I made a mental note to myself about how to find the audience that naturally wanted to respond to a story like that, but also about how you might break through to the ones that thought they *didn't* want to see a film with indigenous characters. From screening *Backroads* around Australia and watching and listening to the audience, a lot of lessons were filed away for another 24 years to be used in making and selling *Rabbit-Proof Fence*.

The two stories are set just 45 years apart, but they are in reality separated by 150 years. One deals with indigenous characters on the eastern seaboard of Australia, where contact started to take place from 1778 with the establishment of the first penal colony, and where by the 1970s Aboriginal culture was almost at its lowest point, almost utterly decimated. Whereas *Rabbit-Proof Fence* is set in the Western Australian desert in the last areas settled by white people. Back in 1931, and even today, Aboriginal people in this area have managed to cling to some of their traditional lifestyle and certainly have managed to maintain spiritual connections to their traditional lands. So, the films are very different. One is about hopelessness, and the other is about hope. Hope being much more possible where the Aboriginal people have managed to cling to just a little bit of what they had when Europeans first came to Australia.

---

[1] David Stratton, *The Last New Wave – The Australian Film Revival* (Sydney: Angus & Robertson, 1980), p. 204.

[2] Stephen Muecke, '*Backroads*: From identity to interval', *Senses of Cinema*, no. 17, 2001.

[3] Ibid.

[4] It eventually ended up in a publicity stunt. 'I towed it out onto the front lawn of Sydney University and then as a stunt to raise interest in the movie I brought

along six sledgehammers and invited the students to wreck the car.' (Noyce cited
    in Raffaele Caputo and Geoff Burton, *Third Take – Australian Filmmakers Talk*
    (Sydney: Allen & Unwin, 2002), p. 149.)
[5] Quoted in Mary Moody, 'Phil Noyce', *Cinema Papers*, October 1977, p. 112.
[6] Stratton, *The Last New Wave*, p. 205.
[7] Keith Connolly, '*Love Letters from Teralba* and *Backroads*', *Cinema Papers*,
    January 1978, p. 262.
[8] Paul Heinrichs, 'Censors re-route *Backroads* signal', *The Age*, 1 July 1977.
[9] Helen Frizell, 'Today's history in form of fiction', *Sydney Morning Herald*,
    4 June 1978.
[10] John Pym, '*Backroads*', *Monthly Film Bulletin*, September 1978, p. 171.
[11] P.P. McGuinness, 'An exciting road movie with a few sermons along the way',
    National Times, 27 June 1977.
[12] Quoted in Moody, 'Phil Noyce', p. 112.
[13] Quoted in Stratton, *The Last New Wave*, p. 205.
[14] '*Backroads*', *Variety*, 6 May 1981, p. 24.
[15] David White, *Australian Movies to the World – The International Success of
    Australian Films since 1970* (Sydney: Fontana, 1984), p. 60.
[16] Andrew Tudor, 'The Aussie picture show', in Albert Moran and Tom O'Reagan
    (eds), *An Australian Film Reader* (Sydney: Currency Press, 1985), p. 213.
[17] Anne Hutton, 'Black Australia and film – only it makes money', in Moran and
    O'Reagan, *An Australian Film Reader*, p. 336.

Chapter 4
NEWSFRONT

Whatever the camera sees, that's real.

Brothers Len (Bill Hunter) and Frank Maguire (Gerard Kennedy) work for rival newsreel companies in the late forties and early fifties; Cinetone is Australian, and Newsco is American-owned. They compete in work and in their love for the same woman – Amy Mackenzie (Wendy Hughes). Len with his assistant, Chris Hewitt (Chris Haywood), covers some of the significant Australian historical events of the period, and the film follows his career up to the Olympic Games in Melbourne in 1956 and the advent of television in Australia.

Newsfront must have one of the longest pre-histories of any Australian feature film – and still enjoys a healthy life 25 years after its original release. It remains a seminal film in its reflection of the Australian collective psyche. And strangely enough, it is still shrouded in myth and controversy.

When I first started making short films, David Elfick was already an icon within the alternative-culture scene of Sydney. He had been editor of *Go Set*, a *Rolling Stone*–type teen newspaper, and later established *Tracks*, a monthly surfing magazine which he edited for about three years. He also ran a cinema called the Manly Silver Screen, which showed alternative movies, and had produced and distributed a number of surfing movies, including *Morning of the Earth* and then a big hit which sold worldwide, called *Crystal Voyager*, on which he was producer and co-director. We had similar experiences in terms of movie making, because while I was shooting and screening short experimental films, he had been producing, directing and distributing surf films, putting up the posters, booking the theatre, taking the money, running the projector and then moving on to the next coastal town.

'By accident some of the experimental films Phil had made at the Sydney Filmmakers Co-op turned up at my office in Whale Beach. I had a 16 mm projector there and so I screened them and was particularly struck by the film about rival bikie gangs, *Castor and Pollux*. This film really impressed me because here was a guy who'd gone out and basically shot a real event but turned it into a drama. Phil has always had a great dramatic sense, even with documentary.'[1]

Bob Ellis recalls: 'Elfick originally had a vague idea of doing a film about Australian pop music of the 1950s and early 1960s. There existed then a lot of footage, principally from *Six O'Clock Rock* (1959–63) and *Bandstand* (1958–72), and by way of research into the music footage, Elfick came upon the Cinesound and Movietone newsreels and began to react to them. Then he thought of doing a documentary like Philippe Mora's *Brother, Can You Spare a Dime?* (1975). Obviously he approached Philippe Mora, who said, "It's a good idea but why not make a drama about the men who shot the newsreels, instead of merely doing a collage film?" The idea originated with Philippe Mora and was based on two brothers called Syd and Ross Wood, both of whom worked for rival newsreel companies and had a sometimes genuine, sometimes ferocious professional rivalry between them. Elfick took that idea first to Richard Neville.'[2]

Elfick had befriended Neville and Andrew Fisher while in London and helped them with the infamous *Oz* magazine. Back in Australia, they would visit with him at his place in Palm Beach, where Mike Molloy, cinematographer on Philippe Mora's *Mad Dog Morgan*, was also living. Mora frequently dropped in at weekends.

'Mike was always talking about the great newsreels,' says Elfick, 'and of course I would remember going to see the Redex cars off at the Sydney Showground and then rushing off to the newsreel theatre a week later to see the same event up on screen. It was on one of these weekends that I decided with Andrew Fisher to write a dramatic narrative involving newsreel cameramen, which gave us a way of working archival footage into the story and also would give us the spectacles we couldn't afford to shoot. Andrew and I then received a trickle of development money from the Arts Council, thanks to Richard Keyes, and we worked on a script whenever we could. We made a living by doing other projects but we always pushed ahead with the *Newsfront* concept, which developed over several years.'[3]

I can't remember exactly when David first told me about the project that was later to be called *Newsfront*, but I think it was in London in late 1974. He said that he, lawyer/writer Andrew Fisher and writer Richard Neville were working on an idea that had initially been a documentary compilation of footage about Australia's post-war history. It had then evolved into a combination of documentary footage, drawn from newsreels and TV, as well as a fictional story, which I believe at the time didn't involve cameramen, but was to tell the story of two kids growing up in post-war Australia.

By the time Bob Ellis became involved, the final protagonists had found their way into the idea. 'David Elfick arrived with the best idea I'd heard,' says Ellis. 'It was about the lifestyle of newsreel cameramen and the stories they covered in the years from 1945 to 1956, with the proviso that newsreels of the day would be inserted into the drama. Elfick approached me after he'd heard a speech I'd written which was delivered by Graeme Blundell for an award night at the Sydney Film Festival. He rang me saying that I was just the kind of person he needed for this project, but had not told me he had already got a script of no great value out of Richard Neville, nor that he'd been ordered by the Australian Film Commission to approach someone like me who had some street credit as a dramatic writer, rather than as a book writer or journalist.'[4]

Elfick explains: 'I met with Bob and found him to be a lively character, but more importantly he shared a great passion for the subject matter and so that's how Bob became our scriptwriter.'[5]

Ellis: 'I was then offered the document written by Neville and I deliberately never read it because I thought it would confuse me. I also read about two pages of a document written by Elfick and it was so dreadful that I threw it across the room, bounced it against the wall and jumped on it. I didn't get more than two or three pages into that one.'[6]

The project initially ran by different titles, as Ellis recalls. 'I think Philippe [Mora] came up with *Newsfront*; Elfick wanted to call it "Useless If Delayed". But it was decided that the word "useless" in the title might attract the venom of lazy critics and so Elfick settled for *Newsfront*. My summary line for the film – "buccaneers on mortgages" – was the shortest way to express the content but it was never considered as a title. It was always just a description.'[7]

Ellis continues: 'I wrote a draft of the screenplay. In those days I wasn't good at stage direction, so I wrote the dialogue and Anne Brooksbank, my wife, wrote the stage directions and a couple of scenes involving Len and his wife Fay (Angela Punch-McGregor). Annie certainly wrote the scene of Len and Fay in bed talking about the children and she says, "I gotta be mother and father to them half the time."'[8]

In late June 1976 David Elfick contacted me again to ask me to read a screenplay written by Bob Ellis entitled *Newsfront*. It was an early draft, but already the project had evolved into more or less the form we see in the finished movie.

I was struck by the uniqueness of the idea and how appropriate it seemed to my own experience as a filmmaker. Combining period newsreel footage with a recreated fictional story seemed to be a natural springboard from *God Knows Why But It Works*, the 1975

Film Australia documentary about Dr Archie Kalokerinos, which combined direct cinema documentary and recreated dramatic scenes.

While I found the script over-long, and the dialogue sometimes overblown and unrealistic, I responded to the characters and nostalgia elements. Although born in 1950 and a young kid during most of the events described by the screenplay, this was the story of my parents' generation, who had lived through fifteen years of disrupted lives with the Great Depression followed almost immediately by the Second World War. As well, it was the story of an Australia which, even in 1977, I could see vanishing, the time before television when we really rejoiced in that tyranny of distance separating us from the rest of the world. Also impressive was the way in which Ellis had mapped out how the film could combine real events with a fictional story, creating both an emotionally involving narrative, a history thesis and a striking political document that described the loss of innocence and the cultural colonisation of Australia.

I was just about to start shooting *Backroads* and was off on a location survey with Aboriginal activist Gary Foley. We were travelling through the outback looking for locations. David still has the telegram I sent him from the town of Bourke: 'Read half the script, great so far.'

Elfick takes up the story: 'Bob produced several drafts of the script but there was a long delay because this was the period of the sacking of the Whitlam government. It was always difficult getting a script from a writer who liked to make good excuses, but it was especially difficult from a writer sympathetic to the Labor Party. He just couldn't concentrate on his work because of the political matters at hand in the nation. That delayed the script for several years, yet we struggled through and managed to get some really good drafts of the script out of Bob.'[9]

Both Noyce and Elfick agree that Ellis's script was too long, something Ellis refutes vehemently. 'I remember a great gloom came over me when Elfick said, "We got the money and the film can be made, but the money is $100,000 less than what is needed to make the film." And because I had printed the script out in a silly format – it was triple-spaced and had come out to about 300 pages – there was a rumour that the script was far too long. But in fact the script was somewhere between two hours and two hours and ten minutes, which I thought was reasonable for a film that covered ten years of history. These days that's a mere bagatelle.'[10]

During pre-production David Elfick and [associate producer] Richard Brennan discussed the problem of not being able to raise enough money to shoot all the scripted scenes.

Although Bob had written a unique screenplay, as the director I was faced with the responsibility of trying to deliver a movie for the budget and also make the viewing experience as compelling as possible for the audience. To achieve both, I knew script cuts would have to be made.

Bob Ellis: 'The problem was that there were primal experiences in the script, and I saw the project more like a snapshot of a whole nation at a particular period of time, but what seemed to be happening was that the script was being pared back to the mere politics of the piece. There were other experiences in the script that were at least as interesting as a tedious left-wing wrangle, which had its place but needed to be supported by a number of other things.'[11]

But Bob insisted that his opus remain intact and started a one-man battle to convince us to reinstate various cut scenes. Like the Ancient Mariner, he would berate anyone who would listen, including some of the impressionable actors who had already been cast. No doubt Bob felt he was doing the right thing, saving his masterwork from these relatively inexperienced filmmakers, Noyce and Elfick, but the situation became untenable.

I can well remember the inertia Bob would induce in me when I heard from our actors that we should put this scene back, or we shouldn't be doing that, or we should be hiring a particular crew-member. It reached the stage eventually where David severed the relationship with Bob and we decided to go it alone, without his day-to-day involvement in the vital pre-production decisions on how to shoot the movie. Although David and I were able to argue about what was right and wrong for the film and then reach agreement, it seemed that as a threesome, Ellis, Noyce and Elfick, we could never reach agreement, just endlessly argue.

By this time Ellis had gained a tempestuous reputation. 'I remember going into the production office at one point and noticing great lines struck through the screenplay and saying to Richard Brennan, "What's all this? What's happening?" I remember Brennan looked at the script with an air of surprise and said, "Oh, I didn't know anything about this!" I thought he was lying. [Then] there occurred the famous incident at Palm Beach when I said, "That's it! I'm taking the film." I seized the script and began to run from the building, and there were workmen in the rafters cheering as Elfick tackled me and brought me down and the script's pages fluttered everywhere like butterflies.'[12]

Other tough decisions lay ahead.

Financing the film wasn't proving to be easy, especially as the main players, Noyce and Elfick, had no experience of making feature films, of proper length, that is. In addition, what became one of the most startling elements of the film – its integration of black-and-white and colour footage – was in fact due initially to pragmatic concerns of one of the funding partners, though Noyce would later offer additional rationales.

The financing for *Newsfront* came principally from two government film agencies, the Australian Film Commission and, majority investor, the New South Wales Film Corporation. The funds were dependent on finding a local Australian distributor. Village Roadshow and head of their Sydney office, Greg Coote, were constant supporters of the project. Roadshow eventually released the film successfully around Australia,[13] but as the security for their investment was going to be the potential sale for screening on Australian television, they wanted a colour movie. With the recent introduction of colour TV to Australia, suddenly black-and-white films were out of vogue, and a no-no for prime-time TV transmission.

But shooting *Newsfront* in colour was an absolute impossibility, as little of the original newsreel footage was in colour. Obviously, all of those sequences, such as the Maitland floods, that involved constant cross-cutting between original newsreel footage and recreated material had to be in black and white. There was no such thing as colourisation in 1977. So I came up with the idea of dividing the chapters of the film between some that would be shot in black and white and some that would be in colour.

Roadshow, as distributor, agreed to these switches based not on chronology but on the emotional tone of each chapter. This decision in turn generated an unforeseen problem for Elfick, who had hoped to have Mike Molloy as cinematographer. He explains: 'Mike felt it should all be in black-and-white, and as a result he declined our offer to shoot the film. That was a big blow to us because our starting date kept on being delayed as it took us longer to get the package together. Eventually Vince Monton came on board as director of photography. We came across him through Richard Brennan, our associate producer, who knew the technicians' market better than Phil or I. Vince was young, hungry, a very smart fellow and technically adept. He fitted our team brilliantly and *Newsfront* really established him as a new breed of cinematographer.'[14]

Monton liked the project from the start of his involvement. 'The first thing I found interesting about the story from a cinematography point of view was that it covered a period of ten years, from just after the Second World War to about 1956, the year of the Melbourne Olympic Games and the arrival of television in Australia. Period films had been done before in this country but they were always set in a period outside of people's memories. I was confronted with a situation where I had to photograph a time and place most people would remember, only twenty to twenty-five years after the events of the story.'[15]

The inclusion of newsreels influenced Noyce's choice of visual style, as the archive footage had to match the recreated scenes.

'The newsreels were predominantly shot on wide or medium angle lenses. They used no long lenses, nothing above 75mm really, so that they were always working with a very long depth of field, compared with what is usual in contemporary films. But we also set out to imitate the slightly stagey feel of so many late forties and early fifties melodramas.'[16]

I decided the film wouldn't have a consistent look in terms of colour. The emotional feeling after the war was more downbeat than it was by 1956, when reconstruction had taken place and the consumer society was completely re-established. So, each chapter of the film was to have a slightly different look to it. From 1956 (the sixth chapter) the film concentrates especially on the way in which Australia fell increasingly into the orbit of America after the introduction of television. Wardrobe and set dressing were to become more garish and outlandish than earlier in the film, and there was to be a degree of caricature in the presentation of people and situations in this section, as opposed to the more realistic, naturalistic first five chapters of the film.

Much had been written about the way the film switches from black and white to colour at various points.

Later on I may have given an emotional and intellectual rationale to the crew about why we were dividing the various chapters, but the decision was forced on me simply by the fact that if we were trying to produce a seamless reality that combined archive newsreel footage with recreated material, then obviously that chapter had to be in black and white. There was no choice.

But when the newsreel footage was used as archive material, such as the Anzac Day celebration where the newsreel makers are watching a cinema screen on which they see black-and-white images of the war in New Guinea shot by legendary newsreel photographer Damien Parer, the sequence could be in colour, even though it contained newsreel footage.

During the early part of pre-production, assistant editor Frans Vandenberg, editor John Scott and I visited the National Film Archive in Canberra (now ScreenSound) to cull through all the newsreel footage that might be relevant to our story. We unearthed a lot of material already mentioned in Ellis's script, such as the Redex trial, the Melbourne Olympics, and so on. But one of the discoveries we made was the footage featuring Chico Marx [of the Marx Brothers] singing 'Waltzing Matilda', which we decided should open the film, as it seemed so appropriate to the theme of cultural imperialism, and evolved into the ghostlike version of the song composed by Bill Motzing for use throughout the story.

We also decided to turn to the living icon of both the Australian newsreel and film industry, Ken G. Hall, who at that time was already in his mid-eighties and living in retirement. Ken had produced and directed seventeen feature films during the 1930s, but when unable to continue directing features after *Smithy* in 1946 spent the next decade making newsreels, before finally leaving the film business to run television's Channel Nine in Sydney for Sir Frank Packer.

'They sought my help, which I said I would be glad to give,' Hall explained. 'They brought a bound script with a well illustrated cover – good showmanship for a start, I thought! – and said it had to do with the "war" between Cinesound and Movietone in the forties and early fifties. In an immediate reaction I said, "Don't make it." When they asked why, I said I did not think anybody in this day and age would be very interested in what Cinesound and Movietone may have been doing in the forties and fifties. How wrong I was!

'I took an immediate liking to these two young men, who had never made a feature film up to this point. Although they were frankly perhaps a little wide-eyed in their approach to the immense problems I could see in what they proposed to do, their enthusiasm was contagious. I responded and I am glad I did. Their story line involved using perhaps a thousand to fifteen hundred feet of the very valuable newsreel library material mentioned earlier. They knew all about it and had already viewed vast amounts of the footage available. I pointed to the immediate problem of integrating the old black and white footage with the colour of today. How were they going to get in and out of it? They weren't exactly sure at that stage – another point I liked about them. There was nothing cocksure about their approach. They left the script with me so that I could digest it and said they would be back in a week.

'I didn't like the script – or to be more exact I didn't like a good deal of it. A film should build to a climax. This script built to a climax . . . and anti-climax after anti-climax!'[17]

I asked Ken for ideas on how to shoot the Maitland flood sequence and he offered a really simple solution: 'You aren't going to be able to flood half the countryside of New South Wales like the real footage, but you may be able to reproduce the appearance of a flood over a limited area. The trick is, it doesn't matter what's outside the frame, son; whatever the camera sees, that's real. So put your camera up high, point it down, and frame up on what you can convince the audience is flooded. Don't show anything else and you will achieve the reality you're after.' If you look at some of the re-created shots of the floods, particularly those where you see Chris Haywood being swept by the torrent of floodwater, you will notice that frequently at the top of frame, the water is quite placid. This is because the jet boats that were simulating water flow didn't reach that high and somehow we framed up an area that wasn't as convincingly flowing as the rest of the shot. As suggested by Ken Hall, the camera is usually looking down on the action.

Ken's other major advice was that we should remove all blasphemy and expletives from the screenplay because he felt that they were offensive to the audience and not necessarily indicative of the way people really spoke during that era. I can't remember whether we followed this advice or not.

Looking to cast the lead role of Len Maguire we first thought of Jack Thompson, who at the time was sort of an Australian superstar, having starred in a number of commercially successful movies, including *Sunday Too Far Away* and *Petersen*. But he turned us down. I know that Bob Ellis now tells the story of trying to convince me that Bill Hunter should play Len and that I supposedly initially said no. I can't say for sure whether that story is true, except that having cast Hunter in *Backroads* and loved the experience, I can't believe I would have been negative about the idea of considering him for *Newsfront*.

Hunter remembers things pretty clearly. 'It was at a pub called the Gladstone on the corner of William and Palmer Streets and it was a strange sequence of events because I think *Newsfront* was the first time I had refused to do an audition. Halfway through *Backroads* [Noyce] said to me, "I've got a part for you," and I said, "Ease up, Phil, I've heard that all my life." [Noyce] walked into the Gladstone Hotel, threw a script at me and said, "You can play one of the brothers." Without having read it, I said, "No, I'm going to play 'the' brother and I won't screen-test and I won't audition." That turned me around a bit because it was a huge punt for me, but I felt it was the right time to assert myself. I didn't do the audition and [Noyce] still gave me the part. Then Elfick asked me to read in for people at Palm Beach. I really thought I was secure, that I had the part. I'll read in for anybody, I don't care, but I didn't realise the reading at Palm Beach was in fact an audition.'[18]

Hunter read for the part and was contracted for the lead, and as the inevitability of actually shooting the film approached, I realised I'd never actually seen Bill Hunter without a beard. David and I decided to coax him up to Palm Beach, north of Sydney, where David had a house in a former beachside tearoom and we were going to encourage Bill to remove his beard. Obviously it wasn't appropriate for a cameraman in 1948 to be bearded. Bill maintained that Len was a bohemian type and we finally agreed, with a lot of persuasion, that Hunter could keep his moustache but the beard had to go.

'I didn't really want to change the way I looked,' says Hunter. 'David Elfick, I think, insisted that I shave. I remember him saying, "Listen, I'm the producer and I don't give a fuck who you are!" I remember that worked. He was right, I was wrong. Forgive me.'[19]

Bill disappeared into one of the bathrooms with a razor and was gone for such a long time that David and I joked he may have used it to cut his throat. Finally Bill emerged and, with horror, we realised that under the beard he'd been hiding four chins. If Hunter had come to us during the casting process without his beard we would have rejected him outright, because he was certainly an unlikely candidate to be the leading man in a feature film. Yet the funny thing is that his unconventionality is what makes his characterisation very, very distinctive and gives the film a wonderful reality.

We thought, 'Well, we've got to get rid of some of those chins before shooting.' So a friend of David's, Paul Jones, who had been cast in a supporting role as the assistant cameraman to the rival newsreel company, was immediately appointed to the newly created role of personal trainer for Hunter, who was to stay at Palm Beach for a few weeks of this training regime. I remember the first morning. Paul set out to jog Bill down the beach to Barrenjoey Point, about three-quarters of a mile away. After 300 metres, one of the two running figures collapsed into the sand. Of course, it was our leading man, who indeed was extremely unfit at the time, but he shed a lot of weight and really pulled himself together over the ensuing weeks.

The collapse was even more serious than it looked to Noyce. 'What you don't know, sir,' Hunter explains, 'is that I had a massive heart attack and Sandy Beach – God love her – took me to an acupuncturist two days before we started shooting. I stopped breathing for a while. Virtually I'm not telling you a fib. This actually happened. PJ knew, Sandy knew, and I certainly knew. Nobody else did. I still saddled up for the part, though.'[20]

'Now, almost twenty-five years later, when I look at the film I see in the part of Geoff, the editor, played by Bryan Brown, who at the time was a relative newcomer to acting, a guy who was probably the obvious leading man. Yet the funny thing I also realise at this point is that Bill's very unconventionality as a leading man is what makes his characterisation very distinctive and what makes the film extremely distinctive. He is an "ocker", an ordinary guy, and that accident of casting was a lucky accident indeed.'[21]

'Having cast Hunter in the lead role we now had to look around for someone to play Len's brother, Frank Maguire . . . Of course, in Australia in 1977 there were only a couple of other actors who had any public appeal and one of them was Gerard Kennedy. Because of his parts in the long-running television series for Crawford Productions, *Homicide* (1964–75) and then *Division 4* (1969–77), Kennedy had for a long time been a favourite television actor . . . Very conscious of the need to cast someone with box-office appeal, we secured Gerard Kennedy, who, when you think about it, is an unlikely brother for Bill Hunter. He was not our first choice, but at least in the Australia of 1977 Gerard was a very visible actor.'[22]

In what would soon become a trademark of Noyce's professionalism, considerable time was spent preparing the actors to play their roles.

Hunter and Haywood – well, all of them – were introduced to their real-life counterparts, whether it was Tony Barry playing Greasy the sound mixer, or Bryan Brown playing Geoff the editor, or Haywood and Hunter playing the cameramen. We found real newsreel workers for them to spend time with, to sort of soak up both the technical as well as the emotional aspects of it all.

And there was other research. *The Australian* newspaper published a report on a minor, but seemingly rather symbolic, incident that occurred while checking locations in Maitland. 'Lo, there was a crick of lightning, and Noyce and Elfick were caught in a deluge, the area flooded and they had to swim across a river, with the copy of the script wrapped in plastic to save it from destruction. This is called getting a feel for the material, or cinema verité, or devotion beyond the call of duty.'[23]

Cinetone was loosely based on Ken G. Hall's original Cinesound company. As luck would have it, Cinesound Studio in Balmain was empty and deserted, but still standing and in acceptable condition. So, with comparatively little investment, it could convincingly become the major set for the film, adding an extra degree of authenticity.

As the start of shooting approached, Noyce became increasingly concerned about his ability to handle the practical side of the production.

'When David Elfick first approached me to read the script and then asked me to direct the film I felt flattered that someone actually thought I could handle a film with a budget of several hundred thousand dollars. But then he started convincing other people . . . that I could direct this film. I actually felt, as more and more money came in, that at any moment the fraud squad would burst through the door to take me away. These people were putting large amounts of money into a project that David had convinced them I could weld into a successful film. But I wasn't completely convinced of that at all.'[24] [However,] I felt very well prepared in the major sense, that is, in my approach to my subject matter, a fundamental prerequisite.'[25]

'There wasn't anything I'd experienced [on *Backroads*], which was shot with a crew of about six, that could ever have prepared me for the first day of shooting on *Newsfront*. I remember driving in a taxi towards the location in Market Street in the heart of Sydney, and wondering what all the cars and trucks and people were doing out on the street, thinking there must be a pageant or parade about to take place. Then it dawned on me just before I arrived at the State Theatre: they were all waiting there for me to say "Action!" I thought, "Oh my God! Can I do this?" I realised that everything I'd done before had been like playing – now I was a film director, I was making a real film, this was the film industry, and they were all waiting for me to tell them what to do. I was scared, to say the least.'[26]

Both Elfick and Noyce were aware early on that the Maitland floods would be the key to the success of the film. Elfick believed that 'If this sequence worked then the whole movie was probably going to work.'[27] But how to afford filming it – given the low budget – was the question that was uppermost in their minds. According to Vince Monton, it was the actors' and crew's determination, dedication and hard work that made it possible. 'I remember sitting in one of the production meetings with everyone in the room throwing ideas around. Every idea we'd come up with, it would always come down to, "Well, we can't afford to do it." But to give you an idea of the level of commitment on this film, David, the producer, then said, "It's pointless going on like this. Here is what I'm going to do. I'll somehow find the money to shoot this sequence because it's an important sequence. You guys go ahead and work out how to do it. If I can't find the money, then we can use my salary. We are going to shoot this sequence and you guys are going to do the best you can, and if it costs my fee, it costs my fee." Up to that point I had never heard a producer say such a thing, and I've never heard a producer say it since.'[28]

Elfick: 'We chose to shoot at Narrabeen Lakes in the north of Sydney because it matched Maitland beautifully and it wasn't as densely populated as it is today, which meant we could build a huge set close to the shoreline, while the newly built housing remained in the far distance. We were then able to put telegraph poles in the middle distance, as well as have a few floating roofs we could push around so that Phil could line up a shot with a roof positioned in the middle background. The location really looked like a flooded valley.'[29]

In trying to work out how to stage the floods, David and I decided to build the facade of two streets in the lake. The shopfronts would supposedly be 12 or 15 feet underwater, but we only had to build the upper portions and not the flooded ground floors that the audience couldn't see. In fact, the water was only a metre deep and we could actually walk around the set.

Combined with the flooded vistas in the newsreel footage that Frans Vandenberg had unearthed, I realised I was going to be able to, maybe, get away with this impossible sequence. To create the illusion of rapidly flowing water, David hit upon the idea of three jet boats running their engines in reverse thrust. These boats were anchored offshore and tied down in the 4-foot depth of the lake. They would all rev up simultaneously and, using Ken G. Hall's idea of limiting the size of the frame, over a very restricted area we were able to give the illusion of rapidly flowing water in the otherwise placid lake.

Working the whole thing out on paper, I realised that if we framed up the street through the opening of a doorway from the chemist shop that Chris Haywood's character rows through, we could create the illusion that this street extended on endlessly out of the left-hand side of the frame. In the right-hand side of the frame, by the arrangement of the camera angle and the angle that the street was built, we could also give the illusion of a much longer street. Of course, movies are all about suggestion, and every frame is surrounded by Scotch tape. As Ken G. Hall had pointed out: what the audience believes they are seeing is what exists.

We built the inside of the Maitland Town Hall on top of a 50-metre swimming pool at a Sydney high school, and then dropped the chemist-shop set into the middle of it. In the morning we shot Chris coming down the steps into the flooded shop, then over lunch the art department dismantled that set and in the afternoon we shot Chris rowing into the town hall. Every day was a tremendous challenge on that film, both because of our lack of experience and the minuscule budget.

Some of the challenges were impossible to overcome, though, as Elfick recalls. 'Our main street of Maitland was basically a very long wooden construction on steel pipes that were set in mud. At the time motorboats were allowed onto the lake, and given that movie-making was uncommon in those days, the local residents were naturally curious. People would come up and speed past the set in their boats, which set off waves and undermined the scaffolding. Inch by inch the whole set started to collapse into the lake, and when I was called down to the set I didn't know what to do. If we had to take the whole set apart and try to reconstruct it, the cost would have been so enormous that we wouldn't have finished the film. We were running out of time and running out of money. We tried winching it but we couldn't get the winches to work. We got a local tow truck in, but it just spun its wheels and couldn't manage to pull the set up. It was quite distressing to watch our movie slowly sink into the Narrabeen Lakes.'[30]

Even the camera department increasingly encountered problems. Vince Monton explains: 'Few people realise just how low the budget truly was. On the last day of filming the flood sequence we only had two rolls of black-and-white film left. That was all, there was no more in Sydney and as far as we knew nobody else in Australia had any more. The last bit of black-and-white film went through the camera when we shot the drowning of the Chris Hewitt character, and if you look very closely where Chris Haywood's hand finally sinks into the water, the film starts to have flash frames, which signals the end of the roll. I was sitting there next to the camera operator begging Chris to just drown quickly, but all actors love to work on their death scene. He would go down and then he would come back up again and grasp for life a little longer, and I was sitting there saying, "Drown, you bastard, please!" I remember just as he went down for the last time the rollers on the magazine on one side stopped rolling, which meant there was a foot of film left, and as he went down, the film ran out and Phil said, "cut." There was talk of doing another take, except I pointed out there was no film left – we had used all of it up. It was one take – it got down to that! Fortunately Chris was perfect on the day.'[31]

Originally, a second major dramatic sequence was planned, which some newspapers and popular magazines reported on.

'"Grasshoppers are extremely bad actors," declares David Elfick . . . as he relives some of the film's worst moments during shooting. The locust plague was to have been one of the two major scenes . . . but the locusts refused to co-operate. The actors were 5000 grasshoppers specifically bred by the NSW Department of Agriculture. The script called for the hoppers to fly around a car carrying actors Bill Hunter and Chris Haywood (Len McGuire [sic] and his young Cockney assistant). The two men as part of the plot were filming the locust plague for their news film house. Their car was to break down and be inundated by flying insects. But the grasshoppers just wouldn't fly.

'The film crew tried moving them with blower fans – they blew away.

'They sprayed the car surface with an insert repellent but the grasshoppers wouldn't hop off.

'They enclosed the insects in transparent containers and tried filming through the car windows. Still the hoppers just sat there, looking bored.

'Finally, the scene was scrapped.'[32]

As it turned out, shooting in black and white wasn't all that easy. 'The film industry at the time had turned its back on black-and-white,' Monton explains. 'Black-and-white was a dirty word, so much so that we had a great deal of trouble getting black-and-white stock to shoot with. Kodak would have made up a batch of many hundreds of thousands of feet that we needed, but we couldn't afford it. We actually ended up having to film with footage left over from different periods, made up of a number of different batches, different contrasts, and some had been lying in refrigerators for fifteen years. In the long run this turned out to be a blessing in disguise. Because the batches of film were so varied, it actually made it easier to match and intercut our material with original archival material that had been shot in different periods. I'm sure we shot with some black-and-white stock that went back in vintage to the original material shot by the newsreel cameramen.

'But because of the difficulty of locating black-and-white film, I do remember there was a great deal of pressure to make the entire film in colour. To give David and Phil due credit, they stuck very strongly to their decision to shoot most of *Newsfront* in black-and-white. This also meant that we could never backtrack and release the film completely in colour, which I think was the hidden agenda of the film's distributor.'[33]

When the last clapperboard had fallen, the production's problems continued. The editing caused Noyce some anguish when the component parts didn't seem to hold together:

When I first saw all the cut scenes strung together in their original scripted order, I came home from the screening stunned by the failure of it all. I took to my bed, where I remained in a catatonic state for about two-and-a-half days, contemplating my future as a school-teacher, certainly not as a movie director. I thought, 'Well, I've been given this chance and I've messed it up. I'll never direct again, not after everyone sees this mess.' The story didn't seem to make sense; it seemed to be made up of so many disparate elements in search of something to glue them together. And we were due to screen the film to our investors about five days later. But eventually I got up out of bed and went back into the city to search for music. I came up with a lot of old 78 records of newsreel music, newsreel fanfares and dramatic film music from the forties and fifties, and came back into the editing room armed with what I hoped might be the glue that would hold the whole thing together, push the story along, provide an emotional thread and the illusion of an intellectual one.

As [editor] John Scott and I prepared for the next screening we also started to lay in some of the music I'd found. I soon realised how important sound was to any movie and also that in travelling directly from the ear to the heart, sound (and music, in particular) has an emotional purity that sometimes supersedes what you see. Music can be more powerful than an image, which has to be decoded by the brain. Sound bypasses the brain and goes directly to the heart and the central nervous system. The film that we screened just five days later with a partially completed temporary music track was a completely different experience, and to my surprise it even showed signs of working as a coherent whole.

'[When] David investigated the rights to the songs suggested by Bob Ellis, he found that purchasing them would have used up more than the total budget of the film. David, however, was also aware that in the 1940s and '50s Qantas and Pan Am crew members would bring in the latest recordings from America to Australia, sometimes months before the original recording would be shipped out here and records pressed. In the ensuing period Australian artists and producers would record cover versions of American hits; Australia had developed an industry based on sound-alikes, much like today's video pirates. Thus most of the songs on the soundtrack of Newsfront, although they sound like the originals, are actually cover versions. David was able to secure the rights to the cover versions for very little money given that they were not really sung by Frank Sinatra or any other of the original American superstars.'[34]

'When I first viewed a cut of the film I realised Billy Hunter's performance was very inconsistent in terms of his vocal delivery. Hunter operated on fear and sometimes his fear came through in the way he spoke. But, of course, the problem was that he was playing a man who never really doubts himself and is convinced of the "rightness" of everything he does. I had heard of a concept called post-synching, which is what we now call ADR [automatic dialogue replacement]. Because of technical deficiencies, or mishaps such as an airplane flying over a scene, it's quite common on feature films to re-record part of an actor's dialogue. But we had to do more than just replace a technical deficiency; we had to even out Bill's performance. Acting on a suggestion from my future wife Jan Sharp, I got him to come up and stay at the Palm Beach studio where we were editing the film and showed him the whole movie on the Steenbeck; in particular I wanted Bill to focus on the last shot of the film, which is a koala bear climbing a gum tree. I remember saying to him, "Bill, that koala bear climbing the gum tree is Len Maguire, and I want you to now think about injecting the warmth we associate with the koala bear into the character of Len." The next day we went into the studio and re-voiced seven scenes, and I think that had a big effect finally on the audience's identification with Len Maguire.'[35]

Before the film was even completed, the controversy about who was the actual scriptwriter blew up, with rumours circulating that Bob Ellis was about to remove his name from the screenplay. Noyce couldn't see any reason for Ellis's attitude.

'After I had decided on which scenes to cut from the screenplay, it became necessary to do a small amount of rewriting to provide continuity for the remaining scenes. Most of the rewriting involved the reworking of the newsreel commentaries that linked various sequences.'[36]

Because these were comparatively small modifications, both Noyce and Elfick still intended to give Ellis due credit.

An investors' screening was held on 13 April 1978 at 10 am with all the key contributors present. '[The] consensus was that [the film] picked up in the last third, won't make a buck overseas, [would be] difficult to sell here,' Richard Brennan recalls.[37] Elfick elaborates: 'At the end of the screening [Ellis] stood up and told the investors that it was one of the worst films he'd ever seen, to take his name off it and that his only satisfaction was that Elfick and Noyce would never work in the film industry again.'[38] Ellis's insistence that his name be taken off the film as screenplay writer was announced in the presence of his agent.

There have been suggestions that Bob was somehow robbed of his screenplay credit, that the credit was denied him by either David, or both David and me. I have since spoken to Bob's agent and Jane Cameron, who was present at the meeting. They confirmed that, in fact, the credits that appear on the final film are the credits Bob Ellis insisted on.

Bob Ellis: 'When I saw the film for the first time all I could focus on were the missing scenes, which to me seemed to be a travesty. Unfortunately I was with Jim McNeil, a well-known "serial murderer" and playwright, who was drunk and said it was a great film and that I should be proud of it. Of course, I didn't believe him because he was drunk! Annie[39] was also there and she didn't like the film either. I went up to Elfick and began to say, "You just should not have left out this or that scene." Elfick, quite abruptly, just said, "Well, is your name on it or off?" Because he was quite abrupt, in that moment I said, "Off!" I was advised a few days later to restore my name because it was stupid not to do so. "Never take your name off anything," was the advice.

'I'm not sure why, but being too clever by half I contrived the eventual credit, which is "Screenplay by Phillip Noyce based on a screenplay by Bob Ellis". But I didn't know the credit was going to be put on the end of the film instead of the front. I should have just put my name back on, but I guess I was young and furious and didn't realise the enormity of what I was doing. I just thought I was having a private quarrel with someone I'd come to dislike intensely for his own untrust-worthiness. You just don't need intellectual dishonesty. You just don't mess around with credits because I think there's a moral bottom line – it's not fair. Life is too short and the business is too cruel.'[40]

Since the day Ellis finished that first draft of *Newsfront*, the project has been surrounded by continuing controversy over authorship. The truth is that there were many 'authors' here, going back to the original discussions that David Elfick described having with Philippe Mora, Richard Neville and Andrew Fisher, through the various drafts and outlines that Andrew, Richard and David produced, and finally to Bob's screenplay, which had a number of scenes written by his wife, Anne Brooksbank. But without a doubt Bob was the principal 'author'.

Plus there were – what Noyce with his usual modesty doesn't mention here – his own, not insubstantial, contributions.

Today Ellis's stance has softened considerably, but there

were times when he publicly claimed almost everything in the film was his brainchild,[41] including the idea of mixing black-and-white and colour stock, and the soundtrack. According to Ellis, Howard Rubie was to be the director of the film but Noyce manipulated himself into the role instead. And yes, there were script doctors employed behind Ellis's back. Today, only the authorship remains a bit of an issue.

It seems that a lot of film writers took the end credits too literally and overlooked Ellis's importance. As well, many may have relied too much on the doyen of Australian film critics, David Stratton, and his extensive elaborations on the matter.[42] On the other hand, when the controversy was reignited – for the last time? – in 1997 in an exhaustive article by Ian Stocks in *Cinema Papers*,[43] it probably didn't help matters that the piece was based almost exclusively on the Ellis archive. Noyce, for example, hadn't even been contacted and asked for his recollections, or, at least, his opinion. But whatever the full story, it should not be overlooked that all of the contributors to the screenplay were prominent cultural achievers of the time – a certain clash of egos seems almost inevitable.

Another unsolved problem was the film's ending.

Bob Ellis: 'The ending as originally written [by me] was to commence with a scene between Len Maguire, Charlie Henderson and Ken (John Dease); while on a fishing boat at night they see the Sputnik come over and reflect on how the world is different. This scene was to be followed by a scene in which Len receives lifetime honours for being a fine cameraman at an event that essentially amounts to being an AFI Awards ceremony. He gives a little speech about how he was a storeman and packer and how grateful he was for having had the chance to work for Cinetone. He says something like, "When I think of the breadth of life we witness and what good times we had, I'm glad I didn't stay a storeman and packer." Then afterwards Len drives past the newsreel cinema, which is now showing Brigitte Bardot in *Et Dieu Crea la Femme* (. . . *And God Created Woman*, 1956).'[44]

One area that seemed to be a real downer was the ending. Bob's original script had called for a coda after the Olympic Games where Len Maguire, having refused to sell his footage of the two communist nations fighting each other in the swimming pool at the Melbourne Olympics, returns to Sydney. On his way home he sees that the era of the newsreels is over as the newsreel theatre is turned into a soft-core [porn] movie house showing Roger Vadim's *And God Created Woman*. The man who had fought all of his life to retain his values, and had achieved some sort of triumph, now realises that it is all for naught because there is no longer a newsreel industry. It was not even bittersweet, just bitter.

We persevered for a couple of screenings with that ending, before eventually deciding to move the sequence up in the story so that Len makes this discovery much earlier. The movie could then end triumphantly with Len's moment of moral strength, followed by a montage of newsreel footage that might have been shot by Len Maguire in the twenty years after 1956 through to the official demise of cinema newsreels in Australia in 1975. To give the feeling that Len would go on working through this era, I shot Bill Hunter against a black background and then superimposed this image of Len with his hand-held newsreel camera over the newsreel images, together with an upbeat version of 'The Road to Gundagai', to suggest that Len's moral steadfastness wasn't foolhardy but rather triumphant.

Someone who worked on the film as a grip later accused me of turning a Catholic ending into a Protestant one. He may be right, in a sense, in that Catholicism encourages its adherents to expect suffering during their lifetimes only to inherit the Kingdom of Heaven, whereas the Protestant ideal is that life is to be enjoyed and then maybe, if you had too much fun, you will go to Hell. For me the rearrangement of that material was crucial to the audience's enjoyment of the finished film.

Ellis is explicit, as always. 'To me the new ending seemed to be seriously disastrous. It gave you something of a happy ending, but also seemed to be another instance of the story having been pruned back to two or three quarrels, one about the Labor Party and one about Australia versus America. So, rather than being about a fuller experience of life in Australia, the film ends on too political a note, on some big issue about resisting American temptation where Len tells his brother to, "Go bite your bum!" Then Len marches off like a Capra hero down a tunnel to oblivion. It was a bit gauche and adolescent for me, thrilling in its own way, but more thrilling as a film of the past rather than a film of the present. It looked too idealistic at that time. It seems okay now, but in the way that you will forgive Capra now for what you might not have forgiven him back then. I resented most of the film's cutting back to the mere politics of the time. *Newsfront* should have been more like a snapshot of an entire era – hot Christmases by the beach, more of the sport, the music we listened to, the way of Australian life generally. Instead it came dangerously close to being an anti-McCarthyist rant when it wasn't intended in that way. That was what hit me between the eyes when I saw it for the first time.'[45]

But Noyce has a clear point of view as well:

There is no doubt of this: Ellis created a masterwork. He took an idea that was one-quarter formed and transformed it into something that worked. In editing I sort of took a straight line, through the political content and because the weakest of his original material was a lot of the family stuff and the contemplative scenes where people were to say deeply meaningful things. I still maintain that Ellis was well served by my editing of his screenplay, because if you look at his later work it could be said to be lacking in narrative focus. There are good characters, but sometimes unrealistic dialogue – a certain excess of poetry in the spoken word. In editing, the attempt was always to eliminate those excesses while retaining his original voice. Not just to reduce it down to manageable proportions in terms of the money and time, but also to strengthen the narrative.

The first public screening was held in Melbourne in early May 1978 as part of the judging for the 1978 AFI Awards. We began to get extremely positive responses. This was followed by a glowing review by Mike Harris for *Variety*.

'In his feature film debut, director Phillip Noyce demonstrates his ability to deal with actors, narrative, and choreograph background activity: he shows remarkable skill and is clearly a talent to watch . . . Tech' credits are uniformly excellent with a particular nod to cinematographer Vince Monton, who had done a monumental job of matching shots and lighting, and editor John Scott who has here a remarkable achievement . . . Coote's production design gives an over-all good look to the film; production values are enormous.'[46]

'The final print was ready on Thursday May 11 at 11.30 a.m. Producer David Elfick [together with Noyce] caught his plane for Europe an hour later,'[47] carrying the film with them off to Cannes, *The Australian* wrote.

At the Cannes Film Festival, the film wasn't shown in any of the competitive sections, just in the marketplace, where anyone can rent a cinema and screen their film. We screened to a quarter-full house at the first screening. This was followed by about four or five full houses with turn-away audiences at all of these later screenings. Very positive reviews followed all over the world, particularly from Andrew Sarris and Molly Haskell in New York, and David Robinson for the London *Times* ['This is one of the best films I have seen this year'] and Derek Malcolm writing for the UK *Guardian*.[48]

Sixteen Australian films were screened at Cannes in 1978. '*Newsfront*, particularly, has been hailed by many as the best Australian film at the festival, and director Phil Noyce is being treated by some of the foreign press as one of the most promising new directors to emerge this year,'[49] *Filmnews* announced proudly.

Bob Ellis couldn't believe what he was reading. 'I was stunned when *Newsfront* was repeatedly voted the best film at the Cannes Film Festival by overseas critics, and I assumed

I was either going mad or it was a cosmic conspiracy,' he told Richard Brennan in 1980.[50]

Even at home, the film set several firsts. One was the astonishing fact that it was nominated in fourteen categories for the AFI Awards – a record that was to stand for 25 years until it was equalled in 2003 by *Gettin' Square*.

I had flown to Perth from Europe for the 1978 Australian Film Institute Awards, where the nominees were staying at the same Perth hotel. After the long flight, I went down in my hotel robe to the basement and sat down naked in the spa. About 30 seconds later, the door opened and in walked a naked Bob Ellis. While we were sweating away in this hot box I said to him, 'This is ridiculous, the film might win tonight. You and I know you wrote the script, I rewrote parts of it and reworked the structure, but it's your screenplay. Let's just cut all the gags out here and, you know, get back to reality.' And that night, when the award for best screenplay was announced, as I rose from my seat I felt this bolt of lightning streak past – it was Bob rushing up to receive the award for a film that a few weeks earlier he had claimed not to have written!

That night the film won in the categories of Best Film, Best Actor, Best Director, Best Original Screenplay (Bob Ellis and Phillip Noyce), Best Editing, Best Supporting Actress and Best Costume Design.

'Soon after, Ellis took out an ad in *The National Times*, a newspaper that's no longer published, saying that he agreed to accept responsibility and credit for writing the screenplay, but still threatened to shoot David Elfick or myself if we ever happened to enter the boundaries of his property on Palm Beach in the north of Sydney. On that note, it appeared the fracas was finally resolved.'[51]

In fact, Ellis has a very different opinion today. As he points out in the commentary to the film's DVD: 'I know now that the kind of film we made with *Newsfront*, a multitudinous chiacking

Australian answer to Capra, might have sired other movies in that style had we not bitterly quarrelled. The loss of that partnership and that immense Australian cinematic future was probably mostly my fault. I know now *Newsfront* is one of the best films I ever participated in. I didn't know then how great and testing a compromise movie-making always is.'[52]

Even abroad the film did astonishingly well and won several major awards.[53] It opened the London Film Festival and was the first Australian film ever to be screened at the New York Film Festival. It was screened at Cannes, where it was the only film the panel unanimously liked.[54] The foreign success came as a surprise to Noyce because the film 'is so parochial. When I made it, I was never looking for an audience further away than Liverpool in Sydney,' he told *The Australian*.[55] 'It's funny that it's struck a nerve in other countries as well.'[56] After the screening at the New York Film Festival it became obvious that 'Its only major setback has been the language barrier. Some New Yorkers simply cannot understand the Australian accent. One critic went as far as to say "There's a case to be made for English sub-titles."'[57] Noyce was clearly amused: 'The flood scene is one that people keep referring to and asking us how we did it. Which is sort of funny when you come to America, the home of big spectacle scenes.'[58] *Newsfront* clearly was an overwhelming triumph as a first feature.

Australian audiences responded warmly to the film and its themes, which *The National Times* identified as 'the fundamental decency of the people involved in the ordinary business of life, set in the context of the political and social history of the time by means of the original and reconstructed newsreel material'.[59] Noyce was absolutely sure of the reason for the film's appeal: '*Newsfront* is the first Australian film that has rejoiced in things Australian; it's a celebration that has allowed Australians to feel really good about their country. It's a no-holds-barred, joyous film about Australia.'[60]

Newsfront opened on 27 July 1978 in the Village Cinema City 2 and ran commercially in Sydney for 42 weeks, that year out-grossing such other Australian classics as *The Last Wave*, *The Chant of Jimmie Blacksmith* and *The Getting of Wisdom*. In fact, it eventually turned out to be the second of only three films – the others being *Backroads* and much later *Rabbit-Proof Fence* – ever to generate Noyce a net profit, and that is including his American films. 'It had audiences queuing for tickets when it opened in Sydney and Melbourne, and brought bursts of applause when the end credits rolled.'[61]

Newsfront is a successful marriage of the documentary and the social drama, mixing elements of British New Cinema with the authenticity of 1950s newsreel. Though it had undergone considerable permutations since its beginnings, the final result has the imprint of both director and writer, and could be described as a writer's project in terms of its literary development. The persistence and management skills displayed by the producer were vital in assembling the cast and crew, as well as in shaping many of the narrative elements of the story. But even though it's clearly the result of teamwork by similarly minded souls, the final result plainly owes the most to Noyce's previously demonstrated skill in handling dramatised documentary techniques. Not least of its achievements is that the *Newsfront* screenplay reveals genuine affection for its main characters, who are distinguished by their 'everyday' characteristics.

The film is about 'my parents' generation, and because those people have exercised possibly the greatest influence on my orientation to life, I have an obsession to comprehend their motivations. I'm fascinated by the influences – social, economic and political that sculpted them,' Noyce told *Filmnews*.[62] He continued, 'I suppose the film is an examination of what we'd call old fashioned, outdated, or conservative ideals. It's also a celebration of naïve nationalism.' And it is also, he added elsewhere, 'an attempt by myself and the others who have worked on it to come to terms with ourselves'.[63]

Very few of the film's shortcomings seemed to bother the critics. 'There's just a minor weakness and that is in the script where in a few places the dialogue is disappointingly dull and occasionally stilted,' *Australian Women's Weekly* noted.[64] *Cinema Papers* added: 'for such a blandly linear, episodic narrative, the story devices are occasionally clumsy'.[65] But the very same article ends: '*Newsfront* is a mighty achievement. On its puny budget of $505,000, it does more to establish the Australian ethos on film than any number of braying caricatures or plodding pastorales.' Even before its success abroad, the film was generally hailed as 'easily our best commercial feature to date ... a testament to professionalism ... a minor masterpiece'.[66]

The film's technical, aesthetic and structural aspects may be of interest to students and critics of film, but they aren't sufficient to explain the 'ordinary' cinema-goers' enthusiasm. Bob Ellis seems to be on the right track when he claims that '*Newsfront* is about how we were – and still are – repeatedly colonised by America in different ways. Whenever we seem to get our head above the parapet, it's then knocked down again.'[67] And it 'had a kind of guilty impact, particularly on the left-wing movie-going community. *Newsfront* had the inside track on a number of things.'[68]

Indeed, it seems that here is a nostalgic film about the perceived Golden Age of Australia – after it had severed some of the chains binding it to its English motherland following the Second World War and before it had become subjected to American corporate power (initially through the introduction of television). When good was still good and bad was still bad – or so it seemed. When life was still simple and values were still Australian. And when the threats that arose – such as the schism in the Labor Party or the communist referendum – could be overcome. In short: when Australia still seemed to be the lucky country it never really was.

Newsfront is a film for grown-ups, not teenagers. It charms its audiences by depicting the life and times of quite 'normal' people – something that seems foreign to Hollywood, in its permanent pursuit of heroes and superheroes. The little Aussie battler always was, and probably always will be, close to the heart of this nation. But while the film depicts the rather stale, conservative Menzies era, it looks like a product of the high-spirited Whitlam years, with its boosting of and pride in all things Australian.

Ellis is now convinced that 'Newsfront is the second, third or fourth best Australian film [ever]. I'd say the best is "Breaker" Morant (1980) and the second best is The Year My Voice Broke (1987), but Newsfront could be the second best. It has an integrity and originality of Australianness, and a level of dialogue and a kind of intellectual attack that few Australian films had in the 1970s and '80s. Newsfront is obviously a classic now in a way that I would say Picnic at Hanging Rock (1975) isn't. It not only holds up, it declares an aggressive, confident Australian content and a colloquial dialogue that probably hasn't survived as a style. At least Newsfront is a measure of what has been lost.'[69]

In short: the importance of Newsfront can't be over-estimated. And it was to have far-reaching repercussions.

Noyce, as he does now, held firm beliefs about Australian filmmaking. 'Carbon copies of American products will only come a cropper. The country's cinema can only succeed by telling Australian stories in a style that reflects the national character. It should be possible to finance the renegade and encourage the outlandish,' he told Sight & Sound.[70]

His debut full-length film catapulted Noyce into the illustrious circle of major contributors to the Australian film renaissance. Key actors such as Chris Haywood, Bill Hunter, Bryan Brown and Wendy Hughes went on to develop impressive careers in Australia, and internationally. The groundwork that was done developing the Newsfront characters helped create a repertory of Australian actors, who were to hone their skills in later screen roles. Newsfront set a benchmark for small independent production groups producing locally relevant material on modest budgets without sacrificing quality or cultural integrity. While the film was in production, another group of tyros, centring around the producers Byron Kennedy and George

Miller, were developing the project that would become *Mad Max*.

And for Noyce – even though this was still a long way down the road – the film would ultimately not only open the doors to, but enthrone him in the Hollywood A league. Harrison Ford approved him for *Patriot Games* because he had seen and enjoyed *Newsfront* at a film festival years before.

But the history of this seminal Australian feature film doesn't stop there. In 1998 the Sydney Film Festival celebrated the twentieth anniversary of the release of *Newsfront* with a forum on the film and a screening that proved its vitality, relevance and ability to inform and entertain.

But Vince Monton and I were aghast because technically the film looked terrible, as it had faded. Then I checked the print I had donated to Columbia University [in New York City] where it is on their curriculum – Andrew Sarris uses it as the basis of a film course.

'The students must have thought the filmmakers of *Newsfront* were incredibly avant-garde, because the image had almost completely faded. It looked like a cast of ghosts wandering through a desert-like landscape. Rather interesting and certainly compelling, but nothing like the film we had originally shot.'[71]

That started a whole process of investigation. Frans Vandenberg, the assistant editor on the film, came over to Los Angeles and we tracked down missing film and sound materials. Eventually we found the image dupe negative in New York. After six years of asking the same company did they have anything, Frans's persistence finally paid off and we found it. It was all a great big detection job. He found the sound elements in Paris and that allowed us to re-master the film in stereo.

All of this was used to strike a proper 35-millimetre theatrical print – painstakingly restored in all its former glory. Likewise it served for the transfer to DVD. Upon its release, the *Newsfront* DVD proved once more how far ahead of his peers Noyce was in terms of understanding the media and its implications.

In marked contrast to virtually all other Australian releases at the time, the DVD contains bonus material that film buffs and ardent scholars usually only dream of, thus transforming the DVD into an invaluable piece of film history.

The ABC took advantage of the media attention generated by the resurrection of a classic Australian film and broadcast it on Saturday, 1 September 2001. Noyce was less than amused and branded the screening as 'vandalism' because the network 'had shown the film in the wrong format, which meant that parts of the title, opening credits and even some characters had been trimmed off the edge of the screen'. He was even reported to be investigating taking legal action under recent moral rights legislation.[72]

And the story doesn't end there. A rare accolade was bestowed upon Noyce when, on 19 August 2003, LAFTA (the Los Angeles Australian Film and TV Association) and the American Cinematheque jointly hosted a twenty-fifth anniversary screening of *Newsfront* at the Egyptian Theatre in Hollywood. The screening was preceded by a reception featuring 'some good Aussie tucker and wine'.[73]

Where will the film go from here? It certainly hasn't reached its use-by date yet.

---

1 David Elfick, quoted in Raffaele Caputo and Geoff Burton, *Third Take – Australian Filmmakers Talk* (Sydney: Allen & Unwin, 2002), p. 131.
2 Bob Ellis, quoted in Caputo and Burton, *Third Take*, p. 114.
3 David Elfick, quoted in Caputo and Burton, *Third Take*, p. 131.
4 Bob Ellis, quoted in Caputo and Burton, *Third Take*, p. 111.
5 David Elfick, quoted in Caputo and Burton, *Third Take*, p. 132.
6 Bob Ellis, quoted in Caputo and Burton, *Third Take*, p. 115.
7 Ibid.
8 Bob Ellis, quoted in Caputo and Burton, *Third Take*, p. 116.
9 David Elfick, quoted in Caputo and Burton, *Third Take*, p. 132.
10 Bob Ellis, quoted in Caputo and Burton, *Third Take*, p. 117.
11 Ibid.
12 Ibid.
13 A detailed account of the changing marketing strategies for *Newsfront* and their impact can be found in Michael Harvey, 'Selling *Newsfront*', *Cinema Papers*, July 1979, pp. 436–39, 477.

14 David Elfick, quoted in Caputo and Burton, *Third Take*, p. 134.

15 Vince Monton, quoted in Caputo and Burton, *Third Take*, p. 138.

16 Phillip Noyce, quoted in Ken Cameron, 'Newsfront – an interview with Phillip Noyce', *Filmnews*, August 1978, p. 11.

17 Ken G. Hall, *Australian Film – The Inside Story* (Sydney: Summit Books, 1980), p. 167.

18 Bill Hunter, quoted in Caputo and Burton, *Third Take*, p. 150.

19 Ibid.

20 Ibid, p. 151.

21 Phillip Noyce, quoted in Caputo and Burton, *Third Take*, p. 96.

22 Ibid, pp. 96ff.

23 *The Australian*, 21 May 1977.

24 Quoted in Cameron, 'Newsfront', pp. 10–11.

25 Ibid, p. 11.

26 Phillip Noyce, quoted in Caputo and Burton, *Third Take*, pp. 94–95.

27 David Elfick, quoted in Caputo and Burton, *Third Take*, p. 135.

28 Vince Monton, quoted in Caputo and Burton, *Third Take*, p. 142.

29 David Elfick, quoted in Caputo and Burton, *Third Take*, p. 135.

30 Ibid.

31 Vince Monton, quoted in Caputo and Burton, *Third Take*, p. 142.

32 Sonya Dobson, 'Trouble with grasshoppers', *New Idea*, 4 November 1978, p. 29.

33 Vince Monton, quoted in Caputo and Burton, *Third Take*, p. 141.

34 Phillip Noyce, quoted in Caputo and Burton, *Third Take*, p. 101.

35 Ibid, p. 97.

36 Ibid, p. 103.

37 Diary of Richard Brennan, quoted in *Newsfront* DVD commentary.

38 David Elfick, quoted in *Newsfront* DVD commentary.

39 Anne Brooksbank, Ellis's wife and co-writer of the script.

40 Bob Ellis, quoted in Caputo and Burton, *Third Take*, p. 118.

41 Richard Brennan, 'Bob Ellis', *Cinema Papers*, October 1980.

42 David Stratton, *The Last New Wave – The Australian Film Revival* (Sydney: Angus & Robertson, 1980), pp. 205–12.

43 Ian Stocks, 'Newsfront', *Cinema Papers*, April 1997.

44 Bob Ellis, quoted in Caputo and Burton, *Third Take*, p. 122.

45 Ibid.

46 Mike Harris, 'Newsfront', *Variety*, 10 May 1978, p. 22.

47 John Philips, 'Behind Newsfront', *The Australian*, 12 June 1978.

48 Andrew Sarris, 'Newsfront', *Village Voice*; Molly Haskell, 'Cannes Review', *New York*; David Robinson, 'When cinematographers got the news but not the politics', London *Times*; Derek Malcolm, 'Parables of Political Times', the *Guardian*.

49 'News and views from Cannes', *Filmnews*, June 1978, p. 1.

50 Quoted in Brennan, 'Bob Ellis', p. 318.

51 Phillip Noyce, quoted in Caputo and Burton, *Third Take*, p. 105.

52 Bob Ellis, quoted in *Newsfront* DVD commentary.

53 Best Film (1979) – Belgium Film Critics Association
Best Foreign Film – British Film Critics Circle

Best First Feature – Paris Film Festival
Best Director and Best First Feature – Taormina Film Festival.
[54] Cf Philips, 'Behind *Newsfront*'.
[55] Ibid.
[56] Quoted in Judith M. Kass, 'Rejoicing about things Australian: Phillip Noyce', *Movietone News*, December 1979, p. 13.
[57] Wally Macmillan, '*Newsfront* captures New York', *The Australian*, 4 October 1978.
[58] Quoted in Kass, 'Rejoicing about things Australian', p. 15.
[59] P.P. McGuiness, 'The way we were', *The National Times*, 12 August 1978.
[60] Quoted in Kass, 'Rejoicing about things Australian', p. 13.
[61] Robin Bromby, 'Test for Australia', *Sight & Sound*, no. 2, 1979, p. 86.
[62] Quoted in Cameron, '*Newsfront*', p. 11.
[63] Quoted in Kass, 'Rejoicing about things Australian', p. 15.
[64] '*Newsfront* director hailed overseas', *The Australian Women's Weekly*, 5 July 1978, p. 11.
[65] Keith Connolly, '*Newsfront*', *Cinema Papers*, August 1978, p. 58.
[66] Ken Quinnel, '*Newsfront*', *Filmnews*, September 1978, p. 17.
[67] Bob Ellis, quoted in Caputo and Burton, *Third Take*, p. 112.
[68] Ibid, p. 119.
[69] Ibid.
[70] Quoted in Bromby, 'Test for Australia', p. 86.
[71] Quoted in Caputo and Burton, *Third Take*, p. 107.
[72] Garry Maddox, '*Newsfront* director tears strips off ABC version', www.smh.com.au, 4 September 2001.
[73] Phillip Noyce, email dated 14 August 2003.

Chapter 5
HEATWAVE

*There was always a very, very strong radical
tradition in Australia.*

*Sydney in the grip of gentrification: Stephen West (Richard Moir) is
a visionary young architect who has designed a $100 million resi-
dential complex, and Kate Dean (Judy Davis) is a radical activist
resisting its construction. But increasingly, an alliance of big business,
organised crime, lawyers, police and journalists forces individuals
into submission and oblivion. Power struggles in a city ruled by
avarice.*

Heatwave goes back all the way to the beginnings of the nation.
The first European settlement in Australia was composed mainly of
convicts and their English gaolers, and the convict population was
made up not only of genuine criminals, but also representatives of
every social, economic and religious renegade group that emerged
in the British Isles between 1780 and 1850, such as the Tolpuddle
Martyrs, Irish separatists, Scottish separatists, religious protestors
and so on. So there was always a very, very strong radical tradition
in Australia.

Because of the split between disenfranchised Irish and enfran-
chised English – or poorer Irish and property-owning English –
Australian society has always been characterised by this incredible
split between working and middle class, or between the convicts and
the gaolers. A split that was also along religious lines, Catholic
versus Protestant – Catholics being the poor who will inherit the
earth after they die, and the Protestants who believe they will own it
while they are still alive.

In the 1960s there was a massive amount of urban redevelopment in Sydney and suddenly a realisation that the most sought-after property would be in the inner-city area, particularly around the harbour. In the second half of the nineteenth century a number of areas in the inner ring of Sydney had been established as housing estates for the poor. During the early 1970s a bitter struggle developed over the fate of some of these traditional workers' houses in the Woolloomooloo and Kings Cross areas of inner Sydney. On the one side were the residents who had lived there all their lives and the various radical groups who were supporting them in their efforts to remain. And on the other side were the property developers and the conservative state government who were supporting redevelopment of the area, tearing down the nineteenth-century buildings and replacing them with modern high-rise apartments for the middle classes. Juanita Nielsen was a middle-class newspaper publisher and social activist, who had become involved in this struggle and subsequently disappeared, presumed to have been murdered by a coalition of Kings Cross underworld figures supposedly in cahoots with some of the property developers.

For about five years before we shot the film in 1981, if you were walking around the Kings Cross or Woolloomooloo areas you would no doubt come across a sign asking, 'Who killed Juanita Nielsen?' So, Nielsen's fate was the subject of a lot of speculation, accusations and rumours. She had supposedly been executed, and the most persistent rumour was that she was buried in the foundations of one of those new high-rise buildings.[1]

Another attraction for me was that just before I read the screenplay I had moved to live in Kings Cross, at 59 Surrey Street. (Judy Davis lived at 43 Surrey Street, before moving to Barcom Avenue.) Also, my mum had grown up in the area and my parents met and courted each other there. The place that I bought in Kings Cross was part of a row of houses that a friend had purchased from a big developer. The developer had originally bought about 50 homes and because they were a high-profile company, squatters had moved into the houses and refused to leave. My friend Jose De La Vega bought the houses and then cunningly sold them to his own friends. The deal was you didn't have to pay anything for a year, and that way he was able to get owner–occupiers into the properties, which meant that the struggle with the squatters wasn't the same as for an absentee landlord who owned 50 houses. So, the moral high ground was suddenly taken away from the squatters. Jose had people moving into the disputed homes within a month and I had to evict some Italian painter from my house in order to live there myself.

All over, the suburb was being rapidly gentrified. Right opposite us was – and luckily still is – a fisherman and his wife; he had grown up in that house. He would go out every night, come back at dawn and we would buy our fish twice a week directly from him. He would come over and knock on the door with a lobster or a big cod, or whatever.

The real-life conflict featured in the film centred on a row of beautiful houses in Victoria Street. The whole of the Woolloomooloo basin was going to be demolished and turned into high-rise apartments, but much was saved by the Whitlam Labor government in the early 1970s and turned into state housing, and many of the original families are still living there.

Mark Stiles – who played the taxi driver who drives Len Maguire home one evening in *Newsfront* and stops outside the State Newsreel Theatre, which has now become a soft-core porn movie house – had written a script that was the basis of the screenplay for *Heatwave*. As Mark had been an architect, his central character was an architect who, like Richard Moir's character in the movie, had designed the building that was to replace the workers' houses.

An architect has a lot in common with a film director, in as much as between concept and reality, there are a million hurdles and a lot of those hurdles can only be overcome through conquering psychological barriers. The architect's power as a personal politician is sometimes as important as their artistic ability. The architect will be constantly called upon to compromise and constantly be trying to measure the worth of their original vision against the price of the compromise. And the architect is, like the film director, always faced with the dilemma that finally their creation is going to be measured principally by the user. So there is this tension between form and function, between personal expression and practicality. Between pleasing the masses and pleasing oneself.

The genesis of the script was a collaboration between Tim Gooding and Mark Stiles. In the finished film, Gooding's work remains in only one scene, when Richard Moir meets the prostitute/dancer played by Gillian Jones, in some of the dancer's dialogue. After Gooding left, Stiles continued to work on the screenplay by himself and eventually approached Noyce. 'But they were unable to raise money on the script that they had,' so Noyce involved Marc Rosenberg.[2]

The Mark Stiles script may have been more dour, perhaps. More realistic, with less panache. Marc Rosenberg at the time was quite a racy writer – light and very ironic. I guess we thought that that's what the story needed, compared to Mark Stiles – who came from a documentary background and perhaps seemed to exaggerate the social realism of the material.

Noyce and Rosenberg knew each other from the Australian Film and Television School, from which Noyce had graduated some years earlier. 'In 1981 Noyce had come to a screening of student films and I had written one of the student films which he liked, called *Gary's Story*. He invited me to his place to talk about various things, and as I recall he wanted me to work on a movie about trucks that he was having problems with. I was interested in working with Phil because he had already established a reputation as a great director. So we talked and then he told me about another film that he was working on called *Heatwave*. The original script had been written by Tim Gooding and Mark Stiles. I was surprised when he asked me if I would like to have a go at rewriting it. And, of course, I did.

'The producer on the film was Hilary Linstead. I think she took some convincing to let me write it, but once she realised how little she could pay me to let me do it she was more enthusiastic.

Phil and I began a relationship that probably lasted about six months, where he would come over to my house six days a week and we would work most of the day on the script. Then, in the evenings I would go back to his house and Jan, his wife, would make dinner for us and then we would probably talk about it some more. We would talk about the development of the script and the characters. I had the advantage that I already knew who the actors that would lead the cast were going to be – Judy Davis and Richard Moir – and I had met Judy. One of the things we were concerned about was making a contemporary film about Sydney, which as far as we knew hadn't been done before. Phil and I spent a lot of days talking, not only about the film, but about our lives or anything that impacted on the characters.

'My relationship with Phil was great. I really did feel that we had become good friends and we became used to each other's rhythms. This was one of the unfortunate things: I worked much better in the morning and he worked much better in the afternoon. So just when I was getting tired, he would be waking up, and that made it difficult sometimes. The other thing was, this was the first feature film I had ever worked on. So Phil was also a mentor and a teacher for me, and set me straight about a lot of the things that I needed to know to sell a screenplay. We became allies against the producer several times, silly ideas that they had about the film. But Phil would always say, "Well, we have to listen to what they say before we reject it, even though we know that we're not going to do it. But we have to give them the respect and listen to what they have to say." I was really impressed with Phil's professionalism and very thankful that he was willing to take the time to teach a new writer what to do and how to do it.'[3]

The script went through many incarnations. In one version, the story started with Richard Moir's architect character among a group of squatters in one of the old inner-city buildings, which they were being called upon to vacate by thugs who were about to break the doors

down. The story was then told in flashback revealing that this man was the architect of the edifice that was to replace these old houses. It told the story of how he had fallen in love with the Judy Davis character, Kate Dean, and become radicalised himself. In that version it was Kate Dean who disappeared, so in a sense he was taking her place. It was neat and probably the most compelling story construction. I don't know why we abandoned that structure, but we did. I have always thought that would have been a better way of telling the same story. More emotionally compelling and direct.

I had known Richard Moir since high school. In my teens I lived in Wahroonga, on the north shore of Sydney, and went to an all-boys school called Barker College at Hornsby, and Richard went to nearby Knox Grammar. Soon after I became involved in movies in my last year at high school, I met Richard, who was also passionate about cinema. He went and got a job as an assistant film editor at the ABC, and I went down and applied as well. To be accepted into that department you had to swear that all you wanted to do in the world was edit television, but I couldn't help admitting that eventually I really wanted to direct movies. So when I refused to swear, they told me I wasn't suitable to be a film editor. Anyway, years later Richard had come to my attention as the lead in Esben Storm's film *In Search of Anna*.

Bill Hunter plays the owner of the architecture firm that Stephen West is working for, a part written for Bill especially, as was Chris Haywood's role as the real estate developer.

Marc Rosenberg: 'Judy Davis was a great person to work with, a terrific person to work with. I got to know her pretty well. She was concerned that I was writing the part too closely to her character, because she's the sort of actress that wants to stretch and be someone else and was always talking about other accents she could do. In fact, when she found out she had to be an Australian, she was going to be an Australian from a specific town, Ballarat, and she would go down there and learn the accent of someone from Ballarat. Well, the truth is, nobody would know where the accent came from, but it made it more exciting for her.'[4]

Judy was never really happy with Richard, who wasn't formally trained, and I think she imagined it was difficult acting opposite him. Judy is also the kind of method actress who tends to take on the personality of the character they are playing, and in Kate Dean she had to assume the feelings of an angry, alienated, middle-class radical, who was typical in Sydney at the time the movie was set – someone like Meredith Bergman who, as the daughter of patrician parents, was one of the leading political activists and women's liberation advocates at Sydney University when I was studying there. The dynamic of Kate Dean's relationship with Stephen West was something I was interested in. This young woman from a middle-class family, who is now an advocate for the dispossessed, in conflict with a young man from a working-class family, who is now employed by the nouveau riche. Preparation with Richard Moir mainly involved introducing him to various architects – in particular, Rick Leplastier, who designs really elegant and ethereal buildings that seem to float rather than stand.

From *Newsfront*, I used Vincent Monton as cinematographer and John Scott as editor. Even though Bill Motzing had done such a fabulous score for *Newsfront*, I wanted more contemporary, electronic-based music, so I decided to use Cameron Allan as composer.

I think I found it difficult to direct my own material. When you are a director working on someone else's script you stand outside the writing, always examining and re-examining it. Now I tended to accept the screenplay as a given, set in stone simply because I had a hand in writing it.

In a – for Australia, at least – rare and rather bizarre turn of events, there was another film being planned on the same subject at the very same time, with an almost identical budget, called *The Killing of Angel Street*, starring Elizabeth Alexander and John Hargreaves. But while director Donald Crombie was still awaiting the outcome of his AFC grant application, Noyce raised the A$1.4 million funding needed, principally through a stockbroking firm in Sydney under the new 10BA tax shelter.

As sometimes happens, there were two films inspired by the same original material. Our story was set supposedly in Kings Cross, theirs was set in Balmain. I guess it might have convinced us that we were on to a hot story [*laughs*], and that might have been a false assumption – I'm not sure. Having a rival project probably also reassured our investors that there would be tremendous public interest in the movie. But I think the fact that there were two movies was more a reflection of the 10BA film-financing subsidy in place at the time, resulting in an excess of film funds looking for legitimate projects.[5]

The two films would eventually turn out quite differently. Other than their basic plot premises, 'the two films are as unlike as chalk and cheese. Where *The Killing of Angel Street* spells out its narrative in strict terms of black and white/good and evil, *Heatwave* consists of constantly shifting shades of grey. It has a far more complex narrative that uses all sides of the conflict to provide dramatic interest and to suggest that motives and actions are more confused and more intricate than the simplicity of *The Killing of Angel Street* would suggest.'[6] 'Noyce's film is altogether tougher, tighter and more subtly intelligent.'[7]

Shooting lasted for 42 days. There was no lack of construction sites to use as locations, and mostly the shoot went smoothly. Marc Rosenberg: 'I would come on set and Phil would yell out, "Okay, back to the lines; the writer's here." He would yell out things like that to the crew and of course they would all laugh because they knew it was a joke.'[8] The perceived connection between the underworld and the developers, however, was a concern. 'Juanita Nielsen disappeared and everyone believed the Mafia was involved in getting rid of her. I don't believe they ever found the body, but even when we were working on the script, there was always this element that perhaps somebody was going to come and try to stop us from making the movie.'[9]

We convinced ourselves that we were afraid of a certain notorious Sydney underworld figure who was supposedly the inspiration for the nightclub owner. The film character was so different in appearance that I'm sure the man in question would never have recognised himself, but among the left-leaning paranoid fringes of Kings Cross society, of which I was one at the time, we all fuelled ourselves with the urban, much-repeated myth that the anti-development campaigner Juanita Nielsen had been murdered by local gangsters, and probably the same crooks would want to eliminate any comment about what had really happened. But there was never any concrete proof that the real-life nightclub owner was the silent financier behind this proposed real estate development, who arranged the death of the project's main opponent. But at the time we all thought it was true and we all thought we were in great danger.

Two weeks before shooting started, Phillip Noyce's 'obituary' appeared in the *Sydney Morning Herald*. His fears grew when, a couple of days later, a classified ad asked 'Where is Phillip Noyce? Reward for information', thus duplicating the actual event around which *Heatwave* was loosely based.[10] Today, Noyce is convinced that somebody played a joke on him.

The film takes place during two weeks of a Sydney heatwave. And ends, as so many Sydney summer heatwaves do, with the arrival of a southerly storm, which precipitates a rapid change in temperature accompanied by winds and rain. The finale of the film is set in the streets of Kings Cross on New Year's Eve. We realised that we would never be able to stage the full scope of the mayhem of New Year's Eve in that red-light and nightclub district, so we decided to film a chase sequence through the real revellers in the minutes before and after midnight on New Year's Eve. The chase was filmed using a steady cam operated by DoP Vince Monton. Unfortunately, on this particular New Year's Eve, some striptease artists from some of the Kings Cross clubs decided to amuse the crowd by performing for free on the balconies outside their clubs [*laughs*]. So as we came to shoot the sequence we realised that everyone was looking up like statues at the naked ladies undressing themselves for the amusement of the crowd below. So we didn't get the kind of visceral material that we would have liked because the crowd was so static and a lot of the sequence had to be reproduced later, using our own paid extras.

After the filming had been completed, Noyce asked Marc Rosenberg 'to write something close to 60 pages of background dialogue, because he wanted to have a full soundtrack. We talked about the idea of trying to create something like a sound painting, where it was more realistic than just having people say "rhubarb" in the background or it was more to work with. And so I got a video of the film and tried to think of dialogue for all the people that were speaking behind the lead actors. So it's really got a very full audio track. It was all scripted dialogue and it was very unusual, and it was really hard work, because there were a lot of people speaking in the background. I don't know how much of it he used, but I think he used quite a bit of it. It seemed to work out okay. A lot of people thought that it might be confusing or convoluted, but it seemed to work out all right.'[11] Obviously, Noyce was experimenting with the soundtrack:

Really, the film should have been in stereo. The Dolby stereo method of sound reproduction hadn't been invented, or was just in its infancy. In a sense it's a stereo film in mono, because there are multiple levels of dialogue in most scenes.

After the success of *Newsfront*, the release of *Heatwave* was met with much interest. Its topic of gentrification seemed to strike a chord with audiences all over the world – wherever the film was released. Marc Rosenberg attended a screening at the British Film Institute in London. 'One of the great pleasures I have had in my life was being in London when it was being screened at the BFI, on the same night that there were the elections for Margaret Thatcher, and the cinema was full. I came out of the cinema behind some people who had seen the film and they were talking about how enthusiastic they were about the film and discussing what had happened and everything.

It was exciting to know that you had participated in something that gave people at least an hour and a half of enjoyment.'[12]

Noyce was applauded for his 'growing technical proficiency',[13] which made the film 'stylish and visually opulent'.[14] 'The dialogue crackles, the performances are good and the pace is vibrant.'[15] 'It is highly skilful in marshalling its narrative elements and deployment of cinematic techniques. Its most striking sequence – Steve's pursuit of Kate through the crowded streets of Sydney's Kings Cross – is a virtuoso triumph in the Hitchcock manner. The celebrating crowd . . . becomes infused with a sense of menace that reaches its climax in a shooting, and ends with the rain that breaks the oppressiveness of a large city sweltering in a heatwave.'[16]

Though hailed as 'cinematically far more adventurous' than *The Killing of Angel Street*,[17] others took offence at just that. 'When Noyce switches from social realism to surrealism, *Heatwave* loses its heat and its hard edge,' lamented *Variety*, labelling the film 'marred – though not fatally – by an unnecessarily convoluted narrative, pretentious directional techniques, and less than perfect casting'.[18] Generally, though, the acting drew particular critical praise.[19] But the new ground that Noyce had tried to break left some commentators confused. 'There is not one simple story but several, all going in different directions,' *Filmnews* claimed,[20] and *Films and Filming* noted: 'A brave but uneasy mixture of narrative styles and moods.'[21]

Noyce concedes that something about the film wasn't quite as he had planned.

'I remember sitting night after night in cinemas in Sydney when the film opened, and I realised I hadn't pressed the buttons with the audience. I hadn't connected with them. I'd mingle with the audience, and they didn't have the buzz that I meant them to have.'[22]

I was disappointed in the end result. I got this sinking feeling at the end of the first public screening that the film wasn't working as I had intended. I think there were certain narrative connections that were never quite completed for the audience. And the one that I am thinking of in particular is the story of the striptease artist played by Gillian Jones, who is killed in a nightclub towards the end. She was the girlfriend of the nightclub owner and underworld figure who secretly financed the Eden housing redevelopment and ordered the execution of the anti-development campaigner. But who was who, and how they were connected to the other characters, was never completely clear to the audience. And I think that was a big mistake, because if you can't make the intellectual connections, you can never make the emotional ones.

Inspired by watching Fellini working on a dialogue re-recording stage during a visit to Rome in 1978, during post-production we added a lot of background dialogue, which became a feature of the finished film. Later I refined that technique as an element in all my movies. But at the time I was just experimenting, and I think in that film I allowed the background dialogue from off-screen characters to almost become foreground and therefore to have too prominent a role in the soundtrack. It became a distraction. This, of course, would become less of an issue later in my career because I would start to work in stereo, where you had the chance to distinctively separate the various elements of your soundtrack.

Heatwave was my first movie after the relative critical and commercial success of *Newsfront* and so there was a lot of anticipation from others and from myself. In particular, there was pressure to prove that I could make a film without the support of producer David Elfick, who had been really important in making *Newsfront*, or of Bob Ellis, who'd written the original screenplay for that film. I felt a lot of artistic pressure, and also commercial pressure, to make a film that was as distinctive as *Newsfront* but still would work at the box office. And in some ways I failed in both regards. Though it was by and large well reviewed, it certainly failed commercially. And it led me to rethink my approach to movie making.

I was touched by my own personal relationship with Preston Crothers, the stockbroker who had been instrumental in raising the private investment to finance the film. Preston was a film lover and was financing the film under a tax minimisation scheme that didn't really put the money at risk as you might in a normal investment.

Nevertheless, when he died a couple of years later from a heart attack, I felt I had let him down personally and vowed that I'd never again want to know the person who was putting up the money [*laughs*], that I'd far prefer to have a highly removed relationship with the financier of a movie. I realised that there's so much money at stake you don't want to be constantly reminded of where that money is coming from.

But I also realised that, following the experiments in narrative and storytelling of *Newsfront* and *Heatwave*, in many ways I still had to learn the rules. In the first two-and-a-half films – the half being *Backroads* – I had sort of broken the rules without knowing what they were [*laughs*], so after that I set myself the task of discovering what the rules were so that I could look forward to one day breaking them again.

---

[1] As an introduction, 'The Juanita Nielsen Case' on the milesago website (www.milesago.com/) is invaluable. The recent publication by Peter Rees, *Killing Juanita* (Sydney: Allen & Unwin, 2004), seems to unravel the truth of this mysterious murder case.

[2] Marc Rosenberg interview.

[3] Marc Rosenberg interview.

[4] Marc Rosenberg interview.

[5] *The Killing of Angel Street* would be released earlier, nevertheless: in October 1981 (disappearing after only a very short season). *Heatwave* was released in March 1982. *Filmnews* rated it 'more designed for a TV audience' and belittled it 'because of the self-conscious concern with accessibility and a cautious conformity to the demands of an audience assumed to be conservative, ill-informed and prejudiced'.

[6] Neil Rattigan, *Images of Australia: 100 Films of the New Australian Cinema* (Dallas: Southern Methodist University Press, 1991), p. 151.

[7] Brian McFarlane, *Australian Cinema 1970–1985* (London: Secker & Warburg, 1987), pp. 102–3.

[8] Marc Rosenberg interview.

[9] Marc Rosenberg interview.

[10] Judy Stone, *Eye on the World: Conversations with International Filmmakers* (Beverly Hills, CA: Silman-James Press, 1997), p. 22.

[11] Marc Rosenberg interview.

[12] Marc Rosenberg interview.

[13] Mark Bould, 'Phillip Noyce', in *The Wallflower Critical Guide to Contemporary North American Directors* (London: Wallflower, 2001), p. 334.

[14] David White, *Australian Movies to the World – The International Success of Australian Films since 1970* (Sydney: Fontana, 1984), p. 60.
[15] David Stratton, *The Avocado Plantation – Boom and Bust in the Australian Film Industry* (Sydney: Pan Macmillan, 1990), p. 215.
[16] McFarlane, *Australian Cinema 1970–1985*, pp. 105–6.
[17] Helen Grace, Pat Fiske and Carolyn Strachan, 'Towards the realm of the merely enjoyable', *Filmnews*, March 1982, p. 8.
[18] 'Dogo', '*Heatwave*', *Variety*, 6 January 1982, p. 16.
[19] Douglas McVay, '*Heatwave*', *Films and Filming*, September 1982, p. 35 ('Pleasure . . . Judy Davis's watchful, astringent presence'); Tim Pulleine, '*Heatwave*', *Monthly Film Bulletin*, September 1982, p. 200 ('expert performances').
[20] Grace, Fiske and Strachan, 'Towards the realm of the merely enjoyable', p. 9.
[21] McVay, '*Heatwave*', p. 35.
[22] Quoted in Michael Singer, *A Cut Above: 50 Film Directors Talk About Their Craft* (Los Angeles: Lone Eagle, 1998), p. 207.

Chapter 6
KENNEDY MILLER

It was a revolutionary workshop.

Back in January 1970, Aquarius, the cultural arm of the Australian Union of Students, had held a one-month film workshop in Melbourne run by director Nigel Buesst. I got a job as a teacher based on the fact that I had made my short film *Better to Reign in Hell*, and sort of knew how to load a Bolex camera, but not much else. At the time in Australia that made me an expert. The 30 students were divided into three groups of ten, and the first exercise I set my group was to make a short film that included a meeting, a chase and a confrontation. On one roll of film. All I did was show them how to load that roll of film, push the on and off button, and focus.

In the group were two guys who would change the history of Australian cinema. One was a medical student who had won a competition for 30-second silent films at the University of New South Wales – George Miller – and the other had won an 8-millimetre documentary competition, and that was Byron Kennedy. Within the politics of the group, Byron instantly became the cinematographer and George the director, and they came back with a 2 mins 40 secs movie that only needed the camera stops cut out. As is characteristic of George's work, the camera was placed in the almost perfect position, and it featured a dynamic meeting between two people, a kinetic chase through the Melbourne markets and a thrilling confrontation in an alley. And it was a movie. A primer of film grammar.

Anyway, Byron and George went on to make *Mad Max*, which they wrote together; Byron produced, George directed. They edited over a long period of time. George was at this stage working as a doctor for a mobile medical service and Byron would drive him around taking calls all over Melbourne, in between editing the film in Byron's parents' house. And then they made a huge amount of money on the movie, which had cost a few hundred thousand dollars, went off to America, looked around and decided to come back to Australia to make movies and TV. They purchased what had formerly been a live theatre and cinema, the Metro in Sydney's Kings Cross.

They really wanted to set up a studio for directors along the lines envisaged by Francis Ford Coppola at Zoetrope back in the seventies in Los Angeles. The idea was that a number of directors would be on permanent payroll, rather like the old Hollywood studio system where directors received their next assignment with the Sunday *Los Angeles Times*. So, working for the studio were myself, Chris Noonan, George Ogilvie, Carl Schultz – they're the ones that I can remember. We used to have weekly screenings and discussions on particular classic movies and would all be looking at each other's scripts in development. It was a campus atmosphere, financed by *Mad Max* profits.

We weren't paid a lot but were guaranteed employment and continuity of work, and opportunity and funding to make movies or television programs. And, even more importantly, a highly creative environment in which to work. Kennedy Miller owned all the rights to the work, because none of us at that stage had any idea of the value of copyright and were just glad to work. Particularly as Byron and George were revolutionary in their approach to research, script-writing and collaboration. It was a workshop atmosphere where everyone was paid to investigate storytelling.

George Ogilvie had been a theatre and opera director who was introduced by George's then partner, Sandy Gore, who was an experienced stage actress. Ogilvie was an inspiring director with many theories on the relationship between direction and performance, and between actors and directors. While we were preparing to shoot *The Dismissal* mini-series, George started some workshops that were essentially an investigation into the nature of performance. I had always done a variation of that sort of preparation, as a result of an approach to working with actors outlined by Fred Schepisi at the film school: trying to envelop the performers in their characters as much as possible. But what Ogilvie was proposing was more oblique in its reference to the specifics of any particular script.

Ogilvie's class was simply about focus, investigating how to focus the audience through the grouping of actors. Another was on leadership, which was of particular importance to the whole *Cowra Breakout* story I would shortly work on. And another was about forming an ensemble, including an exercise I have conducted on the first day of rehearsal for every film project since that time. Everyone chooses a partner and then you nominate one of the two to be blind (blindfolded or simply closing their eyes), and then the whole group forms up and walks around and around in a circle, from which at a given command they break. The pairs have to keep running in and out amongst each other with the blind led and protected by the sighted. In another exercise, the sighted person leads the blind partner on a wordless journey around the whole room, letting them experience the environment as if they can see. That exercise is about trust, which is fundamental to any filmmaking enterprise, particularly the relationship between actors and directors.

George Miller recalls: 'It was Terry [Hayes] and Byron who talked me into doing television. When we began Kennedy Miller we despised television as a lower level of existence. But soon we realised it was just a different level – a different ecology if you like. Now we are addicted to it.'[1] As Noyce likewise would prove time and again during his career, they weren't afraid to tackle the challenge of a different medium with a relatively secure profit margin.

The Dismissal

On 2 December 1972, the Australian Labor Party won the federal election. For 23 years Australia had been run by the Liberal–Country Party coalition – for sixteen of those years under Prime Minister Robert Menzies – leading to political stagnation. Just five days later Gough Whitlam was in office, his government initially consisting of only two members, embarking on a flurry of wide-ranging reforms. But within three years, on 11 November 1975, Whitlam was dismissed in a surprise move by John Kerr, the Governor-General, and Malcolm Fraser of the Liberal Party was installed as interim prime minister. This unprecedented constitutional crisis, and the years of speedy changes that led up to that crucial moment, are still a topic of lively discussion in Australia.

I was 22 when Labor came to power. They were all incredible idealists, and Whitlam saw himself re-creating Australia anew, taking us overnight out of the nineteenth century. So there was a lot of baby boomer idealism invested in that government, who represented a vision of Australia as we would have liked it to have been, not as it had been, and luckily a lot of what they created survived: changes to the divorce law, censorship, maternity leave, support for the arts, Aborigines, the environment, and a recognition of ourselves as part of Asia.

Suddenly, Australians could be proud, and not just of our sporting prowess. There was a flowering, a maturity, that occurred simultaneously with the election, and I don't think the country has been the same since. Whitlam skilfully merged a traditional working-class spirit – an Australian ethos – with that of the intelligentsia, and it was achieved without compromise. Probably that was the cause of his downfall.

Admittedly, people were a bit worried about the speed of change, and Labor had spent so long in opposition that they were very theoretical, with a huge gap between the theory and actually governing a country.

The dismissal of Whitlam's government was as close as Australia ever came to a revolution. I don't think it would have taken much to tip people over into going into the streets.

I had wanted to make a film about the subject since 1979, when Irwin Rado, who was director of the Melbourne Film Festival and head of the Australian Film Institute, had approached me with an outline he had written with Bruce Grant, a Melbourne writer and historian. They wanted to tell the story obliquely and symbolically, through an acting troupe who were performing a play about the dismissal. I approached playwright David Williamson to work on developing the outline and went to stay at his place outside Melbourne for a couple of weeks in 1979. But we couldn't really see eye to eye on how to develop the story and I abandoned the project.

Then, in 1981, George Miller and Byron Kennedy declared their intention to set up a mini film studio (with third partner Terry Hayes, who had been a Melbourne journalist), proposing first to make a miniseries about the dismissal. I think everyone who joined the series admired Gough Whitlam and saw him as probably the greatest leader Australia ever had. We all felt that the premature destruction of his regime was a tragedy for our nation.

As the series reveals, the key to it all was Governor-General John Kerr, played by John Meillon. And the key to Kerr's actions was in his aspirations to be a major player, the pretensions of a man who, ironically, only achieved the recognition he coveted as a result of his own class treachery.

Finally the story all came down to the passage or denial of supply, ending up as a comedy of errors. The Liberal government's ability to block supply, the money bills that give the government funds to run the country, was the issue that necessitated the dismissal. But once Malcolm Fraser was appointed caretaker prime minister by John Kerr, Gough Whitlam was so flummoxed that he forgot to inform the Labor-controlled Upper House that they should block supply and therefore overturn the new illegitimate government. So, supply was passed by a House that thought this was the end of the crisis, when, in fact, passage to supply only legitimised the new government and allowed it to take over.

At the time, only two of us had ever directed television drama – Carl Schultz and John Power. So Carl was to direct two hours, and the rest of us (George Miller, George Ogilvie, John Power and myself) would direct one hour each.

Two weeks before shooting was to commence, we all started a two-week workshop at 'Iona', the mansion in inner-city Darlinghurst now used by Baz Luhrmann as his Sydney headquarters. The actors and directors conducted an intensive investigation into the events leading up to the dismissal. Ron Blair had already written the scripts, but a really interesting process occurred. The actors revolted. They said, 'We can't start shooting, because what we've discovered during this process isn't reflected by the screenplays.' It was a spontaneous revolt. We gave them too much information and one after the other they came to us in dismay. That's how Terry Hayes became a real writer, because he then had to step in and start from scratch. Terry locked himself away and throughout shooting was literally sometimes only a couple of hours ahead of us with the scenes.

What happened was that Ron Blair had been taken on to write the whole six hours by himself. To save time – it was another 10BA production, which meant that the series had to be delivered before the end of the next fiscal year – Kennedy Miller 'started workshopping the more than one hundred actors with five directors, make-up people, production designers and so on . . . It was a wonderful time, like a retreat, and very intensive. The actual politicians whom the actors would play came by to talk . . . By the end of the first week, the actors knew an incredible amount about the characters they were playing. In fact, through this collective osmosis we all knew more about the events of the dismissal than any of the political writers, because they had only looked at it from a political perspective. Unfortunately, what also happened was that Ron Blair, who had been too busy to become part of the process, was like a man left out in the cold. From being the repository of knowledge, he had suddenly become the inexpert; he just couldn't match the collective knowledge . . . Ron [had] eroded his authority.'[2]

The whole process was like running a relay race in as much as the story had been divided into six episodes starting a couple of years before the day of the dismissal, with each of the directors responsible for a particular segment.

For me, the most memorable character was the minister for minerals and energy, Rex Connor, who had the clearest dream, of wanting to develop Australia's natural resources, and to do this he had involved himself with nefarious money-raising intermediaries. Rex Connor was played by Billy Hunter, whom I had worked with three times previously, on *Backroads*, *Newsfront* and *Heatwave*. Connor was a traditional Labor Party stalwart with no experience at the level he was now thrust into, and he had such an irresistibly expansive dream that he destroyed himself and contributed to the destruction of Whitlam's dream as well.

My episode was number two of the six and featured the stories of the then federal treasurer, Jim Cairns, the rise of the future prime minister, Malcolm Fraser, and his overthrow of Billy Snedden as leader of the opposition. Once Fraser came to power, the Liberals finally had a credible leader and skilful manipulator able to exploit the many weaknesses emerging in Whitlam's Labor administration.

The episode concentrated on Jim Cairns' relationship with his secretary, Junie Morosi. John Hargreaves played Cairns, and Neela Dey played Morosi. Cairns and Morosi both came to the workshop and spoke to the actors, and we took the attitude that they may well have had a sexual relationship, but that wasn't the reason why people were attacking them. The reason was essentially that Cairns had the temerity to employ as his assistant an intelligent, attractive, Asian woman. If she had been *ugly* and intelligent, it might have been different.

I don't think Rex Connor was still living at the time [we began the production], but all the others were – John Kerr, Malcolm Fraser, Gough Whitlam, Jim Cairns and so on. We interviewed a lot of the original participants as well as drawing on newspaper articles and such, with two or three full-time researchers.

Perhaps the greatest personal legacy from the series resulted from my exposure to George Ogilvie's theories about working with actors, ideas that I still draw on today when preparing all my films.

The series was shot on 16-millimetre film by Dean Semler, who would later shoot *Dead Calm* and *The Bone Collector* and win the Academy Award for cinematography for *Dances With Wolves*. For me this series was the beginning of a decade-long association with Kennedy Miller.

All six parts were broadcast by the Ten Network on the same evening, on 6 March 1983. The screening emptied the streets of people – no wonder, considering that emotions were still running high less than eight years after the 'most traumatic upheaval in Australia's constitutional history'.[3] Part one, directed by George Miller, has the most cinematic flavour, making heavy use of contemporary newsreel footage to lead into the events. But there is a second reason for its obvious difference from the other parts, as Miller recalls: 'I very blithely went ahead and shot the first episode as if it were a *Mad Max* film. The camera was very subjective, and there were lots of camera movement and wide-angle lenses. But then I noticed that Phil would shoot such a scene with a long lens, the people in profile or perhaps even in shadow. He would just observe them; Carl Schultz the same. Now, it wasn't until the cutting room that I realised all the stuff I had shot, which would have worked fine on the big anamorphic screen with stereophonic sound, was completely wasted on television. The penny had finally dropped for me, whereas the others had known it intuitively.'[4]

The remaining parts – necessarily condensing political history – mostly play out in interior scenes: meetings, conspiracies, more meetings. They look rather like an over-long chamber play with too many characters involved. For non-Australians – and with today's distance from the actual events – the rage that surrounded the broadcast is difficult to comprehend. Still, the Ten Network considered *The Dismissal* such a hot potato politically that prior to the March 1983 federal elections it twice moved the scheduled broadcast.

Most public opinion was enthusiastic about the program. 'It demonstrates, as if [it] needs demonstrating, that Australian film and television is capable of creating better *Australian* film and television than any other nation on earth, if it is allowed to use its imagination,' *The Age* applauded.[5] It continued:

'Of course, the real events were dramatic, but *The Dismissal*, in compressing and telescoping them, makes them achieve a coherence that they didn't seem to have at the time.' Kennedy Miller 'had become a marketable commodity, synonymous with quality productions of an ambitious nature'.[6] And it 'opened up space for the analysis of politics in Australian television drama – a space that was infinitesimal before but has since expanded'.[7]

Obviously, contemporary historical drama has its pitfalls, as was duly noted. 'It is impossible to get to the bottom of recent events. Many of the sources are not yet published and the participants are still lying their heads off. The writers are driven back to the published sources, in the main newspaper reports.'[8] Such sources tend to be biased, and as for the personalities involved, their characters were partially concocted by the media and hence more or less fictional. But if writers try to jettison much of the historical ballast and opt for the purely fictional, 'the greatest obstacle is the laws of defamation. If the version were true it would almost certainly be defamatory in the sense of our restrictive laws of defamation'.[9] It has to be stressed that all the serious critics conceded that the series 'tried hard to avoid taking sides', as Enker observed.[10]

As could be expected, there were some negative responses, though these exclusively related to factual interpretation. The following was typical: 'There was a distortion of enormous magnitude, although in a subtle and underhanded way, in this series.'[11] But it was a different story with the politicians and administrators involved in the events. 'The fitting of a couple of years' real life drama into six hours has dented the egos of some participants, who feel they don't look like that, don't act like that and none of their friends think so either,' as the journalist Garrie Hutchinson observed.[12] Some filled copious column inches with attempts to resurrect their image, show their importance or simply give their point of view.[13] Junie Morosi was pleased with her portrayal, though she would have preferred 'a more substantial portrayal of what she and Dr. Cairns stood for, their belief in "personal liberation"'.[14] And, adds *The Australian* with more than just a slight shiver: 'In her philosophy, monogamy is not essential in marriage.'

But whatever historians eventually come up with in valid interpretation of the Whitlam years, it seems obvious the series served as a catharsis for the directors involved, as they reviewed their common political idol and the shock of his fall.

The Cowra Breakout

After the success of *The Dismissal*, George, Byron and Terry Hayes decided to make more miniseries and the first was to be *Bodyline*, about the infamous cricket series between Australia and England in the 1930s. The second was to be *The Cowra Breakout*, the story of the escape by 1100 Japanese from a prisoner-of-war camp in the Australian countryside on 5 August 1944.

Collectively the two new miniseries would cost more than A$8 million. Judging by early announcements, there was some confusion in the press,[15] as Noyce's involvement was not reported as planned from the start – only Carl Schultz and George Ogilvie were named as directors. Noyce rejects this outright, insisting that only he and Chris Noonan were involved right from the beginning.

The historical background to the program is one of the more horrendous events in Australia's war history. Of the 1100 prisoners who launched the breakout, 334 internees actually escaped. Twenty had already committed suicide within the compound and about another 180-odd died attempting to escape. Four Australian guards from the garrison died and Tadao Minami, the ringleader, was shot dead. Many of the Japanese committed seppuku because they had doubly dishonoured themselves by letting themselves be captured then failing to escape. After nine days, 25 dead escapees were found and the stragglers rounded up by police, soldiers and local farmers. 'No word of the massacre reached Japan till after the war. The Tojo government did not admit the existence of prisoners of war. Families had already mourned the prisoners as dead.'[16]

I was attracted to the story because my auntie was an Australian Army nurse captured in Borneo and bayoneted to death by the Japanese. I had always been intrigued by the fact that my father had been to Japan on a number of occasions and actually liked the country and culture, despite the murder of his sister. I wanted to understand the Bushido Code and its interpretation by Japanese soldiers. I wondered how they could be so brutal to an unarmed nurse and why, once she was captured, they imagined it was acceptable to kill her in cold blood.

It seemed those Japanese POWs had escaped from the Australian camp in order to die, because through indoctrination they believed the indignity of capture turned them into ghosts. Only by reclaiming their role as true soldiers could they live again. Only by dying could they live, so 400 were killed in the attempt to escape.

Given the seeming lack of logic in their actions, I felt the only way to dramatise and explain the prisoners' mindset and make it truly authentic was to locate and interview the many Japanese survivors.

While we were researching in Japan, Byron Kennedy – who had been a friend since I was nineteen – was killed in a helicopter crash. His beloved Bell Jet-Ranger was his one toy from his enormous *Mad Max* profits. Flying without instruments above water, he had crashed into an inland lake and died of exposure twelve hours later.

We conducted almost 100 interviews up and down the Japanese islands, travelling in two teams with two different interpreters. Then all the interviews were transcribed and ten scripts written, based on the transcriptions. We had about fifteen typists working for months, as we wanted it to be primary, not secondary, research, feeling that no one had ever tried to investigate the story from both sides. We spent six weeks back in Australia trying to distil the essence of the story we wanted to tell down to just one sentence.

During one of the more amazing interviews – and there were many – this woman brought out a box containing human bones. During the war, she had been told they belonged to her husband, who had actually been captured and sent to Cowra and finally repatriated in 1946. But rather than admit he had allowed himself to be captured, the Japanese Army sent back those bones.

By the time my fellow-director/writer Chris Noonan, scriptwriter Margaret Kelly and I returned from Japan, we had a strong narrative structure for the series. One of the escapee's stories gave us the perfect story arc for the whole series. This particular soldier had gone to New Guinea with what became known as the Lost Army, Japanese troops who landed at Lae on the east coast, where my mother's godfather was a missionary (and later wrote his book *Prisoners Base and Home Again*, about the landing of 50,000 Japanese troops, of whom fewer than 5000 were to get off the island). They made the mistake of supposing that the 400 miles from the west to the east coast of New Guinea was a straight distance, when in fact it was up into mountains and down into valleys. The temperature at the top was like a chilly Melbourne winter and in the valleys a Cairns summer. And eventually they were starving, low on ammunition, and he was captured and sent to Cowra POW camp. Once he escaped from captivity, he shed his conditioning and suddenly the most important thing became his own survival: he wanted to live. He transcended the Bushido Code and got right back to animal basics. That became our Japanese character's story.

TV and cinema are so different. Once the audience have entered the cinema, most of them are going to stay to the end credits. But on television they're not in captivity and you virtually have to reach out of the TV screen, grab hold of the audience with the characters and the story, and have the characters look the audience in the eye and say, 'Sit there, watch, find out what is going to happen to me.' So, making that series was a real film school, because the medium forced one to learn to communicate directly with the audience, as viscerally as possible.

We intended the series to start with maybe a couple of sentences of Japanese in the first hour and then we'd keep adding to the amount of Japanese-language scenes, until by the time of the breakout the audience are inside the Japanese compound for more than half the story and are now watching a Japanese movie. The Japanese characters start out as very much the weird, dangerous beasts the Australian public and soldiers viewed them as at the time, and then, through one of the characters, we come to know and understand them as humans. By the end of the story it was to be the Japanese the audience were concerned about as much as the Caucasian characters.

While we were in Japan, a soldier told us how he had found himself locked in a deadly battle with Australian soldiers in the New Guinea jungle. It seemed like such a great situation: two men, both starving, suffering from dehydration and malaria, one in the middle of a clearing, unable to move, and the other inside a bunker – just as tired, just as emaciated, just as hungry, just as crazed, armed with a machine gun but himself pinned down. We developed that as the opening of the whole series and once I started to make that story I was suddenly confronted by a new set of dramatic possibilities. Telling that story became an exercise in the creation and manipulation of classic screen tension. That one hour of television was a complete turnaround for me in style. A change in what I thought I could do, and a change in what excited me in cinema. When I started making feature films it was a natural extension of my documentary work to make them reality-based, almost documentary-like. After making this miniseries I discovered another skill.

The battle scenes were shot in little pockets of tropical vegetation at the edge of Narrabeen Lakes to the north of Sydney, near where I had previously staged the flood scenes in *Newsfront*. Like all the Kennedy Miller television series that had preceded it and would follow in that era – *The Dismissal, Bodyline, Vietnam, The Dirtwater Dynasty, Bangkok Hilton* – and the features *Dead Calm* and *The Year My Voice Broke*, it was financed by the 10BA tax shelter system, with financing secured by the guaranteed presale (in the case of the TV shows) to Rupert Murdoch's Ten network.

In those days miniseries were often broadcast over one week, so *Cowra* screened for three hours on Monday, two hours on Tuesday, two on Wednesday and three on Thursday – from 4 to 7 March 1985.

It was an enormous audience commitment to sacrifice four evenings of their week, but the ratings were sensational.

If *The Dismissal* had been controversial, *The Cowra Breakout* seems to have sent out shockwaves among the Second World War veterans. *The Weekend Australian Magazine* ran an exceptionally long story over two weekends, which started: 'Old diggers reacted angrily when *The Cowra Breakout . . .* was previewed in Cowra, NSW, this week. Australia's most controversial war film is expected to divide Australians as never before as old hatreds are exposed.'[17] The main reason is given in the next two sentences: 'Three times unarmed Japanese prisoners of war raise their hands in surrender. Three times Australian guards aim rifles and shoot them dead.' The odd letter to the editor ('Except for a few scenes, the film was largely pro-Japanese, with the Australians shown as part of a slapstick comedy'[18]) looked relatively moderate by contrast. That emotions ran high is understandable in the light of the immense cruelties that Australians had to suffer at the hands of the Japanese, even though by this time the war had been over for nearly 40 years.

It seems that the comparatively clear structure of the series wasn't clear enough for some. What starts out as an Australian soldier's viewpoint on the Pacific campaign of the Second World War eventually ends with an emphasis on the traumas experienced by the Japanese soldiers in captivity. Both groups of soldiers 'have undergone similar experiences, moving from innocent belief in their duties as soldiers to a passionate hatred of the enemy, then to painful self-examination and finally to forgiveness and understanding'.[19] It is 'a story of initial personal and national enmity and later personal friendship'[20]. Possibly even more so than was the case with *The Dismissal*, Noyce and Noonan avoided taking sides.

Historical facts (or fictions) aside, the only recurring negative critical comment was the suggestion that *The Cowra Breakout* could have been a bit shorter. Otherwise, reactions were usually favourable. The *Sunday Telegraph* lauded it for all the most important reasons when it called it 'a creditable television series . . . The gamble of using sub-titles for the Japanese dialogue in such a commercial production pays off.'[21] It conceded brilliant acting by the lead actors (the supporting ones were labelled 'lacklustre') and particularly noted the scene that heralded Noyce's birth as a director of suspense: 'Then suddenly the script (and the acting) picks up for one of the best pieces of war drama I've seen for ages when the two key characters . . . fight it out in the New Guinea jungle.'[22] A jungle, it should be added, that hinted at poor set design due to lack of production funds.

After we finished *The Cowra Breakout*, Chris Noonan and I started to research and write proposals for another ten-hour series tracing Australia's involvement in the American Vietnam War. We interviewed a lot of the original politicians, particularly former prime minister John Gorton, and laid out a framework for the series built around an Australian family divided by their support for or opposition to the conflict.

As it turned out, I was asked to direct a different miniseries called *Saigon*, from a novel by British author Anthony Grey, which the Australian Matt Carroll and the British David Puttnam were producing for CBS in America. *Saigon* traced the rise of Vietnamese nationalism, the war and victory against the French, and then the conflict with America and her allies.

As much as I wanted to do *Vietnam*, I felt this was an even more challenging story to tell. Just as we started casting and finding locations in Thailand, the series was cancelled by CBS's Standards and Practices Division, who claimed the story idealised Ho Chi Minh and didn't provide a comparable figure of historical importance on the American side. As if you could rewrite history and make Westmoreland into Ho Chi Minh. The novel was a sort of docudrama combining the numerous historical figures into one American character.

The time at Kennedy Miller was really important, not only because of the demands that working in television placed on connecting to the audience, but also because of the approach to storytelling that we were investigating there and the search for deeper levels of meaning in the story. Usually when stories work, it isn't because of what happens next, and not even just because of good storytelling – but because a story connects with the audience spiritually and intellectually and answers a need that they have, that they may not even be aware of.

Whenever I do a film, I make the choice based on certain instinctual feelings about the film connecting with an audience.

And when I'm making a film, any of them now, I always go back to that time spent at Kennedy Miller, largely inspired by George Miller and his lateral thinking and his encouragement of us all to investigate our role as a storyteller. To see filmmaking as an obligation in an ancient tradition. And since that time I will always try to define my films in one sentence before starting production.

---

[1] George Miller interviewed by Scott Murray, in Scott Murray (ed.), *Back of Beyond. Discovering Australian Film and Television* (Sydney: Australian Film Commission, 1988), p. 36.

[2] Ibid, pp. 37–38.

[3] Debi Enker, 'Cross-over and collaborations', in Murray, *Back of Beyond*, p. 55.

[4] George Miller interview, in Murray, *Back of Beyond*, p. 41.

[5] Garrie Hutchinson, '*Dismissal* dared to be different', *The Age*, 17 March 1983.

[6] Enker, 'Cross-over and collaborations', p. 57.

[7] Graeme Turner, 'Mixing fact and fiction', in Murray, *Back of Beyond*, p. 72.

[8] Dennis Pryor, 'The dissolution of "*The Dismissal*"', *The Age*, 12 March 1983.

[9] Ibid.

[10] Enker, 'Cross-over and collaborations', p. 61.

[11] Rita Zammit, '*The Dismissal* begged the truth', *Sydney Morning Herald*, 21 March 1983.

[12] Hutchinson, '*Dismissal* dared to be different'.

[13] A striking example is Clyde R Cameron, a former minister in the Whitlam government in 1975, in his 'Inside view of "*The Dismissal*"', *Advertiser*, 22 April 1983.

[14] Bill West, 'They omitted the epic blue, says Junie', *The Australian*, 10 March 1983.

[15] Joanne Sawicki, 'Oz history turns into TV blockbusters!', *Daily Mirror*, 1 July 1983.

[16] Alan Goodall, '*Cowra Breakout*: Old hatreds are ready to flare', *Weekend Australian Magazine*, 23 February 1985.

[17] Ibid.

[18] Nell Gould, 'Cowra comedy', *Sun*, 14 March 1985.

[19] Enker, 'Cross-over and collaborations', p. 59.

[20] Tom O'Reagan, *Australian National Cinema* (London, Routledge, 1996), p. 284.

[21] Pam Corkery, 'Banzai! for *The Cowra Breakout*', *Sunday Telegraph*, 3 March 1985.

[22] Ibid.

Chapter 7
SHADOWS OF THE PEACOCK
(ECHOES OF PARADISE)

I don't think it was anyone's film in the end.

On holidays in Phuket, Maria (Wendy Hughes), a 30-something Sydney housewife running away from heartbreak, meets an alienated Balinese dancer/restaurant owner (John Lone), with whom she starts a passionate love affair. Eventually they both realise they have to go back to their respective societies and keep their promises.

Shadows of the Peacock was a film my wife, Jan Sharp, had written over a period of five years, based on our frequent visits to Bali between 1978 and 1985. It was originally titled *Love on a Tourist Visa*, which was a great title, and was very much about a particular Balinese village called Peliatan, which is renowned as the home of dance in general, but particularly the female Legong dance.

It's the story of a housewife with two pre-teen children, married to an eastern suburbs lawyer in Sydney. After discovering her husband's infidelity while recovering from the death of her father, she goes on a holiday to Asia, where she meets a young and confused Balinese dancer.

Jan Sharp takes up the story: '[I] had been a documentary film-maker for about fifteen years and I think I was bored with my own society. It got to the point where there was almost no area, no story, that I hadn't covered. I could be driving through the western suburbs on the way out of town and in almost every street there would have been a house that I had knocked on a door to talk to an incest victim, or a housewife on drugs, or a prisoner or whatever. So I was terribly bored with the reality of my own world and I went to Bali. It's like a fairytale, like a medieval kingdom, and everything's extraordinarily ceremonial and forthright. And I saw this fascinating story, which was the conflict between individualism and Western ideas of happiness. In Balinese society, one lives one's life in service to one's ancestors. You spend your life replicating the ceremonies, in an observance of that. And there was this particular character called Bagus in this family of dancers. They have been touring the courts of Europe since the 1920s and they're very famous internationally, but they are unmoved by that because they are dedicated to these 500 years of being the dance teachers. This Bagus character was such a glamorous, interesting person that he became my central character.

'Over a six-year period, I would go to Bali twice a year maybe for three or four weeks at a time, and I would just develop my relationship with these people. Really the film was about them, and it was going to be the world itself with everybody playing themselves and doing what they did every day, and then the actors would be placed in that world. But once we lost the setting, the film lost all its meaning – unfortunately.

'I had developed the film over a period of about six years and the first person I offered it to was Jane Campion. She liked it very much but she hadn't made a film yet – she wanted to make her own film first, which I think at that point was *Sweetie*. Then I was thinking of Carl Schultz and I also sent it to Peter Weir, who liked it. Never for a minute did I think of it as a film for Phillip. Thematically there's not anything in it that really interests him and it was never the intention that he would direct. I can't remember now the process by which he came to do it, but it was one of those situations where I was on a roller-coaster making another film. I can't remember precisely, I think he was supposed to be doing *Saigon* – anyway, he had some big project that he was going to do that fell through. And then it just happened and I wasn't thinking. I was too busy and I also had two little children. It happened like that: you're not thinking, and there are too many other things going on and obviously Phillip didn't think either.

'Six years before we made the film, I was in New York and I saw John Lone in a play called *The Dancer and the Railroad*. And it struck me immediately he was my Bagus, so I gave him the script and he was totally crazy about it, so devoted to doing this thing. Eventually he made a film with Michael Cimino called *The Year of the Dragon* that became a hit, and that's what enabled me to make the film, because suddenly John Lone wasn't nobody – suddenly, John Lone was a star. Overnight, things changed after years of no one wanting to make a film about a Balinese dancer.

'I don't think at that time a feature film had been made in Bali. Just getting permission to shoot in Bali was difficult. I think I must have gone to Jakarta half-a-dozen times and waited in my hotel room for weeks on end for the Department of Information to see me, because they were very reluctant.'[1]

For the part of the Balinese dancer, on Jan's suggestion, we were lucky to cast the quite wonderful John Lone, a Chinese actor with incredible charisma and screen presence who had trained as a dancer in Hong Kong. I took him to Bali, where he spent a couple of months living in the village that was to be his fictional home in the film.

'John went and lived with the family in Bali for a month, and it was extraordinary – when he came back, he got off the plane and he *was* Bagus, and he was in love with Bagus, of course. He was saying he was the most complete and evolved human being he had ever met. He was completely besotted with him. He had become that character and it's just so sad that, when we didn't make that film, instead of being that character he became a gigolo – it was a total turnaround.'[2]

Unfortunately in mid-1986, while John was in Bali and after I had already cast Wendy Hughes as Maria, David Jenkins, an Australian journalist, wrote a now famous article in the *Sydney Morning Herald*, comparing Indonesian President Suharto to the just-ousted Philippine dictator Ferdinand Marcos and exposing what we now know was the truth of the corruption at the heart of the Suharto ruling clan of Indonesia.

As a result – at least for a time – Australians were denied visas to enter Indonesia. And a planeload of tourists was turned back. Eventually, that overreaction developed into a rather extended denial of visas to members of the Australian media. About eighteen months previously, Jan had gone to Jakarta and secured permission, in principle, to film in Bali based on the screenplay. But now she was off shooting *The Good Wife*, a film she was producing from Peter Kenna's screenplay, and Jane Scott was now producer of *Shadows of the Peacock*. So Jane and I both went to Jakarta, but under the circumstances it was impossible to get permission, as none of the bureaucrats would dare help us at that particular time. Unfortunately, we were locked into dates with John Lone, who was about to start six months' shooting in China on *The Last Emperor*. So we had a stop date, meaning he couldn't film past a certain date. And there was no guarantee we'd get back into Bali, as no one could predict the political climate. Additionally, we had accepted investment in the film from over 50 private investors, who needed a finished product within fifteen months in order to guarantee their tax breaks.

What was to have been the first-ever Australian feature film to be shot in Bali threatened to fall apart. Antonia Barnard, the production manager, had already paid deposits for hotel accommodation for cast and crew, and the building of sets was well under way. The first response was that the whole film was rescheduled so that the Sydney scenes and the interiors could be shot first.[3]

As we had to make a decision, I went up to Thailand and saw the local producer I had met while preparing to shoot *Saigon*, and he took me down to Phuket, a resort island in the south. Initially I was looking for somewhere to re-create Bali, but I soon realised that was beyond our resources. As John Lone had spent a couple of months in Bali training to be a Balinese with rigorous dance training for many hours a day, I finally made the decision to try to slightly reinvent the story.

The givens were John Lone is a Balinese dancer alienated from family and culture, and uncertain whether he wants to continue in the tradition of dance master that is his obligation; Wendy Hughes is an Australian housewife running away from heartbreak, disillusionment and loss, and they meet and have a romance. I decided that John should be so alienated that he has actually left Bali and is now running a little Balinese-style restaurant on Phuket and that, in a sense, through the relationship with Wendy Hughes' character, he realises that he has to go back, just as she realises that she has to go back – that they both have promises to keep.

Jan Sharp partly disagrees with Noyce's reasoning. 'They still could have made the same story. But I think the problem was that Phillip didn't believe it, and because he hadn't been involved in the development he didn't realise that until he was in production. I think this often happens with a project when it doesn't come from the director. Like, you have these things at the end of a film when the writer says, "It's nothing like the film I wrote." When you actually get on the set, that's when you want to express yourself.'[4]

The transition to Thailand wasn't an easy one. As Jan wasn't available, Anne Brooksbank (who was married to *Newsfront* writer Bob Ellis) came in. She wasn't completely sympathetic to the project and there was a certain residue of tension inherited from the *Newsfront* arguments. Also, out of necessity, every change was made with incredible haste. I flew to Thailand, made the decision to film there, then came back and started shooting the Sydney scenes while we went through the red tape of obtaining shooting permissions, but most of the locations had to be found in Thailand after the crew had arrived. As well, Bali has a spiritual quality which was then (as now) very different from the tourist areas of Thailand.

Brooksbank wrote the new dialogue and faxed it every day to the location in Thailand. Consequently, the actors had difficulties grasping their characters.[5]

As a result, Wendy and John both lost confidence in the project, perhaps because I myself was working overtime to hold everything together and truly didn't know whether we were going to film the next day. Everything was constantly up in the air and I was pretending to them that things were under control, but not successfully hiding my extreme anguish.

But there was more to it, because of Jan Sharp's non-involvement due to the simultaneous production of *The Good Wife* (which for international distribution was renamed *The Umbrella Woman*). 'John got very upset about that because he had always had this relationship with me,' Jan says. 'He felt that I had abandoned him in favour of another project, and then when the plot started to change so radically and became such a different story, he got very, very upset, because, as he said, he had waited six years, he had left Bernardo Bertolucci to come and do this, and now he was just a gigolo. So he got very upset and very uncooperative and very resistant to the way things were going. I think it was a desperately unhappy shoot.'[6]

Events culminated in a crisis meeting. Sharp continues: 'I had to come down from the north coast and it was my 40th birthday. I think it was one of the worst situations in my entire life. We had this meeting because John Lone had refused to continue with the picture, and Richard Soames, the completion guarantor, was there, and Bill Shanahan, Wendy's agent, and everybody was there, and John just said: "I came here to be this particular character, all these years, and now I'm just a gigolo. I don't want to do this." And I didn't know that Phillip had thrown out the script and told them they had to have a new script. This was the first time I'd heard of it. I just went home and took sleeping pills so that I would sleep for 48 hours just to recover, because it was such a shock after six years of work.'[7]

The film could have been a complete write-off, but it's what it is. Somehow we got through and it more or less made sense, but it wasn't the film it could have been if we had kept on the same carefully planned path. I don't think it was anyone's film in the end, compared to what we had wanted it to be.

The film was made under the 10BA tax incentive program and cost A$2.1 million. There are some big set pieces, but they weren't the ones originally intended. For example, we filmed a big scene at a Buddhist temple, whereas the original had been at a Balinese funeral ceremony. But the cap on the budget wasn't really the problem. If you plan to shoot a film around a very particular setting – and it has been written around very, very meticulously chosen locations and personalities in Bali – it automatically becomes the sort of telemovie version of the original when transferred to Thailand.

Shadows was released by Village Roadshow in Australia in 1987. Until then, it had been known as either *Love on a Tourist Visa* or *Promises To Keep*. But now 'they didn't want an ironic title as the film was no longer ironic. It was supposed to be all kinds of other things.'[8] Once it went on release in the United States, the title was changed again, to *Echoes of Paradise*, though no clues can be found as to why.

Despite the misgivings of Noyce and Sharp, the film did relatively well abroad, though not at home. The colourful portrayal of Thailand still provides a stark contrast with the framing scenes in a Sydney that has seldom looked more miserable on screen. The film has a rather old-fashioned quality to it, although this is hard to define. Its subject matter continues to strike a chord with women of a certain age,[9] unlike most of Noyce's films.[10]

Upon its screening in Cannes in 1987, *Variety* ran one of its rare positive Noyce critiques, calling it 'a well made, high-toned soaper . . . and it's much to the credit of the production team that the resulting pic shows few signs of the troubles it encountered' during production.[11] But the one crucial problem – the temple-dancer-turned-restaurant-owner – was apparent right from the start. 'John Lone never really convinces as a passionate lover. He certainly looks the part, and scenes in which he performs a traditional Balinese dance are delightful, but the sparks, which should be there in the love scenes, aren't.'[12]

Though labelled as 'not totally satisfactory',[13] the film 'did fine,' says Jan Sharp. 'It keeps coming back on cable all the time. It's on BBC at least once a year. And so is *The Good Wife* and so is *Wide Sargasso Sea*. It's funny because these three little films go on and on and on, and unfortunately we don't get any of the royalties, but they're in every video shop.

'I'm constantly meeting people who say, "Oh, I saw that film last night," and I go, "Aww." It was just very sad, really, because of the enormous effort, which was completely disproportionate to the film. It was the sort of film I should never have put in that place. It was silly, the whole thing was misjudged, but that happens so many times. Maybe I was really overreaching. It was kind of like I was presuming to comment on a society which, as a tourist, I probably shouldn't have been doing.

'But I think Phillip feels even worse than I do, because he's got much more of an identity as a filmmaker. That film is just nothing; it doesn't fit in with his body of work at all. I don't mean just in subject matter; everything about it – it's not a Phillip Noyce film. First of all, it's not Phillip's material. It was quite a delicate thing, and I don't think he believed in it and I don't think he realised this until he was in production. You can't do something insincerely as a director, it's impossible. I think he had a total crisis about the validity of the story. And I think that he wouldn't be inclined to think of it as part of his body of work, really. As I said, both Phillip and I are ashamed of the film and it will probably be haunting us for the rest of our lives.'[14]

1 Jan Sharp interview.
2 Jan Sharp interview.
3 David Stratton, *The Avocado Plantation: Boom and Bust in the Australian Film Industry* (Sydney: Pan Macmillan, 1990), p. 113.
4 Jan Sharp interview.
5 Stratton, *The Avocado Plantation*, p. 113.
6 Jan Sharp interview.
7 Jan Sharp interview.
8 Jan Sharp interview.
9 International Movie Database (IMDb) reveals that women aged between 30 and 44 rate it a 9 on a scale of 1 to 10, though the average rating is only 5.5.
10 *Rabbit-Proof Fence* is the other notable exception.
11 David Stratton, 'Shadows of the Peacock', *Variety*, 20 May 1987, p. 42.
12 Ibid.
13 Ibid.
14 Jan Sharp interview.

Chapter 8
DEAD CALM

He had a very good bedside manner.

Rae (Nicole Kidman) and John Ingram (Sam Neill) embark on a recuperative voyage on their luxury yacht Saracen *in a bid to forget the traumatic accident which killed their young son. Their solitude is broken by the delirious Hughie Warriner (Billy Zane) and his sinking schooner* Orpheus. *According to him, its whole crew died of food poisoning. But when John rows over to check, he finds not only badly mutilated corpses but also a videotape that reveals Hughie as the killer. Warriner, meanwhile, has taken control of the* Saracen, *leaving John to his fate. A deadly showdown with Rae leads to a gruelling finale.*

Dead Calm was originally a novel written by Charles Williams in 1963. Desi Arnaz, supposedly a Hollywood player, immediately snapped up the rights but they then transferred to Orson Welles, who, in 1969, started to shoot the film, called *The Deep*, on the Dalmatian coast of Croatia, which was then part of Yugoslavia. His version starred himself as Bellows, his long-time de facto Oja Kodar – an actress and sculptress – as Rae, Michael Bryant as Captain John Ingram, and Laurence Harvey as Hughie Warriner. Jeanne Moreau was in the picture as well. Laurence Harvey's sudden death 'eventually caused Welles to abandon the project, claiming it unfinished although, according to Jeanne Moreau, Welles had in fact completed it. Some said that Welles actually suppressed it.'[1] Welles died leaving his version incomplete. Oja Kodar, who was Yugoslavian, retained the rights but was reluctant to sell them to anyone in Hollywood because of 'Tinseltown's treatment of Orson'.[2]

Tony Bill had directed *My Bodyguard*, produced *The Sting* and acted in films like *Shampoo*. For years he tried in vain to buy the rights from Kodar, but was considered by her to be part of the Hollywood establishment who had supposedly persecuted Orson.

Tony and I had become friends after he saw *Newsfront* back in 1980. In early 1985 I was visiting his Venice Beach studio and, as I was leaving, he threw a manuscript towards me. 'You've got water in Australia. See if you could make this down there.' It was a photocopy of Charles Williams' novel, which I kept in my brief-case for six months before reading it on a return plane trip to Los Angeles.

The story reminded me of the second hour of *The Cowra Breakout* miniseries – a high seas adventure in which all extraneous information is eliminated, an elemental tale of survival, in which the director would be manipulating a very restricted palette of story elements and the audience's attention was going to be very focused on just a few characters. It was pared down so much it seemed to obey that Mies van der Rohe theory that 'less is more'.

I told the story to George Miller, who immediately offered to pro-duce the film. I said, 'Well, first of all, Tony Bill gave it to me, so we'll have to ask his permission. Secondly, this woman doesn't want to sell. She has resisted his efforts for ten years now.' Still, I approached Tony, who said: 'Fine, go ahead. You can run with it and you don't owe me anything', which was really kind because he had the moral lien on the material. Then George came to see Oja in Los Angeles and, being an ex-doctor with a very good bedside manner, he convinced her that we wouldn't make a Hollywood version. Ironically, we eventually sold the finished film to Warner Bros. for worldwide distribution.

It may well be that Miller's bedside manner provided just one of two good reasons for Kodar to sell the rights: 'Oja regarded the Kennedy Miller organisation as being a kind of maverick outfit of which Orson Welles himself would have heartily approved.'3

It was to be another 10BA tax-break film, so the finished print had to be delivered by 30 June of the year after you raised the money, otherwise the tax break didn't kick in for investors. So, as was to happen later in my Hollywood career, I found myself on a treadmill, with a date to start filming and a date to finish, but no script. Terry Hayes was to write the adaptation. We decided that all those people alive on the *Orpheus* in the novel served no purpose, so we eliminated them all except Hughie. And we felt there needed to be a more specific purpose for the journey, so the therapeutic nature of the voyage for Ingram and Rae was invented with the loss of a child and the fact that they are out at sea to repair her wounded psyche.

Nicole Kidman wasn't our first choice as Rae. That was the very 'hot' Greta Scacchi, who didn't want to do an 'exploitation movie' and turned us down. Our second choice was a combination of husband and wife Bryan Brown and Rachel Ward, but Bryan said no – I can't remember why. Terry Hayes then suggested a young actress from the Kennedy Miller ten-hour miniseries *Vietnam*. I took a look at a couple of episodes. Nicole Kidman played the part of an anti-war agitator whose brother had been drafted to fight in Vietnam. In about the ninth of the ten hours she is in a radio station conducting a talk-back program, speaking against the war, when suddenly the caller on the telephone is her estranged and deranged brother and she breaks down. I found myself crying as well, just because of the way she used her voice. As I hadn't seen all the story I wasn't as invested [in it] as I might have been, but she reduced me to tears. I remember Nicole as possessing a single-minded determination to do good work and to succeed. She was just so ambitious. And focused. Still is, so I guess it works.

And so we screen-tested her. I wish I could find that test now. She did a couple of scenes, including the one where she confronts Hughie with a spear gun towards the end of the movie. She was great, utterly transformed herself into Rae Ingram, but was clearly a child at only nineteen and this was to be the story of a married couple. But her talent was simply irresistible and once we had cast her, the story evolved to become very much about the rite of passage for her character.

Or, as Noyce put it back then, Kidman had 'the purity we were looking for. She had to show a certain guile and yet needed to be a woman that women can love. Nicole had beauty and sexuality and innocence and vulnerability.'[4]

Sam Neill seemed right to play a Naval captain and projected a certain stoicism that seemed appropriate.

Neill had no doubts about taking on the role. 'I'd always wanted to work with Phil since we first met in 1979. I think he is a very good director. And a very nice guy to be on set with, which is just as important in my book. So it was a matter of really waiting for the right thing. This was a script I couldn't put down – there wasn't any question in my mind if I were to do it or not. It's another one of his films where it's the less showy part, you know. I often get the less kind of . . . I don't know, but it's a kind of a tricky part because it's less obvious than the bad guy. It's easy to be boring in those parts. That's the trap. But I was happy with how it turned out.'[5]

The last character to cast was the madman Hughie Warriner. Wallis Nicita, a Los Angeles casting director who is now a producer, was employed to introduce us to all of the bright young actors in New York and Los Angeles. We'd been at it for a couple of weeks and I must have seen 200 people but didn't really think I'd found someone who truly inhabited the role. As I was due to go back to Australia that night, I thought I'd just settle for the best of those we had seen – I can't remember who that was. Then Wally's assistant brought in a photograph of a young man who looked remarkably like Marlon Brando. But it was Brando with a twist. I mean, twisted. He'd played small roles in both *Critters* and *Back to the Future*. Apparently, his

agent had sent the photograph to Wally for consideration, rather late. I said, 'Well, if he can get in here within the next hour.'

At that time, Billy Zane was doing theatre in Los Angeles. But he was 'depressed about the state of my career and living in Los Angeles. I was on a kind of Gauguin trip – I wanted to go to Tahiti to paint. You may not believe this, but this is a key part of the character, as it turned out. I wanted to take off, I was really sick of it. I just wanted to split for a while, charge my batteries and do something else and then return to it. And enter this film, this character and suddenly that's exactly what the background of the character was, exactly what was needed for me and was provided.

'I was at an audition at the Thalberg Building, at the time MGM. The casting director was casting a few pictures simultaneously and I was meeting on another movie. And just before I left she handed me this script with this yellow script cover. I don't know why this colour is so memorable to me. So I walk into this room and simultaneously realise that Phil and I are wearing the same suit. That can either make or break a meeting. Fortunately, it made it. We both had a good laugh at that. I remember it was blue. I think it was some early prototype of microfibres, I don't really know – maybe crushed silk. He was wearing his usual big, comfortable style, this massive man with these big sandals, an imposing figure with a warm laugh. He was a constant contradiction and that was very attractive. He was just a sweetheart from the get-go and invited the improvisation that came out of necessity, merely because I had no time with the script before meeting him.

'We did the scene just after Rae woke up when I'm at the helm. And we just had a laugh. I think it was the uncertainty I threw into it that he really responded to – he seemed to appreciate the slightly twisted character in my Hughie and the crude humour of the situation.'[6]

I told him the story and asked him to do an improvisation, and a lot of what he invented after about ten or fifteen minutes' preparation ended up in the movie. I flew back to Australia that night, knowing we'd found our Hughie.

Zane continues: 'He said, "Oh great. I'm taking these tapes back to Australia tomorrow." And I said, "Okay, I'll see you.' But I had a hard time believing I'd hear from someone who was going down the hall to another hemisphere. And four days later I got a phone call saying, "Pack your bags and get your visas to come here." It was incredible.'[7]

Billy had the rakish attractiveness, and an out-of-kilter sanity that could simultaneously be seemingly sane or seemingly insane, completely connected or completely disconnected. A lot of the dialogue spoken by Hughie in the movie is improvised by Billy. Hughie listens to cassettes, and that was music that Billy brought to the set, composed and sung by his friend Tim O'Connor. So Bill made the character an extension of himself.

We spent a lot of time choosing the right location. For a film set on the ocean you have to have workable water, and we considered all sorts of possibilities – including a shooting tank in Malta – and all parts of Australia, before finally deciding on the Whitsunday Passage off the Queensland coast. The Great Barrier Reef is about 50 miles out to sea, and just below the surface, acts as a breakwater, holding back the strong undertows of the Pacific and giving the best workable water, particularly for maintaining dead calm conditions. We found an island where the hills surrounding a particular inlet would provide cover from the prevailing winds.

The big task with filming exteriors on any film is to keep shooting every single day. This problem is exacerbated at sea, given that the film's title is *Dead Calm* and most of the story is set under calm conditions, with the water like a pane of glass, absolutely flat and still. The prevailing winds were northeasterly, so the bay we chose was protected from most of the gusts. We arranged three different anchor points, one out to sea, which gave us more or less a 230-degree horizon, and then, depending on the winds and the choppiness of the sea, we could move back into the bay, reducing our horizon and camera angles, but at least guaranteeing that we could keep working. If there were whitecaps out at sea, with longer lenses we could keep those out of focus, but right back in the bay just off the beach there would almost always be calm conditions. And then if the wind changed, we'd move around to another bay offering protection from the other direction.

While training Nicole to sail the *Saracen* we realised it was silly to expect constant mild weather, as every few days there was a squall and rain and heavy seas, and on every one of those days we wouldn't have been able to film. That's when we decided to incorporate a storm into the screenplay, giving us every climatic condition all the way from dead calm to ferocious storm, so it didn't matter what Mother Nature served up – we could film something.

We decided to base ourselves on Hamilton Island, a resort with a twice-daily jet service to Sydney, so rushes could come back and forth overnight, just as conveniently as filming in a city suburb. We also decided that what had defeated previous ocean movies was restricting the time available to shoot at sea. For example, you might have a quarter of your scenes actually taking place on the open sea, but if you allocate, say, four weeks out of sixteen just to open sea work, you'll never be able to complete it in that time, because you will always be waiting for another shot under some other weather pattern.

So we decided to give ourselves access to water and boats for the entire shooting period by building a swimming pool right beside the jet landing strip on Hamilton. It was probably 60 metres long and about 15 feet or more deep, and we filled it with water and then built a sound stage over the top. That became our studio. All the underwater sequences were filmed there, with the sets dropped down into the pool, just like I'd done the flooded interiors in *Newsfront*.

The boat cabins were built 35 per cent bigger than the real ships just to give a little bit more room. The sets were floating on 44-gallon drums in the swimming pool and a team of footballers came across from the mainland every morning and would gently move the sets as we were shooting, so the interiors were constantly mobile, as if you were at sea. If you place the camera on the set you don't see any movement, so the camera was on a crane on the stationary studio floor.

Whenever the first unit was working in the studio, the second unit would have the boats out at sea. And whenever the main unit was working with one boat the second unit would be working with another. Some of those shots of the boats at sea, the aerials and everything, would take a day just to get two boats and the camera into position.

One of the very first decisions I made with cinematographer Dean Semler was the format that the film was to be shot in. We test filmed on a yacht in the 1:1.85 standard cinema screen size, and also in anamorphic, the wide-screen format which the film was eventually shot in. The anamorphic format best captured the majesty of the sea and helped the film to not seem small or claustrophobic, even though most of it would be set in fairly confined spaces on board two boats with mostly one or two characters on screen.

Minute preparations were required not only from the crew, but from the cast as well. Part of this was sheer physical fitness. 'I was rowing, basically,' explains Billy Zane. 'I was stuck on an oar detail. In Rushcutters Bay and in Double Bay I spent mornings rowing my assistant around the harbour, and then when I got to the island I would do a little more rowing. It was necessary for that opening sequence to be able to haul ass for a few hundred yards.'[8] Nicole Kidman spent six or seven weeks learning to sail a yacht. She could turn it single-handedly as she does in the film.

The far more important part of the preparations, however, concerned the development of the characters. Neill was put in touch with the Navy, and Zane spent time with the chief psychiatrist at a mental hospital in Sydney learning about psychopathic behaviour.

I designed about five months of preparation for Nicole. She trained with a voice coach every day, trying to deepen her voice and make it sound older. Also, she worked intensively with a movement coach, studying the changes that occur in body language between late teens and late twenties. The object was to make her seem as though she was, say, 27 or 28 and believably married to the 40-year-old Sam Neill. Nicole trained for four weeks to sail the hero boat, so that it's really her turning the *Saracen* around in those mountainous waves.

Billy Zane recalls: 'I love the way Phillip preps – he gets the actor the opportunity and the tools to build a foundation. He gave me an assistant and sent me shopping for arts supplies and any other research material I might want, and then he sent me to Airlie Beach alone for a couple of days. I just kicked around these weird little tropical bars and was trying to project a sense of propriety. And then I wasn't allowed on Hamilton Island until I'd been alone for a bit. When I showed up, they secured a 30-foot sailboat and put all of the *Orpheus* crew on board that and Phillip came and hung out with us for a bit. He set us adrift with a big bag of weed and a couple of video cameras and you know . . . Basically, we weren't allowed on land for a while.'[9]

I thought that the best preparation would be to isolate Billy on a boat for a couple of weeks out at sea with the fellow travellers he has supposedly murdered. So they were put on board a small yacht, with stimulants that they'd purchased for themselves and our video camera and food, plus a radio so that if they got into trouble they could contact us. Billy Zane came off the boat on a Friday and we started shooting the next day. He was seasick, sunburned, strung out and had now completely transformed into Hughie Warriner.

Though the back story – the events on the *Orpheus* before it becomes a ghost ship – only plays a minuscule role in the film, it developed a life of its own. The other people on the boat were models, and actor Rod Mullinar, who played the skipper, Russell. They all improvised. There was an original screenplay by Vince Monton, the director of the second unit, but Noyce believes from memory that it was pretty much like the novel; whoever was in the book was in the screenplay. But for Zane, the book story posed a major challenge.

'The most interesting challenge was to try to find when the laws of man give over to the laws of nature. That's what we really tried to capture a sense of and that's what's so great about Sam's character: what saved him was order, what saved him was human law, and it's what persevered in the end for him. I succumbed to the human will of these others and ultimately we came to the conclusion that it wasn't murder as much as liberation. The Russell character was a kind of a darker figure as we were trying to paint it. And I was more like the sorcerer's apprentice to a degree, because I was on the outside observing his manipulation and the psychological games he played with these girls once we were doomed. We went so far as to consider the notion of creating – he wanted to make this final photographic essay to be celebrated postmortem – knowing we were dying, knowing we were sinking, he was trying to capture all this video and all these stills and put them in a waterproof pouch to be found, and then it was the ultimate performance art and that's where it started to get just a little dark, you know. When he was having the girls denounce their families. They gave their bodies, they gave their minds, their hearts; I thought, their souls. I was like, "No, this is off. Better to die than this slow, warped deterioration." So I snapped, basically, and that was rational to my character. That was the result of weeks of discussion and playing with Phillip.'[10]

Sam Neill was separated from the back story. 'That was very kind of method stuff they were into there. I was glad I was away from that. That was like a cult thing that was happening there for a week or so.'[11]

Zane has a decidedly more positive impression. 'Cutters were going to and fro, it was good, clean fun on board. And it was Phil's refuge as well. I'm sure there was many a meeting that didn't have to take place on the boat, but any opportunity he could find he certainly came out to us – I guess eyebrows were raised when there was a production meeting and he was nowhere to be found. They finally figured out he'd hit the boat. Phillip and I were a united front. Terry came on board with it eventually, but it was an us-against-them situation for a while. But for the most part, I was encouraged to be a wild man and got well skilled in the art of hot-wiring golf buggies . . .'[12]

Initially we travelled to the principal location every day for about an hour on a giant catamaran. As we set out from Hamilton Island we would radio ahead to find out the prevailing winds and weather conditions, and then the actors would be instructed to dress for particular scenes. Out at sea the weather and light change constantly, so you've always got to be changing from one scene to another.

We became Zen filmmakers. All your training and experience on a land-based production tells you that willpower and a loud voice can accomplish most things, but at sea you quickly learn that it doesn't matter how loudly you shout or how much you will her, the sea won't do what she is told. She has a mind of her own and you had better get with the program – her program, not yours.

At the end of six weeks, no scenes were complete – not one. We would film for half a day in the sun, go to lunch, come back and suddenly there were clouds and it was quite moody and dark, so we had to go on to a different scene. It was really shot not by scene numbers but shot numbers. Each of the storyboards was numbered, and a lot of times the call sheet would say we'd be shooting not scene numbers, but storyboard numbers. I had used storyboards on *The Cowra Breakout* to pre-plan action sequences and also to define visual ideas. For *Dead Calm* the script and storyboards were sort of done simultaneously. Sometimes I would first do storyboards with artist Ty Bosco, and then Terry Hayes would write the script afterwards, using the images to guide him.

Dean Semler's documentary experience was a great asset. Dean and I had first worked together at Film Australia and he really came into his own with his 'catch as catch can, ready when you are' background, which allowed us to film on the spur of the moment and take advantage of the full range of climatic conditions offered up by nature.

The other ace up Noyce's sleeve that enabled him to deal with the rapid changes in weather conditions was a computer device that, for the late 1980s, was rather sophisticated. 'As a counter-measure, Noyce fed his shooting script into a computer system which allowed him to match up his shots to the brooding scenery, the shifting light and varying seas. By cross-indexing his shots, quick switches could be made and appropriate scenes swiftly found when he encountered sudden doldrums or squalls.'[13]

The shoot lasted about sixteen weeks plus one week for the opening sequence back in Sydney. The opening sequence was not, as suggested by Scott Murray in his book on Australian cinema, directed by George Miller, but George did make important directorial contributions to the film. Vince Monton directed second unit for the first thirteen weeks and then George took over from him for the last month, shooting some key scenes of Sam Neill alone on the *Orpheus*.

'The film was shot over a four-month period. Initially, we would venture out each day. Eventually, we just all moved out to sea and lived on a flotilla of boats parked in one of those bays that I spoke about. We would just transfer to our master boats each day. Eventually, we cut the crew down because just transferring from boat to boat takes so long. Eventually, we had a very tiny crew and we all lived onboard each of the boats and would go to sleep, then get up and start filming. It was quite a wonderful experience. Wonderful because you're out there with nature. But it was also wonderful because it was whale-mating season. The whale-mating season is a thing to behold, because the male dances for the female. He dives up out of the water, turns and twists like a peacock before finally partnering for life.'[14]

But the shoot provided unpleasant encounters as well, as Sam Neill explains: 'When we got through the storm, falling sails and things – it was quite scary, hairy stuff we did – stuff I don't think the insurance company would have been happy to hear or see [we'd] been doing. You know, in big seas sometimes. Being a New Zealander I quite like boats, but I don't like being at sea much. I hate getting seasick and I was seasick a few times – I threw up between takes.'[15] Neill wasn't the only one affected – Kidman suffered, too. 'On the way back a storm came up and I threw up over the side for ten minutes. I couldn't work. I just thought: yeah, this is glamour!'[16] Noyce had tried to take precautions against seasickness: 'Everybody took pills and wore various acupuncture devices on their wrists and ears, but that still didn't stop some from getting sick.'[17]

But even in more general terms, the shoot was long and taxing. Kidman: 'It was brutal. We filmed from sun-up to sundown. The weather was hot and sticky. We were all drained and exhausted.'[18] And Neill: 'It was a difficult film to make because it was at sea. There were days you were doing well when you got three shots. Some shots were logistically a nightmare. It was a very vivid time, partly because we were isolated on this damn island for months. It was quite a long shoot given the scale of the film. So there was quite a bit of craziness and some bad behaviour, but a lot of very good friendships were made.'[19]

In fact, there were more than just friendships made:

While on the boat, Billy fell in love with Lisa Collins, one of the actors chosen to be in the murdered *Orpheus* crew, and married her immediately after the shoot. From shooting commercials I hired a Japanese-born make-up artist called Nariko Watenabi, and she and Sam Neill fell in love and later married. And then (as told to me by Tom Cruise), Tom saw the film and fell in love with Nicole. So all the key cast members found spouses through that film.

On the professional side, however, none of the actors complained about the difficulties of making the film. 'It was a very vivid time and I'm thankful for that. I'd do it again,' says Neill.[20] Kidman said of Noyce, 'We established a fabulous working relationship and understanding of each other.'[21] And Zane recalls: 'Phillip is so funny, so into it. He gets so, so involved. He knew which buttons to push – he knew how to court Nicole and suit her and play with her. And he knew that I liked a little bit of conflict and spontaneity, so we'd push each other's buttons and then have a laugh. He just knew how to stir me up and I knew him well enough to let him. It was a great dynamic.'[22] Noyce, however, has slightly more complex recollections.

I recognised from the very first encounter – when he came in and was screen-tested – that Billy had an enormous contribution to make because of his ability to invent dialogue that was consistent with his character. Sometimes actors come up with dialogue that seems to have been sent special delivery from Mars – having nothing to do with the way the character would think or the language you could imagine the character using.

Giving an actor that power of invention can be very dangerous, because when you don't agree with an idea they have introduced, they can feel resentful, even though they may have been empowered by the fact that you are listening to them more than they have ever been listened to in their working lives.

What happened was that Billy at one point just couldn't bring himself to play the scenes as scripted. He wasn't being a bad guy, it was just that he had been over-empowered by my directing methods. We sent everyone home and he and I just stayed on the set, shouting at each other. We argued for four or five hours. I made it clear that unless he did what I said we weren't going to keep filming even if it meant recasting with someone else.

Even the boats were more or less stars in their own right. For the *Saracen*, Noyce explains:

'[We] chose a racing yacht that was built in South Africa in 1961. For the *Orpheus*, the abandoned ship, we found an old Merchant Marine sailing ship from Tasmania that was built in the early part of the twentieth century. In order to film the sequence where the *Orpheus* goes up in flames after Sam Neill sets fire to it, we actually built a replica of the *Orpheus*. Because we were not able to always use the real ship (it was out taking tours around the Great Barrier Reef), most of the shooting that you see was done on that replica. Then, of course, one night in June 1988, with seven cameras filming, Sam Neill threw the torch into the water and the whole thing went up in flames. It was spectacular but just another part of the make-believe world of moviemaking. That replica ship had to be towed everywhere it went, because it was just a balsa wood replica.'[23]

Eventually, the choice of boat would determine the location for shooting a new ending:

We reshot in Port Douglas because that was where we found a yacht to double for *Storm Vogel*, the original *Saracen* in the first shoot, which by now had returned to Thailand.

After shooting ended, the soundtrack became Noyce's major concern.

When I was in Tokyo researching *The Cowra Breakout* I first saw Nagisa Oshima's *Merry Christmas, Mr. Lawrence*. I loved the movie but even more exciting was the score by Ryuichi Sakamoto. I wanted him to compose the *Dead Calm* score, but Sakamoto had never heard of us.

Then one of our assistant sound editors showed me a reel of the film with some music he had composed and it was quite mesmerising. He was about 23, had never written a film score before, but it seemed as though his musical style was perfect. It seemed to have mood, grandeur and great psychological tension, so he was given the job. We set him up in a studio with technicians and I spent weeks going through the film explaining what I needed. After about four or five weeks we asked to hear just one of the tracks he'd been working on and that's when the terrible truth was revealed: he couldn't actually write music. The music we'd first heard had been played spontaneously after a night of smoking dope, and clearly he wasn't going to be able to compose a whole score to specific images.

Martin Fabinyi, who then ran a music company called Regular Records, was listening to this whole sad story at my place one night and said: 'Well, you've got to hear this guy Graeme Revell. He has this band called SPK that we've just signed.' And the next day he sent over a vinyl LP. And it seemed to me and to George Miller that this composer (who had also never done a film before) had produced a unique and appropriate sound. After checking that he could actually write music, we hired Graeme.

Probably his most effective music underscores the chase sequence where Sam Neill's character is rowing back to the *Saracen*, having discovered on board the *Orpheus* the mutilated bodies of the crewmembers and realised that his wife is stranded with a homicidal psychopath. In this sequence, which he revised many times, Graeme came up with the idea of using the human voice. It was disturbing in many ways because it had a certain sexual quality, like someone masturbating. It expressed the anxiety of Sam Neill's character, with the microphone seeming like it was inside someone's mouth, not like the usual use of a human voice in music, which tends to be calming. And he combined those breaths with a really deep, fast drum track.

After we finished the film we brought it over to America to try to sell it to Warner Bros. I wasn't at the meeting, but George Miller and Terry and the other producer, Doug Mitchell, told me that Warners' response was very enthusiastic, but they wanted a new ending.

The original film was structured around the relationship between John and Rae Ingram and the way in which the dynamic of that relationship changed. In the beginning, she is emotionally, and to a certain degree physically, shattered, and while comforting her, he says, 'When you're better, we'll go home.' And then at the end of the movie, *she* saves *him*. *He* is the physical and mental wreck, and she has found her strength, mended her psyche, is very much in control, and she will now be his nurse. In the original ending, when they came upon Hughie Warriner's life raft he was nowhere to be found, but unlike the finished version, they let the raft drift off and nobody knew where

Hughie was. Rae then said that it was time to turn around and return home, symbolising that she was mended.

Warner Bros. felt the audience were conditioned to expect that, because of Hughie's determination throughout the movie, he would be back, and that when he didn't reappear they were disappointed. So nine or ten months after the original shoot, I took Billy, Sam and Nicole up to Port Douglas to film the new ending where Hughie returns. I call this a '*Carrie* ending', because it was pioneered by the film *Carrie* – you know, the murderer suddenly comes back to life for a final thrill, only to be despatched once and for all by the hero. Because I was preparing to shoot *Blind Fury*, the rescripting for the new ending was worked out by George and Terry, with George producing some elementary storyboards. With the strong influence of a different directorial sensibility, what we shot would always have a certain tacked-on quality, as it does in the finished film.

This new ending seemed to be well received in the US, where 'audiences were prone to shouting vociferously for Hughie's blood as Rae became increasingly desperate',[24] but audiences in some other countries considered it silly. Noyce's version was never released anywhere in the world. Still, Sam Neill certainly isn't the only one who is aware of the possibilities provided by DVD: 'It was the Americans who said, "We don't like this [original] ending. It's not good enough. We want more punch." That's why the flare gun fires into his face and all that stuff. It would be great if they could put out a DVD version with the original ending, which I thought was much better. In addition, a lot of stuff that I did is missing from the film. There is a whole sequence where a shark invades the sinking boat, and Rae's fighting for her life with a maniac on her boat and I'm fighting for my life with a shark on mine. It would be good to get the whole thing entire.'[25]

Neill had always thought that the audience should be made aware that there was a shark menace, and George Miller executed the idea.[26] John Cox, who built the replica shark, recalls: 'In the film you'll see Sam Neill put his foot through the bottom of the *Orpheus* and then back in and then he swims out of the hull and escapes the boat. The entire sequence that's now missing was cut from the point when Sam pulls his foot back inside the boat. A shark's head comes ramming through the rotten timber to try to get him, and then the shark gets inside the boat and swims up and down inside trying to eat Sam. The only thing that remains in the movie is a point-of-view shot moving through the water towards the boat, which gives you the sense that there is something in the water and you never get to see what it is. It just sort of gives a sense of menace.'[27] John Cox today runs Creature Comfort, a Gold Coast–based animatronics company, and was an Oscar winner for his special effects in *Babe*, directed by Chris Noonan.

'Brian Cox [the special effects coordinator] – whom I had known for a long time in the film industry – needed someone to actually build the shark. I looked after the sculpting, moulding, casting and finishing of the shark, and he and Dave Hardy and Dave Young looked after mechanising the inside of it. I hadn't yet started doing the robotic side of things at that point. We built a big ramming head section of the shark and also a full 12-foot-long tiger shark. I didn't end up going to Hamilton Island – they didn't have the money to spare. So we handed it all over to Brian and Dave, who looked after all the physical effects on the movie. They took it up to Hamilton Island and rigged it up there.

'It was the first time anyone in the world had done silicon skins for this type of stuff. The Americans were still using urethanes like they had used on *Jaws* – which started to deteriorate instantly when they put it into the water; it was just an unsuccessful material. And our shark didn't, it was fine. Then we went on to refine that technique and refined painting silicon, which no one in the US had figured out how to do, and we started to use other materials. So it's no longer just a moulding material, it's actually a casting material.

'I heard that the shoot on the shark went really well and everyone was happy with it. It was just that at that point in the film – the mast has come down over the hatchway so Sam Neill can't get out of the boat; it's sinking, so the water level is rising and he's running out of air – the tension is already fairly high. And they thought it was just too much.'[28]

In the original screenplay we had invented something that wasn't in Charles Williams' novel, and that was the presence of a marauding shark shadowing Sam Neill during the time he was on the *Orpheus* alone and later when he was marooned on his little raft hoping to be rescued by his wife. The idea was to increase the tension.

But before shooting started, Terry Hayes and I dropped the shark, for two reasons. First, we didn't think the shark looked realistic enough in the water; and secondly, we thought the idea was a little bit hooky. We felt we were trying too hard to inject tension when there was sufficient tension from his isolation on a raft in the middle of the Pacific, let alone having to add a horror-film shark element.

Anyway, George Miller came to Hamilton Island about four weeks before the end of the shoot. And as he was travelling to his hotel, he passed the studio we had built right next door to the Hamilton Island airfield and saw out the back this animatronic shark sitting there. As the producer and biggest investor in *Dead Calm*, he was concerned about how much tension we could create out of the conflict between the three characters, and how much threat the audience would feel from Hughie Warriner. So George asked the special effects team to put this shark in the water and show him what it could do.

George then came on board as second unit director, and had to film the sequence where Sam Neill is underwater in the *Orpheus,* checking the hull to see what damage has been done, and discovers the source of the leak. The main unit with myself were out at sea filming on the *Saracen* with Billy Zane and Nicole Kidman. And every night we would get VHS copies of the second unit material that George was shooting. And suddenly, to our horror, appeared this sequence that George had invented where the shark follows Sam Neill from under the water and chases him through two cabins of the *Orpheus*. It was quite a fantastic sequence, but also very, very unrealistic within the context of the rest of the film. This was a scene out of a shark horror movie with Sam running at 100-metre sprint pace through the cabins of the *Orpheus* and the shark was chasing him in a ten-second 100-metre dash. It was kinetic and scary, but it just didn't fit within the tone of the rest of the film, which was mainly about implied threat.

Terry and I told George that we thought his material was dynamic but unnecessary and at odds with the rest of the movie. I then went back to Sydney and started editing the film with Richard Francis-Bruce. I invited George to come in one night and edit his material. He worked with Richard and looked at the shark sequence within the context of the film and decided without any further discussion that it didn't fit the rest of the movie. So, eliminating the footage from the first rough cut was a decision that was entirely made by George. And I totally agreed.

Warner Bros. were so confident the film would be a success that they released it in the United States before they released it in Australia in 1989. On the first weekend it took more than US$3 million at the box office, making it the sixth-highest grossing film that weekend.

Aside from the glued-on new ending, the film generally attracted excellent reviews, with *Variety* calling it 'a nail-biting suspense pic handsomely produced and inventively directed'.[29] A clear minority, however, attacked Noyce for delivering 'a routine woman-in-jeopardy chiller'.[30]

Other critics thought the film 'rarely thrilling' due to a perceived lack of tense action between only three characters.[31] The film does, in fact, contain little action. Yet, it is a rare masterpiece of sustained tension up to the very end – tension created mostly by the psychological development of the characters.[32] For this reason 'the film has hardly dated and can still be enjoyed as much today as when it was released'.[33] David Stratton wrote of the film, '[It] shows technical mastery at [its] finest, but Noyce never allows the technical flourishes to overwhelm the trio of fine performances.'[34]

But virtually every critic commented on Noyce's visual style – 'all deep focus and crisp light, finely composed'.[35] The influence of other directors and films on Noyce is apparent in *Dead Calm*; for example, in the use of very big close-ups. The cutting between extreme close-ups and extreme wide shots for dramatic effect was a style originally developed by Sergio Leone in his 'Spaghetti Westerns'. Inspiration from Roman Polanski's *Knife in the Water* can be perceived, for instance, in one shot where the camera is placed high on the mast and looks down on to the yacht.

'I watched a large number of films in trying to work out how to approach the material. One that gave me the most inspiration, surprisingly, was a Hitchcock film, although I certainly wouldn't say *Dead Calm* was any sort of homage to Hitchcock. Nevertheless, I gained inspiration from watching Hitchcock's *Notorious* . . . by considering the technique he employed to generate an enormous amount of disquiet in me . . . I also noticed how he was able to manipulate the elements to produce this feeling of tension within me, and was able to do it without resorting to any of the tricks that have become so commonplace in the horror or suspense films of, say, the last 15 years. There was no spine-tickling music; no rapid cutting a la *Psycho* (which of course came much later than *Notorious*); no special visual effects, no extravagant use of sound effects to try to disorient the audience or shock them. It was in fact the opposite: the cutting patterns were quite relaxed, and this gave me the biggest clue on how to treat the material in *Dead Calm*, because it seemed that with so few elements, if we tried to beat the film up . . . you were soon going to have to work up such a frenzy of filmic manipulation that you would have nowhere to go.'[36]

Dead Calm was all about the ebb and flow of tension, the manipulation of audience response through camera placement, camera movement and montage.

Steadicam was used extensively.

Steadicam can approximate the point of view of a moving human. And because the camera seems to glide, there is a funny malevolence about that movement. It seems to be hovering restlessly and yet stealthily, and, unlike a camera that is on a dolly, it feels like the camera is stealing its viewpoint; the movement of a camera on a dolly seems to be very deliberate and has more of an objective feel to it. Steadicam produces a subjective quality even when used for an objective shot.

The dolly is much more formal; you can read stories into the dolly movement, but it doesn't yield the same emotion as a Steadicam. That's because of the human factor of the Steadicam movement, but also, I think, because of the association the audience has with the early use of Steadicam by John Carpenter in his horror films – certain shots that have become a part of the audience's decoding of film language.

Zane says of Noyce's visual style: 'All of Phillip's films have this particular flavour. Even in the colour palette. He has a sense of style prevalent in his work that I really appreciate. It's a texture that is almost completely different, on a par with the consistency of Hitchcock, who was a total fashion whore. He was great. He would hire the "it" girl, always the A-line skirt, the shoes, the hairstyle. And Phillip infused his own sensibilities within it while employing the very current perspectives of his wardrobe department. It's rare to find someone who has a style beyond a very signature filtration system, really going into the fabric and the make-up of his setting.'[37]

It is impossible to judge how similar or not Welles's and Noyce's treatment of the story were. Noyce avoided viewing Welles's version prior to finishing his own, as he explained in 1989: 'We wanted to say we were not the least bit influenced by his script.'[38] But 'after I finished making Dead Calm, I was lucky enough to see some of Orson Welles's footage. Actually, it was a trailer that he had made to try and raise more money. It was quite funny to watch the same story with different actors – although, oddly enough, a lot of the shots he had chosen originally were very similar to my angles. I guess you're restricted on a boat to how many angles you've got. Both Orson and I chose, as one of the more dramatic shots, a shot where the camera is up on the mast and looks down on the deck. It's almost geometrical in its properties, and it's distancing. I use it in *Dead Calm* just before a shock moment to sort of take the audience away from the character. Orson used it in his version during the sequence where Rae Ingram is kidnapped.'[39]

Some confusion still surrounds the production side of the film. Though based on an American novel, there was solely Australian financial involvement during its production in 1987, which cost A$10 million. Only after it was finished did Warner Bros. buy it and insist on the new ending.

The film's repercussions for Neill, Kidman and Zane, as well as for Noyce, were considerable – not only personally, as pointed out earlier, but professionally.

For Zane 'it was a blessing and a curse. I owe Phillip my career, and I owe him my career. It apparently left an endurable impression with the entertainment community and certainly, I guess, the public. It's tough to step away from that label of villain. But I welcome it, it's been a great gift. I mean, the world over, that movie has moved so many people and they see it again and again and again. It's a great feeling to know that people really respond to the work.'[40]

Dead Calm single-handedly catapulted Nicole Kidman into the international star orbit. At the age of 21, she was hailed as 'the next big thing'. Before her, only male Australian actors had made it in Hollywood; now Kennedy Miller flew her to the US to meet possible agents, among them Sam Cohn, co-founder of International Creative Management, arguably the most influential agency at the time. 'Something of a demigod in Hollywood, Cohn was used to doing business in a no-nonsense fashion. He arrived in Los Angeles on the night flight from New York, met the young actress for breakfast, told her he had seen her work and announced that he wanted to represent her. Nicole signed the contract as Cohn finished his coffee. Then he was gone, back to New York to start work. As simple as that.'[41]

For Noyce it was a crucial film in many ways. It marked the successful end of his apprentice years, which had led him through so many different genres before he found his genuine cinematic skill. The film clearly established him as a distinctive director with punch, enabling him to work in the Hollywood candy store for the next ten years – and possibly even longer.

---

[1] Tim Ewband and Stafford Hildred, *Nicole Kidman* (London: Headline, 2002), p. 52.

[2] Ibid, p. 53.

[3] Ibid.

[4] Ibid, p. 55.

[5] Sam Neill interview.

[6] Billy Zane interview.

[7] Billy Zane interview.

[8] Billy Zane interview.

[9] Billy Zane interview.

[10] Billy Zane interview.

[11] Sam Neill interview.

[12] Billy Zane interview.

[13] Ewband and Hildred, *Nicole Kidman*, p. 62.

[14] Noyce, cited in Robert J. Emery, *The Directors – Take Four* (New York: Allsworth Press, 2003), pp. 71ff.

[15] Sam Neill interview.

[16] Quoted in Lucy Ellis and Bryony Sutherland, *Nicole Kidman – The Biography* (London: Aurum Press, 2002), p. 48.

[17] Noyce, cited in Elizabeth Drucker, 'Dead Calm – Phillip Noyce at the helm of a thriller', *American Film Magazine*, April 1989, p. 78.

[18] Quoted in Ellis and Sutherland, *Nicole Kidman*, p. 48.

[19] Sam Neill interview.

[20] Sam Neill interview.

[21] Quoted in Ellis and Sutherland, *Nicole Kidman*, p. 49.

[22] Billy Zane interview.

[23] Noyce, cited in Emery, *The Directors*, p. 72.

[24] Ewbank and Hildred, *Nicole Kidman*, p. 65.

[25] Sam Neill interview.

[26] David Stratton, *The Avocado Plantation* (Sydney: Pan Macmillan), 1990, p. 264.

[27] John Cox interview.

[28] John Cox interview.

[29] www.variety.com.

[30] Verina Glaessner, 'Dead Calm', *Monthly Film Bulletin*, November 1989, pp. 332–33.

[31] Scott Murray, *Australian Cinema* (Sydney: Allen & Unwin, 1994), p. 101.

[32] An extraordinarily lengthy and detailed approach to 'the shadowy origins of fear and desire' can be found in Rose Lucas's 'Deadly ambivalence or the family romance in *Dead Calm*', *Literature Film Quarterly*, vol. 21, no. 2, 1993, pp. 121ff.

[33] Ellis and Sutherland, *Nicole Kidman*, p. 50.

[34] Stratton, *The Avocado Plantation*, p. 265.

[35] Murray, *Australian Cinema*.

[36] Noyce, cited in Brian McFarlane, 'Phil Noyce – *Dead Calm*', *Cinema Papers*, May 1989, pp. 61–2.

[37] Billy Zane interview.

[38] Noyce, cited in Drucker, '*Dead Calm*', p. 78.

[39] Noyce, cited in Emery, *The Directors*, pp. 72ff.

[40] Billy Zane interview.

[41] Ellis and Sutherland, *Nicole Kidman*, p. 61.

Part II

HOLLYWOOD
(1989–2000)

Working in a candy store

Chapter 9
BLIND FURY

It was always intended as a comic strip.

Nick Parker (Rutger Hauer), blinded and lost in action during the Vietnam War, is trained by a friendly jungle tribe to use his remaining senses to survive. Finally, he becomes a master martial arts warrior. Twenty years later, Parker is back in Miami to look up an old army buddy, Frank, who is in trouble with the mob in Reno. He arrives in time to prevent the kidnapping of Billy (Brandon Call), Frank's son, but not to stop the murder of Frank's ex-wife. The rest of the film is a road movie that takes us across the United States to San Francisco in a series of fights and chases as Parker tries to reunite Billy with his father.

Hollywood. The myth. The magic. Probably every film-maker gets tempted – some sooner, some later. Maybe the thought first occurred to Noyce after graduation from the Australian Film and Television School, when he organised screenings of his film-school works in a cinema that held 700 people.

I was really nervous about the cost of hiring this cinema for eight days and ten screenings. But then, right from the first night – and I charged the then unheard-of amount of A$2.50 to see the movies – people were streaming in. As you can see, I am very tall . . . and the money is coming in and eventually it's right up here to my waist. I'm surrounded by one-dollar notes and people are fighting to hand over cash to see my movies. I guess that was when the idea of going to Hollywood first came to me [*smiles ironically*].

In reality, however, Noyce's path to Hollywood proved to be a much longer, and definitely very winding, road.

After *Newsfront* was shown in 1978 as the first Australian film to be screened at the New York Film Festival, I was approached by agents in America who wanted to represent me. The very idea of an agent was almost completely foreign to me and at the time I wasn't really interested in working overseas, because it seemed like Australia was Nirvana. There was freedom and there was money, or there appeared to be, and as I had just directed a big success, I expected to be making many more films. But I did sign with Joan Scott, from Writers and Artists Agency, who had started in New York representing playwrights and stage actors, and then branched out to Los Angeles. Initially, I was mainly interested in her trying to find money to make films in Australia.

My second full-length feature was to be *Heatwave*, starring Judy Davis. Joan Scott sent the script around to various producers in Hollywood, who had expressed admiration for *Newsfront*, to see if any of them were interested in coming in as a co-producer to secure some American finance. As a result I got to meet Tony Bill, who read the script but didn't want to invest in *Heatwave*. Five years later, however, he gave me the manuscript of a novel he had been trying for years to option, and this was Charles Williams' *Dead Calm*. So, it was my long-time association with the American film industry that finally led to *Dead Calm*, the film that allowed me to work in Hollywood with a higher profile.

I had already worked in North America – not in the States but in Canada – in 1985, when during one of the periods of famine in the Australian film industry I had accepted an offer to make a half-hour anthology story, a self-contained drama for HBO [Home Box Office] as part of the popular television series called *The Hitchhiker*. Each episode was directed by a different non-American director, for stylistic reasons and, I suspect, in order to avoid paying US Directors Guild residuals. Mike Hodges, who did *Get Carter*, Roger Vadim, Paul Verhoeven, the German Carl Schenkel and myself all worked on the series.

I had discovered some talent for thriller elements while shooting the Australian miniseries *The Cowra Breakout* in 1983. Joan Scott had shown it around in Los Angeles and this was the project that caught Tri-Star's attention.

When I had shot *Dead Calm* but not yet completed editing, and before it was sold to Warner Bros., I was offered the US$5 million *Blind Fury*. I didn't like the script at all. It seemed much more lightweight in story content than anything I'd attempted – an action–comedy film. But as I wasn't confident about how *Dead Calm* was going to turn out, I wanted to establish a beachhead outside Australia.

It seems that Noyce had developed a deep-rooted understanding of the underlying mechanisms that propelled Hollywood to success after success. And he had valid reasons for considering a change in his career.

In visiting America and living in the quasi-American colony of Australia, I had become aware that the city-state of Los Angeles had colonised us all in a way that even the Romans couldn't have achieved, because Rome ruled through the sword and never truly owned the hearts and minds of the peoples it conquered. But Hollywood didn't need a sword; it hypnotised with packaged entertainment and very smart business practices, which have enabled America to control film, TV and music distribution in the majority of nations worldwide. A multinational such as Coca-Cola, which is headquartered in Atlanta, is able to control the distribution of its product right into the stomachs of hundreds of millions of people all around the world. The Hollywood studios have been able to do the same thing: co-opting talent and then exporting their productions with the various product stamps which are looked to by people worldwide as a seal of good housekeeping. 'MGM', 'Columbia', 'Paramount', 'Warner Bros.' and so on stamped on the film means *Yes, Good*; *Yes, Guaranteed Entertainment, Action, Excitement*. Each of these studio names is like the names of certain actors and directors – a guarantee of a certain level of pleasure in exchange for your hard-earned money.

The Americans have erected an incredibly ruthless and efficient financing and distribution machine, subject only to the laws of supply and demand – normal laws, as opposed to the abnormal ones of government policy. The choice is yours whether that machine eats you up and spits you out, or whether you use it. Around the time of *Shadows of the Peacock* I just got this terrible feeling that I didn't have a big future making movies in Australia. And when I made *Dead Calm* and embraced the thriller genre, I suspected that the way my interests were now developing and the kind of films that I could make in Australia weren't really compatible.

After *Newsfront* it took four years before I made *Heatwave* and then another four for *Shadows of the Peacock*. The reason wasn't only indecision on my part, but also because the Australian film industry is subject to the whims of bureaucrats, politicians and government officials, in as much as it has always been financed mostly by government subsidies. Only occasionally are Aussie films financed according to real market forces, to laissez-faire economics. As a result, at least during the first twelve years of my career, I had to ride the roller-coaster of feast or famine, the flood-or-drought cycle of our film industry, see-sawing from easy production money to none at all. The amount of politicking and inevitable disappointment that I could see up ahead made me think that, having got a foot in the door in America, I should take the opportunity to establish a beachhead there. As it turned out, many directors of my generation felt the same: Peter Weir, Bruce Beresford, Gillian Armstrong, George Miller, Roger Donaldson, Vincent Ward, and so on.

While we were trying to put together the casting for *Dead Calm* I was in Los Angeles and, despite my script reservations, I met with the producers of *Blind Fury* and Tri-Star. I did some work on the script with writer Charles Robert Carner. While we were in a hiatus during the editing of *Dead Calm*, looking for a composer, Tri-Star green-lit *Blind Fury*. So I decided to come across to America for a few months to shoot it.

Thinking back, it seems that *Blind Fury* is about Nick Parker trying to find a home for himself and realising that his lot is to keep on wandering. He is trying to mend himself but realises he can only do that by moving on. Initially, he is searching for a home, but he realises that what he is searching for goes beyond that, it's something deeper – he is searching for a spiritual home, not an actual place. He seeks out his war buddy, thinking that may be the answer. The character of Nick Parker was adapted from a series of Japanese films starring Shintarô Katsu. The character is called Zatôichi and in the original series he's a blind samurai who wanders across Japan righting wrongs. The script for *Blind Fury* had been inspired by two of the Zatôichi movies.[1]

The World Wide Web may well be a boundless source of information, but it can also contribute to confusion. Some of the information about Noyce on the Net is palpably false. Was *Blind Fury* adapted from a screenplay by Ryozo Kasahara?

I don't think specifically that our script was adapted from one particular screenplay. It was a reinvention of the Japanese character, so I think there was an obligation to give some sort of credit that came with buying the rights.

'Initially I didn't really go for the script – it was more of an exploitation movie. But then it was great to make a movie that had no redeeming social values. The main attraction was that it was so frivolous, that it aimed merely to entertain, and, as an antidote to everything I'd done before, that seemed like a good movie to make. The other films I've made were realistic, naturalistic and deadly serious.'[2]

I cast Rutger Hauer, who has a certain dislocated quality that seemed to make him appropriate for a blind man with an offbeat sense of humour. Rutger was very overweight. He wasn't exactly slim when we were shooting the picture, but he was 30 pounds lighter than when we had cast him. He trained for over two months both to lose weight and to be able to handle the sword.

As on most of Noyce's films, much time and energy was spent on research.

'I took Rutger Hauer to the Braille Institute in Los Angeles, and we spent a lot of time talking to and being with blind people. But then, for the real test, and for several days, all of the cast and myself and the key crew prepared for the film blindfolded. It produced a great camaraderie, and you learn to depend on someone when you're impaired in that way. Then, for the agile sword work, Rutger trained with a swordsman for eight weeks, starting fully sighted during all of those moves and then doing them actually blindfolded.'[3]

During pre-production I returned to Australia to shoot the new ending for *Dead Calm*, just before starting to shoot *Blind Fury*.

The film was shot over six weeks in 1988 and released in 1989. It was a non-union picture, which means you shoot outside Los Angeles with cheaper non-union crews. We shot a lot of it in Houston, Texas, then the gambling scenes and the ski-chalet scenes in Reno, Nevada, with a mostly local crew picked up at each of the locations. Cinematographer Don Burgess later went on to shoot *Forrest Gump* with Tom Hanks, and *Terminator 3*, among other films, but this was one of his first small features. When I found him he was shooting TV commercials. The Vietnam jungle scenes were shot in a small area of tropical greenery near the Houston Zoo.

When we were shooting in Houston it was early summer with 95 per cent humidity and over 110 degrees Fahrenheit heat. We seemed to be the only people that were on the streets.

There was almost a fatal accident on that film. In the action finale, the bad guy is cut in half by Hauer's character and falls down a mountain, which in the end was achieved by a crude form of CGI – computer-generated imagery – rather less sophisticated than it became in the ensuing years. But originally we tried to do something like that with a stuntman, who had to fall backwards about 60 feet. I can remember: the camera is rolling, the guy is coming through the air and he is falling into this huge box filled with bags of air. And suddenly I realised that on the edge of the box, one of the wooden supports is sticking up about 3 feet and the guy is headed straight towards it. Just when he was about to be skewered, the medic pushed him away from possible death.

We had done some stunts on *Dead Calm*, but I'd never attempted anything like the sort of work I was doing on *Blind Fury*, with swords and guns. I myself was a little inexperienced, which is probably how those accidents happen. I realised that although you have safety people and stunt coordinators, finally you have to check everything yourself as a director. You just have to check everything.

Despite the training he undertook for the film, Hauer is not an acknowledged martial arts hero. Information on the Web says that for the climactic fight sequence the producers brought in martial arts star Shô Kosugi (in much the same way that Bruce Lee was brought in for *Return of the Dragon*).[4] Kosugi is considered to be quite good in his small role, but martial arts movie fans may be disappointed, as he has few, if any, real lines.

Noyce refutes the use of a double:

Rutger might have been substituted in some wide shots or second unit shots, but I don't remember him being replaced in fight scenes. Well, no more than in any action film. It's like saying that in *Rabbit-Proof Fence* the kids didn't play the scenes where they walk across the desert – well, they didn't; the wide shots used doubles. Shô Kosugi is the swordsman whom Rutger battles in the final action sequence.

For me there was always an unresolved tension between the violence of that film and the presence of a child in the story. The studio wanted an R rating because they figured that would mean the violence would be stronger and that action would provide the basic appeal of the film. But I thought the violence should be much more restrained, that the film should be PG 13, which would mean it could play to junior teenagers – kids aged from thirteen on.

After I had shot a couple of the action scenes, the producers and the studio had this conference one night and said, 'Look, your shooting style has to emphasise the violence more. You have to go back and shoot more material.' And they even brought in a new stunt coordinator to try and encourage me to beef up the violence. My idea was that everything should be implied. You should never actually see a sword stuck into people, and so on. I think there is still an unresolved tension between the reality and fantasy elements of the movie. I think it pulls in three different directions: one is towards extreme violence; another is towards a comic book quality and the softer elements of the story with the child; and finally, you've got a narrative and character interaction, which you're meant to take seriously. Yet the whole setting is so unrealistic. The idea of a blind man with a sword in America is so unreal. But I'm not sure how you could resolve these opposing elements without a different script, because the way of making the film more artistically cohesive would have been to make it completely comic book in design and execution.

The film's frequent comedic moments should not be over-looked. When Parker sets off on his wanderings across North America, he stumbles across an alligator in the Everglades that he addresses as a 'Nice doggie'. In the camp ground scene, his skill with the sword is observed by an elderly couple who immediately want a sword too; and then there is the scene where the blind Parker is at the wheel of a car driving through busy city streets. These elements seem to be in strong contrast to the prevailing violence but fit well into the concept of a comic strip with its inherent exaggerations.

A couple of pastiches can be found as well, most notably when Parker is offered a home by Billy, the little boy. Or later, when Billy cries desperately, 'Uncle Nick, don't leave me. Everybody leaves me. I need you!', but Parker refuses to give up his wanderings. Like the lone rider in a Western, he chooses to wander aimlessly forever. The film's emotional moments are wrapped in violence.

Some parts of the film evoke a strong sense of déjà vu. This is particularly true of the long scene set in the cornfield, which has a bit of Hitchcock's *North by Northwest* about it, or perhaps even Joseph Losey's *Figures in a Landscape*. And the cable car scene is reminiscent of the James Bond film *Moonraker*. The overall approach of the film, at least to a certain degree, is reminiscent of Bruce Beresford's *Barry McKenzie* films: the character of Nick Parker is definitely a larrikin – a little stupid and a little clever, a little rough and a little smooth, a little funny and a little serious. All this is probably because Noyce had not yet found his personal Hollywood style – if he can be said to have developed one at all.

The strongest and most memorable part of the film may well be the opening Vietnam sequence where Parker wakes up in pain. A flashback reveals he has been blinded in a series of explosions. Later he stumbles through the rainforest, where he becomes caught in a trap set by a local tribe, who befriend and try to heal him. They tease him crudely while at the same time teaching him to use his other senses, such as his sense of hearing, more keenly. Noyce plays with sound wonderfully. We see the flashing explosions – all tinted in blue – but we don't hear them. The air is filled with strange whispers, and Parker is made to listen. The first words spoken in the film come much later, when, in the Everglades, he addresses the alligator he has mistaken for a dog. This effectively kills the mood that has prevailed until then and sets a completely new tone.

The film was meant to be an amalgam – a little bit of drama, a little bit of slapstick comedy, a little bit of pathos, a little bit of action – all rolled into one. I wanted it to be a hybrid film, which may be the making or breaking of it, because when you make a film that attempts to be many things, it's sometimes hard to mesh the disparate elements together into a satisfying whole.

It is not clear whether Noyce succeeded in this task or not – the results are contradictory. Whereas most film critics panned *Blind Fury*, it has found an audience.

We finally tested the film for an audience and, believe it or not, it was the third-highest score I ever achieved: 87 out of 100. *Clear and Present Danger* was 92 or 93, followed by *The Bone Collector* with 89.

Before the film was released, the management of Tri-Star changed (as happens often in Hollywood) and new executives came into the company just as the film was being finished. For a while there was doubt about whether it would even be released. So I said to the studio, 'Let me take it to Australia. Give me one territory.' I went to Queensland and worked for a few weeks with the local Tri-Star guys and the film earned half-a-million dollars in Queensland alone. For Queensland, that was sensational. There's a guy there named Sonny Schattling who has been in the business a long time. He had worked his way up from booking the films, travelling around the outback by car, getting the exhibitors to sign up to the movies back in the 1960s and 1970s. And now he was head of publicity, a charming rogue of a guy who worked on a person-to-person basis. He got me around to all the radio and television stations, the country newspapers, organised competitions and everything. And the film worked.

So then Tri-Star said, 'Okay, now we'll open it in Germany as the next trial.' We took it there and it failed. Finally, in America, it was released in only about 300 cinemas, a comparatively small release for that kind of exploitation genre. It went on to be a big success later on video.

It would have recouped its budget taking into account video and TV. It's hard to lose money on a film that cost so little.

Serious film critics dismissed the film outright. In Germany, it had the lowest ranking of any of Noyce's films released there. Critics took offence at what they called a 'genre-cocktail' of 'war film, criminal film, thriller, martial arts movie and road movie with a disappointing Rutger Hauer as lead actor . . . The film neither offers great actors nor a convincing plot or any other artistic highlight.'[5]

Variety was not much more comforting: '*Blind Fury* is an action film with an amusing gimmick, toplining Rutger Hauer, as an apparently invincible blind Vietnam vet who wields a samurai sword with consummate skill . . . The rest of the film is simply a series of flights and chases as Parker heads for Reno to reunite Billy with his father.'⁶ Other critics – like the one at the BFI's *Monthly Film Bulletin* – found the exact opposite: 'Rutger Hauer is well cast . . . Phillip Noyce, obviously relaxing after his high-suspense work on *Dead Calm*, directs capably, and the film assembles a fine collection of villains for the hero to beat.'⁷

There is another notable difference between this film and Noyce's others: an Internet search for *Blind Fury* produces more hits than one for any of his other films. It appears that the martial arts community has bestowed on it the mantle of cult movie. For fans of that particular genre, it undoubtedly has the advantage of not taking itself too seriously.

What did the film mean to Noyce at the time it was made and how does he feel about it today?

I was always a little embarrassed by the movie because it's such a silly film. During shooting, I was already thinking I shouldn't be doing this film, it's not good for my career. But then I thought if I don't *have* a career, then this is better than nothing. And I was fortunate that *Dead Calm* was released first in America so that when people saw *Blind Fury* they said, 'This is the film he made before *Dead Calm*'. Which is sort of true, because I finished shooting *Blind Fury* and then completed *Dead Calm*.

When I look back on it now, I think a film like that, a low-budget exploitation film, is often the way a foreign director starts in Hollywood. I was lucky enough that it wasn't the way it ended, because it's truly a dead-end journey. But, you know, even John Woo started with a Jean-Claude Van Damme vehicle, so it's a similar situation. I was lucky in that I really loved working with Rutger, who is both a gentleman and a talented actor, and became a very good friend. But I was glad *Dead Calm* came out first.

---

¹ The *Zatôichi* series started in Japan in 1962. *Zatôichi* (literally meaning 'Masseur Ichi') was a blind man in 19th century Japan who earned his money by massaging. However, his true skills lay in the use of his cane sword. The films followed a rigid formula, with Zatôichi usually outsmarting the Yakuza. The

audiences loved this so much that the series went on for a couple of decades, with usually as many as four released per year.

At the time of writing, a film called *Zatôichi* is a huge success. While it doesn't have the same screenplay, *Zatôichi* is based on the same Japanese series. It has been bought by Miramax, and won the audience awards at both Venice and Toronto in 2003.

2 Quoted in Toby Creswell, 'Phillip Noyce's double take', *Rolling Stone*, 1989.
3 Robert J. Emery, *The Directors – Take Four* (New York: Allworth Press, 2003), p. 73.
4 J. Michael Dlugos, www.retailad.bc.ca/videoviews/pages/indies/Blindfury.html.
5 Ralph Umard, '*Blind Fury*', *TIP* (Berlin), no. 17, 1989, pp. 38ff.
6 *Variety* Internet Archive.
7 Kim Newman: '*Blind Fury*', *Monthly Film Bulletin* (London), vol. 57 no. 679, August 1990, p. 219.

Chapter 10
PATRIOT GAMES

In fact, he never left the parking lot.

CIA analyst Jack Ryan (Harrison Ford) is visiting London's tourist sights with his wife and young daughter when they become caught up in an IRA attack against members of the British royal family. Ryan intervenes to protect the intended victims and in the process kills the brother of one of the assailants. From that moment on, Ryan and his family are under constant threat of a bloody revenge.

Patriot Games has to be thought of as Phillip Noyce's first 'proper' Hollywood film: in genre, in style, in budget, and in his dealings with the script and actors. His assured handling of the thriller genre this time around is a far cry from his ambivalent approach to the 'genre-cocktail' that was *Blind Fury*. Suddenly, all the typical Noyce ingredients came together. But the story of how the film itself actually came together through Paramount, the producer Mace Neufeld, Noyce and Harrison Ford, is almost a movie in itself.

Brandon Tartikoff was head of drama at NBC when I was making the pilot for the *Nightmare Cafe* TV series [(in 1992): see US TV work chapter on CD-ROM]. Soon afterwards he came over as chairman of Paramount just when the studio was looking for a director for *Patriot Games*, a further adaptation of one of Tom Clancy's novels centred on the character of Jack Ryan, the CIA analyst who had been played by Alec Baldwin in *The Hunt for Red October*, which John McTiernan had directed into a huge hit [in 1990].

Mace Neufeld recalls: 'I actually asked John McTiernan to do *Patriot Games*. I had already asked Frank Mancuso, who was chairman of the studio, to acquire the rights to both *Patriot Games* and *Clear and Present Danger*. My thought was to do *Patriot Games* first, since it was a more personal story, and then we could go on to do *Clear and Present Danger*. Because I was going off to London to do something, I suggested that McTiernan go in, without me, to meet with the then head of Paramount, Brandon Tartikoff, and discuss *Patriot Games*. To my horror I found out that McTiernan had taken the meeting with Tartikoff and had said that he thought *Patriot Games* was an enormous mistake, that it would kill the franchise and shouldn't be done, and that *Clear and Present Danger* should be the second film. So having heard that, I simply said I didn't want to continue working with McTiernan on the series.'[1]

Neufeld had met Noyce 'many years earlier when he came to the United States looking for a distributor for *Newsfront*. I met him along with some other Australians, like the young Mel Gibson, who came through my office because we had some connection with Hoyts, a company that distributed American films in Australia. I went to see *Dead Calm* and I was very impressed with the film. When we were looking for a director for *Patriot Games* I suggested Phillip and somebody at Paramount said, "Well, he didn't really direct *Dead Calm*; it was done by George Miller." And I said, "I thought that George Miller was the producer. What do you mean?" "Well, the bulk of it was directed by George Miller."'[2]

Sam Neill recalls: 'George had a very high reputation, but nobody really knew Phil, so for some reason the word got around that it really was George's film. Mace Neufeld called me – I knew him because I had done *Hunt for Red October* with him – and said, "Look, I really like this guy Phil Noyce and I like this film and I'm interested in him for this next Tom Clancy film that we are doing. But what do you think?" I said, "He's fantastic, are you kidding?" And he said, "But look, everyone says that George directed this film, that it wasn't Phil." I said,

"That's complete bullshit. George did some nice second unit stuff but that's all it was. Phil is the guy that made this film, no question about it." And he said, "Thank you very much for telling me that. That puts my mind at ease."[3]

Noyce at that moment was working on the script for 'a film called *Trial By Jury* for Morgan Creek when I was sent the screenplay for *Patriot Games* by Paramount. I read it and actually at that time the script was much more concerned with action than the final film turned out to be.'[4]

The script had been written by J. Peter Iliff and reminded me a little of *Blind Fury* in its sophistication. Not wishing to cement my reputation for cartoon action, I was very hesitant to take on the project.

Neufeld: 'What he probably didn't tell you is that he initially turned down the project. I was stunned. We went to a restaurant for lunch and I sat there with him and Steve Rabineau, who was then, and still is, his agent, and I just couldn't budge him on it. I think the Irish question was the problem. And I said, "That shouldn't bother you, you're Australian, you're not English." But at any rate I called him again and he seemed softer, and then eventually we had lunch again and he said he would like to go forward with it.'[5]

But after meeting with studio executives and producer Mace Neufeld, I read Tom Clancy's novel, which I found to be a combination of wonderful documentary reality, rather interesting characters and situations, and incredibly dull, gung-ho, right-wing attitudes. I realised it was the latter that had been mainly translated into the screenplay. So I said that I would direct the film if I could have a say in further script development.

I went to Jamaica to visit my wife, Jan Sharp, who was at the time producing *Wide Sargasso Sea*, a film that she had written and was being directed there by John Duigan. There I met up with Alec Baldwin, who had played Jack Ryan in *Red October* and who was in the final stages of negotiating his contract to reprise the role. Since shooting *Red October* Baldwin had met his wife Kim Basinger, and while they were co-starring in a film for Disney called *The Marrying Man*, the two of them together, for whatever reason, had acquired a reputation as being irrational and unreasonable in their demands and promptness. The whole of Hollywood had been electrified by the stories of Alec and Kim on the set of *The Marrying Man* and Paramount were paranoid – to say the least – about his presence on a big-budget action picture. *Patriot Games* was budgeted at US$42 million – a lot of money in 1991.

So the studio decided to draw the line in their negotiations with Alec. The fee had already been agreed and it was substantial. But the two areas which the studio elected to disagree on were that Alec should have script approval, like many actors at that time, and that he should, of all things, receive a certain number of return first-class plane tickets to London. Aeroplane tickets to locations are one of the perks that studios have allowed actors to claim. It is not unusual for A-list actors to secure multiple return first-class tickets to Los Angeles, London or Johannesburg, or wherever the film is being shot – for their mother, wife, nanny, business manager, assistants, best friend, art dealer, stockbroker – whomever. So Paramount said no to this request for tickets and no to his request for script approval, and a tug of war developed.

At the time Paramount had just cancelled production on a very expensive action–adventure film that was to star Harrison Ford. It was a period film set on trains, to be directed by Harold Becker, and they found that the budget came in too high at around US$50 million, especially given that Harrison was coming off Mike Nichols' *Regarding Henry*, which had underperformed.

Mace Neufeld remembers events slightly differently: 'We were very upset at that point. We had this film we were planning in progress, we had already signed Phillip Noyce as director and like a miracle Harrison Ford had just opted not to do a picture and was open for a film. I had worked previously with him, 13 years ago in *The Frisco Kid*. I had been trying to do a movie with him for 13 years and he kept turning me down. I sent this script out and we got a call saying he loved the idea of doing it, and we had our new leading man. We did offer *Red October* to Harrison and he turned it down – he would rather play the Russian submarine commander. But this time around, he was very enthusiastic.'[6]

David Kirkpatrick, one of the executives at Paramount, gave the script of *Patriot Games* to Harrison, who read it and expressed interest in the character of Jack Ryan.

Neufeld: 'When Alec Baldwin pulled out of the film and Harrison Ford got on board I called Harrison and he asked me if we had a director. My heart kind of sank because I know that Harrison doesn't go out to see a lot of movies. And I said, "Well, we do have a director but obviously you wouldn't know this person." He said, "What's the name?" "It's an Australian by the name of Phillip Noyce." He said, "I haven't heard of him – what did he do?" I said, "He made this film *Dead Calm*". He said, "I didn't see that – what else has he done?" I said, "Years ago I met him when he'd done a little film called *Newsfront*." He said, "*Newsfront*? I love that!" I said, "Where in the world did you see *Newsfront*?" He said, "I was at some film festival and I think I was on the jury when I saw it. Just bring him on down to meet with us." And of course he had director approval. So Phillip ended up directing the film in spite of himself.'[7]

So Mace Neufeld and myself, Don Granger [Paramount vice-president in charge of production] and Brandon Tartikoff, the guy who had come over from NBC and who had originally recommended me to direct the film, flew up to Wyoming in a private jet and met with Harrison at his ranch outside Jackson Hole. Amusingly enough, Harrison, who of course had director approval, had loved both *Newsfront* and *Blind Fury*. So I was pre-approved. We discussed the script for several hours and left with the impression that if and when Alec Baldwin fell out, Harrison would be approachable to play the role.

Alec was offered the part of Stanley Kowalski in the Broadway production of *A Streetcar Named Desire*. At the same time he was insisting he get his script approval and London first-class plane tickets. The funny thing was, the more I told him that Paramount wouldn't back down, the more determined he became to break them. In the end Alec announced he was pulling out of the film in order to work on Broadway. I guess he expected that when he went out the door with his last offer, Paramount would run to the street and call him back into the shop, as often happens. But he walked out that door, down the street, around the corner and nobody called. He left. What he didn't realise when he thought he was calling their bluff was that there was another potential actor in the wings. I think the studio were more willing to stand up to Alec given that they had a superstar on hold.

The studio, in fact, worked quickly. On 12 September 1991 Paramount president David Kirkpatrick announced that they had signed Ford for not one, but three films in the role of CIA analyst Jack Ryan. He didn't mention, however, that the deal was subject to Ford's by now standard script and director approval. 'Accounts varied, but his fee for *Patriot Games* was by common consensus $9 million, with a further $20 million to follow for the two sequels. Harrison's percentage of the gross would be of the order of ten per cent. At near enough $30 million plus the promise of as much again in profit point bonuses, the package eclipsed anything Harrison – or Hollywood – had seen before . . . The $10 million a movie barrier was breached for the first time in Hollywood history.'[8] Understandably, Alec Baldwin was not amused. 'Harrison's not sexy and audiences will not turn out to see him,' he bitched.[9] This off-target remark may be an additional indicator of Baldwin's blurred perception of the Hollywood realities.

So we then started to work on the screenplay with Steve Zaillian, who later was to win the Academy Award for *Schindler's List* and became a director in his own right, with two very good films (*Searching for*

Bobby Fischer, 1993; and *A Civil Action*, 1998). Steve started on a page 1 rewrite of the Iliff script, going back to the book and pulling out what Harrison and I liked about Clancy's original material. Steve wrote the script that we shot. Uncredited, because the Writers Guild decides on credits, and they usually give it to the original writer. In this case, two of them: Peter Iliff and Donald Stewart – the guy who wrote *Missing*. Their names are on the credits, but 80 per cent of what was shot was written by Steve Zaillian.

Mace Neufeld is explicit in his assessment of Harrison Ford's contributions to a script. 'You know that the script that he has approved is not the script we're going to end up shooting, because we're going to work on it every day up to and while we're shooting. Every scene in a film and ergo every line that makes up the scene has got to advance the story and be consistent with the character. He's always looking to eliminate false notes, writer's directions that look good on paper but just don't work.'[10]

Screenwriting veteran Don Stewart, of Oscar-winning fame for Costa-Gavras's *Missing* and feared for defending his material, acknowledges Ford's exceptional professionalism. 'After 20 odd years in this business, I have learned to kind of tune out to a lot of these story meetings. But you don't with him, because you know he's going to say something that you want to remember,' he stated. 'He's the only actor that I really take notes on.'[11]

Even Noyce was impressed with Ford's knowledge of film-making. 'He is a walking encyclopaedia. He's worked with so many great directors, and seen the shots that work and the shots that don't.'[12]

Only during their future collaboration in *Clear and Present Danger* would these feelings partly turn sour. For this project, however, problems arose from a rather unexpected quarter.

I couldn't have predicted the controversy that resulted from the relationship with Tom Clancy, the author of the novel. Clancy had been an insurance salesman who had written *The Hunt for Red October* and sold it to a specialty publishing house, when Mace Neufeld, the producer, read the yet-to-be-published manuscript and bought the movie rights to the material.

Clancy was a relatively obscure author at the time the screenplay *The Hunt for Red October* was being adapted by Don Stewart. Don later told me that even at that time Clancy had taken exception to, or had been offended by, the ways in which it was necessary to abridge his material. All of his books are extremely thick in size and complex in structure, with a large cast of characters.

With the release of the movie and its popularity contributing to book sales, Clancy became the publishing sensation of the 1990s. By the time we started work on *Patriot Games* he had written numerous other novels which had subsequently become number 1 bestsellers.

I went across to Chesapeake Bay, in Maryland, to Tom Clancy's house to talk about the script and the novel and some of our ideas for developing the material for the screen. My then ten-year-old daughter, Lucia, was with me as we drove into his compound. The house was like Jack Ryan's place down on the bay in the film. But Clancy's version was surrounded by high-tech security machinery and laser beams. As we drove up, out came Tom Clancy dressed in army fatigues and I said, 'Why is he dressed like that?' And my daughter hit it in one: 'I think it's some kind of statement, Dad.'

We started to discuss various aspects of the story and how it might be more efficiently adapted. Mace and I wanted to change the character of Prince Charles – who appeared in the novel – to a distant cousin of the royal family, Lord Holmes – as he appears in the screenplay – because we just thought that having an actor playing a real person and then putting him in with fictional characters would be distracting. There was also a number of other points about amalgamations, about changes that we thought were necessary. Clancy became extremely hostile and the more so when he received Steve Zaillian's screenplay. While Steve was basically telling the same story as the novel, he gave more humanity to the Irish and more liveliness to the Ryan family in ways that were more appropriate for the screen.

'It is true that if you are faithfully trying to adapt the novel, changing the central character's ideology from what is a right-wing to a completely left-wing position . . . it is arguable that you are not being faithful.'[13]

Harrison Ford: 'It's important to stay faithful to the spirit of the book and try to match the action as closely as possible. But books and films are such different mediums that there are moments when you find you simply have to change things because it doesn't work in the film, and there were a few of those things in *Patriot Games* – but not too many.'[14]

The scene that most vividly expressed Clancy's belief that 'Hollywood was under siege from communist infiltrators'[15] appeared in an early version of the screenplay, but didn't make it to the screen. When Ryan is visited at home by the head of the CIA, Admiral Greer (played by James Earl Jones), who is attempting to lure Ryan back into the agency, Greer says: 'Jack. I know you have had problems with some of the things we've had to do in the past.' As soon as Clancy read the scene he 'sent us a massive fax accusing us of running some sort of Hollywood, left-wing, liberal, fellow-travelling club. He was always running a fax commentary on everything we did,' says Noyce,[16] who eventually stopped responding to the faxes.

Clancy then started to talk to the press.

So here I was doing my first big Hollywood movie and suddenly I read in the newspapers that this by now four-times *New York Times* number 1 bestselling author is saying, as he did, that this director is at best a B director, and Harrison Ford is too old to play Jack Ryan.

In fact, only a couple of days before the release of the film, Clancy told the press that the script had been bastardised. Even worse, he complained that Harrison, who was only days from his 50th birthday, was too old to play the 31-year-old Ryan. Which Mace Neufeld disputed: 'I optioned *Hunt For Red October* seven years ago, and I came across a letter from Tom

Clancy in my file last week which said "Dear Mace, I saw *Witness* last night. You are absolutely right, Harrison Ford is Jack Ryan. Wait until you read the first chapter of the new book I am writing, *Patriot Games*." I thought that was very interesting.'[17]

As a general rule, all the key players toned down Clancy's hostility when the topic popped up during publicity interviews. In a typical response, Harrison once said: 'I don't think I can afford to be very honest about that.'[18]

Eventually we decided that the only way to cope with this was to cut off all contact with Clancy, because the more information we fed him the more ammunition we gave him to attack us. We decided we had to go ahead and make decisions about what we thought was best and hope for the best. And if the film was successful then more people would see it than had read the novel.

Imagine how relieved I was when a year later, when the film came out, the gist of Janet Maslin's review in the *New York Times* was that she was relieved that the makers of the movie had avoided the worst excesses of the novel. ['Clancy should be grateful, in as much as his fevered, paranoid, right-wing world has been reduced to something that is almost acceptable.'][19] Similar comments were made by the *New Yorker*.

Clancy was so opposed to the screen treatment of his novel he asked for his name to be removed from the film's titles; he agreed to have it restored just before the film's release. The advertising didn't mention his name at all and simply read, 'From the best-selling novel'.

In spite of these shenanigans, Noyce and his adversary Clancy are very similar in some respects. David Hay in *The Bulletin* hints at this when he notes 'the author's obsession with detail, his method of building tension through cross-cutting the narrative and his devotion to his central character'.[20] The same could be said of Noyce and his working style. Perhaps this explains some of the friction between the two?

Given the topic of the film, and Clancy's confrontational approach to it, there was an even more serious controversy threatening from the start:

I predicted it as soon as I first read the script and spoke to Paramount. At least in the screenplay that I read, and less so in the film, but obviously still enough to prove incendiary, I felt that the film was liable to be condemned by elements of the Irish Republican Movement and those on that particular side of the age-old argument in Northern Ireland.

To avoid major political confrontations, Noyce did serious research on Irish history. He even made visits to Ireland to get an understanding of the Irish characters that would appear in the film. As a result the Ryan family's antagonists underwent an interesting switch: the hero develops into a crazy Rambo-type character, the heroine is actually an Englishwoman who has gone over to the Irish side, and their extremist group even kills comrades from the IRA proper.

I don't know if it's apparent from watching the film, but the Irish extremists are a splinter group who have broken away from the IRA, who in turn would like to eliminate them. There was some reference to that in the book, but we made it even stronger in the screenplay.

As well, I tried to portray Sean Miller's character as being justified in his hatred for Jack Ryan. Hopefully we feel that Miller [played by Sean Bean] has a very close relationship with his young brother, and that there is no sign of hate in their eyes when they undertake this kidnapping attempt. In the first scene where we see them loading their guns, they are portrayed as very human in their response to each other, and neither looks like they are enjoying what they are about to do. Jack Ryan's killing of the boy is an extreme and needlessly excessive reaction to the threat to his own family. I tried to be careful in that sequence, with the attitudes of all the characters, so that the audience could hopefully see it from everyone's point of view.

Recalls Patrick Bergin, who played Kevin O'Donnell: 'And of course these characters do not consider themselves as terrorists. They have legitimate political agendas. My character was much more sophisticated in the book and by the nature of film-making the character gets pared down very often and becomes more the essence of a force rather than a well developed character. So there were certain aspects that attracted me and then maybe a little bit disappointed me, but I feel that I am a part of a trilogy of people really, like the brains, the brawn and the beauty, and I had the brains, not the beauty.'[21]

So for me the film tells the story of a conflict between two families, the Ryan family and the Miller family, and it's essentially about the primitive urges that are unleashed when a human animal's flesh and blood is endangered.

Harrison Ford: 'In the character of Jack Ryan I found the opportunity to express a character that was caught in a web of violence and yet resisted by virtue of his intellect and his disposition, resisted being part of that and was finally drawn into it inexorably.'[22]

But then, for Noyce, Patriot Games is not one movie: 'It's about four different movies rolled into one. It's an action–adventure story, it's a very emotional story, it's a political story and it deals with aspects of the C.I.A and their spying apparatus that interested me and it has certain comedic elements that I also thought would be fun to try.'[23]

As soon as Harrison signed on, a release date was set for the movie, which was 5 or 6 June 1992. So once we started shooting in late October, early November 1991, the only days we had off were Sundays, Christmas Day and New Year's Day until the film was finished. That was the beginning of three years of almost continuous production for me, going after Patriot Games to Sliver, then to Clear and Present Danger. As soon as I committed to each movie, I was locked into summer releases, which are the most coveted dates on the schedule because everyone's on holidays, so every day is like a weekend. Friday to Sunday are the predominant cinema-going days all over the world.

'We started our shoot in November as the deep cold of the English winter approached, which was actually quite appropriate for us, shooting all of the English sequences and also using some of the English countryside to double for Ireland.'[24]

But even aside from the weather, conditions in England weren't exactly as expected.

Producer Mace Neufeld: 'They don't roll out the red carpet for you the way they do in most states in the United States where they are anxious to have the kind of money film companies bring in to it, a city or a town, you know. We spend a lot of money when we come into a location, and so they roll out the carpet and they try to sell you on shooting in Des Moines or Vancouver or Seattle or Los Angeles or Texas. In England if you shoot there, they actually couldn't care less. I mean, they feel they've been around a long time [*laughs*].'[25]

The scenes set around Buckingham Palace, where the initial terrorist attack occurs, were in fact shot at the Royal Naval College at Greenwich. Mace Neufeld: 'We were shooting within a hundred feet of buildings that had 15th century windows in them, original windows. We had to be very, very careful with the amount of explosives and the amount of noise that we made. But it all eventually worked.'[26]

Then we moved to Annapolis, Maryland, where the US Naval Academy is situated and where the scene of the attempted assassination of Jack Ryan was shot – where the assailant is following him in the street as he comes out of the Naval Academy. Then we moved on to CIA headquarters in Langley, Virginia.

Noyce was allowed to shoot the exterior of the building and the lobby of the new CIA building, which was the first time this was allowed.

We then went back to Los Angeles. The desert scenes were shot about 100 miles from LA in the Brawley National Park. It's a huge expanse of sand, where lots of desert sequences are shot for movies, TV shows and commercials. Interior offices and high-tech CIA equipment were re-created on Stage 5 at Paramount Studios in Hollywood. The exterior of the Ryans' home, overlooking Chesapeake Bay in Maryland, was actually located on the rocky cliffs of Palos Verdes, California. And right here in LA in the same place where Cecil B. DeMille had parted the Red Sea, we shot the climactic speedboat chase at the end of the movie, in the parking lot of Paramount Pictures.

It was the most remarkable sequence from a logistics point of view. The parking lot is built so that one part of it has a dip, and with a fairly minimum amount of construction we were able to build up the walls and then turn the lot into a giant sea.

So Harrison Ford, who is supposedly out at sea, never moved anywhere. He was, in fact, stationary. There were rain machines, wind machines and wave-making machines and giant hoses pushing water past the characters to give the illusion of movement. It's an optical illusion, intercut with second unit shots with stuntmen out at sea and rear-screen projection in a studio. You get the impression that Harrison is travelling across the ocean, but in fact he never left the parking lot.

Harrison Ford has vivid recollections of the ordeal: 'The real rough stuff was done by the second unit, who spent 29 nights at sea to get the bones of the boat chase at the end of the film into which we could plug close-ups and tighter shots involving myself and Sean Bean and Patrick. But those were the guys who really worked hard . . . some of that was blue screen, rear projection, some of it was shot in a warehouse . . . against a black backdrop, some of it was shot on the back lot, so there were bits and pieces from all over.'[27]

What Ford doesn't relate here are the changes to the ending that took place. In Iliff and Stewart's screenplay, Miller and Ryan fight it out hand-to-hand in a lengthy underwater scene. '"The water was very cold, you can't heat that water, and it was dirty because you couldn't filter it either," said Bob Rehme who spent each night of the shoot working with Harrison. "He was in the water all the time and wore a wetsuit under his business suit to keep warm. We had been doing this for three nights and on the third night he said: 'Gee, I hope we get this done tonight.'"

'Rehme assumed his star was simply tired but as he unzipped his suit realized it was more serious. "He was beginning to get infected by the dirty water – he had broken out in a rash. I'm sure it was very painful and very uncomfortable, but he had silently carried on doing his scenes," said Rehme.

'Then Harrison, an experienced diver, hit his head while grappling underwater with Bean. The on-hand divers had to rush in to his aid as he struggled for air. The incident was serious enough to be picked up by the press days later. By then an accident which had left Harrison with a small cut to his forehead had become a near-death experience.

'The sequence's complex, *Man From Atlantis*-style ballets simply did not work. A month before the film was due to be released, he and Bean returned to the Paramount set and shot a more straightforward fist-fight on board an out-of-control speedboat.'[28]

'The [real problem with the ending], I felt, was that the moment where the two men make contact with each other has to be defined for the audience: they have to be able to feel and see it. And what we unfortunately had was this water, in the middle of the night, dark, and it was like sunglasses. You couldn't feel what Harrison was feeling because you couldn't see it. There was a film, an aqua filter [between the actors and the camera]. It took place about ten feet from where the [current ending] takes place, which is two feet above the water – originally it was eight feet underwater. If Criterion ever makes a laser version, I'll get them to [include the original]. It was similar even in its shots.'[29]

Bean recalled: 'We reshot the ending [of *Patriot Games*] three times, so I kept having to fly out again. The last time was just before we were about to start on *Lady Chatterley*. For continuity, they wanted me to have my hair cut again – a crew cut – which would have been a big problem for doing Mellors.

'But in the end it wasn't the hair that was a problem. I rang the *Lady Chatterley* production and said, "I got some good news and some bad news. I managed to keep my hair, but I've split my eye open." I had eight stitches where a boat hook hit me in the final fight scene.'[30]

It's been noted that 'If one watches the final scenes of *Patriot Games* closely . . . the two different haircuts can actually be seen. The boat hook mentioned was actually swung by Harrison Ford while filming these scenes and the scar remains one of Bean's defining facial features, just under his left eyebrow.'[31]

Noyce's relationship with the CIA was crucial, given the topic of the novel and the secrecy and red tape surrounding this still rather mysterious institution. A lot of research was essential.

Later, on *Clear and Present Danger*, given the content of the story, the CIA refused any assistance. But *Patriot Games* wasn't really critical of their activities so they allowed me to tour CIA facilities and to get a sense of the kind of people who work there and the interior architecture of the place.

On one of these visits I was accompanied by my daughter Lucia, and one of the women in the area where they analyse satellite photographs took a liking to Lucia and offered to mind her. In the car on the way back from the CIA that afternoon I said to Lucia, 'How was it? What happened?' She said, 'It was great. I went on this computer and we looked at images of Cuba and she showed me how to make the images bigger and even though it was night we could see people!' Because they could see the heat from the people. I said, 'Really?' She said, 'It was like playing a video game.'

So a few months later, before we started shooting, I was back there with Harrison Ford and it seemed as though now every door that had been partially closed before was open, taking us everywhere. I said, 'But you haven't taken us to the one place where you have that machine that can see infrared satellite images, and resolve and enlarge them.' And they said, 'We don't have such a place. What are you talking about?' Anyway, I put it in the film. And, of course, during the Desert Storm conflict, for the first time we saw those infrared images.

But extensive research was also done into the other end of the spectrum: the actors playing the Irish extremists were sent to a guerrilla training camp, where they were trained to assassinate, to kidnap and to do other things that terrorists get up to. Remembers Patrick Bergin: 'We had a number of people come who had expertise in all sorts of walks of life, intelligence, counter-intelligence . . . They taught us how to use weapons, and they taught us how to attack houses, how to roll around in the mud and all those sorts of things that people do in that sort of activity. We did a mock kidnapping, which was fascinating, we planned it and executed it, and of course everybody was volunteers . . . It was interesting to feel the way . . . people who are involved in this sort of activity must feel outside of the mainstream of life. It is a terrible sacrifice to have to live in that world.'[32] Noyce's reason for putting his actors through such an unusual ordeal is simple: 'They came back bruised and sorry, but wiser and I think more able to confidently portray their characters in the film.'[33]

Patriot Games was the first of two films in which Noyce used the talents and skills of Australian cinematographer Don McAlpine – the other being *Clear and Present Danger*.

I first met Don back in 1969 when I had a job as production assistant during my university holidays at Film Australia – or the Commonwealth Film Unit, as it was called then, the Australian Government's equivalent of the Canadian National Film Board. At the time Don McAlpine was the senior cameraman, who didn't seem to do much except assign the other photographers to various jobs. I remember him as a man who was extremely lively but who appeared just about ready to retire. But a couple of years later, Don was asked by Bruce Beresford to shoot *Barry McKenzie*, Beresford's first feature, and the success of that film led to a continuous association until Bruce went to the US to direct his first American film, *Tender Mercies*.

I particularly admired McAlpine's work on two Beresford movies, *Breaker Morant* and *The Getting of Wisdom*. *Morant* had a very robust period look to it, and *The Getting of Wisdom* a very romantic, lush period feel. Don's expertise as a cinematographer preceded him. But when I met him I was also impressed with his straightforwardness and lack of pretension, and obviously, speaking the same branch of English, we never had any trouble communicating. Compared to Hollywood cinematographers, he was also extremely fast.

Noyce soon became known for his ability to deal with actors on an artistic level. His demanding professional approach is combined with a compassionate understanding of the particular challenges a certain role imposes on an actor.

When I was working at Kennedy Miller, George Miller created a sort of collective of directors, assigned to his studio. One of them – George Ogilvie, who went on to co-direct *Mad Max Beyond Thunderdome* with George – had been an opera and stage director. And part of the process encouraged by George Miller involved various workshops conducted by Ogilvie – investigations into the process of directing and acting, for actors and directors. 'Hard back, soft front' was Ogilvie's summation of the characteristics that are necessary to succeed as a director. A hard back so that everyone knows that you will push through, you've got determination. But a soft front so that everyone knows that whenever they've got something to say, they can say it, and you are receptive enough to receive their thoughts, feelings and contributions.

Despite the fact that Noyce and Harrison Ford soon became friends, the relationship between the very professional Ford and his equally professional director was never completely free of friction – as would be the case again during the making of *Clear and Present Danger*.

One of the most interesting things was Harrison's crisis of confidence in me very early in the shoot. There are two sequences I particularly like in the film. One of them is when Jack Ryan watches images shot via infrared imaging from a satellite as an English SAS team are destroying an alleged terrorist camp somewhere in North Africa. And the scene in an Irish farmhouse when Patrick Bergin tricks his potential assassin. When Harrison first saw the rushes of the farmhouse he couldn't imagine how the scene was going to be put together and became agitated about my shooting style. So I just said to producer Mace Neufeld, 'Look, I'll cut the scene and Harrison can see it', which we did – and then he was fine. But I guess it was shot in a way he wasn't used to.

Garry Jenkins, Harrison Ford's biographer, elaborates on the first of these scenes. 'In Iliff's and Stewart's script, a room full of staff watched the operation via a powerful spy satellite. Harrison came up with the idea of conveying Ryan's unease at the ruthlessness of the operation by concentrating solely on his facial emotions. Noyce, Neufeld and Rehme had no arguments when they saw him run through what he had in mind. "It was originally a dialogue-heavy scene. Harrison suggested no dialogue except one line at the end of the scene implying 'a kill'. Everything else was played out on Harrison's face," said Neufeld.'[34]

Harrison is generally acknowledged as an excellent actor. But the actor who played Sally, Ryan's daughter, stood out as a genuine discovery:

Thora Birch is the child in the film, and she is now best known as the daughter of Kevin Spacey and Annette Bening's characters in *American Beauty*. She came in for a screen test and we cast her immediately. Once I realised how good she was, we would write extra things for her to do because she had a quality of spontaneity and naturalness; she doesn't seem like she's acting. But she *is* acting and she knows exactly what she's doing, even at that age of eight or so.

As with most of his American films to follow, Noyce was pressed into a rigid schedule because of the already fixed release date.

The major problem for me on the film was fatigue, given that we started to shoot later than we had hoped and were locked into an early June release date. We had to shoot six days a week for sixteen or eighteen weeks with only Sundays, Christmas Day and New Year's Day off. And once the shooting was complete, the film was in front of a test audience within ten days. So there was a rush to get the film edited as well. I employed two editors. Neil Travis had previously cut *Dances with Wolves,* for which he won the Academy Award, and Bill Hoy would later cut both *The Repair Shop* for TV (1998) and the next feature after that, *The Bone Collector* (1999).

Noyce could only cope with the magnitude of the task by working in the editing room during lunch breaks and after the end of shooting each night.

I had felt fatigue before on films in Australia, but nothing like this, and neither had I really ever experienced being part of the Hollywood machine. From the first day of principal photography the publicity people were starting to work on the trailer. The publicity machine seemed to be running just behind the actual production in terms of importance and focus. I realised then that the Hollywood system – based as it is on the employment of branch offices all over the world promoting and selling these movies – is totally dependent on a continual flow of product, and it's been set up to promote that product into the hearts and minds of people all over the world. Something it does with an incredible efficiency, perhaps unmatched by any other American export. In essence, movies represent marketing opportunities for Hollywood.

James Horner composed the music for *Patriot Games*, and later for *Clear and Present Danger*. The music critics were unfavourable towards the score,[35] and even Noyce wasn't totally satisfied.

This was the more successful collaboration of the two from my point of view, even though I hated the way James used Irish music in the score, so that whenever we saw an Irishman we heard an Irish pipe sound. I thought that was way too obvious. James, of course, later won the Academy Award for *Titanic*.

Despite working in Hollywood still being a new experience and the time constraints he was under, Noyce reached the production finish line just in time.

We made it in time. The screening for the critics – who had been brought from all over America – was held with sound separate from image. When the movie started we were still mixing the sound of the final reel, so the critics started watching a yet-to-be-completed movie.

The reaction varied; there were very good reviews and some not-so-good ones. It made something like US$80 million in the States and over US$90 million overseas.

The film, made with a budget of US$42 million, was placed in 2000 cinemas with a promotional campaign that cost an additional US$15 million. It earned US$18.5 million the first weekend, instantly placing it in the number 1 slot. In 1992, the film grossed a total of US$83 million in the US. It was one of that year's highest earners, yet it was about a third down on *The Hunt for Red October*.

When the film was released, a pattern that had started to take shape with the release of *Blind Fury* became established and has changed little since. It's not that the critics pan Noyce's films; rather, they often give his work the cold shoulder. He is criticised not so much for what his films are, but for what the critics feel they should have been. Audiences don't make such a distinction and simply enjoy the films for what they are, which creates a gap between the so-called serious film critics on one side and the ticket-paying audience on the other. This is especially evident when comparing reviews in the print media with those that appear online.

The first critical blow is often aimed at the political correctness of Noyce's subject matter.

The first review [of *Patriot Games*] to appear was from a reviewer in *Variety* called Joseph McBride, obviously an Irishman with sympathies for the Republican Movement. Mr McBride, I suspect, was sometimes talking about the novel on which the film was based, rather than the film itself. Later when I read various articles in the Irish Republican press, I realised that a lot of them were based not necessarily on watching the movie as much as on reading the novel. In fact, they had been preparing themselves for the movie. The novel had already been widely circulated and was a bestseller all over the world, but Joe McBride was extremely bitter in his condemnation of the film, feeling that it was an attack on the Republican Movement.

The potentially devastating benchmark review in *Variety* stated: 'Mindless, morally repugnant and ineptly directed to boot, *Patriot Games* is a shoddy follow-up to Par's 1990 hit *The Hunt For Red October*. Also based on a bestselling Tom Clancy novel about intrepid CIA analyst Jack Ryan, the ultra-violent, fascistic, blatantly anti-Irish film stars a dour Harrison Ford . . . The case is sentimentally loaded by painting the IRA faction as monsters who don't hesitate to attack Ford's wife (Anne Archer) and daughter (Thora Birch) as part of Bean's vendetta. Director Phillip Noyce is way out of his depth here, relying on tight close-ups that eliminate visual and social context and incoherently handling action sequences in the would-be spectacular climax.'[36]

More fair-minded serious critics, such as Hal Hinson in the *Washington Post*, readily acknowledge Noyce's ability 'to let us watch Ryan think . . . The main problem with *Patriot Games*, though, is that the inevitable confrontation between Ryan and Miller takes forever to materialize.'[37]

The general tenor of the reviews was that 'Harrison made a more plausible, wholesome hero than Baldwin's Jack Ryan, but for a thriller from the Clancy canon of high-technodrama it was a strangely cool and clinical film. "Even third-rate Hitchcock exposes the dramatic and psychological feebleness," wrote Philip French in the *Observer*; [who] thought Harrison was "dull" in the Ryan role. Harrison's headline-hogging salary was also fair game for many. *Time Out* thought the film was "so duff you wonder why they didn't ask Roger Moore to star."'[38]

Could the film be said, in the end, to be nothing but a simple revenge story conducted with lots of fancy CIA high-tech gadgetry? Probably not, but of course it all depends on one's expectations and preferences. Noyce's obsession with technology and surveillance – probably most characteristic of his Hollywood films – will be dealt with more extensively later. But it should be noted that here they play an important role for the first time in his career.

The way in which this film might vary from another action film and the way in which it varied from the book is, I think, illustrated by Jack Ryan's response to what he has seen on the satellite monitor. There is no sense of triumph in him. If anything, he has feelings of regret and loss and guilt. Hopefully the audience understands that he feels the enormity and moral complexity of what's been done. That there are obviously innocent people who will be killed in this process – there's been a judgment made here and now there's an execution, but it wasn't in a court of law and the military power that is on his side may be right – or it might not. It could even be the wrong camp. What he is seeing obviously involves danger to those executing the raid, but essentially he's watching a ruthlessly efficient duck shoot. And hopefully, Harrison Ford's character doesn't portray any exultation, no celebration.

The desert camp satellite shots create a haunting overall atmosphere – the feeling that 'Big Brother is watching you'.

Since the events of 9/11 things look different, but back then an evocation of a Ghaddafi/Libya connection may have been perceived as just another cliché. Didn't Chairman Mao, while still en vogue, advise prospective revolutionaries to swim like fish among the population? In plain English: to go to the cities and not the deserts and forests, where they would be more easily noticed?

We researched that aspect, in terms of whether any Irish Republican group had ever received sponsorship from any government in the Middle East, and confirmed that they had. At least, according to our sources.

There was one sentence that slipped through. I seem to recall that the suggestion is made in Ryan's dialogue that somehow the Shining Path group from Peru may also be receiving sponsorship. Later I took that out of the foreign dialogue version of the film because we hadn't confirmed that one point.

One country went so far as to ask Noyce to change the film:

The only request for censorship that I can recall was from Malaysia. They wanted to cut the images of terrorists training in an Arab country.

It is largely pointless to look for remnants of Noyce's experimental background in his feature films – Hollywood isn't like that. Still, the title sequences of his films usually stand out, if not for being experimental, at least for being state of the visual and/or graphic art. *Patriot Games* starts with extreme close-ups of the changing figures in an airport departure timetable followed by aerial shots of treetops whooshing by just underneath. (A near replica appeared nine years later in *Rabbit-Proof Fence*.) The impression is equally abstract in both cases, though the motive behind the first instance is technical, while in the second it is to evoke nature. The visual nature of this opening sequence even bears some resemblance to *The Bone Collector*,

Teaching Vietnamese extras how to handle their weapons for *The Quiet American*, Hanoi, April 2001.

The Quiet American. Seated: Michael Caine, Phillip Noyce. Standing: Sydney Pollack (executive producer), William Horberg (producer), Tran Anh Hoa (translator/adviser). Hanoi, April 2001.

The tenth anniversary celebration of the Russian release of *Dead Calm*, Moscow, 2000. From left to right: Sam Neill, Nikita Mikhalkov, Phillip Noyce and Billy Zane.

Phillip Noyce discusses the screenplay for *Dirt Music* with Tim Winton (author) and Justin Monjo (screenwriter), Sydney, June 2004.

in which the abstract night lights of New York City are contrasted with the book's old-fashioned wood prints.

Something else typical of Noyce's films is revealed when the treetop shot proves to be an aerial shot of the CIA headquarters: Noyce started the shot while the plane is climbing and not when it had reached a certain level, which is the usual practice.

Often a movie will use establishing shots just to tell the audience that you're in such and such a place – to change location, to set the scene. When these are aerials, we usually shoot from a helicopter. But I always try to get the pilot and the cameraman to put some slight forward movement into the shot. One of the most effective devices for inducing unease in an audience is the camera that moves forward almost imperceptively. Because the audience can feel unease but they don't know why. When you use point-of-view shots of, say, someone approaching someone – an intruder, someone spying on someone – it's usually done with a forward slow camera move. The audience knows from their understanding of film vocabulary that a slow move forward often means something nasty is just around the corner.

And in *Patriot Games* you also see what they used to call 'the Noyce Creep', a slow forward camera movement. In that film I used to do it with a dolly. But I realised that, particularly when you're shooting anamorphic wide screen, the focus is very critical. It's very hard for the focus puller to keep guessing when the camera keeps changing its distance from the subject. It's much easier to achieve the same result if you have the camera stationary. Using the auto-zoom, you can still achieve that unnerving forward movement. By *The Bone Collector* I was mainly utilising the auto-zoom.

There is a difference, however, in the psychology of each of the shots. I prefer to actually move the camera on tracks towards someone. It takes much longer and it's more prone to mistakes, but it's much more effective. Zooming in to a person isn't so much about unease, though if you find the right pace of focal move it can be unsettling. Instead, it's more about isolating a person: as you get a longer focal length, the background goes out of focus, so you're actually isolating the subject in the frame. Whereas if you keep the same focal length while getting closer, the background doesn't necessarily go out of focus – the audience moves physically closer to the subject.

More than in most of Noyce's films, *Patriot Games* contains a number of interesting transitions. One example is a threefold parallel montage used when the CNN news is on TV and, separately and on different continents, the CIA, the IRA and Jack Ryan are all watching it simultaneously.

The CNN era was quite young. Now, multiple points of view of one news item have become a cliché in contemporary thrillers, as a method of storytelling. But it was quite unusual at that time, because the idea of people watching the same news item in different parts of the world seemed improbable.

Other notable transitions are from Miller's face to Ryan's face, or from fires in the night to the porch of Jack's home.

It's part of the overall design of the film during your storyboarding and preparation. A lot of the time the transitions that you work out don't turn out to be the ones you use. Probably about two-thirds of the transitions you predict when you're shooting, and one-third are a result of something the editor does or that you discover while editing.

Looking back, what did the film mean to Noyce then, and what does it mean today?

I was most interested in it because of the spy technology. And the detective aspect of the film. A lot of the spy technology was still almost science fiction when the film came out. Particularly the use of infrared imagery that nobody knew about at that time. The wars in Afghanistan and Iraq showed this in action, but remember, it was more than ten years ago when we made that film. In many ways *Patriot Games* was the forerunner of what almost became a genre of movies dealing with the Big Brother aspects of government.

'It was the first of my big Hollywood films. I'd never attempted anything that large before. When you're dealing with so many elements – whether it's the pressure from a superstar, the pressure from a studio, the ability to maintain a coherent narrative even though you are constantly overwhelmed by the distractions of trying to direct traffic. I guess I proved I could exist within that conveyor-belt system. Success in that arena was the best and the worst thing that could happen, because even to this day that's mostly what Hollywood wants me to do. Killing and spying. I am a bit tired of that now.[39]

---

[1] Mace Neufeld interview.
[2] Mace Neufeld interview.
[3] Sam Neill interview.
[4] e!-feature, dated 6 August 1992.
[5] Mace Neufeld interview.
[6] e!-feature.
[7] Mace Neufeld interview.
[8] Garry Jenkins, *Harrison Ford – Imperfect Hero* (London: Simon & Schuster, 1997), pp. 291ff.
[9] Cited in ibid, p. 294.
[10] Cited in ibid, p. 296.
[11] Cited in ibid, p. 297.
[12] Cited in ibid.
[13] Cited in Karl Quinn and Raffaele Caputo, 'Patriotism and other games', *The Age*, 7 August 1992.
[14] e!-feature.
[15] Quinn and Caputo, 'Patriotism and other games'.
[16] Cited in ibid.
[17] e!-feature.
[18] Jenkins, *Harrison Ford – Imperfect Hero*, p. 300.
[19] Janet Maslin, '*Patriot Games*', *New York Times*, 5 June 1992.
[20] David Hay, 'Patriot missile takes on lethal weapon', *The Bulletin*, 23 June 1994, p. 98.
[21] e!-feature.
[22] e!-feature.
[23] e!-feature.
[24] e!-feature.
[25] e!-feature.
[26] e!-feature.
[27] e!-feature.

[28] Jenkins, *Harrison Ford – Imperfect Hero*, p. 298.

[29] e!-feature.

[30] Sean Bean, in *Lady Chatterley* DVD commentary.

[31] http://persweb.direct.ca/wkent/patriot.html.

[32] e!-feature.

[33] e!-feature.

[34] Jenkins, *Harrison Ford – Imperfect Hero*, pp. 296ff.

[35] As one editorial review noted: 'From the sound of the final product, it seems that either Horner was horribly restrained by the command of the film's director and/or budget, or he simply did not have the time or interest in producing a superior score for *Patriot Games*. What Horner did succeed at was effectively killing the superior musical example set forth by [*Red October* scorer Basil] Poledouris and established that the music of the series would take on a secondary role. With so much potential to continue a great franchise, I consider this to be one of Horner's greatest blunders.' (www.filmtracks.com/titles/patriot_games.html).

[36] Cited in *Variety* Internet archive. (It should be noted that *Variety*'s web archive no longer names Joseph McBride as the author of this piece, but only gives '*Variety* staff' as author.)

[37] *Washington Post*, 5 June 1992, cited at www.washingtonpost.com/wp-srv/style/longterm/movies/videos/patriotgamesrhinson_a0a782.htm.

[38] Jenkins, *Harrison Ford – Imperfect Hero*, p. 300.

[39] Email dated 20 February 2002.

Chapter 11
S L I V E R

This film was doomed from the beginning.

Book editor Carly Norris (Sharon Stone) has recently divorced and moves into one of Manhattan's so-called sliver buildings. She soon becomes romantically involved with Zeke Hawkins (William Baldwin), only to find herself tangled up in a psychosexual mystery that tests the fragile boundaries between reality and her deepest fantasies. A story about romance, murder and a fascination for voyeurism that can be addictive and dangerous.

Shortly after Memorial Day 1992, while working on *The Saint* in its very early stages, Noyce received a phone call from his lawyer, Sam Fischer, who told him he had a script he would like him to read. It was written by another one of his clients, Joe Eszterhas.

At the time Joe Eszterhas was notorious as the highest-paid scriptwriter in Hollywood. Together with his agent, Guy MacElwaine, Joe had engineered a series of sales for ever more dizzying numbers – two million, three million and so on – for spec scripts, stories that Joe made up and Guy would sell. One had been *Basic Instinct*, which was an enormous success for both director Paul Verhoeven and actress Sharon Stone. Anyway, Sam Fischer sent me the script, which I read, and my two daughters and wife also read it, all on the same day. An erotic thriller, freely adapted from the novel *Sliver* by Ira Levin, who had also written *Rosemary's Baby*. And I liked the script a lot. Or at least I liked the idea of jumping on the Eszterhas bandwagon.

As it turned out, the producer was Robert Evans, who had recently returned to Paramount after a number of years out in the cold in Hollywood. He'd gone through various personal difficulties, including a bust for cocaine possession, financial upheaval and association with a notorious murder case – the Cotton Club Murders. But now he had a rich deal and a suite of offices back on the grand old Paramount lot on Melrose Avenue. *The Saint* and *Sliver* were both Robert Evans projects. But for different reasons, Evans wasn't the day-to-day producer on either film. More about that later.

Though on very good terms with Noyce, 'a big fan of his talent',[1] and actually already working with him on *The Saint*, Evans had other thoughts initially. Like Ira Levin, he was convinced that only Roman Polanski, who was living in Europe, having fled the country after he was found to have had sex with an underage model in 1977, could tackle the topic successfully. (In Hollywood lingo this boils down to 'bringing most change into Paramount's coffers'.[2]) This was not only because of Polanski's infamous reputation, but also because of his extraordinary achievements in adapting *Rosemary's Baby* for the screen. Still, there seemed no way to get Polanski back to the United States – unless he wanted to end up behind bars instead of behind the camera. Evans wasn't prepared to give in easily. Similarly to *Rosemary's Baby*, most of the action in *Sliver* took place indoors. Therefore, 'Why not have a top second unit director shoot exteriors, entrances, and exits in New York and re-create the interiors in Paris?' where Polanski lived.[3] But nothing came of this plan.

Even though *Patriot Games* had not yet been released (although it was completed), Paramount was extremely supportive of Noyce's desire to direct the film, and they wanted to start work on it immediately. Evans recalls: 'I'd never been given – or gotten – a quicker or more enthusiastic thumbs-up.'[4] But it seems the enthusiasm was less for the script itself than for the prospect of a promising 1993 Memorial Day release.

Noyce agreed to make the film. Immediately the race was on to find the female lead. Notwithstanding whatever else was said in public, for Evans there was only one logical choice: 'Sharon Stone was one, two, and three on my dance card.'[5]

Sharon Stone was the hottest mature female actress in the world at the time, having risen from years of relative obscurity in B movies, to become a major box-office star with *Basic Instinct*. So she was the first person we approached. As it happened, her agent was Guy MacElwaine, who was also Joe's agent, but initially Sharon was reluctant, explaining that she had worked hard to be taken seriously and was afraid that with two erotic thrillers in a row, she would be tagged as a box-office draw only in sexually themed movies.

Negotiations with her dragged on with no result. Repeated threats by Robert Evans to cast Demi Moore, Michelle Pfeiffer or Julia Roberts instead didn't bother her. Finally, the studio gave her a deadline: no commitment by Friday, no role for her; another actress would be chosen.

At this point a meeting took place at the Four Seasons Hotel in Los Angeles, of which all the major players in the ongoing drama that surrounded the making of the film have very different recollections. The only undoubted fact seems to be the presence in the same room of Sharon Stone, Joe Eszterhas and Phillip Noyce.

We hired the hotel room so that we could all sit and talk about this script. I don't know why we did it there, maybe Joe was staying there.

In his memoirs, Evans hints at a possible reason for the choice of the hotel room. It seems Sharon Stone had accused him of a strange, undisclosed sexual incident involving one of her friends and had resolved never to enter Evans's home or office.[6]

As the man who, in a sense, created her superstardom status, Sharon had good reason to be respectful of Joe and, according to Eszterhas (in his 2004 memoir *Hollywood Animal*), they had previously enjoyed a drunken, drugged night of sexual games together. Sharon walked out of that room having agreed to appear in *Sliver*, which was remarkable, given that she entered telling us there was no way she would do the film, stating that she had come to apologise. But I don't think that from that day on Sharon was very comfortable playing that particular character in that particular story, at that time in her career.

In his autobiography, *American Rhapsody*, Joe Eszterhas focuses on the sexual aspects of life in Hollywood – for example, Stone is quoted as saying of Noyce: 'He's a big goon. He doesn't know anything about sex.'[7] He recalls that in his original screenplay Carly was supposed to look at a Calvin Klein advertisement featuring a scantily clad male and to use this as a stimulus for the scene in which she masturbates in her bathtub. Sharon Stone took exception to the idea that a woman would look at a photograph of a man to stimulate herself. Eszterhas claims that he, Noyce and Stone discussed the proposed scene at the Four Seasons Hotel. While he professes not to care all that much either way about the scene, for Noyce it was a big issue, he says. He goes on to claim that during the meeting Stone offered to give him, Eszterhas, a massage. 'Sharon was straddling my back with her legs, moving up and down. I noticed she wasn't wearing any underwear.'[8] He further infers that Noyce was so moved sexually by watching Stone massaging him that he stopped talking and broke out in a sweat. And then at the end of her massaging him, Noyce 'said to Sharon in a flat, dull tone "do the scene how you want" . . . She did it as she wanted through the entire shoot – not just that scene but every other one, too. She was the director of the movie.'[9]

Joe has mixed up a number of different meetings and a number of different issues. In fact, the three of us met only once at the Four Seasons Hotel. And that was to convince Sharon – despite her well-grounded misgivings – that she should take the part. On that occasion, which was quite tense going in, Sharon asked Joe if he'd like a massage. And then the scene proceeded as Joe has described it. It's true that I stopped talking. But not because I was sexually moved by the sight of a 50-year-old man lying on the floor moaning as Sharon Stone was massaging him while sitting astride him. I stopped talking simply because he was so grotesque in the sounds he was making that it seemed ridiculous to continue trying to convince Sharon to do the part. And so I stopped talking and let the two of them play with each other on the floor. After massaging Joe, Sharon agreed to take the part of Carly.

Evans, on the other hand, claims that Stone only accepted the role of Carly after Geena Davis appeared that week on the cover of *Vanity Fair*, heralded as 'Hollywood's new femme fatale'. He lied to Stone's manager that Davis would start shooting the film on Monday. According to Evans, 'Sharon didn't want the part, but she sure in hell didn't want Geena [who, he'd heard, was first choice for *Basic Instinct*] to have it.'[10] So she finally agreed to take the lead role.

Only six weeks remained before shooting was scheduled to start on the US$30 million project . . .

Having cast Carly, I then had to find Zeke – her lover, who has secretly placed cameras in every room of the apartments in the building he owns.

I had admired Billy Baldwin's work in Mike Figgis's police thriller *Internal Affairs*, where he played a young cop, and also in Ron Howard's *Backdraft*, and I thought he had a very sneaky sexuality.

At the time, a young man named Brad Pitt was on everyone's minds. He had appeared in a sensational love scene with Geena Davis in Ridley Scott's *Thelma & Louise*, but talking to him he just didn't seem to project the qualities I had in mind for Zeke. Possibly he was just overwhelmed himself, as everybody was telling him he was the next big thing. I couldn't see it.

Paramount and Sharon Stone weren't convinced about Billy Baldwin. Sharon wanted Brad, whom she had worked with in acting classes. I decided to test Billy with Sharon and we shot a number of scenes of the two of them together, and that seemed to convince everyone. However, Billy knew that Sharon hadn't wanted him and their relationship was always tense. I ended up having to shoot many of their close-ups with only one of them in the room at a time, because they didn't want to look at each other. I suspect this film was in some ways doomed from the beginning by the star's deep-down feeling that she was in the wrong movie, as well as her deep-down feeling that she was playing opposite the wrong actor.

To judge from Eszterhas's memoirs, Stone didn't keep her feelings to herself. 'When we were casting *Sliver* and the studio wanted Billy Baldwin, she said "He's a boy. Give me a man. Give me Alec. I'd let Alec throw me over the table anytime".'[11] And Bob Evans recalls: 'Miss Stone was underwhelmed by our choice' of the male lead.[12]

During pre-production I travelled to New York City with Sharon to introduce her to various publishing editors and executives, so she could research her role as a literary editor. On the MGM Grand Jet, which was the nearest thing a fare-paying passenger could come to a private plane, she remarked that she had read the book by Ira Levin and much preferred Ira's story over Joe's. Robert Evans had bought the manuscript of the book before it was published, and when *Basic Instinct* became such a box-office hit, he hired the red-hot Eszterhas to adapt Levin's book. Joe had never written an adaptation before and found it very difficult. Having read the book, he put it aside and started from scratch, refashioning his own story using elements from the original that he remembered, but not actually cross-referencing back to the novel as he was writing. The book ended quite differently, from memory, more like the film does now, except, as I remember, she kills Zeke. In Eszterhas's original script, of course, Sharon's character ends up with Zeke, who has been revealed as the murderer. That story is essentially the story of her coming to terms with her own dark side. Her original attraction to Zeke is revealed to have been a natural selection, because she's the perfect mate for him; it's just that she's been denying her real instincts, the same as Michael Douglas's character in *Basic Instinct*.

So we visited various publishing houses, met numerous role models and investigated the character. Sharon and I went to dinner the next night and I rather forcefully answered her objections to the screenplay: 'Well, we're not doing the novel; we're doing the script. That's what we've signed on to do and I don't want to talk about it.' So she resigned, saying the director is unreasonable and not sympathetic to her point of view.

The most powerful and respected agent in New York at the time was Sam Cohn, the senior agent at International Creative Management, the agency that represented Joe Eszterhas, Sharon and myself. So Sam arranged a detente meeting in his office where he acted as the counsellor and she was able to give vent to her complaints. And I was sufficiently contrite. She agreed to go on.

It was this far more important issue in terms of his own authority as the storyteller that Joe has confused with the meeting at the Four Seasons Hotel. We were only a few weeks from shooting and basically Sharon was saying she wanted to start back at square one. My own loyalty to Joe, as well as the practicality of the situation, meant that I had to say, 'No, we're not gonna do that.' That was the issue – whether we were going to rewrite the script from the first page, and that was the issue on which I took a stand. I gave her the appearance of submitting, whereas in fact we did shoot Joe's script. But I allowed Sharon to feel she had won – that she was the most powerful person in the relationship.

Joe has failed to understand that you can often achieve exactly what you want by appearing to let the other person win. My own directorial style can be described as 'nudging' – nudging people. I don't believe much is achieved by confrontation, except resentment. I mostly get exactly what I want. But the secret of doing that in movies is to allow the other person to think that what *you* want is what *they* really want.

At various stages, nevertheless, changes were made to the script. Evans mentions a complete rewrite by Joe Eszterhas that

Stone disliked even more than the original.[13] Undated notes in Noyce's archive register Noyce's concern about story development and are addressed 'dear Joe, written in extreme haste', complaining that 'Each draft has become a little more talky', wondering if 'Jack can be just a little bit more charming?' and reasoning: 'We've added the idea that Jack is impotent, but are all impotent men murderers? . . . We need something more and maybe it's as simple as defining the photos of Naomi and Carly found by cops in Jack's bedroom, e.g., porn, bondage . . . or whatever.' Noyce's style of working can clearly be observed in these notes: between typing them out and sending them off he has altered and added in handwriting nearly one-quarter of the text.

Stone's final agreement to continue was far from the last of the most immediate problems.

There were other things that for me made this movie-making experience less than enjoyable.

When looking for the right cinematographer, I was most impressed by Vilmos Zsigmond, who had shot, among other films, *McCabe and Mrs. Miller* for Robert Altman and also George Miller's film with Jack Nicholson, *The Witches of Eastwick*. I thought Vilmos had a very lush, romantic style. Anyway, I phoned George Miller and his advice was *not* to work with Vilmos because he felt that our personalities wouldn't mesh. Since working with George, Vilmos had unsuccessfully tried his hand at directing and I should have perhaps taken that as a warning sign. For we never achieved a truly harmonious working relationship.

In Australia, I had previously worked with cinematographers who tailored the lighting needs to the time available. Without studios to pay for budget overruns we Aussies were all aware of the privilege of being able to spend someone else's money making cinema. But Vilmos would get the set ready, when he was ready. So we were moving at a laborious pace. When that happens, the director has to change the shooting style with less takes, less shots and less complicated shots.

Sharon was very happy because Vilmos excelled at making

women look good, and perhaps he felt that unless she looked her best the film would fail. So he may have been very right to take his time. He was like the old cinematographers from the forties, using mainly the direct lighting method to transform his star into a screen goddess. The modern style of indirect lighting is based on the idea that instead of shining the light directly on the actor, you bounce the light off a reflector. The old style was that you had a fill light which illuminated the subject and the whole room, a key light which essentially put light in their eyes, and a backlight which gave shape to the body and face. Indirect lighting allows the actor much more freedom with hitting predetermined marks, which are placed on the floor by a camera assistant. For direct light the marks become really crucial, and if the actors don't land on them it can all look completely different.

So this film started to become about hitting marks.

There was a third factor that turned the studio shooting into a pressure-cooker situation.

There are two famous brothers – production designers – who work in the American film industry, called the Sylbert brothers, identical twins. Richard was the production designer on such films as *Chinatown* and has been the more successful of the two. His brother, Paul, started with Hitchcock on *The Wrong Man*, as art director. I hired Paul because of his deep appreciation of the story's themes and his previous design of New York interiors, most recently for Barbra Streisand in *The Prince of Tides*.

We started in October 1992 in New York City with the exteriors and some shots in the real apartment building. 'Sliver' is the name given to the thin apartment building style which grew up in New York City in the sixties and seventies to take advantage of the small blocks that were available, given that the only way to increase square footage was to go up.

The principal location was the Morgan Court building, located on Madison Avenue in the Murray Hill area of Manhattan. This 32-floor edifice was completed in 1985 and is situated on a 33-by-100-foot plot of land. One of the last sliver projects constructed in Manhattan, it was chosen by Sylbert 'to take contemporary architecture and give it a gothic turn'[14]. The structure was modified for the film, with the addition of an entrance from 36th Street, a glass arcade and redesigned garden. Then the crew and cast returned to Paramount Studios in Hollywood, where Sylbert had designed the courtyard, lobby and interior apartments of the sliver on four separate sound-stages. The interiors were defined by strong columns, circles and curved walls throughout the edifice. Sylbert explains: 'I wanted to give the sense of looking through a lens at all times – a legitimate way architecturally to lend unease.'[15] Noyce, however, soon encountered another kind of unease.

In Australia I'd never spent a lot of time talking to the designer about which walls of a set would 'fly'. In my experience, usually when you construct a set, the production designer tries to make everything movable – you can remove any wall you need to for ease of shooting. I had assumed that Paul would do the same thing. But when we got back to stage 15 [at Paramount] I discovered that sometimes none, and usually only one, of the walls in any one room of the set were movable. Paul explained that he thought the film should have a reality about it and in a real apartment you couldn't move the walls. Which was fine as a theory, but it didn't take into account how we were going to shoot the film, and really slowed things down because Vilmos couldn't get his elaborate lighting easily into the room's scheme. Instead of taking the roof off, he had to erect poles inside the set, just like in a real location. Normally the advantage of being on a stage is you can quickly remove the roof and then light from above.

The need to employ a certain lighting style and restrictions due to the apartment design were only the beginning. The set had been built right above a huge water tank, left over from Esther Williams's days, and when the actors or camera moved in dialogue sequences the floor would creak, and we were in danger of having to re-record all the dialogue in post-production. The carpenters would work on the problem all night but it seemed that nothing could be done. At the end of the first week back in Los Angeles we were almost a week behind schedule.

Eventually the animosity between Sharon Stone and Billy Baldwin turned into outright hostility. By the last month of the shoot they wouldn't talk to each other except to say their lines, and often one or the other would ask me if they could act close-ups to a stand-in – someone reading the lines – because each were so perturbed by the other.

Joe Eszterhas recalls that Sharon Stone 'did the same eviscerating trip on [Billy Baldwin]. She'd wipe her mouth after kissing him or rinse it with mouthwash. She bit his tongue during a kiss; he sounded cotton-mouthed the next day.'[16] Baldwin countered in an unrestrained interview by calling her 'a paean to lipstick lesbianism'.[17]

In the original ending, Zeke Hawkins and Carly Norris celebrate their honeymoon by flying a helicopter across the molten lava lakes of an active volcano in Hawaii, then plunging into the volcano towards the fiery centre, before disappearing.

To cut costs, Vilmos Zsigmond proposed the old technique of rear projection for the volcano flying scenes, where you actually project the image that's behind the actor onto a screen. So when you photograph the scene you can see what's behind them at the same time, and you photograph the actors in the foreground, and the plate (the background scene) behind. It has the advantage of immediacy but the disadvantage that once you've shot it you're locked into what you've got.

Nowadays we would either shoot those plates in the same manner or animate the volcano in a computer, and the actual shooting of the scene would be done against a blue screen with the background matted in behind the actors during post-production. Using computers now, we can change the background, the colour or the density and have relative control over every individual picture element.

So I went to Hawaii and hired a helicopter pilot, who took me down into the cone of the Kilauea volcano. I took a lot of photographs and knew what I wanted the second unit to bring back on film. In fact, it wasn't even a job for a second unit director. I sent my assistant and associate producer on the film, Laura Viederman, over with Michael Benson, who'd shot so well for me on the second unit of *Patriot Games*, and with Craig Hoskins, the helicopter pilot, who had done a lot of work on *Patriot Games*. I knew I had a good team there.

It was just halfway through the shoot, just after the New Year, Saturday afternoon. I was editing and I called the production office in Hilo, on the main island of Hawaii. I was giving them instructions, and they were in contact by radio with 'the bird'. And I can still remember the voice of the production assistant as she said, 'Just a minute.' I said, 'What's wrong?' 'Just a moment,' she said again. Then she came back after a long absence and said, 'The bird's down. We've lost the bird.'

The 'bird' she was referring to was the helicopter, and 'down' was inside the active Kilauea volcano. Coming over the cone the helicopter had somehow lost power. Because Craig Hoskins (who went on to shoot with me on *Clear and Present Danger*) was so experienced a pilot, he was able to auto-rotate, using what rotation he had left to make a controlled landing. Without this ability you just crash. He landed inside the volcano, but over to one side. What could have happened without control is that they could have ended up in the molten lava. But as it crashed, the blades hit the wall and sheered the helicopter in half, just behind the compartment. At the time there were a lot of clouds around, and together with the sulphur and the fumes that were coming out of the volcano, the clouds closed over soon after they crashed. They couldn't see out at the time, so of course no one could see in there either. The production office at this point didn't know where they even were. They knew they were in that vicinity, that's all.

At this point Michael Benson and Chris Duddy, the cameraman and assistant, decided to try to walk out and climb up the edge of the volcano. They started out before the clouds closed over and while they had good visibility. They were only about 15 feet apart from each other, but suddenly the fumes closed in and they couldn't see past their arms; they couldn't see each other anymore. The pilot had decided to try to stay and get the radio going, and he managed to talk to a helicopter that was flying over on a sightseeing tour. The clouds parted, and that helicopter came down and landed and picked up Craig Hoskins. Then the clouds came back again and the pilot couldn't see how to get out, and of course you need sight to navigate up when you're so close to the edge of the rock. But then he decided to go up blind – and got out. This happened about an hour after the crash.

For Michael and Chris, a nightmare ordeal began. They were trapped and blind inside the cone.

The next morning a massive search operation was launched. But nobody could get in there and nobody could see the wreck. I mean, you can't just move blindly around a volcano, because you don't know when you are going to put your foot on a 1000-degree updraft of gas! It would kill you instantly, burn through you like a laser. Craig climbed up the outside of the volcano and put some red markings there, near the point where he thought he had crashed. At the end of the second night, Chris shouted out to Mike, 'I can't stay here another night, I'm going to try to climb up. If I die, I die.' He climbed up in the dusk. A park ranger who was trying to come over from the other side found him, so he survived.

Mike Benson was stranded alone in the cone that night. Next morning the Navy came in with a helicopter equipped with sonar, so it could fly blind, as well as a team with special heat-resistant suits. They tried to fly into the volcano but it was surrounded with clouds, sulphur and fumes. They couldn't see anything and they even reported that it was too hot to fly. A notorious daredevil on the island of Maui heard about the whole event and, although he crashed his car on the way to the airport, he flew his helicopter over. When the civil defence director who was in charge of the rescue operation heard that this guy had come, he just refused to let him have anything to do with the rescue, so notorious was his reputation. He ordered no further rescue flight attempts, otherwise not only one man but another helicopter and crew might be lost. But my assistant, Laura, distracted the guy so that the pilot could take off, carrying underneath him a basket at the end of a rope. Using the red flags that had been left by the pilot, he dragged the rope where he thought Michael might be.

At one point, Michael actually got himself into the basket, but the helicopter took off before he could gain his grip. The pilot had to fly right up in the air before he knew whether he had anything. He had nothing, except this feeling that something or someone had been there, that he felt a slightly different strain, so he returned for another attempt. At the beginning of the third night Michael was pulled out. We had already adjusted to the idea that maybe he was dead. The irony, of course, is that the footage was never used in the film.

Michael had survived without food or water. Ironically, he was saved from freezing in the mid-winter cold by the volcanic heat. He was very lucky that he somehow found a pocket of air. He had lung problems for a while afterwards, but he was back shooting within a couple of months, and went on to shoot second unit on *Clear and Present Danger*, *The Saint* and *The Bone Collector*. During the second night, Michael swears that he was visited by Madame Pele, the goddess of the Kilauea volcano, who only agreed to spare him after Michael pleaded for his life. Michael's descriptions of the goddess exactly dovetail with ancient Hawaiian folklore, but Michael says he had never previously heard of Madame Pele.

However potentially tragic these events undoubtedly were, the film's main battlefield was still located below the Hollywood Hills. What began as a mutual dislike between star and producer had now accelerated. As Evans recalls, she had let Noyce know that Evans' presence on the set made her uncomfortable: 'Not wanting to cramp Miss Stone's style, each day I'd pay a momentary visit to the set and, like a plague, quickly disappear.'[18] 'I would rather clean toilet bowls than make another film with her,' he said on a different occasion.[19] Yet, still more was to come.

I knew that for years Evans had turned his Beverly Hills mansion into a mecca for small-town beauty queens seeking to rub shoulders with the powerful men of Hollywood. I remember trying to have a script meeting at Bob's place one morning while he was wandering around the room shuffling Polaroid photos of naked women, shot – from the shoulders down – the previous evening. Evans was infamous for the wooden chest in his foyer filled with thousands of Polaroids like that. After he was warned off by Sharon, in order for Bob to check progress on the set I had a video feed installed from stage 15 through to his nearby office. Like the character of Zeke, Evans was able to 'watch' everything that Carly was doing in her apartment.

Towards the end of production we celebrated someone's birthday at a place called Dominic's, an old diner on Beverly Boulevard. I'm not sure whether it was Sharon's birthday or one of the producer's, Bill MacDonald. At the time Sharon was going out with the son of Jon Peters: Chris Peters. Jon Peters was the hairdresser to Barbra Streisand and had became her lover and then her producing partner, and later a studio executive. That night Sharon spent most of her evening talking quietly with Bill MacDonald, who had been married for just six months. Joe Eszterhas was there too. As soon as we finished the shoot, Sharon told me she had fallen in love with Bill. Soon afterwards Eszterhas eloped with Bill's wife, Naomi, and it was reported in the press that he claimed to have set up Sharon with Bill in order to steal Bill's wife. Obviously *Sliver* was a rocky, emotional ride in front of and behind the camera.

But for Noyce it was a rocky physical ride as well:

A movie wears you out physically and, as a result, mentally as well. And in the end you're clinging to your ideas and just trying to get through. On *Sliver* I just became so tired I couldn't get off the floor. I had to have doctors constantly injecting me with vitamins.

I was trying to give up smoking at the time and I don't think I was all that stable myself, as I had been inhaling up to six packs a day previously. If you look at any of the television documentary footage of *Patriot Games* it's very hard to find anything without me smoking in it. I was terribly addicted and had decided to give up before *Sliver*. This probably wasn't a good idea for my equilibrium, but nevertheless I stayed a non-smoker until the beginning of *The Saint*. But every day of pressure on the *Sliver* set caused bad nicotine-induced panic attacks, so the chaos of the whole thing was not something I could blame on others. The film had become a Hollywood nightmare – with a producer who, from the beginning, had dreamt of his movie being directed by someone else, a writer who had abandoned a bestselling novel to pen his own version of the story, an actress who I couldn't communicate with and who loathed her co-star and producer, and a cinematographer who was creating beautiful images at a snail's pace, on a set that made more noise than the actors when they spoke their lines.

At night I dreamt of turning up to a schoolboy rugby match and then running onto the field only to discover I'd left my football boots at home. I'd wake with a deep sense of dread. Facing another day at the factory that filmmaking had become.

When we finally finished after about three months, I think we were at least ten days behind overall, and that meant a lot of money. Once you get behind, you're always cutting corners. As the story progressed – and this is truer in the original version – Sharon's character became more and more distracted from reality, more and more drugged by the experience and less in contact with the real world. I think, by a certain process that often happens to actors, Sharon was becoming like that off screen as well. It was very difficult to communicate with her. She would take hours to come out of the trailer. I think it was part of her process to be so vulnerable, as the character was, and to be distracted and ethereal. Sometimes you find that the actor isn't able to switch off. Although we finished the shoot as friends, she became very upset when the film didn't preview better. She blamed me for that. And I accept the blame.

Yet she said Noyce was 'mind-bogglingly supportive, and provided a space where I could try stuff, let this kind of honest female behaviour be filmed'.[20]

Five months of research, planning and design went into the construction of the secret monitor room. The preparation of the voyeuristic footage that would be used on the 50 monitors in the hidden room took several weeks. At first, over a period of six weeks, a separate film unit shot 250,000 feet of film and video to expose the life of the building's tenants. Bill Hoy, who had worked on *Patriot Games*, was assigned the task of editing this mass of footage into 540 individual videotapes representing a realistic progression of events for the inhabitants of the sliver. 'Phillip wanted to show a combination of spontaneous activities from the mundane to the shocking – activities that dare the voyeur and the audience into watching,' says Hoy.[21] The voyeuristic footage went through six steps of preparation by the time it was ready to be projected in the monitor room. Supervised by Richard Baskin, a twenty-member video and sound crew orchestrated a symphony of visuals and sound for three weeks of filming in the monitor room. While it's pretty unobtrusive, the first-ever appearance of Noyce in one of his films is among the many short flicks.

Although you can't see it in the shot that I chose to keep in the movie, there is other footage from that same day showing me naked in a bathtub. I was trying to encourage Sharon Stone and Billy Baldwin to be a little less protective of their own nakedness. We were yet to shoot the lovemaking scenes, so I thought, 'If I'm going to ask them to take their clothes off, I should set an example.' In the scene, I'm looking in a mirror cleaning my teeth, and the camera, of course, is behind the mirror. That scene was directed by Sharon Stone. I said, 'Look, I'm going to be in one of these surveillance camera scenes and I want you to direct me taking a bath.' So I'm in this bathtub and, unexpectedly, a beautiful young woman comes into the bathroom, takes off her clothes and hops into the bath with me. I tried to just look straight ahead and keep acting. Then I hear Sharon's voice through a loudspeaker saying, 'It's your wife. You're glad to see her.' I was horrified because I'm thinking, 'I'm not an actor, I'm a director and there is a naked woman here and I'm meant to be acting with her like she's my wife. I'm having a bath with her and I'm glad to see her, but I can't be too glad or I might get into real trouble.' That's why you only see the shot of me in the mirror; it just wasn't a very good idea for the director to be naked with an actress.

(As will be seen in later chapters, Noyce makes a cameo appearance in two more of his American films – his own little Hitchcock syndrome.)

I started editing *Sliver* with Richard Francis-Bruce, who had cut *Dead Calm*. He was one of the editors on *Road Warrior*, and has also edited *Seven* and *The Shawshank Redemption* among numerous other Hollywood films (including *The Witches of Eastwick* for George Miller). As soon as I had a cut of the film I sent it to Joe Eszterhas. And he loved it.

Then we did the first screening for a recruited audience on the lot at Paramount, as was customary for a Paramount film. The guys from a company called National Research Group, run by Joseph Farrell, would go out to malls and cinemas and recruit an audience for these previews. In Los Angeles people are pretty used to being invited. It's a way of getting the lowdown on films many, many months before their release, and, in a town devoted to the entertainment industry, it's also become a way for the ordinary man and woman to have their say. They can become not just a film critic but a film executive. The tick of their pen, the cross of their pencil, can decide, as has been the case since the early thirties, the fate of the movie that they're judging. The preview audience's power has been further increased since the late 1990s by advance reviews appearing on Internet sites such as Ain't it Cool.

The research companies have developed strategies for accessing responses, but basically it goes like this: viewers are asked to rate the film as excellent, very good, good, fair or poor. The top two boxes, excellent and very good, are the two that people are interested in, nothing else. Unless a film scores over 70 per cent in those top boxes the studio will be really worried, and it's liable to affect not only how much they meddle with the cutting of the film from that point on, but also how much they're willing to spend on promotion. If you're over 75 you're pretty clear and they let you finish the film on your own. Under 50, you're in deep shit.

We scored, I think, 48.

Now, of course, the system isn't infallible and is no prediction of box-office success; it only tells us how a film played to that audience on that night. An example is, as producer Jeremy Thomas told me many years later, *The Last Emperor*, which won nine Academy Awards, didn't even score 50. Interestingly, *Clear and Present Danger* and *The Bone Collector* scored about equal to *Blind Fury*. Now, *Blind Fury* is an enjoyable film at a particular time of the week, to a particular kind of audience, but you could never claim it was of the same quality as *Danger*. We went through a lot of tension over *Dead Calm* because it was scoring in the 60s and low 70s, so Warners were very anxious about that film. But you couldn't say that it was of inferior quality to the higher-scoring *Blind Fury*. With these anonymous research sheets you must keep in mind as well that the audience don't censor themselves; often they say things simply because they're given a forum in which to vent.

Anyway, the first screening scored very low. The studio – Sherry Lansing was now head of Paramount – was nevertheless very supportive. They said, 'Well, we'll get it up there. Don't worry.' They had recently gone through a similar experience with *Indecent Proposal*, directed by Adrian Lynne, which had also started off with very low test scores, but then with cutting and restructuring they got the score up, and the film became a box-office hit. The score isn't an indication of how many people want to see the film, only a measure of their pleasure. A film could score 98 but take no money, because no one actually wanted to leave their house to see it.

The studio was helpful at first, and we would recut and recut and screen, and recut and recut, but it didn't seem to make any difference. Then Joe Eszterhas came and looked at the film with an audience. We thought perhaps the problem was that people found it difficult to sympathise with Sharon Stone's character. She is a relatively innocent person, whose dark side is unlocked by her relationship with the Billy Baldwin character – a man who shows her that she has a very strong repressed sexuality and a repressed perversity as well as, ultimately, an amoral nature. The audience found that all difficult to accept. None of this would have been a problem if the film had been made for a lower budget. Because then you can be more unconventional with the material.

So, I was discussing with Joe what we could do to try and help the audience to become involved in the Carly character's transition, in a way which didn't change what happened to her, but allowed them to stay with her and be sympathetic. One of the things that worried Joe was that it appeared the audience spotted from the beginning that Billy Baldwin was really the killer and not Tom Berenger, and that Berenger was just a red herring.

One day Sherry Lansing, Joe and myself were talking in Sherry's office and Joe said, 'Wouldn't it be a good idea if we made Berenger the killer?' I guess I was so frustrated at the time that I thought, 'Maybe this *is* a good idea.' I felt that I had failed, too, because the audience were guessing that Billy Baldwin's character was the killer. Of course, I thought right back to originally casting him, and thought to myself, 'Well, of course it's a game of poker that you play with the audience, but maybe Brad Pitt would have been better because he's more angelic, whereas dark-haired, devilish Billy Baldwin perhaps appears guilty from the beginning.'

So Joe began drafting some new scenes and, just a few weeks before the film was due to open, we scheduled to reshoot. As Joe rightly points out in *Hollywood Animal*, Sharon's last line of the new ending, 'Get a life', was invented by the actress herself. What Joe doesn't mention is that, having suggested the new ending, he became embroiled in the break-up of his marriage, and fled to Hawaii before finishing all the new scenes necessary for the new version. We were left having to practically improvise the final scene. Joe also lays the blame for the changed ending on the Paramount Studios chairman, Stanley Jaffe, claiming Stanley forced us to change the film. I wish it was so easy to deny responsibility for something Joe and I conspired on. True, Jaffe pressured us to revise the film's morality, but Joe was the person who thought up how to achieve that. And I was the one yelling 'Action' and 'Cut'.

At that point we were also fighting another battle, for I had sent the first cut to the censors of the Motion Picture Association of America and they had indicated that it was not going to get an R certificate.

The MPAA have a phobia about seeing people joined together in lovemaking. So they wanted us to cut down on the amount of material where Sharon and Billy seemed to be truly coupling. I would cut it and they would say, 'No, no, no, still too much.' I would try cutting it again – 'No, no, no, still too much' – and this went on endlessly. Yet in any film that I have made in the US, there has never been any discussion with the censors about violence.

America has always had a very, very skittish relationship to films involving sex. The English settlement was founded by pilgrims, and there's still a strong religious fanaticism and a moral majority. Now that we've come through the porn era where America seemed not to be a censored place, we realise that what Americans can see in films shown in multiplexes is quite restricted compared to much of the Western world.

While squabbling with the censors and struggling with test-screening audiences, another front opened – though on a minor scale – between Noyce and his producer.

Robert Evans had previously served as head of production for Paramount Pictures and had always encouraged the story that he was responsible for the re-editing of *The Godfather* when Francis Ford Coppola was supposedly having problems making the story work during post-production.

After the first preview Bob approached Sherry Lansing and convinced her that the film wasn't being edited properly. Part of his sales pitch was that neither myself nor editor Richard Francis-Bruce understood sex. So, Sherry rang me and said, 'Do you mind if Bob goes into an editing room and does his version, which we will all see?' And I said, 'Fine, as long as I don't have to listen anymore to his suggestions.' He had been making suggestions, but none of them were really dealing with the problem. They were all over the place and mainly to do with sexual content, but very little with character or story.

For the next several weeks, each night Bob would come into an editing room set up down the hallway, and, together with line producer Howard Koch Jr, he would sit cutting an alternate version of the film. Sometimes he would emerge from the darkened room as I arrived to start work next morning, often with his face covered in white powder, as if he had collapsed into the stuff.

Eventually Sherry went to see Bob's version. The agreement was that she would look at it and if there was anything in it, she would tell me. Afterwards she said, 'There was maybe one shot that you ought to think about using.' They had found another shot of Sharon Stone in the bathtub, which I also found and eventually incorporated, but otherwise nothing came of it. But, of course, usually the producer doesn't go off and try to produce their own cut. But given that Bob was so persistent in his argument that he knew how to make the film work, I guessed this was the only way to silence him. But it was extremely disruptive to the whole process, because we had to give our staff to him at night, which meant they couldn't work during the daytime, and so the whole thing became a little fractured, which didn't at all contribute to making the wisest choices.

For the final reshoot we had to wait until the last minute, because Sharon was shooting another film up in Canada. Then finally the cast reassembled on rebuilt sets and for about four days we reshot, mainly the material in the last twenty minutes of the movie. As fast as we reshot, it was edited and sent out to the composer for composition and recording. The revised version was put together with undue haste because the film was locked into a release date and there wasn't the time to consider what we were doing – it was really shooting and editing and completing all at the same time. As it was, the film opened on a Friday and was only completed on the Monday before. The prints went out the day before the opening, arriving in the cinemas the night before or on the actual day of the opening.

The film wasn't well received by the critics. Despite some horrendous errors (Laszlo Kovacs is credited for cinematography), *Variety*'s approach was pretty typical: '. . . *Sliver* proves all flash and no sizzle – a thriller that simply changes gender on the *Basic Instinct* formula to did he or didn't he? . . . a cold, inaccessible yarn about murder and voyeurism that's too leisurely about getting where it needs to go and doesn't fully develop what should be its core: a just-divorced woman (Sharon Stone) drawn into a kinky, voyeuristic relationship with mysterious younger man (William Baldwin) . . . Blame it on the editing and reediting, but even the sex scenes aren't all that steamy, and the movie suffers from some choppy moments and high-rise-size lapses in logic.'[22] Even in foreign countries the response was similar, as this German critic illustrates: 'What starts out as an updated version of Hitchcock's *Rear Window* soon turns into a tamely tired and hackneyed idea of a thriller. Psychological consistency and therefore finally suspense are too obviously sacrificed for the sole target: to make the audience a voyeur on Sharon Stone.'[23] Still, the film generally fared quite differently abroad.

The film didn't do well in the US, but as soon as it opened overseas it was a big success – I think its domestic take was US$37 million and somewhere in the nineties outside America. The finished film was perhaps still too unconventional for the American audience, even though it was a lot straighter than the original version, but much more to the taste of Europe.

For the international version we cut in about three minutes of extra footage with slightly more sexual content. There is a little bit more of the scene where Zeke approaches Carly and makes love to her against the column in the apartment, and there is a bit more in their first sexual encounter, when they make love with her sitting astride him on the floor of the apartment. And maybe some other shots throughout, but it's not significant. A number of cuts that were made for censorship reasons even at the last minute in the American version were reinstated.

As there were so many changes and recuts, even with access to different versions it is hard to determine what was changed, when and why. However, a few sections that had major remodelling stand out. For once, the international version is roughly four minutes longer and looks much more 'erotic' than the version released in the US. The passionate love affair between Carly and Zeke is much more convincing, and this isn't due only to the more intense lovemaking scene against the column between the two protagonists.

The sudden about-face between hero and villain that occurred as explained above in the very late stages of post-production is surely a very rare instance in film history. In another twist, Carly and Zeke at one stage even got married. (There was a wedding scene on top of the sliver building about which Noyce proudly recalls: 'There was an incredible shot from a helicopter. It starts on a close-up of Sharon's finger and comes out.')

The most visible change, however, is the ending, in which the honeymooning couple fly in a helicopter across Hawaii and voluntarily dive to vanish in the red-hot lava of a perfectly shaped volcano cone. This may look a little too Freudian; yet, it captures the obsessive passion in their relationship in a very conceptual way. The final dialogue between the two reflects, as well, their trust/distrust: they are bound to each other by fate/passion/crime. Still, they struggle to stay independent, not submitting to each other – as is usually the case in a more conventional relationship.

Helicopter rotor blades. Carly shoots down with a video camera. Both sitting in a flying heli, Zeke at the wheel.
    Zeke: *Take that seatbelt off.*
    Carly: *Why?*
    Zeke: *Trust me. It's more fun this way.*
    Lava flows down to the sea. Heli follows the streams uphill.
    Zeke: *Don't be scared.*
    Carly: *I'm not – I kept the tapes.*
    Zeke: *[puzzled expression]*
    Carly: *The one with you and [the model] in the shower.*
    Zeke: *Where did you see that?*
    Carly: *In the fireplace mirror.*
    Zeke: *Where is it now?*
    Carly: *It's safe. Trust me. It's more fun this way. Don't be scared.*
    Zeke: *I'm not.*
    Zeke: *Here we go –*
    PoV shot diving into volcano.
    Monitors in sliver building empty (white noise).

Some of the trouble with *Sliver* may be the result of a certain ambiguity in the film's perspective, which somehow never makes it quite clear what it is aiming to be about: a passionate love affair or a crime story with several murders. Considering that the US version attempted to be less 'erotic' than the export version, it is surprising to learn that a clearly more 'criminal' opening of the film ended up on the editing-room floor. In this opening an electrician – obviously on a routine job in the building's lobby – incidentally discovers some cables. Curious, he follows them until they lead into the elevator shaft and further upwards, probably to what we now know is Zeke's monitor room. Climbing upwards, he is killed by a large object thrown from above.

The different public remarks by the film's key players are only partly enlightening and not always consistent. 'Carly . . . becomes romantically involved with Zeke . . . only to find herself being seduced into a mysterious and clandestine world that tests the fragile boundaries between reality and her deepest fantasies,' claimed the press kit.[24] Noyce added: 'This is a story of a woman who starts out straight jacketed in her attitudes to the world and her self. And who through a relationship with a man unlocks herself to all sorts of experiences that most of us keep hidden, except in our own personal fantasies.'[25] Bob Evans stated that the film is 'an electric shock on audiences by exploring the single most secret fantasy everyone has but won't discuss – voyeurism.'[26] Joe Eszterhas admitted: 'I have always been drawn to the theme of people being intimate strangers to one another . . . The story is really a high wire act about temptation and vulnerability.'[27] Noyce preferred still another angle: 'I wanted to make this film partly as an antidote to *Patriot Games*. That film featured a very large cast and played on a very large canvas, with many disparate story elements. I longed for something I could hold in my hand as it were – something containable, something more intimate and psychological and in particular a woman's story. There are very few of them.'[28] At the same time, he claimed: 'This film is also potentially a wonderful candidate for film mythology, being a sort of 1990s' version of *Rear Window*.'[29]

Browsing through recent European photo publications about the career of Sharon Stone,[30] it is easy to see that she has never been shown as more beautiful and erotic than she was in *Silver*.

That was the particular skill of Vilmos Zsigmond, which was a great asset to the film. He lit the film to emphasise the erotic and the romantic aspects of the story – with Sharon as a goddess at the centre of it all.

Stone's costumes, which included very delicate lingerie, were designed by Deborah Scott, who later went on to do the costume design for *Titanic*, for which she won an Academy Award.

The inference is: Carly was always that way – and maybe we all are, too. All we need is the litmus paper or the stimulus to draw it out of us. Just because we wear fancy clothes doesn't mean we aren't just animals, and also maybe *because* we wear fancy clothes we are more than animals, in as much as we are very, very complex in the way our animal nature is acted out.

It may well be that Europe was better prepared for a passionate, erotic piece of cinematic art, due to its long experience of eroticism in literature and – to a slightly lesser degree – in art. *Sliver* came close to being a masterpiece of erotic film; yet, something is missing.

It seems the film's relative failure in the US 'was due more to moral outrage than anything else, since overseas – where people were less concerned with what Sharon was doing to whom than what she was doing on screen – *Sliver* was a big hit, giving the film a world gross of [US]$114 million'.[31] Still, part of the film's enormous success outside America must be credited to its soundtrack, which earned Noyce a platinum disc:

As always, the songs are initially suggested by your music supervisor, but then the director chooses them according to the type of sound that one sees in totality for the movie. I have many times rejected songs that have gone on to become hits, simply because they didn't fit. The first criterion always has to be 'Do they fit into the film?' If they don't, then you are best not to use them.

Four of the songs that we had chosen for the soundtrack of *Sliver* became number 1 records in other parts of the world. 'Can't Help Falling In Love' by UB40 was number 1 for six weeks in America. And other songs were number 1 in various other countries. The drawing power of these songs really helped us overseas, because when the film came out in America, the soundtrack was only just becoming known and most of the success with the soundtrack came after the film had already played there.

And on the home front? *Sliver* doesn't appear to have sparked much in the way of open controversy in the US. Perhaps those people who objected most strongly to its erotic content kept their views to themselves. As well, as the film didn't have big grosses in the States, it was not the subject of much discussion.

In Hollywood, most things are allowed in a successful film; nothing is forgiven if it is unsuccessful. So how did Noyce survive the backlash?

I screened the first cut of the film – as I have always done – to my daughter Lucia. At the time she was about ten or eleven. She looked at it and said, 'Have you done the deal on your next movie? Have you got a contract for your next movie yet?' I said, 'No, why?' She said, 'Listen to me, this is for the family, you know. I want you to do the deal. Don't show this film to anyone else until you've got a contract on your next film.' I said, 'Okay.' Paramount had approached me to do *Clear and Present Danger* as the second of [my] Clancy films. So I said I would do it, and we signed a basic agreement before I showed *Sliver* to the studio.

It is extremely interesting that as recently as 2004, ten years after its release, the film's key background players still seem to be extraordinarily eager to publish their differing views of what happened with *Sliver*. In that way, the film is obviously still pretty controversial. But why?

A lot of reasons, including the past histories of the major players and the fact that major changes were made to the storyline during post-production. And also because of the behind-the-scenes sexual theatre where Joe Eszterhas was supposedly manipulating Sharon Stone and producer Bill MacDonald into an affair in order to steal MacDonald's wife – as reported in a *New York Times* article, but later denied by Eszterhas.

And, in addition, it was the first film of Bob Evans's comeback, a legendary Hollywood producer, a man associated with numerous scandals – not the least of which was the Cotton Club Murders but also *The Godfather* editing controversy. Bob, of course, claims he had a big hand in the final content of that movie. Coppola, on the other hand – who is a friend – says that's a fantasy of Bob's and that actually Bob never contributed to the editing at all, other than in the normal course of studio/film director comments.

Sliver is a *film maudit* in the true sense of the word, and will probably remain so. (Interestingly, it is the only one of Noyce's major films that has not been re-released on DVD.) Bob Evans probably gives the best wrap-up: 'What started out as a platinum project with a solid gold screenplay and seasoned with the flavour of the year's femme fatale ended up being no more than a silver-plated flick . . .

'Poor Phillip Noyce . . . Given the luxury of another week to deliver the international version, he added four minutes of sizzle. What a difference a sizzle makes. Around the world, except in the good ole U.S.A., *Sliver* was a huge box-office smash, bringing heavy change into Paramount's coffers.'[32]

Whatever is fact and whatever is myth, if Noyce were to release a 'director's cut' of *Sliver*, it would really be something to look out for.

---

[1] Robert Evans, *The Kid Stays in the Picture* (New York: Hyperion, 1994), p. 402.
[2] Ibid, p. 408.
[3] Ibid, p. 401.
[4] Ibid, p. 402.
[5] Ibid, p. 403.
[6] Ibid, p. 404.
[7] Cited in Joe Eszterhas, *American Rhapsody* (New York: Alfred A. Knopf, 2000), p. 90.
[8] Ibid, p. 90.
[9] Ibid.
[10] Evans, *The Kid Stays in the Picture*, p. 403.
[11] Eszterhas, *American Rhapsody*, p. 87.
[12] Evans, *The Kid Stays in the Picture*, p. 404.
[13] Ibid, p. 402.
[14] Cited in Carol Sewell (ed.), '*Sliver Production Notes*', dated 15 April 1993, p. 5.
[15] Ibid, p. 6.
[16] Eszterhas, *American Rhapsody*, p. 91.
[17] Cited in Michael Munn, *The Sharon Stone Story* (London: Robson Books, 1997), p. 101.
[18] Evans, *The Kid Stays in the Picture*, p. 406.
[19] Cited in Munn, *The Sharon Stone Story*, p. 98.
[20] Ibid, p. 99.
[21] Cited in Sewell, *Sliver Production Notes*, p. 7.
[22] Brian Lowry, '*Sliver*', *Variety*, 24 May 1993.
[23] *Zoom* (Zurich) September 1993. Cited in Lothar R. Just (ed.), *Film – Jahrbuch* (Munich: Heyne, 1994), p. 282.
[24] Sewell, *Sliver Production Notes*, p. 2.
[25] Noyce, cited in Carol Sewell, *Phillip Noyce comments* (attachment to production notes), 1993, no page numbers.
[26] Cited in Sewell, p. 2.
[27] Cited in Sewell, p. 3.
[28] Cited in Carol Sewell, *Phillip Noyce comments*.
[29] Ibid.
[30] David Sandison, *The Unofficial Sharon Stone* (Bristol: The Book Company, 1996); Tom Kummer, *Sharon Stone* (Munich, Paris, London: Schirmer/Mosel, 1997).
[31] Munn, *The Sharon Stone Story*, p. 128.
[32] Evans, *The Kid Stays in the Picture*, p. 408.

Chapter 12
CLEAR AND PRESENT DANGER

They're not watching TV – I am the program.

A prominent US businessman who has been dealing with the drug cartels is killed. The American president (Donald Moffat), a close personal friend, is embarrassed and has Jack Ryan (Harrison Ford) officially pursue the matter, while secretly setting loose national security advisor James Cutter (Harris Yulin) and CIA hardliner Robert Ritter (Henry Czerny) to send a paramilitary force against the drug lords. When Ryan discovers he has been tricked, he decides against personal loyalty and sides with the Constitution – he faces down the president.

While I was shooting *Sliver*, John Goldwyn, Paramount head of production and grandson of one of the gentlemen who started Metro Goldwyn Mayer (MGM), gave me the script for *Clear and Present Danger*, the latest adaptation of a Tom Clancy techno thriller. This time the story was much more interesting and complex than *Patriot Games*. I read the screenplay, which at the time was written by Don Stewart, who had previously won an Academy Award for *Missing* and who had been one of the writers on *Patriot Games*. I also read the source material and found that, like the first script of *Patriot Games*, the novel was much more interesting than the screenplay suggested.

One of the principal problems for a screen adaptation of this story was that when the novel was written, there wasn't yet a series of films featuring the character of Jack Ryan. The story hadn't been conceived with Ryan as the dominating central character that a movie starring an acknowledged superstar would require. So the story needed to be refocused around the part to be played by Harrison Ford. Clancy's novel was about a situation involving many different characters, one of whom was Ryan.

In Clancy's 700-page novel, Ryan doesn't appear before page 200. This sort of thing is possible on the page, but a film has to focus around a main character. On the other hand, the novel – originally released in 1989 – had sold six million copies, so there was a danger of alienating a large portion of the potential audience if changes to the novel's storyline were too profound. Clancy, with his usual forthrightness, had made it clear to Paramount that he expected his most successful book to be converted into the best adaptation yet. A first script by his friend John Milius had met with his approval but was dismissed outright by the studio. A seven-figure fee had convinced Donald Stewart to come on board again, but Clancy disliked the result. 'If you shoot this script, *Sliver* will look like *Citizen Kane* [by comparison],' he grumbled in one memo. In another he wrote: '*Clear and Present Danger* was the No. 1 best-selling novel of the 1980s. One might conclude that the novel's basic storyline had some quality to it. Why, then, has nearly every aspect of the book been tossed away?'[1] The general consensus at this point was that it just might not be worth the trouble of working with Clancy again.

Still, Noyce agreed to do the film.

After taking a short holiday at the end of *Sliver*, I went straight into pre-production. This involved bringing in screenwriter Steve Zaillian, who, uncredited, had written the shooting script for *Patriot Games* and by this time had also written the as yet unreleased *Schindler's List*. Steve and I again journeyed with Mace Neufeld to Harrison's ranch in Jackson Hole, Wyoming, and spent a few days talking about the novel, the existing screenplay, and what we liked and disliked about both.

I saw the film as being principally about patriotism – which in its

Latin derivation refers to family – and about responsibility – about Jack Ryan's responsibility to himself and his country. In counter-manding CIA rules is Ryan not serving his country, or is his own morality the only rule he needs to abide by? If he makes moral choices, can that be an expression of patriotism, as opposed to following the law of the land?

We decided at those meetings to rework Clancy's material so that Ryan is flattered and seduced by his closeness to the most powerful political leader in the world, the American president, and then has to make a choice as to whether he is going to speak up and act when he detects morally reprehensible behaviour by those above him. Steve spent a lot of effort building up the early scenes between Jack Ryan and the president.

Interestingly, these moral issues in the plot later caused major grievances. In the book, Ryan eventually confronts the president in the privacy of the Oval Office over his illegal war and threatens to go public if it is not called off. Ford, however, thought the book's ambiguous ending was 'insufficient enter-tainment',[2] and he seems to have persuaded Zaillian to change it to an accusation in front of the assembled Congress. 'Clancy and Milius, both right-wing Reagan-ites, hated the idea and called it "ridiculous . . . Anyone in this day and age who thinks that Congress is an honourable organisation is a fool," Milius moaned.'[3]

But these problems were still far in the future in these early stages of pre-production.

During pre-production I decided to go down to South America and work out where we could shoot the film. I went first to Colombia – to Bogotá and to Medellin, where the real Pablo Escobar's drug cartel was operating, and also to Cali, where the guys who had taken over from Escobar lived. And in Medellin together with Terry Marsh, my production designer, I went incognito, pretending to be a tourist. We were taken around in a small tourist minibus by the brother of Doug Mitchell (one of the producers of *Dead Calm*), who is an insurance salesman in Medellin. He and his wife had already warned us on the phone not to refer to any of the cartel personalities by name, but rather just to call them 'magicians' and their houses 'castles'. We went on a tour of the various cartel holdings, Escobar's compounds, the village outside Medellin where he grew up and the gaol where he had been held until his recent escape.

In the film, Escobar is called Escobedo, so it's a thinly disguised portrait of Escobar. The character was a combination of Escobar and the personalities and styles of some of the Cali cartel members.

From seeing the way people were living there it became pretty obvious that it would be impossible to shoot in Bogotá – mainly because of crew and actor security. In a bar after work you would realise there were men with loaded submachine guns standing guard over the revellers. Journeys to and from work were favourite times for kidnapping businessmen.

So I went to Quito, in Ecuador, which, like Bogotá, is perched high up in the Andes. In the film you see Ryan's plane landing, supposedly at Bogotá, but in fact we took the shot in Quito. We also went to Costa Rica, Puerto Rico, and then to many other cities in Mexico. Finally, I decided that in order to shoot the scenes that supposedly take place around Cali and Bogotá, we would need to film in several parts of Mexico – Mexico City for the Bogotá scenes, and then a combination of Cuernavaca and Tepitzlan, which had previously been used by Oliver Stone to shoot *El Salvador*, Coatepec and Jalapa in the south – and all of these country locations would in combination substitute for the Cali scenes in the movie.

In Bogotá I visited the American Embassy and there I discovered that one of the Drug Enforcement Agency agents was in fact a woman of about 50. She became the model for the hard-talking but feminine red-headed DEA agent in the film.

While at the embassy I also discussed strategy for providing security to visiting American dignitaries, and some of the embassy protection staff outlined how they would transport people from Bogotá airport into the city. Their strategy was based on travelling in convoy with multiple motorcycle escorts and the key was never to stop, even if it meant ramming vehicles that seemed to present obstacles.

The vehicles carrying the dignitaries would hand out name cards to anyone they bashed into, advising them to come to the American Embassy to have their vehicle repaired. So, it was based on the idea of just pushing through, no matter what the obstacle.

As soon as they told me this plan I realised its potential flaws. One was that if the bad guys could substitute their own rider for one of the escort motorcyclists, then the convoy would follow the wrong man. And second, if it was based on the idea that the Chevy Suburbans that were carrying the dignitaries could ram through any obstacle, then obviously one had only to come up with a sufficiently large barrier to trap them.

So I invented the idea of a rogue motorcyclist leading the good guys into a street that was barricaded at both ends by large buses. The victims were then like rats in a trap, surrounded by missile-firing assailants.

The ambush had been briefly described in Clancy's book, but it was a much smaller event and didn't involve Jack Ryan at all. At first we tried to find a real street in a Mexican city, but given that we were blowing up vehicles and destroying parts of buildings and needed complete control over the location, we finally decided to build our own street, based on photographs that Terry Marsh had taken in old Bogotá. Terry designed a street which we built beside a soccer field in Mexico City, made up of facades only, allowing us to shoot tracking shots along the tops of the buildings. The whole sequence was elaborately planned with many different versions of the storyboards drawn, edited, then redrawn six times by David Negron, almost like it had been shot and edited and then reshot and re-edited and then re-edited and reshot. We even produced an animated version of the scene to gauge how the proposed shots would play.

Interestingly, after the film was completed, the sequence was then used for training US foreign service protection staff, because it described an elaborate ambush and posed some of the problems that attack victims might have to try to avoid.

One of the things I like to do when I'm portraying any subculture is to try to meet people from that group, whether they're working for the CIA, for the cocaine cartels, the IRA, the New York police or in book publishing – whatever. With a good model, you then can portray fictional characters on screen with confidence. Also, you often see foibles in real people, little character traits that you would never think of, because truth is definitely stranger than fiction. For example, the indomitable powerhouse of this little red-headed woman, who wasn't afraid of anything despite having one of the most dangerous postings in the world as a drug enforcement agent in Bogotá, where the drug cartels had assassinated the judiciary and politicians. Only by going there to Bogotá itself and seeking out people would you ever get the idea for a character like that.

One thing that happened to Terry and me while we were in Bogotá was quite amusing – but only in retrospect. I had approached an American journalist working for a newspaper in Bogotá, who specialised in writing articles about the various cocaine cartel members and their activities. I told him I wanted to mix with these people. He knew a woman who was the money launderer for one of the cartels – she ran a gem shop in Bogotá, buying and selling precious jewellery, which provided the cover for money laundering. He said that he had arranged for me to meet her at a certain time. I said, 'What did you tell her we were doing?' He said, 'I told her you were making a film about . . .' and he mentioned the name of a very famous gem dealer. I forget the name, could never remember it – that was the problem. And he said, 'Jack Nicholson is going to play the guy in the movie.'

So we were travelling to the meeting, and every ten minutes or so, Terry and I would ask each other, 'What was the name of that guy we're making the movie about?' And of course, probably because of nerves, neither of us could remember the name. About 300 metres before we got to the shop, Terry bailed out, saying, 'I can't remember the guy's name and I've got a bad feeling about this.' So he left and the last thing he asked me was, 'What's the guy's name?' I said, '. . .' and I got it right.

So I went into the shop. We sat down, me and the journalist, and we started talking to this woman. I can see three young guys in suits watching television in this room next door, but I couldn't hear them or anything. It must have been that either we or they were behind some sort of soundproof glass. I'm talking to the woman and then suddenly I look over again and I realise that they're not watching TV – *I* am the program. It's me they're watching on the screen. And that's when I could no longer remember who I was making the film about, which coincided with her asking about the subject of the film, and I just went to pieces. Within seconds I had an Uzi in the back of my head, a cocked, loaded Uzi pressed up against my neck, and we were told to leave and never to come back. I did leave and I didn't go back. To the shop. To Bogotá. Or to Colombia.

More serious problems were encountered during pre-production. As with *Patriot Games*, the film would be heavily dependent on the cooperation of the Pentagon, particularly as all kinds of military equipment would be needed, from Black Hawk helicopters to an aircraft carrier. This time, however, the military was much more reluctant to help. They feared being portrayed 'in an irresponsibly gung-ho light', and Noyce and Stewart 'had to agree to a series of script changes before they got clearances'.[4] These clearances finally arrived – but more than a week after principal photography had started in Los Angeles on 3 November 1993.

Luckily, the scenes set in the White House didn't pose a problem. 'For the shooting of his White House comedy *Dave*, Ivan Reitman had constructed a realistic, full-scale replica of the Oval Office. This same set was reused by Alan J. Pakula for his film *The Pelican Brief*, so it was relatively inexpensive for *Clear And Present Danger* to rent the set.'[5]

Once the production had switched to Mexico, another potentially devastating problem arose. Only about a week before, a rebellion had erupted in the southern state of Chiapas and was bloodily suppressed by the army. Now the Mexican government was reluctant to issue permits granting the import and use of most of the weaponry and explosives needed to make the action scenes look authentic. The permits eventually came through about 48 hours before the scheduled start of shooting.

As time went on in 1993 without a finished script, it became clear that we would have difficulty completing the film in time for the summer 1994 release that we all wanted. So in the end I approached John Milius, who had written *Apocalypse Now* and had the year before directed a film for Paramount and for producer Mace Neufeld called *Flight of the Intruder*. It hadn't been a success and John wasn't on good terms with Mace or the studio. But John had written the first draft of *Clear and Present Danger*, which reflected the multiple characters of the book and wasn't really about Jack Ryan as much as it was a true adaptation of Clancy's story. John had been replaced by Don Stewart before I joined the project. Don invented the structure that integrated Ryan into the story.

I thought that in Milius's draft the action sequences were really strong, as was his understanding of military jargon and the interaction of the military characters. I could see from the material that Steve Zaillian was giving me that those two areas weren't really capturing Steve's imagination. So I approached John Milius and he said, 'Well, right now, I hate the studio, so I'm not inclined to do anything. But I like you, so who knows?'

The first scene I nevertheless asked him to look at was the introduction to the sniper, Chavez. I was at my office at Paramount late at night and suddenly the fax machine sprang to life. I went over and saw that the fax had no markings of origin, but I realised that it was the script of the scenes I'd requested. While still officially refusing to help, John had written the scenes. Now he was mimicking a scene from the novel, where the corrupt national security advisor receives a fax from Cortez, the double-dealing Cuban, late at night.

Eventually I revealed to Paramount and producer Mace Neufeld that the sniper scenes they admired so much had been written by John Milius; so I approached John again for help with the ambush sequence, this time offering to pay him. He said, 'Well, I'm not going to do it. I still hate the studio, and I won't accept a penny from them.' I said, 'What would you accept?' He said, 'I want one of those ambushed Chevy Suburbans, one that's left over, but I want it filled with Cuban cigars.' When we were filming I had to make sure that I didn't destroy all the Suburbans, and then one was loaded in Mexico with banned Cuban cigars and delivered to John Milius in Santa Monica, California.

Steve Zaillian left to resume work on *Schindler's List*, but we still hadn't quite worked out the ending, so Don Stewart came back. The funny thing was that in my office at Paramount we had Steve Zaillian, John Milius and Don Stewart, the three writers, talking about the ending. There was a great feeling of camaraderie, which was unusual because mostly in Hollywood when a second writer comes in, the first writer takes umbrage and they don't talk to each other. But here we had three writers working simultaneously and all in communication with each other. On the credits you see 'Screenplay by Donald Stewart and Steve Zaillian and John Milius' and they all worked both separately and together, even though particular parts were written by one or the other.

Harrison and I now were pretty confident with each other. We both share the same approach to the work, which is that even if you've really got confidence in the script you have a responsibility to explore the possibilities during the day that you're shooting that scene and see where it will go. Until you get on the floor with actors and exchange ideas, you don't know what's going to happen. There's always the possibility of coming up with a new idea and you shouldn't close yourself off. That's the way I've always liked to work and Harrison has been my greatest single teacher of commercial cinema techniques.

Still, as with *Patriot Games*, frictions arose between the two seasoned professionals.

Harrison and I had clashed during the shooting of the ambush sequence in the Bogotá street. He has always wanted to do as many of his own stunts as possible. There is one great shot in there where he is driving and you see an explosion as one of the rockets hits one of the shops nearby. We argued when he wanted to drive that car for real and I said, 'Let a stunt double do it.' He said, 'I like the audience to feel that I'm really there,' so I let him drive. After the shot had been taken we found this gaping hole in the wall opposite the explosion. And then one of the special effects team found a huge piece of wood about 100 metres away in the middle of the next-door soccer field – it had been blown there in the explosion. Then when we looked at the footage we saw this projectile speeding past the front of the Suburban, just a little bit over a foot from hitting Harrison. He was protected by Lexan [a transparent bullet-proof material], but the force projected this thing such a distance that the protection wouldn't have been sufficient to prevent it from decapitating our star.

In another shot when Harrison was escaping, he backs through a wall and comes out in the adjacent street. Again I explained that he didn't need to drive because the shot of the Suburban emerging wouldn't identify the driver. It could be driven by a stuntman and I just didn't want to take a chance. Harrison got very upset. I later realised that he enjoys doing these action films in part because he likes the thrill of risk-taking. Hence his passion for flying helicopters, light planes and jets. When I went up to visit Harrison in Jackson Hole again in July 1999, he met me at the airport and showed me his collection: planes for landing on top of mountains, planes for landing on short landing strips, helicopters, a jet – all of which he is well equipped to pilot.

Later we did a shot that wasn't used in the finished film – Harrison supporting the FBI director, who dies in his arms. When we were filming this particular shot, a Mexican actor driving a motor-cycle at a very slow speed almost collided with Harrison and he was justifiably upset with me. So by the last couple of weeks of production everyone was a bit frazzled from exhaustion and there was a lot of tension between the two of us. I was certainly operating at less than full mental capacity due to the exhaustion of the long shoot.

Maybe the tension was exacerbated by Harrison's reaction when nominations for the Academy Awards were announced for *The Fugitive*. The picture received six or seven nominations but not one for him, and from what I had heard, he had truly played a key role in crafting the film from script to casting and shooting. And, of course, his performance is what holds that story together. I think he was just feeling a little bit unloved as an artist. He was a little frustrated because he had been in so many money-making films, and *The Fugitive*, which was a straightforward action film, executed brilliantly, had been awarded the rare accolade of Academy Award nominations – but Harrison had been ignored.

Even though the frictions were clearly noted by the press at the time, Noyce played them down. ' "It is more stressful. We had less of a script this time, so we had more to argue about," [Noyce said] before going [on] to compare his relationship with Harrison to a marriage, polite the first time around, less so the second.'[6]

Still, the production went pretty smoothly until the last section of shooting, which was in Jalapa, a city in southern Mexico. Actually, we weren't even filming in Jalapa city but in a small village nearby. These were the scenes that supposedly take place in and around the coffee factory owned by drug boss Escobedo. The studio started to become extremely worried about cost overruns. The film was, I don't know, a week or so over at the time.

And one day, suddenly this fax arrives, giving an absolute stop date. It says that any shooting over that date will be paid for by the director and the producer.

The fax, on Paramount letterhead and addressed to 'all concerned', was dated 1 March 1994 and unsigned. According to Noyce, it was sent by Don Granger, vice-president in charge of production, even though he was listed on it as one of the recipients. The fax read as follows:

Important
Due to new projections for overruns in the first unit schedule and the budget for the entire film, and per today's conversations with Mace Neufeld and Ralph Singleton, the following is to be instituted immediately:
1. First unit shooting at the coffee factory location will finish at the end of normal shooting day on Thursday March 3rd. Any shots not completed by the first unit will be attained by the second unit if this is within the second unit budget.

First unit, without exception, will move to its next location to shoot on Friday March 4th. If, for any reason, first unit decides unilaterally to remain on the location to shoot on Friday, the cost of the day will be borne out of the director's and producer's fees. Paramount will not pay for the day.

2. Harrison Ford's last day of filming on this project is, absolutely, Tuesday March 8th. It's up to Mr. Ford's discretion if he wishes to return to the United States at the end of the day on the 8th, or the morning of the 9th. Harrison Ford will not be available to shoot with any unit after the close of the day on March 8th.

3. First unit principal photography on *Clear and Present Danger* will finish at the end of the shooting day on Wednesday March 9th. This is absolute and non-negotiable. Again, if a decision is made to shoot with the first unit after the end of the day on March 9th, Paramount will not pay for any more days. These extra costs would be borne from the director's and the producer's fees. The second unit budget and schedule will be discussed between Ralph Singleton, Mace Neufeld, and Paramount.

4. Phillip Noyce will return to the United States on Thursday, March 10th.

Thank you for your attention to this. We appreciate all the hard work everyone is putting in, but feel it's time to set some absolute definition to this final week.

Addressees in Mexico were Mace Neufeld, Phillip Noyce, Harrison Ford, Ralph Singleton (line producer), Itsi Atkins (production manager) and Susan Towner (accountant). At Paramount they were Sherry Lansing, John Goldwyn, Donald Granger, Bill Bernstein (president of business affairs), Fred Gallo (president of physical production), and Larry Albucher and Mike Hill (vice-presidents of physical production).

Noyce, understandably, was worried by the sentence 'Paramount will not pay for any more days.'

I wasn't worried about who else was paying – I just knew that it would be me, and one day of shooting would cost something like [US]$200,000.

So I looked at the date they said we should finish by and spoke to my first assistant director, Alan Curtiss, who was in charge of the schedule, and we both agreed that we couldn't finish the film in that time.

Unfortunately, at this time, producer Mace Neufeld had to leave Mexico because his wife had been diagnosed with cancer, so he wasn't there to adjudicate. We had already filmed part of the sequence where Harrison escapes from the coffee factory, in perfect sunshine and involving several days of complicated stunt work. So we had to wait for sun to film the other half, and thank goodness the sun didn't appear for nine days, because that's how long I needed to film the rest of the interior scenes. The second unit, which usually takes aerials and stuff like that, came in, with DoP Michael Benson, who shot for me on *Patriot Games* and *Sliver*. Basically, I worked two units at once, shooting two scenes simultaneously, setting up with the second unit for a shot, while the first unit were lighting, then I'd run from set to set, filming all over that coffee factory. After nine days the sun came out and we went outside, and again I split the unit into two, sending half to shoot the explosion of the hacienda, while the other half stayed with me to complete Harrison's getaway from the coffee factory.

It was a ridiculous situation. The studio were saying, 'Pull out', and I was saying, 'But we'll have to come back.' As it was, we still had to return later to shoot a couple of days around that sequence with a small second unit.

You always reach a point on every movie shoot where, through fatigue, frustration, cost overruns and everything else, people start to behave irrationally. On one shoot, lasting sixteen or eighteen weeks, with people constantly putting their egos on the line, there is probably more pressure than most people might feel in a whole lifetime in most occupations.

I think the studio probably imagined that we were going too slowly and that they had to really put the screws on – particularly on me, the director. And that I would then make decisions about how to shorten the script or abridge the way I was shooting the picture, and eventually things would turn out okay. My own feeling was that it was a very complicated film and each of these parts was inter-dependent. When I looked at the film in Germany at the Würzburg Film Weekend, where they were holding a retrospective of my work in January 1999, I was quite amazed when I saw the complexity of its story construction. And I tried to imagine what would happen if we pulled out any of those cards – it seemed as though each one, like an elaborate card trick, was dependent on the other.

But the premature end of shooting wasn't all that worried Noyce during this stage of production.

The frictions with Harrison continued during the editing. A lot of directors hide their cut from everybody. I always like to get the cut in front of an audience as soon as possible. Whether it looks sleek isn't the point, because the story only exists when it speaks back from the screen to the people that are watching it. As I had done on *Patriot Games*, I sent a tape of the very first cut to Harrison, who felt it didn't work.

Ford articulated his irritations in a twelve-page fax dated 15 April and transmitted two days later to Noyce, Neufeld and Neil Travis, the editor. In the fax, he revises the film sequence by sequence in some detail, raises questions, suggests changes in dialogue and images, and even suggests some new shots and scenes. The tone of the document is highly professional; there are no personal remarks in it at all. He focuses particularly on three sequences: the Coast Guard opening sequence, the kill zone, and the interiors of the coffee factory.

I still had four weeks before I was obligated by my contract to screen the film to anyone else. Harrison had started to pressure the studio and say, 'I need an editor to come up here and work with me, because it's not working.' I thought the only way around this was to get the unfinished movie in front of an audience.

So, well ahead of time, we held a test screening. It was a big risk, particularly after *Sliver*. But I was buoyed by my secret weapon – my daughter Lucia. I had already screened the film to her and she had told me, 'Don't sign up for your next movie until after you have shown this film all around the world, then agree to do another movie.' Harrison came to the screening as well, and it scored 80. Suddenly, the studio who had issued stop work orders, the actor who had declared that he needed to bring in his own editor – suddenly, everybody was happy, everyone was on the same team again. My team.

To judge by documents in Noyce's archive, there seems to have been still another preview, dated 24 May, as Ford, again by fax, comments on this to Noyce, Neufeld and Travis. This time, however, his remarks took just two pages, and were mainly concerned with small changes in dialogue lines or the attribution of dialogue lines to certain shots already used in the film.

Still, at the time Noyce's public comments on Harrison's attitude had become pretty blunt. ' "Anal", was the word that stood out as he described his star's fretful behaviour to the *Sydney Morning Herald*. He amplified on it later in London. "He is morally brave, doggedly obsessive, detail-oriented. Harrison can be a bloody pain," he complained.

'Harrison attempted to put a more positive spin on their differences in the weeks that followed. "We try to meld our energies together, that's the ambition, for him to keep his strong point of view and for me to keep my strong point of view and for us to end up with something twice as strong", he said. "We usually come to an accommodation. But directors have a point of view and I have a point of view about what to do."'[7]

This vendetta aside, at least Noyce generally had a more conventional editing period for this film. While he had to work quickly, the schedule wasn't ridiculous. 'I think we finished the film about a month before it opened.'

On the Web – always prone to publishing myths and unsubstantiated claims – it is reported that during post-production five reels of the film were destroyed in a film lab in the Los Angeles earthquake.

Not post-production, but during shooting, the LA earthquake struck. It wasn't five *reels* of the film, it was five *rolls* of film damaged when everything stopped and they were cooked in the processing.

Noyce comments on some particularities of the camera work in the film:

From my memory the framing and the size of the close-ups is similar in *Clear and Present Danger* and *Patriot Games*. In fact, just based on memory, I would say that maybe there are more big close-ups – meaning from the eyes to just above the chin – in *Patriot Games* than there are in *Clear and Present Danger*. The use of an extreme close-up in a film that's shot 2.35:1 – that's anamorphic – can have the effect of heightening the tension. Because of the size of the frame you can still see into the background, but the background image is very much out of focus. Sergio Leone was the first director who really called this technique to my attention: ultra-wide shots followed by extreme close-ups – instant tension. I started doing that on *Dead Calm*.

There is a lot of Steadicam work in the film but none as obvious as when the American helicopters are heard in the distance as they land the Special Forces troops in Colombia. This 360-degree continuous track around Escobedo was executed by Ian Jones, the same Steadicam operator that I employed on *Dead Calm*. I actually brought Ian over from Australia for *Danger*, and he later directed and photographed second unit on *Rabbit-Proof Fence*. Today he's one of Australia's leading DoPs, having photographed many films for Rolf de Heer.

Again, music was of great concern to Noyce.

The sound effects, atmospheres and music make up a lot of my work on every film. Music is an enormous tool for the filmmaker as storyteller. Since *Patriot Games*, the temporary music tracks for most of my films have been constructed by American music editor Joe E. Rand. The music editor provides a track for the various test screenings before the composer has recorded the final score. Joe wasn't available to work with me when I did *Sliver* and I've often wondered whether we would have gotten into the same problems if he had been there. A good music editor can make a huge difference to the way an audience responds to an unfinished film.

When Joe joined me again for *Danger* and first laid up temporary music, I realised how much he was teaching me about my own movie. This time I didn't have time to discuss much of what I wanted, so he took the film straight from the editing room and completely tracked it on his own. Joe literally defined the musical possibilities for the film and allowed the drama and the story to more or less work, even in a first rough cut.

Interestingly, when Harrison Ford was sent that first cut, which he was so ambivalent about, he saw the movie without music. When we test-screened it a few weeks later, the audience saw it with Joe E. Rand's temporary music track. A huge difference.

The official previews – always of utmost importance in Hollywood – were conducted on five different occasions. Four of the previews were held in Los Angeles (on 31 May, and 3, 4 and 5 June) and one in a so-called rural area (on 13 June in Tempe, Arizona). The reports are classified as 'absolutely confidential' and, together with attached tables, are between 22 and 37 pages long. Though legal concerns prevent quotation in detail here, some findings are highly significant:

- The response was in general enthusiastic although there were some remarks about the slow pacing and the length of the film.
- For those who had seen the previous Jack Ryan films, *Clear and Present Danger* was clearly rated the best of the three.
- The unresolved ending particularly irritated the older age group.
- The best-liked scene was, predictably, the ambush in Bogotá, with the computer showdown between Ryan and Ritter a pretty close second.

Additionally, the test screenings were used to determine the look of one of the final key scenes. For the scene very near the end in which Ryan walks out of the president's office, two different versions had been prepared. In the first one, Ryan punches the national security advisor in the face. In the second version he simply walks by. The audience made the final decision, which can be seen in the film.

Compared with the average of 55 that test-screened films score, it received between 74 and 91 per cent 'excellent' and 'very good' ratings, with the ratings being higher for each successive preview screening. Consequently, *Clear and Present Danger* stands out as Noyce's most popular film with the public. The results of the previews were corroborated once it hit the theatres.

The reception to the film was very strong in America. Within a month it had made US$100 million and it went on to make US$127 million in the States.

In the first five days after its release, the film earned US$28.8 million and eventually went on to top *The Hunt for Red October*. This success clearly left in its wake a contented Harrison Ford – who all the time had been engaged in a second vendetta: with Tom Clancy. In an interview conducted in Mexico in January, he 'made no secret of his impatience with Tom Clancy . . . He pulled up short of declaring open war, but intimated that if the author wanted to start one, he was more than ready to oblige.'[8] By the end of the year, the *Forbes* Top 40 list – the benchmark of financial success – showed positions held only a year before had changed drastically. 'While Clancy had slipped to 27th in the table, falling behind arch-rivals Michael Crichton, Stephen King and John Grisham, Harrison had leapt to the very top of the Hollywood heap. His 10th-place ranking and his annual earnings of [US]$27 million – $44 million over two years – dwarfed anything anyone else had earned in acting. The lion's share of his millions had come courtesy of salary and his 11.5 per cent profit-share from *Clear and Present Danger*.'[9]

For once, the critics' responses were pretty much in line with the film's public success story. The more serious national papers, in particular, compared the Noyce film favourably with the Clancy novel. Janet Maslin wrote in the *New York Times*: 'Taming the eyeball-glazing prose of Tom Clancy's *Clear and Present Danger* with the same brisk efficiency they brought to *Patriot Games*, the makers of this latest espionage thriller have made their first-rate work look easy. And clearly, it was anything but . . . As directed by Phillip Noyce . . . this becomes another fast, gripping spy story with some good tricks up its sleeve, and with a much more economical style than that of Mr. Clancy's best-selling novel.'[10]

Even *Variety*, generally critical of Noyce, remarked: 'To [the screenwriters'] credit, and that of director Phillip Noyce, repeating from *Patriot Games*, the far-ranging plot isn't confusing, and many characters who are allotted only a few moments of screen time manage to make the required impression.'[11]

There were, of course, dissatisfied voices as well – particularly those of the Clancy addicts – but they were few. Such criticism usually arises from the necessary condensing of a voluminous novel's story into an action film. Still, mostly they concede, 'It's probably the best adaptation of a Clancy story to date.'[12]

The same two outstanding scenes contributed considerably to the success of the film. Much credit is given to the ambush sequence in Bogotá, but the paying public – generally younger than the film critics – responded much more to the computer chase. The scene has an interesting pedigree:

During pre-production we again turned to the CIA (as we had done for *Patriot Games*) to help us with research. But given that the novel and screenplay described illegal activities, the CIA politely declined to assist. They did allow us one tour, just to catch up on the changes to the architecture at CIA headquarters. Although this was 1994, one of the things I noticed was the introduction of personal computers for storing files. And that observation really did change a crucial part of the film.

In the book, Jack Ryan steals information from the office safe of another CIA worker that allows him to detect an illegal operation involving American troops in Colombia. I realised that with the way things were moving, by the time the film came out our audience would expect that a technology dependent organisation like the CIA would more likely store information on computer. And this led to one of the sequences in the film that I enjoy the most – which I guess is the equivalent of the satellite raid from *Patriot Games*. Ryan is desperately trying to break into his co-worker's computer files and extract the relevant information, while at the same time his opponent has discovered that someone is poking around in his backyard and is trying to delete the files. A marvellous race in cyberspace.

I only started working with a computer very late, in 1999, but it was probably this sequence that gave me the most enjoyment, because I realised in visiting the CIA that we were on the eve of a whole new technological age and way of communicating. And people would be doing this for the next ten or fifteen years – trying to break into computer files and steal information. It was one of the sequences that most pleased audiences as well. When the film was screened around America, applause would break out during the scene and the audience were very, very involved, much more than in a more traditional heist.

It wouldn't be an exaggeration to call this computer chase today's equivalent of an old-fashioned showdown in the dusty main street of a Western town – but instead of guns, the protagonists fight with keyboards. Surprisingly, in the same year, Barry Levinson's *Disclosure* (based on a novel by Michael Crichton) was released, which includes a very similar scene: while Michael Douglas is searching for a certain computer file, Demi Moore is rapidly deleting them. Even if Levinson or his scriptwriter, Paul Attanasio, weren't influenced by Noyce's film (which was released earlier than theirs), it seems clear that at least the time had been ripe for an update of a time-honoured movie cliché.

The computer-hacking showdown aside, key ingredients such as the appearance of voice analysis are proof of Noyce's interest in high-tech surveillance gadgets. With his use of a satellite phone, Noyce was again at the cutting edge of what was in the air technologically.

The voice analysis machine was based on existing technology, but was more complex than anything officially being used in 1994. Now, a decade later, a machine can analyse voices to that degree, but nothing like that was on the market in 1994, at least not that the FBI or the CIA or any of the police agencies would reveal to us.

In the movie – in a scene we didn't take from the book but invented – Cortez is identified by a CIA voice analysis machine. While we were shooting, Pablo Escobar was apprehended and shot dead after using a cellular phone to speak to one of his children. It was later revealed that the Colombian police had identified Escobar's voice using similar equipment to the fictional machine depicted in the film. So, almost the same thing happened in real life, even as we were shooting.

In a so-called techno thriller, we filmmakers have an obligation to make projections, particularly given the speed of technological changes. For example, when working on early scripts for *The Sum of All Fears* we were projecting the types of palm pilot devices that might be available in the following decade, where you'd have mini-computers in your hand that are combined TVs, computers, communicators and telephones. We had developed a palm pilot for the story, which was all of those things, as well as a GPS navigational guidance and so on. This combination wasn't science fiction, just valid future projection.

Usually, I employ two or three researchers on a project. When we're writing the script we'll have a researcher on full-time, then I usually task one of my assistants to do further research. When we were preparing the early screenplays for *The Sum of All Fears*, producing partner Kathleen McLaughlin had been doing a lot of the research. But we also employed a specialist military researcher and someone in Russia to research the current state of the Russian nuclear arsenal.

In a film like *Clear and Present Danger* or *Patriot Games* or *The Sum of All Fears*, there is a level of reality demanded by the audience. They want to be reassured in two ways that seem to be in conflict with each other. They want a good, entertaining escapist story, but given the context in which the stories are told, they have to believe that everything that happens is possible in the real world.

Strangely, the UK version of *Clear and Present Danger* appears to be shorter, though there seems no really convincing reason for this:

I really think it's just credits. When length is calculated in America you measure from the start of the picture to the very end – the logo at the end. It could be that someone is calculating story length – start of story to end of story. I'm not aware of any cuts, not even in Malaysia. The studios are very systematic in their notification of any cuts, even for censorship.

Probably quite naturally, the film fared less successfully outside America, where movies that touch on American politics tend not to be so popular. Critically there were the usual misinterpretations: 'Another one of those thrillers produced with gigantic expenditure which offers nothing else than other thrillers produced with gigantic expenditure.'[13]

Still, foreign critics generally viewed the film favourably: 'A perfectly set up political thriller which shows not only interest in the usual effects of this genre but as well in the conflicts of the characters and their motives and which as well is critical about the authorities of the country.'[14]

It was the film's critical approach to the authorities that many Americans seem to find fascinating and appealing. 'This is the first important negative portrayal of political authority in the movies.'[15] That foreign markets could relate to this too may come as a surprise. But the topic of what authorities tend to do to the public (and to cover up) isn't only relevant to the United States; ethics and morality are subjects of universal interest. This combined with the film's extraordinary action elements, meant *Clear and Present Danger* was predisposed to do well abroad, if not quite as well as in the US. Still, as Noyce explains:

The issues that the film dealt with were obviously much more pertinent to American audiences. The use and abuse of executive power by the US president is something that has been very close to the American experience since Kennedy's days. The idea that the president has absolute power, but is still a human; a human with the power of God. The leaders of other democracies aren't accorded the same demigod status as the President of the United States.

The issue of America as policeman to the world is also something the American audience lives with daily. In a sense it's been fundamental to American foreign policy since the Second World War. This issue of whether to intervene outside America: it was exercised with extreme caution back in the First World War, and then only when pushed in the Second World War. But after leading the victory in 1945, in the next fight, the fight against communism, America saw herself as needing to be vigilant for all of the so-called free world. And that's continued into the post–Cold War era, where America – given that she is the melting pot of all tribes – sees herself as policing the world militarily, politically and morally. But whereas American audiences will view a story about that issue with pride, foreign audiences most usually will see the issue as demonstrating America's hubris, a misguided belief that they know what's good for the rest of the world.

When in the early part of the film the president is speaking to his national security adviser, he says: 'I determine that these drug cartels represent a clear and present danger to the national security of the United States.' That is the code through which he speaks to the adviser to tell him that he's just been authorised to conduct a covert operation – but he hasn't really been told anything. It's a phrase from the book and not a legal term from the Constitution. If the president felt there was a clear and present danger to the people of the United

CLEAR AND PRESENT DANGER 267

States he could authorise a white – as opposed to black – operation. But that would be through authorised, official channels. It may be for certain eyes only, it may be a secret. And the fact that something represents a clear and present danger would be justification for initiating an action. But in this case it's merely the phrase that's used to initiate an illegal black operation.

And that is basically what the film meant to Noyce during its making and why it is still of importance today:

What interested me most at the time was the examination of the use and abuse of executive power by the most powerful country in the world. The power that's vested in the president and the government of America. That's still the most interesting aspect of the film and one which probably has become more relevant in the early part of this century. The fallibility of the human being that is called the President of the United States. The film reminds us that around that person are a collection of equally fallible humans also vested with enormous power. With the current war in Iraq, this issue has perhaps never been more relevant.

---

[1] Cited in Garry Jenkins, *Harrison Ford – Imperfect Hero* (London: Simon & Schuster, 1998), p. 323.
[2] Ibid, p. 324.
[3] Ibid.
[4] Ibid, p. 323.
[5] Director's commentary on *The Saint* DVD.
[6] Jenkins, *Harrison Ford*, pp. 325ff.
[7] Ibid, p. 326.
[8] Ibid, p. 328.
[9] Ibid, p. 330.
[10] Janet Maslin, 'Ryan spies again, this time as C.I.A. battles drug lords', *New York Times*, 3 August 1994.
[11] *Variety* Web archive.
[12] Cited at www.ohms.com/bpst043.shtml.
[13] Walter Schobert (ed.), *Fischer Film Almanach* (Frankfurt: Fischer, 1995), p. 196.
[14] Katholisches Institut für Medieninformation (ed.), *Lexikon des Internationalen Films* (Hamburg: Rowohlt, 1995), p. 2971.
[15] http://support.cas.muohio.edu/eekman/page2.html.

Chapter 13
THE SAINT

It needed just a few more million dollars.

Russian billionaire Ivan Tretiak (Rade Šerbedžija) hoards Moscow's heating oil in order to trigger a revolution that will make him the first post-Soviet tsar. Fearing a new source of energy, he hires the freelancing Simon Templar (Val Kilmer) to steal the formula for the so-called cold fusion from nuclear physicist Dr Emma Russell (Elisabeth Shue) in Oxford. Templar succeeds, but unexpectedly falls in love with Russell. He switches sides and fights to topple Tretiak and save the embattled democratic Russian government.

Noyce had been toying with *The Saint* since his childhood in rural Griffith.

'Like most kids in that town I spent every Saturday afternoon at the movies, swapping comic books and also swapping ordinary novels with other kids. We would bring all our books and our comic books, and at interval you would meet the other kids outside the cinema and you would have a look at what he or she had – "and I'll have one of these, you have one of those" – and in the end you went home with a whole new stack of books to read and comic books to look at until the next Saturday afternoon matinee. And I can remember reading my first Saint story, it was called *The Saint in New York*, and in this story Simon Templar, Leslie Charteris's character of *The Saint*, was hired by a New York businessman to assassinate the six most notorious criminals [in] New York. I remember reading about the first assassination . . . Simon Templar was dressed as a nun, and he waited outside the bad guy's house and then pulled a gun out of his habit and sent the guy to his maker.

You need to understand the context to appreciate why a character like this would appeal to a young Australian boy. Australia was originally established as a penal colony where the best and the worst of Britain's criminals were sent. Some of them for quite serious matters, but mostly for minor infractions. In addition, just about every religious, social and political renegade group that sprang up in the British Isles in the first half of the nineteenth century had a representative among those transportees sent to the penal colonies down in Australia. So I guess you could say that that original experience of transportation of a criminal class produced a certain ethos that still survives today.

So, when I found a guy called Simon Templar, who, like Robin Hood, stole the ill-gotten gains of the evil rich and redistributed them to the poor, but – unlike Robin Hood – who always kept something for himself, who charged a toll, who kept some of the booty, who was, in essence, a criminal, I thought I had found my ideal hero.'[1]

It took many years, however, for Noyce's appreciation to result in adaptation.

After completing *Patriot Games* and before I embarked on *Sliver* I was approached by my compatriot and friend Terry Hayes, who had written the scripts for *Mad Max 2: The Road Warrior* and *Dead Calm,* as well as serving as producer of *The Cowra Breakout* miniseries along with George Miller. Terry was now writing an updated version of *The Saint.*

The film was being produced by legendary producer Robert Evans, who had been an executive at Paramount back in the 1970s, when he worked on the first of *The Godfather* pictures and then produced Roman Polanski's *Chinatown.* Even in his seventies, Evans was extremely handsome and charming, and, as revealed in his autobiography *The Kid Stays in the Picture,* not shy when it came to talking about his sexual exploits in Hollywood.

Originally I was attracted to two ideas. One, being able to bring to the big screen one of my childhood and teen heroes: Simon Templar, The Saint. I had read the books in my pre-teens and watched the television series in my teens. The other thing was the chance to create my own franchise, my own cinema character in an action–adventure story.

For about two or three months I worked with Terry Hayes on a story that revolved around Simon Templar's estranged son discovering that his father was a man called The Saint. The story evolved from the contract Paramount had with the rights holders, one of whom was Roger Moore, who had played Templar in the original TV series. The contract stipulated that Moore should have a significant role in the cinema reincarnation of The Saint. The only way that could happen seemed to be if Roger played the old Saint, and the new Saint was his son.

So I met Roger Moore. I had always found him, even in the TV series, to be rather bland; it appeared to me that nothing was hidden, what you saw was what you got – and when you have an actor who only gives you what's there, your enjoyment is severely limited. There's no subtext to the performance. I felt very uneasy making Roger a major player in a big-budget film, contract or no contract. He's a very straightforward and nice man – but that didn't make him, in his early seventies, a star for movies.

I left *The Saint* to direct *Sliver*, followed soon after by *Clear and Present Danger*. While I was editing *Danger*, John Goldwyn asked if I'd be interested again in *The Saint*. *Fatal Attraction* writer James Dearden had written a new screenplay, which I read along with Terry Hayes's original, which had been set in Russia. I said to Paramount, 'Well, I'm sort of interested, but I do think the story should be set in Russia. I think audiences will be interested in the new Russia.' Also, I wanted to visit Russia and the idea of making a film there intrigued me, even though I knew the place was considered to be quite lawless.

The first problem was that Bob Evans was the producer. I found his editing during post-production of *Sliver* – even though he did it with my knowledge – very offensive and disruptive. It was terribly distracting to have this alternate movie being made down the corridor while I was trying to get the best movie out of the material that we were working with.

Bob's presence had been disruptive and chaotic. The girls, the parties, the photos of naked women were all amusing, but terribly distracting. So I said to Paramount that I didn't want Bob to be the day-to-day producer, because I didn't think I would then be efficient as a director. We weren't a good team; he didn't bring out the best in me. When you're in a vulnerable situation like trying to make a movie, you need a producing partner who is strong but encourages you in the right ways. It seemed to me that Bob encouraged all the wrong things in me.

So the studio approached David Brown, then in his early eighties and still a very, very active producer, a legend. Among other films, he produced *Jaws* with Richard Zanuck. David was brought on to produce on Evans's behalf. Later, David had to split his time between our shoot and *Kiss the Girls*, so Mace Neufeld, my mentor in Hollywood from the Clancy films, came on additionally as one of the producers. Bob Evans was the silent producer, but my contract stipulated he could only work through David Brown.

As Terry Hayes was off writing *Fahrenheit 451* for Mel Gibson, David suggested we bring in Jonathan Hensleigh, and we started to work together on revising the story. Terry's script was the story of a young Simon Templar, who gives up his polo-playing playboy life when he discovers that his estranged father is The Saint, and the two embark on an adventure that takes them to Russia. When the older Saint is killed, young Simon becomes the new Saint.

For inspiration, Noyce went back to the Leslie Charteris novels.

'I realised what we had to do in order to reinvent the Simon Templar character was to tell the story that had never been told – how Simon Templar became a saint. In his hundreds of stories . . . Charteris had never revealed the genesis of the character.'[2]

'We also started to investigate the world of our reincarnated Simon Templar. Taking clues from Leslie Charteris's descriptions of Templar's back-story we decided to make him a master thief who sells his services to the highest bidder. And so I started searching for criminals, thieves. And the guy that seemed to combine most of the credentials that I was looking for had, in fact, started his professional life as a thief and then had been given the opportunity to go to gaol or continue doing the same thing but getting paid for it and working for his country, and had ended up as a special operative for the British Secret Service. This guy detailed many of the techniques he used to break into buildings such as foreign embassies, sometimes to steal or photograph documents, maybe to place listening devices, and he also described technology developed to avoid laser or heat detectors, how to utilise miniature TV cameras to keep track of guards, as well as sophisticated computerised machines developed to quickly crack the locks on safes and safety deposit boxes. And he also described surveillance techniques, which became the basis of the way that Simon Templar's character invades the life of Emma Russell, the character played by Elisabeth Shue.'[3]

Jonathan and I talked and talked, and eventually came up with the basic story that you see in the finished film. Simon Templar is a heartless thief who is hired by a Russian to steal the life's work of a brilliant young female scientist. But in the process of seducing and hoodwinking the woman, the thief himself loses his heart. They end up becoming lovers and he is redeemed by her love. He changes from being a heartless thief to a man who now uses his talents to help people. We wanted to reinvent the story by telling something that had never been told by Leslie Charteris – how Simon Templar originally came to be The Saint.

Jonathan Hensleigh in turn left the project to work on *The Rock*, so I brought in Wesley Strick for further script work on the prologue. I felt that our sympathy for the adult Simon's larceny might be greater if we could establish a compelling back-story. So, growing up in an orphanage, Simon develops a skill for lock picking and breaking-and-entering, both as a way to establish an identity for himself and also to impress a young girl, who dies when one of Simon's pranks goes wrong. When, as an adult, he meets the female scientist, Simon has a feeling, as do hopefully the audience, that she is the same little girl reincarnated, the angel that will be the catalyst for his rebirth.

Our problem for almost a year was finding someone to play Templar. Initially I approached British actors, given that Templar was originally a Brit, and had been played by Brits – and an Australian – in the various TV series. Hugh Grant thought the character was too physical for him, at least in the early draft that he read. (Lots of action sequences that I had storyboarded early in the piece were subsequently cut out for budget reasons.) Ralph Fiennes didn't relate emotionally to the character. For three or four months, Mel Gibson toyed with the idea. Mel was in post-production on *Braveheart* and he wouldn't say yes but he wouldn't say no. Eventually, when Mel was doing press on *Braveheart*, I arranged to get the number of his bodyguard so that the phone could be handed to Mel and I could say: 'Mel, I don't care, but correct me if I'm wrong. You're not gonna do *The Saint*, are you? You don't really wanna do it, do you?' So, I did that and he said, 'No, actually I don't.' I said, 'Good, that's all I need to hear, because now I can move on.' At one stage Russell Crowe approached me to play Templar but I utterly failed to see Russell's potential as a star and rejected him, despite Russell telling me that I would look good later in my career for casting him when he was still a relative unknown. So I turned down the chance to cast both Brad Pitt and Russell Crowe before they were household names.

I also met with George Clooney, who was just beginning the second season of *E.R.* George wasn't a big enough name to carry the projected budget of *The Saint*, but with the frustrations of trying to find a star I decided to jump ship and direct Clooney in his first big feature, *The Peacemaker*, for Steven Spielberg at DreamWorks. But Paramount exercised an option they had on my services and I was forced to return to the task of finding a lead for *The Saint*.

Sherry Lansing suggested Val Kilmer. I sent the script to Val, who was at the time shooting *The Island Of Dr. Moreau* in Australia, outside of Cairns in far north Queensland, so I arranged to fly there. I booked into a hotel and Val rang me and he said, 'Meet me at such and such a place at 7.30,' and I said, 'Fine.' So, at about seven o'clock, I left the hotel to walk down the street to this café and I became aware of someone following me. Each time I would turn there would be no one there, yet I could feel the person right behind me. I went to the café and Val wasn't there. He arrived later and told me he had been following me all the time. He said he had set himself the task of watching me, just to see what it was like to be The Saint.

He basically agreed to do the film and we started pre-production in Moscow, casting and looking for locations.

Just before Christmas 1996 I was to meet Val down on the location of his next film, *The Ghost and the Darkness*, on a game reserve in South Africa. So I left Moscow, flew to London and then on to Johannesburg, where I met up with Wesley Strick, the writer. Val picked us up in his Land Rover at about nine o'clock at night and drove us back to the game reserve, saying he wasn't going to do the film unless we took his ideas for the script seriously. When we finally reached Val's campsite, a luxury tent complete with outdoor bathtub, at about eleven o'clock, Wesley was white with fear because the drive had been so horrendous with Val driving quite recklessly on the rough roads, all the time drinking and smoking and talking.

Val then built a campfire and we sat down to listen to his ideas. He didn't stop talking until the sun came up. At about 9.30, after we'd had a few hours' sleep, Wesley in the tent next door to me, several hundred yards away from where Val was staying, said to me, 'I want to go home. I don't like this guy and I've had enough of this.' And I said, 'Wesley, the only way you can leave now is to walk, and if you do that you're probably going to get eaten because you're surrounded by wild animals. So, you *can't* leave. You've got to see it through with this guy.'

There had been some use of a disguise in early drafts of the script, but the idea that Templar should have multiple personalities – which he uses almost to hide behind – was something that came from Val. I think he had wanted to make a film about a character like that for many years, and he realised that this film was a vehicle for his own obsession. He seemed so insecure about his own ideas and how they might be received that he was way too excessive in terms of forcing them on us, not realising that I was quite open to exchange and change, and not closed or locked into the screenplay that we already had. In fact, when I realised on that first night that the sun was coming up and the actor had been talking about his feelings about the character for six-and-a-half hours, I wasn't horrified but rather amazed that a guy who hadn't even signed the contract yet could be so passionate and deeply into the character even at this point.

'There was Val, living on a nature reserve in a tent and living with him was a wig maker, someone that he had . . . brought out from London to start constructing wigs for the multiple characters that he had started to imagine he might play in *The Saint*. They had already started work on about seven different wigs – a long dark wig, a long blonde wig, a short blonde wig, a bald cap – and I said to Val, "Well, we haven't actually got the go-ahead on this movie yet. Who is going to pay for all this?" And he said, "Don't worry, I'll pay for it if the movie doesn't actually get going. I just wanted to start . . . imagining characters that I could play."

'Also working on the movie was Tim Monich, a really amazing dialect coach who is used by so many actors when they are trying to work in other languages or with other dialects, and together the two of them had begun to collect various accents. The accents and the wigs hadn't yet been put together, but, for example, they had collected the accent of this Spaniard that Tim had met on his travels and Tim would play the various tapes – a Spaniard, an Englishman, a South African, a Russian, an Australian – and Val would sort of listen to the tapes and then he would choose a wig and he would put it on and he would say, "Well, how about this accent with this wig?" And it was free-ranging sort of speculation on what could be. A bit daunting to me, because I already had a screenplay, and now I had an actor who seemed possessed . . .

'So I left Val in South Africa with his dialect coach and his wig maker, and went back to Europe to try to put together the other members of the cast and I thought that I would look not in Hollywood, not in New York, not in London – but to find Russian actors, I thought I would look in the former Soviet Union. In Russia itself, in Yugoslavia, in Czechoslovakia, in Poland, all countries that had, under the Soviet system, had extremely active film industries and with these film industries, produced many fine actors. And in Croatia I found Rade Šerbedžija to play the part of Ivan Tretiak. Rade had starred in over 40 movies in the former Yugoslavia and I first remember him from

Dušan Makavejev's film *Manifesto*, but he probably came to the attention of Western audiences for the first time playing the Macedonian journalist in *Before The Rain*, directed by Milcho Manchevski. For the part of Tretiak's son, Ilya, casting director Elisabeth Leustig searched through the Moscow theatre scene, and at the Moscow Arts Theatre she found Valeri Nikolayev. Valeri had formerly been a hockey player, a stage combat instructor, a gymnast, a dancer, as well as having served in the Soviet Army.'[4]

Val was a nightmare to work with from beginning to end, but I always felt positively towards him. Even when I hated him for his self-centredness, for his selfishness, for his narcissism, for his rudeness, for his lateness – I still always enjoyed working with him. I admired his acting ability, even while I may not have admired his human ability. He was alienating to people and often made it very difficult for others to make rational decisions. It's not necessarily an experience I would like to repeat. But as a director I find it difficult to blame the actors when things go wrong. Your job is to work with people; you are supposedly a svengali. Personalities are very, very different, and what it takes to draw the best performance out of one actor will be different from another. And some actors are good no matter *who* directs them.

I was constantly telling Val that I wanted him to be responsible for his character, to arrive on set and just let his mind speak. Unfortunately I unleashed a monster, because whereas Harrison Ford would come out with lines and ideas that were true to the essence of what we were trying to do, Val unfortunately would often come out with psychobabble completely unrelated to the story and themes. Then I would spend half the day trying to convince him that in this case we weren't going to improvise; that we had to stick to the screenplay.

A rumour circulated during shooting that Kilmer insisted that extras avoid making eye contact with him while on the set. It popped up again in January 2000, when *People* reported it during Kilmer's filming of *Red Planet* in Australia.

'Well, the truth was something like that, but I guess that I was really the culprit, because what I found was that the inexperienced Eastern

European extras who had been chosen for the scene, chosen mainly for their look rather than their film experience, would often try to elevate their roles by sometimes even stopping inexplicably in front of the camera, or trying to establish an artificial relationship with the central performers. So I was constantly having to stop and shout and demand that the extras remain absorbed in their own worlds and not try to elevate their parts.'[5]

The female lead had not been decided on when Noyce met up with Kilmer in South Africa.

When I arrived in Johannesburg, a British Airways representative gave me a note saying, 'Please call Paul Hitchcock' – the line producer – 'in Moscow immediately.' I managed to get through to Paul, who informed me that my casting director, Elisabeth Leustig, had been killed by a hit-and-run driver in Moscow the previous night, while I was in the air, flying to Johannesburg. She was with Joe Nemec, the production designer, who had also designed *Patriot Games*. They were about to cross the road in downtown Moscow and were standing together, only inches apart. But she was struck by the bumper of a passing car and died instantly. She had always supported the idea of Elisabeth Shue playing Emma, particularly when the studio were suggesting Jodie Foster. Elisabeth felt that Jodie didn't have the right sensuality needed to make sparks fly in the relationship. At this point we were still thinking of other actresses, but once Elisabeth died, I became determined to fulfil her wishes and cast Elisabeth Shue, because on the day that I'd left Moscow she had said again to me, 'We've got to get Elisabeth Shue. She's smart and sexy and a good actress. I believe in the relationship.' So, once Elisabeth lost her life, that sort of tipped it for me.

I had admired Elisabeth Shue's performances over the years in many films such as *Adventures in Babysitting*, *Cocktail* and *Soapdish*, and just as I started to search for someone to play Emma Russell I was lucky enough to catch an early screening of Elisabeth's breakthrough performance as the prostitute in Mike Figgis's *Leaving Las Vegas*. She came into my office at Paramount and we sat down and talked about the character for over an hour, and after she left I thought, 'My goodness, I think I've just spent an hour with Emma Russell.' And later I realised that so much of the character as written dovetailed with Elisabeth's own personality. Her intelligence, her infectious enthusiasm, her charm, her vulnerability, but most of all, her completely disarming honesty. Working with Elisabeth, Val seemed to find a vulnerability that was so important to the character of Simon Templar.

During its various script incarnations, the story had been set in New York City and in Russia; at one stage we were preparing to shoot in New York; at another point, Los Angeles, then Toronto. But we ended up changing the story so that it was set in England – London and Oxford – and Moscow, and so we shot on those locations. I moved to England. I ended up renting a house there with my family for three years until Lucia finished high school. Britain is to many Australians the mother country, politically and culturally. I had shot a bit of *Patriot Games* there, but being able to live as well as work in London was very, very attractive. So we filmed for about three weeks in Moscow and for about thirteen weeks in London and Oxford.

In early 1995, together with Jonathan Hensleigh, the second screenwriter, and producer David Brown, I'd gone to Russia for the first time and my impressions had a lot to do with the way the script developed. I remember one evening when we went to a club, it was like a place out of the Wild, Wild West. Rats were racing around a miniature track and people were betting on the outcome of these races. That became the basis of a scene in the movie. I remember middle-aged and elderly gentlemen with their beautiful young girl-friends and trophy wives.

I made contact with Nikita Mikhalkov, Academy Award–winning director of *Burnt by the Sun* (1995), and a much-loved and revered figure in Russian society, both for his artistic and his political endeavours. He has a permanent studio in Moscow, called 3T. He and his team arranged for me to meet a lot of politicians and businessmen. The first thing that I realised was going on, was a massive sell-off of formerly government-owned resources – gas, oil and so on – in supposedly open auctions, but it seemed as though the same groups of people were always winning the bids, so you had this strange phenomenon of new billionaires who were formerly a part of the communist machinery.

I visited the second-in-command of the Russian Communist Party in his casino. He was an avowed capitalist, or at least liked making money, and yet he was also a communist. So, those experiences and meetings became the basis of the Ivan Tretiak character, a former Communist Party boss who now runs an oil and gas company and has political aspirations. It seemed as though Tretiak represented aspects of many of the characters I had met, all rolled into one.

Paramount were very loath to give us permission to shoot in Russia. The American press at the time was full of stories of lawlessness, and I went to many other former Soviet bloc cities – Prague, Warsaw, Berlin – to see if any of them could double for Moscow, realised that they couldn't, and decided to go to battle with the studio. There followed about a six-month debate, as two or three guys from the studio came over to Russia to try to assess how orderly the whole thing could be. As it turned out, the three weeks of shooting in Russia went as smoothly as any three weeks of any shoot that I have ever done. That was despite the heavy snow and rain and all sorts of impediments that in any other situation may have brought shooting to a halt. But given the Russians' resilience and the fact that they're used to inclement weather and hardship that might stop others, and because they have learnt over many years to operate cheaply and efficiently, the shoot proceeded without a hitch. This despite the fact that we were filming in the Kremlin, and took over Red Square for several days and nights, with enormous logistical requirements.

In the end the Russian production team saved us $1 million and even refunded us some of the money that we had paid them for certain costs. The Russian experience was completely the opposite of everything all the naysayers had predicted.

Noyce's experience of filming in Russia was, indeed, one of the most amazing parts of his career to date: the challenges of shooting a movie in a country that was being torn apart by contradictions, by the tensions between communists, nationalists and the Russian Mafia. As it turned out, Noyce's ability to relate to the people working with him – both on a professional and a personal level – earned him a dedication that would be hard to find in a Western country. And it opened doors that helped him to achieve wonders that, unfortunately, only a few people may have noticed while watching the film. As well, it earned him the compliment, in August 2000 during the Moscow Film Festival, of a retrospective screening of his major works and a major party to celebrate the tenth-anniversary of the Russian release of *Dead Calm*, with Noyce, Sam Neill and Billy Zane all in attendance. Noyce left the shoot of *Rabbit-Proof Fence* for this occasion, which required him to fly on seven different aircraft from the Flinders Ranges to Moscow. The partying with his Russian co-workers went on almost incessantly for about 30 hours, before Noyce hopped on another plane to start the arduous trip back to South Australia.

Tatiana Petrenko, a director of documentaries, started out as Noyce's Russian interpreter but within days was made his Russian adviser. Her memories are fond and very detailed: 'What struck me at first sight was that Phillip showed great knowledge of and great interest in Russia. And Russia at that time was changing so rapidly that it was difficult even for us Russians to grasp the changes. But since he was coming to Moscow rather often during that period, he would notice every change that was happening and he would make you aware of it. At some point I thought, "He knows my country better than I do." He saw things from a very different point of view, which made every contact with him so interesting and so enjoyable.

'I also realised from the start that he's a very, very interesting film director. Since my background is film, it was a particular pleasure for me to work with him – it was like going to film school again. He immediately sensed my special interest, having been trained as a director though I was taken on as his interpreter. My interest was pure, with nothing financial in it.

I agreed to do this just because my friends from 3T Studio talked me into helping Phillip, and Phillip appreciated all the knowledge of Moscow I could share with him. I organised a number of meetings so that Phillip could meet people from all the different social layers in Russia at that time – from bandits and racketeers, up to New Russians – the richest guys in the country, and then up to the political elite. For example, we met Gaidar, who had been the prime minister and had just been sacked. We went to his office and spoke to him. And then we went to see Vladimir Semago, who's a communist in the Duma. But at the same time he is one of the richest people in Moscow. Phillip said, "He is exactly like Tretiak."

'Sometimes it was very scary, because Phillip is fearless. On Soviet Army Day, 23 February, a huge meeting of thousands of communists took place in Pushkin Square. They were all very angry and scary, and were going to march down to Red Square – they were former officers and Cossacks. Phillip wanted us to be in among the crowd, holding up banners showing Tretiak's face, so that it would kind of be documentary footage that he could shoot for our movie.

'I was scared to death and tried to talk him out of it, because I knew those guys could easily kill you. And Leonid Vereschagin, from 3T Studio, said: "Phillip, you have to be very cautious. We can do it as a documentary; they would love it. But we definitely can't have anyone holding up a portrait of Tretiak." The whole idea was really dangerous. We ended up applying to the highest level of authority for permission and for security for our people, but they said they couldn't guarantee we would be safe. Phillip said, "I'm going to do it anyway." All of us Russians were scared, because we knew we would be risking our lives.

'We gathered at Pushkin Square with our posters of Tretiak, neatly folded and closed. Phillip put up the cameras all the way down for the rally. He told us beforehand that all our stuntmen would protect us. But instead, he placed all those stuntmen to protect the cameras – and we were left naked. We said,

"We can't do it, Phillip. We'll be dead in half an hour." When we said that, he said he would do it himself. "Give me the poster," he said. "I'm going." I called 3T and told my husband, Sergei Gurevich, what Phillip was planning to do. So Sergei and Leonid Vereschagin rushed to Pushkin Square. Phillip said, "Tatiana, are you with me?" I said, "Okay. Farewell to my life, but of course I am with you." I was nearly crying, I was so scared. I had two kids at home. And then he said, "Leonid, are you with me?" Leonid stepped forward, saying, "Okay, Phillip." Then Phillip said, "Sergei, so you are not with your wife?" Sergei had no choice but to take a poster of Tretiak and be in that crowd. Then Leonid luckily met the officer who was in charge, a very nationalistic guy. He said to him, 'We're from Nikita Mikhalkov's studio and we want to film a documentary of your march, sir." "Okay," he said. "Stand in front of these officers who are opening the parade." So there we were, standing just behind their first line of officers and just in front of the Cossacks. Can you imagine? We were all trembling.

'We started marching. When we reached the spot where our cameras were positioned we held up our posters of Tretiak that you can see in the film. Immediately, the Cossacks were going, "Who is this? Whose portrait are they carrying?" And maybe it was Leonid who said, 'It's a Serb communist who wants to support your march." And somebody approached my husband, who said, "It's Stalin's son, who you know wants to support you." By this time we had the footage that Phillip wanted.

'They realised it was all bullshit and we were immediately surrounded by very tough guys and somebody shouted, "Traitors! Kill them!" And they set upon our men, who were then saved by the Special Security Forces who were in plain clothes. Leonid has probably never told Phillip that he secretly arranged to have this protection. The Security Forces guys moved in between us and the Cossacks, saying they were from the KGB. They pretended to arrest our guys but actually saved their lives. "You men, carry on with your march," they said. "We'll take care of these bastards."

'You can't imagine what it was like. The storyboard artist, who had also been there, was hysterical in the car later. The Russian location manager was found curled up in a corner, trembling. I will never forget it. I am telling you this story to illustrate what a great director Phillip is. When he wants something, he will do anything to get it. And after that, somehow we felt like a family. I will never believe that he wasn't scared deep in his heart. But isn't it amazing that he got all the footage he wanted?

'He didn't use extras for this scene, because he wanted it to be authentic. He said, "You can never find extras with those faces." Because the faces were very special. It was all their lives behind those faces, and Phillip wanted it to be authentic. That's why he took all those risks. I remember that as I started marching I thought, "How nice, my mother is at home with my children." I thought it would be the end of it. At the same time I couldn't refuse Phillip. I can't explain it to you. Actually, I didn't go with him to Chechnya, probably because of that experience. I just couldn't risk it; my children were too young. Phillip just wanted it to be really authentic. He's like that. He's always trying to do the best.

'Production services for *The Saint* were provided by 3T. The head of 3T, Nikita Mikhalkov, is an extraordinary person, a living legend in this country. His father was a very famous poet during the communist era and won all these awards and was the author of the state anthem of the former USSR. But Nikita himself comes from what I would call a Russian heritage, because his grandfather was a very famous painter, as was his great-grandfather. He's something that has to be, you know, preserved, taken care of, and all the people love him. Even the people in the government adore his films, and they love him. So Nikita's name opened a lot of doors for Phillip in Moscow. We were able to achieve a lot of things through Nikita, such as getting permission directly from Prime Minister Yeltsin's office to film in Red Square for six nights and a day. So, Phillip got Red Square. I don't remember any Russian film director being allowed to do the things Phillip did in Red

Square. (You would be allowed to do things lower down, as probably you can see in many Hollywood pictures like *Air Force One*. But that was not really in Red Square – it is what we call the slope, between St Basil's and the River Moskva.) We were able to film in the square right opposite the president's offices. Phillip didn't even use all the opportunities 3T provided him with, such as the opportunity to film inside the Kremlin, in places where the public doesn't have access. That was all fixed by 3T. But then, for some reason, those interior scenes were moved to London and they were filmed on a sound stage. But being able to visit the Kremlin helped him to create a very authentic atmosphere on the sound stage.

'Things happened on *The Saint* that had never happened before. The only occasion when armoured vehicles are permitted to be in Red Square is Soviet Army Day during the parade. Unless Phillip Noyce is shooting there. It's unbelievable. We had several armoured vehicles. Phillip and I went to see the vice-commandant of the Kremlin, who even ended up giving us permission to fire a gun in the square. We assured him that it would be just one shot from a gun. On the night, there were shots being fired all over the place!

'3T also got permission for Phillip to build Tretiak's mansion just 100 metres from the Russian White House, the seat of the government. Again, that was unbelievable. He was allowed to build it on the site of an actual working power station in the centre of Moscow. These things are like military objects in Russia, because if you destroy them it means the central city has no heat, no electricity. And then he was able to explode a Range Rover in the centre of Moscow near the Peking Hotel. 3T got permission for him to do that. It's the only time in the history of Russian cinematography that that's happened. For 3T it was a great experience, too. They were forced to find ways to do things just because Phillip wouldn't take no for an answer. They didn't want to lose face with Phillip, or with the world of cinematography. And it was a kind of ambition for them to manage to do things.

'My children were very interested in what was happening during that production. Alex, who was eight or nine years old, wanted to come to Red Square and spend a night with us while we were shooting there. There was a lot of stuff he was interested in – cameras, tanks, armoured vehicles. And of course, as a little boy, he was very interested in the gunfire and explosions. So one night I took him there and there was a lorry for Phillip to sit on, so that he was a bit higher than everybody else. And the moment Alex came on to the set, Phillip, who hadn't met him before, felt what the small boy was feeling. He immediately stood up from his director's chair that said 'Phillip Noyce', put that little boy in it and then continued his work. So Alex was in the director's chair that night, kind of supervising what was happening on Red Square. I don't think he will ever forget it in his life. For him it was something very great.'

'Another thing about Phillip that surprised us Russians was his ability to work around the clock. We had several nights when we had night shooting. During the day we did a lot of other things, but then after we finished shooting we went to see the daily rushes and then we had to go to the set again to change sets, or to do other things. And it was very interesting for us to see the new working methods in cinematography. Everyone from 3T who worked with Phillip loves him, and remembers him fondly. He would come up to everyone, shake their hands, say, "How are you?", explain what he wanted from them. He's so nice to people. They'll never forget their experience of working with Phillip Noyce. And Russian actors love him because for them it was a great chance to show that Russian acting was good enough. And, of course, they were happy working with him.[6]

Originally the project was much more of an action–adventure story. The original budget was well over US$80 million and contained many elaborate action set pieces.

In fact, looking at the very elaborate storyboards, it's obvious that big chunks of highly promising action had to be dropped. The headlines for the outtakes from shooting read: Jillian's parachute landing sequence; Templar's parachute jumping sequence; Motorcycle stunt sequence; Train to St Petersburg sequence; Kids on the rooftop, Leningradsky Station. And then there are the outtakes from the script including: US Embassy street sequence; Lear Jet landing; Tretiak headquarters exploding.

Sherry Lansing came to Paramount when I was shooting *Sliver*, so I had already effectively done two films with her. She sort of had in her mind certain budget figures according with the so-called bankability of the leading men. So, for Mel Gibson I could have a budget of above US$80 million, but for Val Kilmer it had to be down in the fifties somewhere. She had given me budget figures all the way down to U$40 million. I knew I couldn't make the film for $40 million. I think it ended up costing about $58 million, and may have gone into the low sixties by the time we were finished. Fifty-eight million was the projected budget.

In the end I think the budget was cut a little bit too extremely, because the film was always on the edge of being thrilling and having huge scope, but it never quite made it. It keeps promising, but doesn't quite deliver. I think it needed just a few more million dollars, because it takes so much just to get your crew out into the field, hire your actors and everything, and then there's a certain point where every new penny goes straight on to the screen. It's like once you've built a house it doesn't look any good until you've put the paint on it. Well, this film is a bit like a house that hasn't quite been decorated properly, and a couple of the rooms were cut off as well. But there it is, it's a house, you can live in it, it sort of works – but it's not really whole.

Production was centred at Pinewood Studios, about an hour north of London. The principal reason I used Phil Meheux as a DoP, apart from his enormous talent for lighting action films, was that he was British. I was shooting out of Britain, with a lot of shooting in London, and I needed to get a complete camera crew out of the UK.

Vilmos Zsigmond and Phil were the only non-Australian cinematographers I have used in my career, and the British Phil was a lot easier for me to communicate with than the Hungarian Vilmos. Phil did a good job, but still I felt disconnected working with him. You can never say all the things that need to be communicated with a cine-matographer – a lot of it is just based on shared aesthetics and life experience. So, inevitably, it's much more productive to work with someone of your own nationality and background.

The music was again by Graeme Revell, the avant-garde composer whom I had offered the job of scoring *Dead Calm* after I'd listened to some of his recordings. And, of course, he's gone on to have a very, very full career in Hollywood feature films as a composer. He came over to live in London for a few months while working on the score. I was very happy with his work.

Under the complicated financing of the film all post-production also had to be carried out in the UK, but of course test-screenings, due to Paramount's feeling that they could only trust the American audience, took place back in Los Angeles. So we brought the film over to America in late 1996, and we screened it for the studio the night before we were to screen it to the public. At the end of the first screen-ing Sherry Lansing was genuinely crying. She said it was a brilliant film and it was *Doctor Zhivago*-ish and could achieve a US$200 million box office. Sherry was crying because Elisabeth Shue's char-acter had died in that version and Simon Templar had gone on to avenge her death and bring her dream of cold fusion to fruition. Sherry left messages all over town with various people announcing what a brilliant film it was.

I remembered what had happened with *Sliver*, and the more she said that it was great, the more I thought, 'Oh, my God. This is terri-ble. This is gonna be terrible, it really is.' I just had a bad feeling. I said to Terry Rawlings, the editor, 'Just wait till tomorrow.' So we screened it the next night to a recruited audience. It scored 69, which is right on that magic line where it's not really a great score, but it's not bad; it's in the area where the studio thinks, 'Well, we can get this to really work.'

So, for the next six weeks we would go back to London to make changes, then fly back and screen it again, but all the cutting didn't really change the movie. It would go up two points, down three, up a point, then we would cut a scene out, or restore a different scene. But in the end the test scores remained in the mid to high 60s.

Then, for one of the screenings, I produced another version where I kept Elisabeth Shue alive, achieved just by changing the order of scenes. And suddenly the score jumped. That raised a whole problem because clearly the audience found that story more enjoyable than the one we had been screening.

Maybe it was also because the tone of the rest of the film was at odds with the terrible reality of the heroine dying. But also I think the problem was in the structure. Emma's death occurred at the end of the second act, a full 40 minutes before the end. If a death occurs at the beginning of a story, then the film becomes about adjusting to death, but if at two-thirds of the way through a main character dies, the audience may feel that the film has lost its momentum and focus unless the story that follows really resolves all the issues surrounding that death.

I spent two or three weeks thinking, 'What am I going to do here? On the one hand I've set out to make an escapist entertainment, so it's almost like this film has failed if the audience doesn't respond to its main elements. So should I stick to the original structure, or should I change it?' And finally I thought, 'Well, the change is in the spirit of the movie. The tone of the film will be consistent, whereas in the original there were two movies: a light-hearted film about two lovers getting together and then there's another film about someone who is revenging the death of a lover. Two different movies.'

I think the problem may have been inherited from way back at the beginning of the process, when Jonathan Hensleigh and I sat down and worked out the architecture of the film. We tried to imagine the story in its bare bones and we'd always thought of it as having a death at the end of the second act. And maybe it would have worked if the death had been closer to the end of the movie – if she died, for example, just before the climax – and then, propelled by what has happened, Simon Templar does something which provides his final canonisation as The Saint.

There was another problem. The audience clearly didn't feel that Val Kilmer showed enough emotional response to the loss of the woman he loved. It's a failure in direction and performance, because I think the audience felt that the character didn't show enough heart-felt emotional loss, he didn't seem as remorseful and shattered as they themselves felt. I should have pushed Val to open himself up more.

For Noyce, script development is a process of carefully working out the psychology of the characters, the details of the subplots and so on, so it may seem surprising that Noyce might have overlooked this aspect of the main character. But, on the other hand, the film has a bit of a comic-strip character that Noyce says was always intended. His Simon Templar can jump from high-rise buildings or produce a new wig out of thin air. And a comic-strip hero doesn't really deal with emotions.

Death, for such a sweet, angelic person like the character Elisabeth Shue was playing, is very real. At the time, I convinced myself that the tone set by her death was at odds with the comic-book tone of the whole film.

Anyway, I changed it and that became the version that was finally released. That required shooting some new shots of Emma in that lecture at the end and a different ending with Templar in the audience and escaping.

Later I did feel resentful that Sherry Lansing had initially been so enthusiastic about the movie, only to eventually talk me into cutting those things which had most moved her when she first saw the film. As with *Sliver*, Sherry had been influenced by the results tabulated by Joe Farrell at test-screenings.

Noyce wasn't absolutely convinced that this was the right decision:

'In the months since, I have often asked myself: did we make the right choice? Well, the original ending was saved and some time in the future, maybe yet another special-edition video will appear and we will all be able to decide.'[7]

Due to financial considerations and climatic constraints, almost every contemporary visual effects technique was used in the film. 'We shot blue screens for stunts and falls and car driving sequences,' the film's visual effects supervisor would later say. 'We used motion control, we added textures to set pieces, removed wires, we added birds and vehicles and clouds, we inserted computer screens, we inserted imagery in the huge screens in Red Square, we did matte paintings, explosions, all sorts of things, it was just a huge asset to the production. And then, of course, the big sequence that we got involved in was the crowd replication in Red Square. Two thousand extras had to be expanded to look like a wild crowd of 500,000 . . . We determined that the smallest group of extras that we could get away with was 2500 people and that in one night we would have to shoot them in at least fifteen different positions, like a checkerboard . . . By the time we actually started filming we really only had about five hours to do what I believe is the largest crowd replication scene ever done for a film.'[8]

There is one scene in the film that is supposedly set in Berlin – or rather, Berlin's Tempelhof Airport. In the German-dubbed version, however, it looks like Copenhagen Central train station, and Kilmer talks with an odd Danish accent.

Well, I'm sure they changed it because it didn't look like Tempelhof for Germans. Actually, you know why they changed it? Because he is pretending to be a gay German and they thought the German audience would get upset at this.

However, a different second version of the film exists as a kind of gift to his Russian co-workers.

After the sequence near the end, in Red Square, where the cold fusion machine works and causes a riot, originally Tretiak and his son had retreated back to their mansion beside the river, and they were followed by Templar and the Russian Army, and while the army pounded the mansion with tank shells, Templar went inside to capture Ilya. Now, once we cut out the fact that Ilya, the son, had killed Elisabeth Shue's character, the need for this man-on-man fight was lost and it just felt like the film was more whole without the sequence. Again the sequence was a carry-over from the original movie that I had set out to make, which was full of wonderful elaborate action set pieces. Anyway, I decided to cut the sequence from the film, even though it was the most expensive action sequence. But because so much work had gone into shooting in Russia with the army, and people had gone through such elaborate arrangements to facilitate all this, I decided to put the scene back in the Russian version of the film, so that the people who had worked with me could enjoy all the work they'd done. So there exist two versions of the film in release.

'A director forms close relationships on every film, but perhaps because of the time you spend locked up together in a tiny room over such a long period, the strongest memories are etched from a director's relationship with his film editor. On *The Saint* I was lucky enough to work with Terry Rawlings, editor of such movie greats as *Chariots of Fire*, *Alien* and *Blade Runner*. Nowadays most films are edited not on film, but by utilising computer editing machines where the editor doesn't actually have physical contact with the celluloid. That job is left to assistants who conform the film to match the computer printouts generated by the editor. But Terry Rawlings is one of the old school: he cuts film. And the joy of working with him was that just when I thought that I knew all the editing tricks, this guy took me back again to film-editing kindergarten. And he did this by putting me back in touch with the medium itself. You see, so many of the techniques used in filmmaking today have worked to produce a generation of film directors who are making TV for a big screen. Those directors who I remember as having inspired me to make movies in the first place, like David Lean or Akira Kurosawa, were inspirational because they produced breathtaking wide-screen images, worthy of the name "cinema". They didn't compose these shots by watching a TV monitor while they were shooting or editing from a TV screen. And for reminding me of that, I say thanks to Mr Terry Rawlings and his 1960s-era upright Movieola film-editing machine.'[9]

The Saint was released in the United States in early April 1997.

The film eventually took around US$60 million both in the US and outside America – about $122 million worldwide – which meant that it would have made a very small profit in the end, with that profit coming from TV and video earnings.

The critics were lukewarm, but the exit polls were among the best I ever had, surprisingly. On the opening night, they poll the people who actually go to the cinema, around the country, and this was 91 per cent 'very good' or 'excellent'.

And mixed – or undecided? – the critics were, indeed. *Variety* set the tone: 'A generic suspensor that doesn't taste bad at first bite but becomes increasingly hard to swallow, *The Saint* comes off more as a pallid imitation of Paramount's Eurothriller *Mission: Impossible* than as anything resembling the further adventures of Leslie Charteris's charming rogue.'[10]

The more positive critics focused on the qualities of Val Kilmer, as well as the film's lack of sensational stunts. 'There isn't a contemporary film actor more crafty than Val Kilmer – or one who reveals less of his true self. That is why Kilmer is so perfectly cast as Simon Templar', according to Edward Guthmann in the *San Francisco Chronicle*. Sometimes even Noyce is getting the honours: 'Masterfully assembled by director Noyce', Leslie Rigoulet wrote in *Film Scouts*; 'Noyce keeps things moving at a kinetic, involving pace', said Desson Howe of the *Washington Post*.

The Saint starts with an intertitle stating, 'Once Upon a Time in the East' – even though the film has no ties whatsoever with the Far East.

A European like Simon Templar growing up in the Far East could have been any nationality – Russian, Australian, English, American, German. His parents could have come from anywhere. We wanted the reinvented Templar to have an undefined nationality.

The first scene of the film, set in a Catholic orphanage, is only slightly related to the main story – in a similar vein to the dramaturgic structure of some James Bond films, which offer one-and-a-half plots for the price of one. But more than this, it is a clever trick to let audiences know about the private life and background of the hero. Slightly tilted angles give the sequence a dream-like quality. In fact, as many critics observed, the opening is promising: witty, with impressive images.

The same can be said of the 'proper' opening sequence when Templar is portrayed 'at work' in a Moscow high-rise. 'The agile, stylish camera of Phil Meheux, the flowing editing (Terry Rawlings) and the music of Graeme Revell meet to form a breathless rhythm that doesn't allow for boredom, not even for one single second,' a German critic remarked.[11]

But soon, it seems, the plot gets a little lost, apparently no longer going anywhere. This is partly caused by an overall indecisiveness: *The Saint* looks like an action movie but is, in fact, a love story. Or vice versa, if you like. The film is partly a comic strip, also. The action component works well; not so the love story, unfortunately.

In the technically accomplished action sequences Noyce's skills are, as always, obvious. Sure, there are chase sequences (particularly the one in the middle of the film), a bit of shooting and the inevitable jumping from roof to roof. But the real strength of these sequences is their revealing exteriors. (By contrast, all the interiors were shot at Pinewood Studios in the UK.) Noyce 'captures an atmosphere of menace and decay in the streets of Moscow',[12] revealing his deep insight into the situation in contemporary Russia. But the average movie-goer probably doesn't appreciate, or even care, that certain shots were filmed outside the Russian president's office in the Kremlin; that community apartments really do look the way they do in the film; or that the New Russians really do spend their money on mistresses and rat races. In short, the average movie-goer is unlikely to care about the lengths Noyce went to, to portray a Russia in transition. Film, after all, is about make-believe.

The love story fares worse, because we are not given a convincing reason why Templar feels differently about Emma Russell than he did about any of the many girls he has used and discarded in the past. Perhaps she reminds Templar of his long-lost first love. She, a nuclear physicist, offers to reveal the secrets of cold fusion to him after a one-night stand. Surely she didn't need to conceal the secret formula in her bra! Other details, like Russell's heart condition, are introduced and not developed. Even allowing for problems caused by the late change of ending, all of the above surely contributed to the mixed perceptions people have of the film. 'The show has no character worthy of our love or hate,'[13] as Steve Rhodes put it on the web. But at least, thanks to Noyce's skills, in the romantic scenes Elisabeth Shue looks gorgeous in close-up. This is truly erotic.

Val Kilmer's use of different appearances adds significantly to the film's comic-strip character. His make-up and disguises are simply extraordinary. Kilmer's acting divides public opinion, with some finding him hilariously funny; others self-indulgent. In any case, there is some justification for the perception that Templar 'seems more like a disguise fetishist than a formidable international operative'.[14]

With the many different appearances he could have had, why does Templar approach Dr Emma Russell in the guise of a long-haired hippie?

He saw a photograph on the wall of a romantic poet with long hair, and he also saw a photograph of her father with the same sort of hair.

As well, Lord Byron is on the cover of a book on Emma's bed, together with some delicate lingerie.

He conjures up the idea of this ethereal, romantic guy, because he figures that that is the sort of person that is going to appeal to her.

Some of the flaws – or rather, inconsistencies – in the film can hardly be attributed to budget cuts. When talking to each other, sometimes the Russians speak Russian – creating the need for subtitles – and sometimes they use English. 'If it was far-fetched for Tretiak to offer big bucks in the first place for what was only an alleged formula, it is ludicrous when he brings pressure to bear to make cold fusion work on a 12-hour deadline after decades of frustrating failure, then laughable when the strongman pins his hope for a coup on a public demonstration of cold fusion (or lack of same) at a rally in a jammed Red Square.'[15]

After a long chase, Templar can only escape Ilya Tretiak by diving into the icy waters of a canal. Near to death by freezing, he then huddles in a hidden pocket of an apartment house, warmed solely by Emma's bare body. Only minutes later, while Ilya and his cronies search the house, they are given away. But by now Templar has recovered his strength and his clothes are dry, so off he and Emma go into the Moscow winter. *Chain Reaction*, by Andrew Davis, released in August 1996, eight months before *The Saint*, contains a sequence similar to the one described, when Keanu Reeves and Rachel Weisz break through a frozen lake into icy water. The film's premise concerns cheap energy made from water, and its heroine is a female scientist, Dr Lily Sinclair. The similarities end there, however, with *The Saint* being a superior film, despite its flaws.

The character of Ilya may seem a bit out of step with the usual picture of the Russian environment, but Noyce insists that 'he is based on a lot of Russian guys that I have met, the young ones . . .' Costume designer Marlene Stewart added that the sixties gangster look is definitely fashionable: 'They are Russian street boys and have very sharp suits. They are sophisticated and sleek in a very dark way.'[16]

In Noyce's films, we have come to expect surveillance cameras and other high-tech gadgetry. Simon Templar's equipment includes special goggles, and a penknife that doubles as a blowtorch, compass, a lock pick, flashlight and camera. He uses an Apple Powerbook and a Nokia palmtop computer to check his ever-expanding Swiss bank account.

'I just stumbled on it by accident. One of our computer guys was rigging up Simon's laptop for use in the scene and I noticed that he was carrying with him this little portable computer phone. And I said, "Why don't we use that prop instead of the laptop?" And he said, "Well, it's not a prop, that's my personal phone." I said, "Hey, it's your personal phone, but it's better than any imagined prop, so let's use it."[17]

With the Nokia 900 we were, without realising it, maybe eighteen months ahead of the market. At the time you couldn't access the Internet on it, so we invented this portable phone that allows you to do so.

The Saint at the time was an opportunity to try to create a franchise. Although in the end, what I really found attractive about it was the opportunity to choose my own location to set the story. So, it became as much about the adventure of making the film as the adventure of the story of the film. It was as much about the adventure *off* the screen as the adventure *on* the screen. I satisfied my curiosity about post-Soviet Russia during the making of that movie and now I would say that the escapist popcorn elements that were necessary to deliver the franchise were probably inconsistent with my real interests. So, it was an awkward fit for me as a filmmaker. The combination of elements never quite coalesced. I wasn't able to deliver the necessary comic-book elements because in truth I wasn't really interested in those elements.

[1] Director's commentary on *The Saint* DVD.
[2] *The Saint* press kit, p. 4.
[3] Director's commentary on *The Saint* DVD.
[4] Ibid.
[5] Ibid.
[6] Tatiana Petrenko interview.
[7] Director's commentary on *The Saint* DVD.
[8] Robert Grasmere's commentary on *The Saint* DVD.
[9] Director's commentary on *The Saint* DVD.
[10] Todd McCarthy, *Variety*, 6 April 1997.
[11] Thomas Wollmann, www.artechock.de
[12] Edward Guthmann, *San Francisco Chronicle*, 4 April 1997.
[13] Cited at www.all-reviews.com/videos-2/saint.htm.
[14] Roger Ebert, *Chicago Sun-Times*, 4 April 1997.
[15] McCarthy.
[16] *The Saint* press kit, p. 11.
[17] Director's commentary on *The Saint* DVD.

Chapter 14
THE BONE COLLECTOR

Unfortunately, the movie previews were incredibly successful.

Lincoln Rhyme (Denzel Washington), one of the world's foremost forensic detectives, is paralysed from the neck down after an accident while on duty. Though suicidal at first, he is reluctantly recruited to aid a rookie cop, Amelia Donaghy, (Angelina Jolie) in her investigation of a series of brutal killings. The killer, who is obsessed with old New York, uses the guise of a taxi driver to abduct his victims and leaves clues behind that only a brilliant mind can interpret.

In 1990 I had been approached by New York producer Martin Bregman to work on a comedy script set on the moon, *Pluto Nash*. Never having directed a comedy, naturally I was intrigued. The film was eventually made years later and released with disastrous results in 2002. Directed by Ron Underwood and starring Eddie Murphy, it's the story of a nightclub owner up on the moon colony some years in the future. Back then we could never get the script to work, but in late 1997 Martin Bregman rang again with another project. Affected by polio at an early age, Martin had developed a bulldog approach to life. His offers were always hard to dismiss.

The screenplay Martin sent me was by Jeremy Iacone, adapted from the novel *The Bone Collector* by Jeffrey Deaver. I thought, another serial killer film, not for me . . . how can I better *Seven*? After a few days I had second thoughts, because, while I wasn't interested in the serial killer story, the characters remained with me: Lincoln Rhyme, the bed-bound quadriplegic, and Amelia Donaghy, his protégé. There was something about the spirit of each of them and the relationship that the screenplay described that really attracted me.

In some ways it was a variation on the same relationship I'd attempted in *The Saint*. A man starts the movie with one intent, changes his life's direction and, in this case, his death direction, as a result of his deepening relationship with a woman. It's also a story of resurrection – he wants only to die and then finds the will to live again. And she finds her vocation and what she really wants to do with her life. In *The Saint*, Simon Templar found that he didn't want to be a sinner, but a saint. He found his vocation as a born-again Robin Hood. The two films had similar themes and in some ways I think it was because I felt *The Saint* wasn't successful in exploring those themes that I wanted to try again to conquer them.

The price for doing that was I had to make a serial killer film, which obviously I could accomplish with my thriller experience, but I never really enjoyed that part of the story, which shows in the final film. It's the relationship, and watching the two actors work with each other, that propels the viewer through the film. On the other hand, it's a relationship that's told against the story of the hunt for a serial killer, and maybe that setting allows the story of a quadriplegic who wants to die to be something everyone can watch. Movies about quadriplegics aren't usually the stuff of bestsellers, but this film has been quite successful. Maybe the formula setting was a way in which the unusual relationship and characters could be digested by a mass audience.

By this time, Noyce had changed studios. After generating US$300 million in domestic takings alone for Paramount, he switched to Universal.

When I first came to Los Angeles I chose to live in Hollywood, which is near the Paramount studios – just down the road. Paramount is in Hollywood, I lived in Hollywood, so one thing led to another.

Paramount offered me a contract to stay there after *The Saint*. Unfortunately, the deal stipulated that I direct a set number of films for Paramount, which could have forced me to do a film chosen by the studio. I can make bad choices all by myself but if, like a director of the 1940s, I'm forced to choose only from studio-nominated projects, then perhaps I could really get into trouble. On the other hand, that studio system produced some classic movies, even where the directors were more or less assigned to projects.

My assistant at the time, Jonathan Goldman, showed me a tape of a Home Box Office movie called *Gia*, the true story of a famous supermodel back in the seventies, who had succumbed to drug addiction, contracted HIV and eventually died of AIDS. The lead actress was someone I hadn't really heard of before, Angelina Jolie. I was only vaguely aware of her from the poster for a film by Iain Softley called *Hackers*, which she starred in with her first husband, Jonny Lee Miller.

Martin Bregman, who was really enthusiastic about Angie for the part of Amelia Donaghy, arranged a meeting and once I had met her I thought she was perfect. It was a no-brainer. She oozed talent and charisma; some people have it, some don't. She had spunk, fire, youth, something *je ne sais quoi* – the unknown quality that would make people want to see her in this movie.

However, the studio was reluctant because of her lack of proven star power. The script was relatively hot around Hollywood; there aren't many good female roles. Usually you have to push any script, but in this case people were pushing themselves on us. A lot of young actresses wanted this role and some of them were very well known – like Demi Moore. The studio was jumping up and down saying, 'Demi will do it for a million bucks, her usual price is much, much more. You've got to take that.' It's sort of like when you hear people who have gone to a dress sale saying, 'I bought this dress for $1000, and the usual price is $3000,' as if the sale price isn't still a lot of money. We told them they could get Angelina for $350,000, and she was going to be worth more than anyone else, because she's right for the part. I said, 'Look, I'm telling you this is a star – not now, not in a year, but in a year and a half when the film comes out.' But Universal would willingly have paid a lot more in the belief that what's proven makes them sleep easier; a known star provides more of a guarantee that people will actually turn up.

In terms of the male lead, I thought, 'We may have a real problem.' You've got a guy who spends the whole story lying in bed, and half the movie wanting to end his life. He can't move from the neck down. That could be a real downer. The movie is going to cost over US$40 million. To make its money back, it's got to take over US$100 million worldwide. So casting is crucial. The terrible reality of quadriplegia is mixed with the terrible fantasy of a serial killer movie. If you are seen by the audience to be belittling the experience of a quadriplegic, then they are going to reject the whole movie.

So I asked myself, 'How do I make an audience want to see this?' And always my thought was that the *only* way was to get a great performance from the actor playing Rhyme. This part gave the actor a stage from which to mesmerise the audience with technical and emotional power. But it's no use giving the stage to someone who can't command it. There are many film actors who are essentially personalities, not performers.

Martin Bregman, who had once managed Al Pacino, approached Al, who declined. He was also offered *The Insider* at the same time. Sean Connery, who would have been terrible in that bed, read it and just said, 'It's not for me. I don't think it'll work.' I thought of Russell Crowe, sent him the script; he was shooting *Mystery, Alaska*, an ice hockey film, in Canada. I rang him and he said, 'I'll consider it if you agree to script changes and think about casting Nicole Kidman as the girl.' And I said, 'Well, I've already cast the girl and secondly, I'll consider any good suggestions, but I'm not promising to make particular changes.' And he said, 'I'll think about it.' Then Ed Limato, agent of Mel Gibson among others, said he had given the screenplay to Denzel Washington and were we interested? And it immediately clicked for me: Denzel Washington, an amazing actor with great charisma.

'Denzel has command of his instrument, which is his body. And he can play it like a violin,' Noyce commented.[1]

'While the character of Lincoln Rhyme only uses 2% of his body, his mind works at 600% capacity. I've been watching every major star for weeks, imagining what a performance limited to the upper body would be like. Acting skills alone are not enough – the performer has to have the ability to energise a room/scene with his eyes and spirit. In my opinion, I've got one of the best actors of our time: Denzel Washington. Not only is Denzel a master of his craft, he has a life-force that you can literally feel when he's in the room and see on the screen. From a purely visual standpoint, the image of Denzel – a man of such vigor – condemned to a bed perfectly captures the tragedy behind the character he will portray.'[2]

I could suddenly see the idea of Angelina and Denzel: he gives the film a seal of quality, she gives the film pizzazz. And I thought, 'That's it, in eighteen months' time, with that cast, I will definitely want to see this film.'

Denzel was at that perfect age where he could be both a father figure and a surrogate lover to Angelina's Amelia. If Rhyme had been older, it might have been offensive. The dynamics of the father–daughter, professor–student combination could have been off-putting as well. So, for me, casting those two wasn't really a gamble.

However, it seemed that the studio were afraid audiences would reject a relationship between a crippled African American man and a white woman. I think they would have preferred *any* white guy to Denzel, just because of this fear that the audience would reject the coupling.

I always took the view that this was very much a *Pygmalion* story. Henry Higgins is the Lincoln Rhyme character, the professor who takes a woman from the wrong side of the sticks and trains her to be himself. We needed someone in the part of Rhyme who radiated intelligence.

'There was something about the coupling of Angelina and Denzel that somehow moved me. I just felt that the audience would respond to that *Pygmalion* story, the tension between the two of them. Here was a woman who I felt people would feel is ripe to be taken over, to form a relationship and who has some sort of spiritual quality that is going to ignite the male character, ignite Denzel's character. So before we cast Angelina I arranged for her and Denzel to have dinner at a restaurant in West Hollywood, and Denzel arrived late. Angelina was there probably twenty minutes before him, and incredibly nervous, and later that night I realised that the way they were relating exactly mirrored their scripted on-screen relationship. I mean, Angelina was nervous because of her respect for Denzel as a proven master of acting and I realised that this was what she was going to use to fuel the on-screen relationship.'[3]

Jolie recalls the evening: 'Denzel had to meet me. He had watched my films, and I was so nervous. I was filming *Playing by Heart*, and I had this pink hairdo that was all spiked up. So I tried to cover it with a scarf, and halfway through the dinner I accidentally pulled it off and didn't realise it, and they were all staring at my head, this pink thing. Here I was trying to be like a lady, a cop and an adult. But he approved me and that said a lot.'[4]

Noyce eventually had to pressure Universal Studios' president, Casey Silver, in between takes on the New York set of *The Repair Shop* TV series in May 1998 (see the chapter on US TV work on the CD-ROM). Universal had indicated they would accept Angelina Jolie 'but only if we have an even more bankable actor than Denzel Washington . . . I also explain that by the time the film comes out, Angelina Jolie will be an established female star in her own right. Cast Denzel and Angelina or count me out.'[5] The ultimatum worked.

Jolie: 'It took months. I had to basically wait and wait and wait and beg and not take another job. But I don't blame them – I'd certainly never had a money-making film. They took a big risk.'[6] While Noyce's ultimatum did eventually succeed, he indeed had to take a risk.

Finally the studio suggested a 'compromise': 'We'll let you have Denzel and Angelina if you agree to a US$45 million budget.' If we went over, then we had to pay, and I had to put up a US$1 million bond – an agreement that I would pay the first US$1 million if the film went over.

I thought it was worth the bet and that, if we watched our costs, we could bring it in under US$45 million. Even if I had to pay a little bit of this money, I thought, 'Those two actors are the best.' Thanks to some tenacious work by line producer Lou Stroller, we came in well under budget – US$42.5 million, maybe . . . and both Martin Bregman and I were paid bonuses by Universal.

In order to do it cheaply we decided to shoot in Montreal. All of the interiors were shot there. We built Lincoln Rhyme's apartment, which is meant to be a loft on the corner of Great Jones and Lafayette in SoHo, in a very small studio with models of the surrounding buildings outside the windows, and sometimes a blue screen outside as well. We were able to superimpose the real New York location on to those windows, so you see moving traffic, and so on, beyond Denzel.

The idea of shooting in Canada is that you bring your key crew, cinematographer, production designer and most of the actors with you. But then 95 per cent of the crew, and all the supporting actors and extras, are Canadian and they're much, much cheaper than Americans.

Denzel was coming off a series of under-performing films. He hadn't scored a hit since *Crimson Tide* [in 1995]. We also could get him relatively cheaply because we agreed to shoot all his scenes in 25 shooting days, the first five weeks of the shoot. We were able to say, 'Well, we'll pay you by the week, so you'll end up getting more per week than you might on a sixteen-week shoot.' So, we shot in his apartment set in scene order, and he was able to enjoy the rare luxury of going from scene 1 to scene 150 in order, allowing him to build his performance through the story, scene for scene.

This was also great for me as a storyteller, because usually you shoot the ending first and the beginning last, and if you're lucky the middle's in the middle, but it's never in the order that they appear on the screen. One of the skills of a good director is to be able to unravel the jigsaw that you find yourself assembling as you shoot the film.

I started researching about six months before shooting started, trying to understand the reality of a quadriplegic so that I could present a realistic portrait of that experience. What is the day-to-day routine of someone who can't evacuate his or her own bowels? What are the opportunistic diseases that might strike a person who's immobile their whole lives? And what is their mental state at various stages of recovery and adjustment? This last one being of particular importance in a story about someone who has lost his will to live.

Meeting these people was also an incredibly uplifting experience, because I was reminded both of how lucky we are to have kept our health, and of how human beings will rise to conquer even the worst dilemmas.

I thought there were elements of universal truth in this screenplay, and though that's mixed up with ugly murders, within this piece there are some messages to humanity that I thought people would want to see.

Like Noyce, Washington prepared exhaustively by visiting quadriplegics in Los Angeles, New York and Montreal. Together, they conferred with leading spinal cord specialists at Mount Sinai Hospital in New York City.

'Even Christopher Reeve is generous enough to consult with Denzel. We have a wheelchair brought to Denzel's home in Los Angeles so he can get used to limited mobility and during rehearsals he will either be in the wheelchair or lying down, barely moving a muscle below the neck. Later, on set, we will have a full time nurse acting as a consultant for both Denzel and Queen Latifah, who plays his caregiver.'[7]

Washington remembers another important aspect of his discussions with quadriplegics: he 'learned how they use some of their increased senses of smell and sight to compensate for their disability'.[8]

Another important part of the research was investigation into forensic police work. To that end, Noyce approached Detective Hal Sherman from the NYPD, who had been in the force for seventeen years and had investigated close to 2000 crime scenes. 'Hal was right over my right shoulder, offering expert advice, telling me how it would really be done.'[9]

The screenplay is credited to Jeremy Iacone, but in fact some very important work was executed by another writer, Christopher Crowe. Jeremy wrote the screenplay that I first read. As a former playwright, he established strong characters, but it read more like a play. Christopher Crowe then came in and wrote two drafts, transforming the play into a film script. Later I brought Jeremy back and we only finished the shooting script at the end of the first week of shooting. We had about a week of rehearsals, maybe a little longer. Hearing the actors speak his lines allowed Jeremy to make some crucial last-minute adjustments.

By mid-June 1998 Noyce became aware that Dean Semler was again considering working as a cinematographer. They had worked together on *Dead Calm*, but, following his Academy Award for cinematography on *Dances with Wolves*, Semler had embarked on a career as a director. Noyce sent him the script immediately and Semler accepted.

'So many times during the hurly-burly of production, I will look back on that day as being one of the best decisions I made . . . I've always admired not only his fine, naturalistic lighting style but also his calm, no-nonsense efficiency born out of our shared documentary background and low-budget filmmaking in Australia, where, without a studio backer, filmmakers had to come in on time and on budget and still conjure up spellbinding images.

'Dean and I decide that, like *Dead Calm*, the film should be shot in the 29:35 anamorphic ratio. When you're dealing with a claustrophobic situation, where over one-half of the story takes place in one room, the extra money spent shooting in anamorphic is the cheapest production value available to a filmmaker. Even a relatively static dialogue scene between three people can be invested with a glorious big screen panorama for the audience. They literally see more for their money. We also agree on a natural, reality based lighting scheme that will be more about the relationship between the central characters than the darker aspects of the serial killer side of our story.'[10]

Principal photography started on 21 September in Montreal. Starting the shoot with the interiors, because of Denzel's other commitments, caused several problems.

Denzel Washington: 'It was an interesting challenge as an actor to play a role that [didn't allow you] to use your hands, body, or anything other than your eyes and mouth to convey the emotion of the character. But there was a particular challenge, as I was laying in bed for hours at a time for *The Bone Collector* while at the same time training for another role (Rubin 'Hurricane' Carter in *The Hurricane*). I had to stop working out with weights completely and just focus on the aerobic aspect of my training program [so as] not to get too bulked up while filming *The Bone Collector*.'[11]

Another problem caused headaches for Noyce.

Normally you shoot your exterior shots early in your shooting schedule so that when you are lighting your interiors you can match the exterior light for scenes set on that same day. If you shot the interior assuming an overcast day, and then you shot the scene outside in full sun, it would look odd when you cut the two together. Because of our contract with Denzel we agreed to shoot with him for the first five weeks, and assumed that on arrival in New York for exteriors in mid-November we would be greeted by grey, early winter days. But instead New York was experiencing an Indian summer, with brilliant blue skies and people wearing T-shirts and shorts.

Sometimes you wait it out. But we couldn't afford to not shoot. We always had this sword of Damocles hanging over our heads, and over mine in particular – which was the US$1 million I had to pay of the first overages. So I decided, together with Robert Grasmere, my long-time second unit director and visual effects supervisor, that the solution would be in CGI work – computer-generated images – altering the contrast of various shots in post-production. Clouds were added to the sky, and basically the contrast was altered so that it doesn't feel like a sunny summer's day.

In the second half of the schedule I was shooting predominantly with Angelina Jolie. Usually in the morning when I woke up, I couldn't wait to get to the set to work with her. I was impatient to continue what became a sort of love affair, being connected in this weird manner, through the lens, through the story, through the strange relationship between performer and director. I had the same connection with Nicole Kidman. I loved her, adored her; she was an angel who couldn't do a thing wrong. It wasn't like that with Sharon Stone, even though I respected her as an icon. Maybe I had been intimidated by her stories of how she was a member of Mensa – the group whose members all have extraordinarily high IQs.

'In the scenes between Amelia and Rhyme where she becomes his eyes and ears and legs, we had a particular problem. Not only were the two of them connected only by radio, but also Denzel had already completed filming when these scenes with Angelina were undertaken. To overcome this problem, my assistant, Jonathan Goldman, produced a CD, an edited version of all of Denzel's previously recorded lines. Then during the shooting of the scene the lines were piped into those headphones that you see Angelina wearing, and so Jonathan Goldman became the on-set embodiment of Denzel Washington, having to, in a sense, play the scene with Angelina, guessing the appropriate moment to bring on the next line, to press the button, to feed her his response.'[12]

When I first met Angie I felt a sense of discovery, of being there when something wonderful is still being formed. You could see tremendous talent as well as hunger, a hunger for work, good work, a love of trying things, a love of giving herself up to the character, to the lens, to the moment. And that's what also separates the good actors from the okay ones. The good ones love it; they don't just like it, don't just enjoy it. They're hungry like someone who hasn't eaten for weeks. They love the work and they don't want to be in any other place but right here in front of this lens playing this part right now. There is nothing else they would prefer to do.

'Porcelain isn't fine enough to describe how fragile she is. She's not burned out with the joy of performing. She's in her element because she can set parameters for a character, whereas I suspect she doesn't know her own boundaries emotionally and physically. I suspect she's happiest when she's not being Angelina Jolie.'[13]

'She's very courageous as an actress. She never says, "My character wouldn't do that," which is often something that actors tell you when they are afraid of going there. Angelina will go anywhere, or at least she'll try going anywhere that the director suggests.'[14]

In the original screenplay it was mentioned that her father had committed suicide. But the idea that she had discovered his body was something which Angelina and I decided in our discussions before the film was shot. In some ways I think this is the key to her character – at least, the way she intersects with the opportunities presented to her in the story. In the scene at the steam junction, where she's approaching the scalded body of Mrs Rubin, walking slowly down the stairs towards the corpse, I can remember, just like in a silent movie, talking her down the stairs, saying to her: 'Well, you're coming towards your father's house. You can feel a dread inside you. You know there's something horrible in the air, seething out of the house. And you open the door and then you smell something terrible, not an actual smell, but now you're walking down the corridor and in your heart, but not in your brain, you know what it is, and now you round the corner and you can now see the blood on the wall, and you know whose blood it is; and know whose brains it is; and now you turn and you can see it's your father, dead, gun in his hand, a hole in his head, carpet is full of blood. His body's lying in a pool of blood and it's just the most horrific thing you have ever seen or could ever imagine seeing, and you will never forget it', and so on.

What you see in the movie of her walking and finding the body of that woman and then walking down closer towards the corpse, was all done to a track of me describing that fictional event.

In post-production I shot some footage of a computer screen with the words 'Body discovered by daughter Amelia Donaghy, NYPD officer.' The whole idea was that death and the investigation of death is her natural vocation, but also the thing that she was most repulsed by and most deeply disturbed by. Lincoln Rhyme could sense there was a barrier that she needed to cross in order to free herself.

Suicide deaths by cops are not unusual and the causes are usually stress-related. Anyone who commits suicide is obviously disturbed and vulnerable and unable to cope with all that is disturbing them at that time. We can see that she is basically a very strong and determined woman, but we suspect that she has a breaking point. So the specifics of why her father committed suicide aren't really important, it's the fact that he did – and therefore broke. And hopefully you get just from her acting, just from the way that she's coiled up, the feeling that she could break too. She's determined, but not necessarily tough. The fact that he committed suicide is going to have an enormous psychological effect on his child, both to make her feel that she failed him and to make her feel that he failed her and abandoned her, and to make her feel that she may be subject to the same imbalance that might lead to an impulse to end one's own life.

When she says that 'Forensics is not my area', it's because the crime scene unit only deals with death, and death isn't where she wants to go at all. Yet Rhyme recognises from her instinctive actions at the first crime scene that she's a natural, and death is where she should be going. Because of the catharsis of discovering her father's body, it's where she needs to go to surmount that and stop it eating away at her. That's why the addition of that one little sentence, which probably cost 300 bucks to add, was worth so much to our understanding of her, in the absence of an elaborate back-story.

One of the more memorable events during shooting was the December day in New York when Jolie was injured.

'We were set-up beside an Amtrak railway and in the scene Angelina's character comes across a gruesome crime scene with forensic evidence lying on the tracks. When a train barrels around the corner – heading towards the evidence – she stands in the middle of the tracks and flags it down. We had our own train and had rehearsed several times with her stunt double to make sure the train could run at reduced speed and consistently stop on its mark just a few feet in front of Angelina. But for an hour, Angelina stood on the tracks literally staring down the locomotive. She was like a bullfighter – rather, a bull – staring down its opponent, trying to will it into submission. Nothing could take her away from that spot or break her concentration. Ironically, it wasn't the train that hurt her but one of our safety men. On one take the train missed its mark by a few feet, but Angelina didn't budge. Our safety man tackled Angelina, knocking her off the tracks and twisting her ankle.'[15]

The setting of this scene beneath the Westside Highway, and the use of certain other locations in the film, provokes a discomforting feeling that, even in a bustling city like New York, places exist that seem to invite murder.

Most of the interior crime scene locations were invented, but they were inspired by old photographs of real locations, as well as by visiting some similar locations in 1999's New York City. Everything is pushed a little – it's reality-based, but pushed for dramatic purposes – by production designer Nigel Phelps. I first saw his work on *Alien: Resurrection* and although I believed his spaceships and all of his designs, I was also haunted by them because they had a psychological edge, or something – both real and yet out of a nightmare. I thought we could make the movie mirror old New York City and what is there now, but I thought there had to be a subtle extension of reality in order to get under the skin of the audience.

Creating the sets posed some difficulties.

'For the interior shots one of my biggest concerns is recreating the distinct New York skyline that will be seen from Rhyme's windows. Nigel Phelps has created models of the surrounding buildings with forced perspective, giving us a believable view of downtown New York. The models have their own interior lights, plants and furniture on balconies and steam coming from smokestacks on rooftops. The models also give the actors something to play off, rather than staring at a blue screen.'[16]

In regard to Denzel Washington, one of the highlights during the shoot was a scene that was described in the script as Lincoln Rhyme pushing himself to a point of near-exhaustion.

'But none of us were quite prepared for the Denzel Washington that actually appeared on set that day, covered in sweat by make-up artist

Carl Fullerton. And none of us were quite prepared for the perform-ance that Denzel unleashed. I would like to say that I contributed as a director to the depths of despair that he plunges his character into, but I didn't. It was all the actor's own work and he literally took over the set. The usual babble of off-set conversations were absolutely silent that day. Just like the characters in the scene itself. After the first rehearsal I said to Dean Semler, "Let's set the cameras up. Let's not move them. Let's just capture the performance like we were shooting a documentary." And so it was, in one take Denzel did everything that you see. And after he had finished I said, "Do you need to do another take?" He said, "I've got nothing more." And, of course, nothing more was needed.'[17]

As the lead actor is motionless, preventing the film from look-ing static was a particular challenge.

'We could have artificially moved the actors, but I decided not to do that and let them play the reality instead. We also could have arti-ficially moved the camera, but I decided not to do that either because each camera move needs to be motivated by something within the scene. In fact, the only time the camera moves in a shot involving Rhyme is when he's talking to Amelia via radio and she's moving, working a crime scene on his behalf. We shot twice as many camera setups and camera angles as you would for a normal dialogue scene, so that when the scene is cut the audience will get the impression of kinetics or movement simply because the camera is always cutting to somewhere new, and we hope to always be one step ahead of the audience.'[18]

The film allows as well for an insight into the way Noyce approaches production design.

Although it is dark in places, essentially *The Bone Collector* is lit as a love story – it is quite soft and romantic, not hard-edged. Well, it's blues and golds, really. In *Patriot Games*, for example, there were two colour schemes: outside of America was predominantly blue, cold, unwelcoming; and the scenes in America were warm, like home, homely, warm, comforting. And then within that there are other colour schemes scene for scene. I will usually spend time with an artist and we will try to work out key drawings to give to people in colour that indicate the mood of the piece. We will always shoot tests beforehand to try to pin down the look of the film. *The Bone Collector* we test-shot for two weeks.

As more than half the movie takes place in that one room, we were testing the room and its colour scheme. Sometimes three times a week it would be repainted. I mean, it started as exposed and quite dark brick, then the brick was painted over and green was the predominant colour of the room, and the furniture was completely done three different times, different kinds of furniture and dressing. Usually, getting simpler and simpler all the time and warmer, and more homely and less cluttered. The colour of the sheets, all the costumes, are usually tested against the predominant scenes that will be shot. You may not have noticed but his sheets keep changing colour in the movie, and the furniture keeps changing in the room even though it's the same room. His bed keeps changing position in the room. That's so that we could open up the scenes to different staging. I mean, it's logical that they move his bed out so that he can be in the centre of the room when all the people are there, and then when they leave he goes back to his position against the wall, and so on.

Principal photography wrapped in January 1999 and Noyce went off to London to start work on the editing with William Hoy, thereby renewing their working relationship from *Patriot Games*. In April, dialogue was re-recorded in Los Angeles, which was followed by a test-screening there on 14 April and in small-town Paramus, New Jersey, on 22 April.

The part of the film that I was most unhappy with, and which caused lots of arguments with Martin Bregman, was the ending where the killer's identity is revealed. Martin had produced a film called *Sea of Love*, where the killer was unveiled almost from left field. But when director Harold Becker and writer Richard Price revealed the killer as having been the ex-husband of the woman Al Pacino had been having a love affair with, the bad guy's motives became immediately apparent. In our film the killer had to explain himself to an audience who had never really been given the opportunity to participate in guessing his identity. I wanted to change the prologue where Rhyme is injured so that it referred to his original testimony in the killer's trial, so that when this guy is unmasked at the climax, the audience would feel a sense of completeness, because only then would they realise that the events at the beginning of the film were the catalyst for this man's dementia.

Martin Bregman didn't like it, so I agreed to shoot the original screenplay, but there was this constant argument between us about the need to change it. I was pretty confident that after a test-screening the studio would support me. Unfortunately, the movie previews were incredibly successful so nobody wanted to listen – they just felt that the director was completely insane. He wants to change the movie, but the audience loves it. Whereas I had previously been fucked by low scores, now I was fucked by high scores.

But at least there was one major relief. With shooting finishing on time and no extra costs involved, by July it was clear that Noyce wouldn't have to pay anything out of his own pocket.

The film cost US$42 million to make – relatively cheap for a studio film with stars. It was financed 100 per cent by Universal. But because they needed to raise money to finance their debt, they sold half of it to Sony/Columbia just after we finished shooting. So it was distributed by two studios. They agreed to split it down the middle – they paid US$21 million per studio and each got half of all the profits. But the final cost that it is carrying is US$77 million. So US$34.5 million has been spent on prints and advertising.

Even before the official premiere on 5 November 1999, Universal was eager to publicise the first rave reviews, in a memorandum dated 6 September. These had come from the press screenings held months before, as well as *The Bone*

Collector's inclusion in the Montreal Film Festival. 'A chilling, jump-out-of-your-seat thriller,' raved CBS,[19] while CNN simply changed the likely direction of viewers' bodily movement: 'A fast-paced, jump-in-your-seat, terrifying thriller.'[20] And ABC added: 'Joins *Silence of the Lambs* and *Seven* on the decade's short list of great thrillers. Denzel Washington's performance is superb, a star-making performance from Angelina Jolie.'[21]

Once the film was released, however, the critics weren't as enthusiastic, even though the ticket-paying audience loved it. *Variety* – in its longest critique so far on any Noyce film – highlighted the film's clear strengths and weaknesses: 'The obvious difficulties in making an action thriller out of Jeffrey Deaver's best-selling fiction . . . aren't entirely surmounted in Phillip Noyce's glossy adaptation . . . Denzel Washington delivers a convincing central turn . . . perhaps more serious flaws, however, lie in Angelina Jolie's credulity-straining role and a narrative that keeps the killer's identity and motives unknown until a hyperbolic, contrived climax.'[22] 'Noyce has the skill to keep the plot percolating and overcome its occasional missteps,' remarked the *Los Angeles Times*,[23] whereas the *New York Post* lambasted the film, saying 'Jeremy Iacone's script is riddled with plot holes you could drive a train through.'[24]

In short, there was praise for the individual performances ('Denzel Washington is fine, Angelina Jolie is more than fine, and Phillip Noyce's direction is frequently astute'[25]) but some disappointment in the film as a whole

As a thriller – or, more precisely, as a whodunit – the film leaves something to be desired, particularly in its lack of clues, as already mentioned. It's true that 113 seconds into the film, with the title credits still rolling in superimposition, a newspaper article appears, revealing the later conviction of the killer, under his original name of Marcus Andrews. But the viewer can be forgiven for overlooking this clue when the film hasn't even properly begun. Noyce, as already indicated, is dissatisfied with this aspect.

'In my alternative version of the film, which you will never see, the preamble which opened the movie would have served a double purpose. Not only would the audience have discovered how Lincoln Rhyme became a quadriplegic, but the events surrounding that accident would have been linked to his testimony at the trial of Marcus Andrews, the real name of the medical technician who he would later know as Richard Thompson. In my alternative preamble the audience would have briefly glimpsed Richard, but due to his beard and long hair wouldn't have been able to recognise him when about six minutes later in the present film he first appears tending Rhyme's heart pacing machine.'[26]

In contrast, the end of the film seems overdone.

'As originally scripted the final scene of the movie, in Rhyme's apartment, took place just between Amelia, Lincoln and Dr Lehman, his personal physician, who right at the beginning of the story had agreed to facilitate Lincoln's final transition. Sometime during production you started to feel that the audience may appreciate the chance to be reunited with the whole cast of characters, around Rhyme and Amelia, and we asked Jeremy Iacone to write this feel-good Christmas party scene. With distance, and looking at the movie now and maybe for the first time feeling the loss of Thelma that so much of the audience must have felt, I probably would be more inclined to favour the original scripted final scene, which also more specifically addressed Rhyme's newfound determination to go on living.

'In a footnote to this scene, we actually did film a shot of Thelma [Queen Latifah's character] to be inserted right there, as Rhyme's niece kisses him. We did at one point cut to Thelma, not dead but alive, seated over to the right in a corner, smiling, bandaged, but alive, but it seemed when we tried it out, not for an audience but just for ourselves, that it was too much. It was enough that Lincoln, when we had convinced the audience that he might be dead, was now alive. But Thelma seemed to be, well, just too much of a feel-good ending.'[27]

Even though Noyce refers to the film as a love story between the two protagonists, one obvious obstacle to this was the impossibility of any physical exchange.

'When I was researching the film I met a quadriplegic in England and asked him about his sex life. And he said, "Look, your genitals are your usual place where you feel sexual response, but for me, paralysed from the neck down, that's not possible." But, of course, that isn't where sexual response originates. In spite of what many women might think, men's brains are not in their penis, so when a woman turns me on, and these are his words: "My head becomes a giant swollen penis. I experience orgasm up here in the head, the only part of my body that I still have feeling in, just as strongly as I ever did when it was centred in my loins. All the pleasure cells are still operating, but they are restricted to the upper part of my body."'[28]

The nearest thing to a 'sexy' scene occurs about 88 minutes into the film, when Lincoln is asleep and Amelia is by his side, gently stroking his one good finger.

At the very first screening the audience laughed, for a variety of reasons – the finger appears almost phallic, just sitting there; it sort of feels like she's stroking his penis. After the screening, music editor Joe E. Rand said, 'Well, I decided that I should go for some different music in that scene.' I said, 'Why?' And he said, 'I think you need to distract the audience at that moment just when they feel like they're going to laugh and you'll get them through it, and then it will be fine.' So he found a certain track which achieved that without interfering with the drama of the scene . . . an invisible distraction.

The film has several obvious similarities to the work of Hitchcock, the master of suspense. As in *Rope*, much of the action is confined to an apartment. Then, there is the long, fast, tracking shot about 87 minutes into the film, going from where a policeman is shot outside the killer's cab, to Rhyme's room.

'I guess in the old days the shot would have had to be done mechani-
cally – that is, actually hauling the camera through physical space.
I guess that is how Alfred Hitchcock did it in *Frenzy*. I must admit
that's where I got the idea. There is a shot in that movie where,
retreating, similarly, from a crime scene, the camera goes down a
stairway, out the door and ends up on the opposite side of the
street.'[29]

Another Hitchcockian ingredient is Noyce's cameo as one of
the customers in a bookshop.

I wanted someone to be in there that would make the audience
uneasy. They gave me some extras and I looked at them and none of
them unnerved me. So I thought, 'Maybe I had better get in there in
a big black coat and the audience would go "Whooo! What is he?" It
wasn't that I wanted them to think that I was the killer; I just wanted
them to be unnerved momentarily before they meet this bookseller.

Whenever the killer is preying on a potential victim, this is
shown point-of-view. Noyce claims to have 'borrowed the idea'
of using the subjective camera from Michael Powell's *Peeping
Tom* (1960).[30]

The peregrine falcon is clearly a symbol in the film.
However, the symbol isn't coherent; at least, not as a fixed
annotation in art or literature.

First of all, the falcon arrives at the beginning when Rhyme is talking
to the doctor and it's clear from Rhyme's smile that this is a regular visi-
tor. Later, when Rhyme is suffering a disreflexia attack, he looks up as
the falcon comes to the window. At the end, when the falcon soars up
into the sky, the audience might think it is actually Rhyme ascending to
heaven. But it's also intended to represent his spirit soaring; he's
renewed himself. And it's the bad guy that has now been vanquished.
I didn't invent the falcon, it was already in the screenplay, but it was
never really clear what the falcon meant. Interestingly enough, listening
to the encounter groups after the test screenings – they get twenty

people together and they ask them questions and discuss the movie – it appeared that the audience members always had plenty of suggestions as to the meaning of the falcon.

The second unit camera work is on a par with Dean Semler's impressive first unit footage. Most notable are the aerial shots, but even otherwise, New York is ravishingly depicted.

We flew around New York City for five hours to shoot them. I had previously seen some stills looking straight down on those sky-scrapers and I thought the perspective looking down like that would work for us. But when I shot them I always tried to get the helicopter to be moving sideways and the camera to be panning and zooming a little, so the audience becomes slightly disoriented. I always imagined that it's the peregrine falcon flying over New York City and the fight between good and evil, between life and death, that's going on inside Rhyme's brain.

The day after principal shooting finished, the second unit cameraman and I shot panning shots across the skyline of New York for hours and hours, collecting material which was then fed into an AVID digital editing machine to compose the opening titles sequence. It became a project which the assistant editor would return to day after day over a three- or four-month period, refining with me all of the strobing lights and then adding as we did, various images that complemented the story to follow.

In a way reminiscent of Noyce's experimental-film past, the colour streaks of the opening titles were created with a camera that ran not with the usual 24 frames a second, but with only three frames per second. This way, the images shot from the Brooklyn side of the city look blurred and appear to be abstract and strobing.

Unconsciously you draw from those experimental images when you're making films, even these days. This opening sequence with lights flashing across the screen was inspired by a hand-painted film I saw and distributed way back in the early 1970s Co-op days, called

Sonata For Pen and Ruler by Barry Spinello. Spinello scratched the emulsion off black film and then coloured it in a crude form of animation of lines and dots moving across the screen.

When the aforementioned zoom was created, another experimental technique was used.

'It is actually three zoom shots combined. The first zoom shot was shot in New York City. We placed the taxi and the stuntman in the real street, surrounded by real people, and real cars, and on a cue, the stuntman fell to the ground and the assistant cameraman zoomed fast back with his hand, a manual zoom, as fast as he could. Then in Montreal, on stage, we actually repeated that action, zooming out from the blue screen that was placed behind the window. Later, the second unit shot a shot of that canyon of buildings, actually the camera was again on top of the public theatre in Lafayette Street, and then in the computer many months later, those three shots were combined to produce the appearance of a single 5-mile-long tracking shot.'[31]

The Bone Collector is the first, and so far only, Noyce film to make generous use of modern digital techniques, particularly computer-generated imagery. Still, there is some similarity with earlier films in his approach to the aesthetics of the opening titles – one of his trademarks. The openings of *Patriot Games* and *The Bone Collector* are structurally identical. The abstract night lights that appear can be compared directly with the rather abstract images of the rolling figure columns. They are superimposed with newspaper clippings, old photographs and prints in the case of *The Bone Collector*, and with unidentifiable treetops in the case of *Patriot Games*. So, 'modern, technical, abstract' is contrasted with 'old-fashioned, natural, realistic' in one image. *Clear and Present Danger* is slightly different in its opening titles, but even in that film an abstract image and a realistic one are double-exposed on top of each other.

To my mind, that's a coincidence. But maybe it's because there are a lot of similarities between the character played by Denzel Washington in *The Bone Collector* and the character played by Harrison Ford in both Clancy films. Both are highly analytical men, both are detectives in their own way, both have encyclopedic and photographic memories, both are able to make intuitive leaps to solve problems, both have a tenderness that's combined with what we suspect is a very strong determination, so they're both soft and hard personalities. Both are humanists we can rely on to make sensible, enlightened, reasonable decisions, who we can believe won't lie to us, because they are decent people. Also, both are stories of a search to confront someone who may harm you or those people close to you. So, it's natural there's going to be a similarity in the images that are used in the theme sentences of the movies, the titles.

The Bone Collector turned out to be particularly important to its actors. Denzel Washington might have been hoping for recognition in the form of an Academy Award of his extraordinary achievement in portraying Lincoln Rhyme, though he won't admit this. Today he is philosophical about it. 'The role didn't have as much effect on my career as the success it had at the box-office. That's the nature of the entertainment business at the moment.'[32] Angelina Jolie for the first time had her name above the film title on the marquees, indicating she was on her way to becoming new Hollywood royalty. She gave due credit to Noyce for this, particularly praising his ability to see things from a female perspective and to make her character both soft and strong at the same time.[33] Although in this, her breakthrough film, she played a vulnerable character, from then on she would assume a tough and brash image that would propel her to tabloid-weirdo fame.

It was actually a turning point for me as well. The screenplay for the movie combines two seemingly disparate elements: an exploitation slasher movie with a heartfelt examination of the psychological and physical trials and tribulations of a paralysis victim. So, in a sense, that project, launched as a thriller, was a bridge to making a film like *Rabbit-Proof Fence* – a film that's about emotions, a film that has softer elements which are going to appeal to an audience. In other words, after *The Bone Collector* I think I wanted to make less testosterone-driven movies. That desire was a result, in a way, of being touched by the humanity and the fragility of the characters in *The Bone Collector*'s story.

---

[1] Cited in Bruce Fretts, 'Washington', *Entertainment Weekly*, 24 December 1999, p. 43.

[2] Phillip Noyce, Diary, *Fade-In*, 1999.

[3] Director's commentary on *The Bone Collector* DVD.

[4] Cited in Anne Bergman, 'A proverbial adventurer', *Los Angeles Times*, 7 November 1999, p. 15.

[5] *Fade-In*.

[6] Cited in Andrew Essex, 'Girl uncorrupted', *Entertainment Weekly*, 5 November 1999, p. 43.

[7] *Fade-In*.

[8] Denzel Washington, email dated 12 June 2003.

[9] Director's commentary on *The Bone Collector* DVD.

[10] *Fade-In*.

[11] Email dated 12 June 2003.

[12] Director's commentary on *The Bone Collector* DVD.

[13] Cited in 'Rebel without a pause: Volatile, outspoken, aggressive – Angelina Jolie is Hollywood's favourite wild child onscreen and off', *Time*, 24 January 2000, p. 72.

[14] Cited in Bergman, 'A proverbial adventurer', p. 15.

[15] *Fade-In*.

[16] Ibid.

[17] Director's commentary on *The Bone Collector* DVD.

[18] Cited in Kathleen Tracy, *Angelina Jolie* (Toronto: ECW Press, 2001), p. 133.

[19] Dan DiNicola, CBS, cited in Jeff Sakson, '*The Bone Collector* – quotes #2 memorandum', 6 September 1999.

[20] Paul Clinto, CNN Interactive, cited in Sakson, '*The Bone Collector*'.

[21] Mike Cidoni, ABC Rochester, cited in Sakson, '*The Bone Collector*'.

[22] Dennis Harvey, *Variety*, 31 August 1999 (updated version), '*The Bone Collector*'.

[23] Kenneth Turan, 'Thriller elements make "Bone" thrilling', *Los Angeles Times*, 5 November 1999.

[24] Lou Lumenick, 'It's got chills and thrills, but don't expect meat on this "Bone"', *New York Post*, 5 November 1999.

[25] Philip Wuntch, '*The Bone Collector*: Villain doesn't have a spine', *Dallas Morning News*, 5 November 1999.

[26] Director's commentary on *The Bone Collector* DVD.
[27] Ibid.
[28] Ibid.
[29] Ibid.
[30] Ibid.
[31] Ibid.
[32] Email dated 12 June 2003.
[33] Tracy, *Angelina Jolie*, p. 133.

Part III

IN TOUCH WITH
THE WORLD
(2001 –)

Chapter 15
RABBIT-PROOF FENCE

Everything had to fit around the children.

A true story from the 1930s: a fourteen-year-old Aboriginal girl, Molly Craig (Everlyn Sampi), and her younger sister and cousin are taken from their mothers to be trained as domestic workers for integration into white society. They escape from a mission in Western Australia and try to find their way home on foot, chased by the government across 2000 kilometres of mostly barren desert, by following the rabbit-proof fence.

I was completing post-production on *The Bone Collector* and reworking the script for *The Sum of All Fears* when in July 1999, at 3.30 am, the phone rang. Thinking it must be an emergency, I answered and heard this strange female voice that sounded like a crank caller. Later I realised she was just nervous, having miscalculated the time difference between Sydney and Los Angeles. She thought she was ringing my office in the middle of the day, not my home in the middle of the night. It was documentary maker Christine Olsen, who five years earlier had purchased the rights to the book *Follow the Rabbit-Proof Fence* written by Doris Pilkington-Garimara, the daughter of Molly Craig, whose story it told. Christine was convinced I was the perfect director for the first dramatic screenplay she had written. I was convinced she was a script stalker and tried to get rid of her by telling her to ring my office, which she did. She sent the screenplay over and eventually my business partner, Kathleen McLaughlin, read it and told me the story. I found it compelling but I was already contracted to shoot *Sum of All Fears* and just wasn't ready to embrace the idea of leaving my life as a Hollywood director to make a low-budget movie back in Australia.

But Kathleen kept insisting that I would love this story and eventually, after three or four months, I read the screenplay and agreed it was marvellous. It was the kind of story that kept coming back to me over the following months, as if I was being drawn by an invisible voice. A voice, I later realised, that was telling me to follow the lead of young Molly and make the journey home myself.

What primarily appealed to Noyce was the story's universality.

'Although when I started to read I was very aware of the children's Aboriginality, about halfway through, they ceased to be black or white, they were just children in distress, powerless, fighting back and finally triumphing . . . With this film there is an added bonus in as much as it's telling a very significant part of Australian history that by and large has been denied us."[1]

I was very moved by the kids' determination to get home. But I said to Christine, 'Look, this is a great story. It's very timely for an Australian audience, but it's unlikely I'm going to be able to direct it in the near future because I have an obligation to Harrison Ford and producer Mace Neufeld now we've set our sights on a third and last in this Jack Ryan series, so you'd be better to find another director.'

But my agent in Australia, Jane Cameron, and Kathleen both encouraged Christine not to take it anywhere else.

I continued work on the screenplay for *Sum*. Paul Attanassio (*Donnie Brasco* and *Quiz Show*) wrote another draft with a lot of input from myself and, particularly, Kathleen. He was paid more than US$1 million to rewrite the screenplay, which, due to another commitment, he ended up doing in about ten days. Nice work if you can get it!

Anyway, we delivered the new script to Harrison, who felt that it was merely a second-rate rehash of elements we'd already worked with on the two other movies. In March 2000 Kathleen and I found ourselves in a hotel off Wall Street working on further story changes and knowing we wouldn't leave New York until Harrison agreed without reservation to commit to a start date. Together with the new writer, Trey Calloway, we would rework the story line and then travel uptown by taxi every second day to Harrison's Central Park West apartment, describing the changed plot and leaving him with the latest four or five-page outline. But on alternate days he'd either be enthusiastic or pessimistic. On Tuesday he'd respond positively to our new ideas and give us some more feedback. We'd go away, make more changes in response to his comments, and then return on Thursday to find that now he was completely pessimistic. Then we'd go away and do some more work, come back on a Sunday and he'd be optimistic again. He was up and down like a yo-yo. Probably because he wanted to make it work, but the source material just wasn't inspiring him, the novel having been written back in the early 1990s when a nuclear stand-off between Russia and the US was much more likely than at the turn of the new century.

After about ten days of this, I began to feel frustrated with the whole Hollywood system and my place in it. The studio wasn't really concerned about what changes Harrison wanted, only that we got him to commit. And we were very much caught up in the power play of the star system. We weren't going to make the film until Harrison agreed. But no matter what he said and what we did, we couldn't please him.

Throughout all this manoeuvring the story of *Rabbit-Proof Fence* – a very elemental, simple story – had stayed with me very strongly. Here we were, trying to manipulate *Sum* to increase audience empathy with the central character, increase his jeopardy, and his triumph at the end of the movie – and we were failing. Yet the true story of *Rabbit-Proof Fence* contained all the elements of classic invented fiction. I was simultaneously working on the budget for *Sum*, which was up around US$100 million, and the whole thing just seemed overwhelming in its complexity. And one day I just said to Kathleen, 'You know what? I've had enough of this. I'm gonna go back to Australia and see if I can get that film going – *Rabbit-Proof Fence*.' And she said, 'I was just thinking that myself.'

So I flew from New York to Sydney, stopping in Los Angeles to pass the screenplay over to London-based producer Jeremy Thomas, an old friend who also rents space for his Recorded Picture Company in my Los Angeles office. And by the time I got to Australia he'd read the script and indicated he would offer a distribution guarantee to kick-start additional funds. In Australia I hooked up with David Elfick, who had produced *Newsfront*. David now came aboard as executive producer to pull the remaining money together so that I could shoot the picture before the impossible heat of the Australian summer and before *The Sum of All Fears*, still scheduled to shoot in early 2001. Catriona Hughes, head of the government-funded Film Finance Corporation, was incredibly helpful and flexible at this and every stage of production – the best 'studio executive' I've ever worked with.

On my return to America, Harrison Ford officially announced he was passing on *Sum*, and the chance to continue playing Jack Ryan. Paramount head Sherry Lansing was keen for Ben Affleck to take over and thought she could reinvent the Ryan franchise with a much younger actor, and continue the series for another decade. So I met with Ben Affleck, who I thought had a great presence, but I must admit I was very concerned about how to direct him, because for me Jack Ryan was Harrison Ford and the process of making the films had been such a team effort between Harrison, producer Mace Neufeld and myself.

So in the back of my mind I wasn't at all certain I would do the film, but I thought 'Well, if I'm gonna make *Rabbit*, I might need the fee from *Sum of All Fears* to finish *Rabbit* with my own money.' I was desperately trying to get the actors for *The Quiet American* and I sent the script to Michael Caine on the day I met Ben. Michael responded very quickly and very positively, but the financiers, Intermedia, indicated that Caine wasn't enough to green-light that movie for a US$25 million budget. We still needed to get the quiet American of the title – an American actor from a pre-approved list. So I met John Cusack and Ryan Phillippe. Even when I met Affleck for *Sum*, I was thinking maybe I should slip him the script of *The Quiet American*.

I went back to Australia in June 2000 to begin pre-production and casting of *Rabbit*. Still – as far as the studio knew – I was going to direct *Sum*. In August, a month before shooting started on *Rabbit-Proof Fence*, Brendan Fraser read *The Quiet American* and accepted the role of Alden Pyle. And overnight that project was green-lit to start shooting in early 2001 and I had to officially pull out of *Sum*.

Once Noyce had arrived back in Australia, in June 2000, he immediately embarked on his usual intensive research. In Perth, he met up with Doris Pilkington and visited the remains of the Moore River Native Settlement to soak up the atmosphere of the place. Following in the footsteps of his heroines, he went all along the rabbit-proof fence right up to Jigalong, where he met the real Molly Craig and Daisy Kadibil, now in their eighties. They told him their stories and answered his many pressing questions.

In the official press release, dated 15 July 2000, announcing his return to Australia, Noyce gave his reasons for taking on this film project:

'This is a marvellous adventure story and thriller, celebrating courage and the resilience of the human spirit. It tells the story of three unlikely heroines who refuse to let an uncaring bureaucracy destroy their lives and must trek across thousands of miles of the most exotic and forbidding countryside in the world.'[2]

In some ways the film was chosen as an antidote to everything I had been doing in Hollywood: tiny budget, no studio, self-produced, no stars. So I was freed from all those things which for ten years had gradually imprisoned me. I knew the hardest hurdle would be to find kids to play the three children, because there is no casting directory of Aboriginal children. No obvious reservoir of talent to draw on.

So began a three-month search across Australia, aided by casting director Christine King – who had done *Moulin Rouge* and *Two Hands* – but also helped by community leaders, schoolteachers and parents deputised to interview children in the four corners of the continent. Of about 2000 kids interviewed I probably saw 800 personally, touring by four-wheel drive and light plane around numerous outback settlements.

We were looking for very specific children, who had to be of mixed parentage – not full blood – and possess the charisma of movie stars. Eventually, seventeen kids were chosen from all over the country and flown to Broome in northwestern Australia for two days of intensive casting workshops.

During that weekend the kids were usually surrounded by up to seven cameras. Lucia was shooting for her own 'Making of', a piece that eventually became part of a documentary put together by indigenous director Darlene Johnson, and Channel Nine Australia was shooting for a five-part series to be shown on the *Today* breakfast show, which also became a twenty-minute story on the *Sunday* current affairs program. Publicist Emma Cooper was also shooting stills for magazine stories on the casting of the film. Being surrounded by cameras was an essential component of the tests given to the kids, because we needed three youngsters who could hold their focus in the pressure-cooker situation that awaited them in just four weeks' time when shooting was scheduled to start. Only those kids with vivid imaginations who could also maintain equilibrium under extreme pressure could be expected to make it through the shoot.

As it turned out, one of the chosen leads – Caitlyn Lawford – dropped out after arriving in Adelaide two weeks later. Only seven years old, and from the remote community of Fitzroy Crossing in Western Australia, the distractions of big-city life, plus the discipline required to spend eight hours a day preparing herself to be in a movie, proved just too much. She was replaced at the last minute, just five days before shooting. That's when Tianna Sansbury, a seven-year-old from Adelaide, who had originally come in for a casting session for extras, was retested and offered the part of Daisy.

Given that we had unknown and untried leads, I thought it important to secure one name performer to help with sales. I approached Geoffrey Rush, Hugh Jackman and then Russell Crowe to play the part of A.O. Neville, but none of them was available. And then Christine King suggested a Brit on the grounds that Neville was born in England and came to Australia in his early twenties. The first actor she recommended was Kenneth Branagh.

Branagh's participation was officially announced on 30 August 2000. In an email dated 25 September of that year, Branagh presents to 'Dear Phillip' important additional aspects of Neville's character. 'My intention is to offer up a few observations about him that I hope can support and enhance the main thrust of the story. It's not meant to be a crude defence of a man or to unbalance the film's adventure quality by making it too political. However it does seem to me that in looking at his scenes and particularly what he says that there may be a chance to render him more vividly and to up the dramatic stakes overall.

'In broad terms, I think it might be useful to see Neville under more pressure, and for the recapture of the girls to be of much greater symbolic importance for him.

'As you will know much better than me, he seemed to spend much of his professional life under siege. Often a political scapegoat. Constantly under-funded, his policies constantly challenged (he might say undermined) and continually having to justify his actions and in so doing often masking his genuine fascination with the Native culture. He loved the country and the people, and yet had through his empire background a paternalistic, sometimes ruthless attitude, towards a race that he also had tremendous compassion for. I feel that the more extremely we can see these contradictory forces in him, the better. A man torn between what is ideal, what is necessary and what is possible. If we can see his shock at their treatment, his admiration for the full bloods, his deep concern for the young girls, we should more powerfully feel the intense force of his vision. His dangerously flawed vision. A subtitle for his role in the film could be "Neville in Crisis".'[3]

Branagh then goes into detail, over several pages, about each scene he will be in, making suggestions and sometimes even giving alternatives to his own suggestions.

For the role of the tracker, David Gulpilil – the quintessential Australian Aboriginal actor since he first appeared by the name of 'Gumpilil' in Nic Roeg's *Walkabout* in 1970 – was chosen. His seasoned face, combined with his oft-proven acting skills, adds immensely to the serenity of the character he plays. Immediately after *Rabbit-Proof Fence* he was offered the title role in Rolf de Heer's *The Tracker*, which won him an AFI Award for Best Actor in 2002. The two films resurrected what had been his rather quiet career of recent years.

David Gulpilil was the obvious choice to play a tracker because he lives in a remote part of Arnhem Land, in northern Australia, and really hunts for food using traditional bush craft – he's the real thing. So his body language is 100 per cent genuine. He's a superb actor. Very subtle. But some aspects of that character could never be acted.

John Scott, who'd cut *Newsfront* and *Heatwave*, came on as editor. Roger Ford, who designed John Duigan's *The Year My Voice Broke* plus *Babe* and *Babe: Pig in the City*, joined as production designer/costume designer.

I had met Chris Doyle back in 1979 in Taiwan when I was there to shoot *Attack Force Z*, a film on which I was replaced as director by Tim Burstall before shooting started. Chris, who spoke fluent Mandarin and Cantonese, had been assigned as my interpreter and subsequently became a friend. At that time his dream of becoming a cinematographer seemed very remote. Over the years we exchanged postcards and his messages chartered his rise and rise in the new independent Asian cinema. I remember once going to the set of one of Wong Kar Wai's films in Hong Kong and realising that Chris's crew consisted of one other person for camera and lighting, so I was struck by his flexibility, portability and spontaneity. He subsequently came to America to shoot *Liberty Heights* for Barry Levinson and then Gus Van Sant's remake of *Psycho*, and became kind of an extended family member, moving into my house in Los Angeles for several months.

I imagined that for shooting with children, we'd need to be very flexible and not weighed down by excess equipment. The success of the film would be dependent not only on finding the right children, but on how we managed to interface with them and the flexibility of the working environment. Usually the actors fit around the camera and other equipment. But with untrained children, everything had to fit around them; everything had to be subordinated to them. They couldn't necessarily be relied upon for take two, or hitting marks, or any of the usual acting disciplines. The DoP had to be ready when they were ready, and he had to get it when they got it. Chris was always ready.

Doyle was mostly known for working with a hand-held camera, utilising close-ups and capturing the confined spaces of urban Asia. Now he was being given the task of capturing wide-open spaces with wide-angle shots.

Over the years a very predictable style for shooting the Australian landscape has developed, with pretty pictures and classical composition, but I wanted this film to evoke a different feeling of Australia. The audience shouldn't think that once the kids have escaped from Moore River Native Settlement they are safe. There's still a hell of a long journey ahead of them and for the major part of that trek you should fear for them, because it's not just the authorities they have to battle, but also their own personal limitations and unfamiliarity with the land. That's why I didn't want the landscape to look welcoming. And I wanted Chris to give the film a quasi-documentary look with his hand-held camera and off-centre framing. As he himself isn't at ease with nature, the viewer feels Chris's own alienation from the outback. Chris just prefers the landscape of neon lights, bars and fast-food joints.

Chris Doyle recalls his work in very similar terms. 'The look of the film is God-given, I guess, pretty much outdoor . . . a road movie on foot. For me, all films are made by the circumstances of their making. *Rabbit-Proof Fence* is very dependent on the spaces we're working in and what God gives us in terms of climate and weather conditions.

'That said, what I'm trying to do as cinematographer is give things a certain look. I think the Rochester, Kodak, Norman Rockwell kind of look is other people's reality, not mine. I was looking for something that suggested the torment, the cruelty of the journey, the loneliness, the isolation and the expanse. We've gone for a washed-out look because it's very different from a traditional Australian outback painting or an image with this beautiful blue sky we see here. In our film we don't want blue sky because [the characters'] skies are not very blue. They're harsh and cruel and tormenting, so it's a washed-out look. There's a lot of extremity, of whiteness to the landscape. There's a bleakness to what lies before them and we achieve that by desaturating the colours, by certain exposures, little tricks and by the way we process the film.'[4]

The shoot started on 18 September and was pretty uneventful, really. I don't remember anything in particular.

The *Rabbit Bulletins*, however, sometimes tell a slightly different story, at least those from the location in the Flinders Ranges. The bulletins were released, mostly to family, friends and business associates, once a week during the seven weeks of the shoot and were edited by Lucia Noyce.

'The first six days . . . of shooting in the Flinders Ranges presented many challenges to the cast and crew. Unpredictable weather, unforgiving sun, winds, and overall barren and hostile terrain made the change in working conditions a noticeable one. However, the new environment has its advantages as well. The open air makes the days go faster and for many provides a visual link to the film's story; bringing us all a small step closer to understanding the experience of the characters.'[5]

'During the final week of filming the cast and crew faced some of the most formidable challenges of the shoot. Unpredictable weather, unscheduled re-shoots, and technical difficulties created unforeseen problems that were somehow avoided thanks to the communal efforts of a group that had grown particularly close during the *Rabbit-Proof Fence* shoot. AFI winner Deborah Mailman spent over six days in the Flinders for her portrayal of Mavis, a domestic servant on a farm who offers the girls a place to sleep quite early in their journey home. Damage to the film negative made re-shoots of this difficult scene necessary. This opportunity to refine what is a key emotional moment in the script was not unwelcomed by director Phillip Noyce and screenwriter Christine Olsen.

'Another technical difficulty created problems as well, but this time for the 2nd Unit team. Helicopter aerial shots of the Torrens River salt lake were abandoned and then rescheduled due to an electrical malfunction in the chopper. The sequences utilised two sets of doubles for Molly and Daisy shot in two separate locations. This footage is then to be cut with Main Unit footage shot with Everlyn Sampi and Tianna Sansbury, the "real" Molly and Daisy.

'A foretaste of the flash floods that began days after we left the Flinders, leaving many of our production office team stranded, also provided another testing moment. Heavy rains on the third to last day of shooting slowed the speed at which the crew was able to work. However, the creative thinking and organising of Assistant Director Emma Schofield prevented it from being a threat to the film's scheduling.'[6]

The greatest challenge during shooting was working with the eldest of the children, twelve-year-old Everlyn Sampi, whose mother was a part of the Stolen Generations, having grown up in a church-run institution. Everlyn was a very highly strung young girl – proud and seemingly confident, but underneath extremely unsure of herself and overwhelmed by all sorts of fears. She was perfect for the part of Molly because of her natural rebellious personality and healthy disrespect for authority, coupled with remarkable determination. So everything that was potentially a negative within the context of making a film was a positive within the context of creating a character, so long as we could settle her sufficiently to be herself and allow the camera to capture that extraordinary determination, wisdom, energy, vulnerability and psychological complexity. She ran away a couple of times during pre-production – just like the character she was playing. So a lot of my energy was spent filling her with confidence, nurturing her, guiding her, trying to get her to believe in herself.

Although he was used to the attitudes and mood changes of Hollywood stars, Sampi's tantrums were trying for Noyce. At the workshop in Broome, she once left the room supposedly for ten minutes, only to return hours later. The press reported: 'she refuses to put on her costume. Another time she storms off and slams the door behind her . . . At the age of 13, she already smokes. She dresses like Britney Spears and dances like a woman.'[7] The problems became so difficult that Noyce seriously considered replacing her just days before filming was due to start. But as 'no one had Sampi's talent or the fire in her personality so necessary for the role', he decided to put up with her temper tantrums.[8]

Noyce's professional instincts clearly alerted him to the discovery of a gem. 'In Everlyn I see that star quality I have seen twice in my career, once in Nicole Kidman and then again [in] Angelina Jolie, and now for the third time I have seen it in Everlyn.'[9] Still, she wasn't there yet.

Between a beginner and an experienced actor there is a huge gap. And often it's better not to fill that gap, because someone with absolutely no experience, and therefore no technique, can be just as good as the most experienced actor. With experience come actorly tricks, acting techniques that can make a performance false. Each of these children had been typecast to play characters like their own real-life personalities.

The children had been chosen because of their ability to concentrate and maintain focus, but also because of their vivid imaginations. As long as they feel free, children can take themselves anywhere in their minds, inventing friends or alternative parallel universes, turning a chair into a spaceship or creating a battlefield in their minds. Kids can transport themselves anywhere. So a lot of preparation was simply about encouraging the children to free their imaginations by asking them to improvise. The only formal training involved forcing them to use their voices a bit better, to project, and just getting them slowly at ease with the machinery and crew that would surround them during filming. So, in preparation, they progressed from reacting to a still camera, to a video camera, to a small movie camera, to a large movie camera and an ever-expanding crew, who gradually became their extended family as well.

As they were children from remote communities we even brought their mums, and often dads, as well as sisters and cousins, so they wouldn't get homesick. And we used the other family members in the Moore River sequences as actors. For example, the tracker's daughter is played by Tracy, the sister of the middle lead actress Laura Monaghan.

There were absolutely no black–white frictions during the shoot. The three real children of the story came from Jigalong in Western Australia, so the elders from there sent representatives to the set whenever we were depicting their country and people, to advise us on cultural matters. Doris Pilkington-Garimara, the writer of the novel, was the script adviser, and she participated in the editing by looking at various cuts and giving her comments. At all stages and everywhere we filmed, local elders and representatives were also consulted.

Locations were spread around South Australia but were mostly in the Flinders Ranges. The Moore River Native Settlement was constructed just south of Adelaide, the Jigalong set east of Leigh Creek. The total production cost was A$10.5 million.

Peter Gabriel didn't join the team until after the movie was shot. I'd been a fan since hearing his score for Scorsese's *The Last Temptation of Christ*. I have always marvelled at that composition because it works for a remote period setting, even though the music is modern and innovative. I had gotten to know Peter while living and working on *The Saint* in London, and later approached him for *The Bone Collector* but that film just wasn't his cup of tea; though he did sell me one of his tracks for the final credits, 'Don't Give Up'. After I shot *Rabbit-Proof Fence* I immediately went to Vietnam for pre-production on *The Quiet American* and to start casting for the lead actress, and that search took me to every city in the world where there were Vietnamese diaspora, including Paris and London.

While I was in London, the music supervisor from *The Saint* and *Bone Collector*, George Acogny, a mutual friend, arranged a meeting with Peter again. And I gave Peter the choice of composing for either

The Quiet American – the story of which he was familiar with from Greene's novel – or *Rabbit-Proof Fence* – a project he had never heard of. But I told him the incredible story of *Rabbit* and said that there was little or no money to pay a composer for that film but I'd really love him to do the score for either project. Two days later he rang back and said he wanted to do *Rabbit*, despite the budget barrier. Peter loves to use ethnic elements drawn from a wide variety of sources that somehow coalesce, and I think that his personal support for human rights issues also attracted him. Also, George Acogny had been deeply moved by the story, which mirrored his own African grandmother's experiences, so he had encouraged Peter to participate.

That began a nine-month collaboration on the soundtrack with Peter, although I never saw him in person again from that day to the film's London premiere eighteen months later. It was mainly done by email, by the exchange of MP3 files of music and sound effects. My team of sound editors working at Soundfirm in Fox Studios, Sydney, emailed natural sounds of the Australian bush – birds, wind, rain, crickets – over to Bath in the UK, where the crew at Real World would copy, program and synthesise musical notes based on those sounds, incorporate them into the music and then email the files back to us. And we would mix them into the film soundtrack together with the dialogue, so that we could keep building organically from each other.

The cooperation with Gabriel continued, in fact, to the last possible day: the very last piece of sound arrived only the day before the premiere screening in Sydney's Fox Studios on 4 February 2002. This event was pretty colourful, with Noyce paying due homage to Doris Pilkington-Garimara. The three girl actors, together with the Jigalong mob and local Sydney elders, took to the stage. Among the audience were other well-known Aboriginal Australians such as Olympic gold-medallist Cathy Freeman. Everyone seemed in a very conciliatory mood.

But with a prime minister in office who still denied the Aboriginal community a gesture of reconciliation, it was hardly surprising to find Australian conservatives on the barricades even before the film was released. Similarly to events surrounding Martin Scorsese's *The Last Temptation of Christ*, Lismore mayor Bob Gates attacked the film even though he hadn't seen it yet – and wasn't ashamed to reveal that he had no intention of seeing it.[10]

The mayor had based his verdict on a newspaper article by hardliner Andrew Bolt, who had even been attacked in Parliament over his right-leaning views. Bolt objected to the film calling itself 'a true story', and to the disgusting fact that A\$5.3 million of taxpayers' money had been wasted on its production. He concluded with a personal blast at the director: 'Your film shames not us, Phillip Noyce, but you.'[11] He also attempted to point out what he considered to be errors of fact – for example, he argued that the children weren't removed because of Neville's plan to 'breed out' Aborigines, but instead were taken from squalid camps for their own good.

Noyce and scriptwriter Christine Olsen refuted Bolt's claims comprehensively in a public statement dated 20 February 2002, which was published in the Melbourne *Herald Sun* a week later.[12] But Bolt was in no mood to give in. Instead, he tried to have the last word by writing two nearly identical responses published in the *Herald Sun*[13] and the *Courier-Mail*[14] (which had published his earlier attack on Noyce as well). In these he demanded the same amount of factuality from a feature film as from a documentary, and expressed his conviction that children of mixed racial parentage in general, and the girls in the film in particular, were not taken from their families as such but were resettled to improve their welfare.

Piers Akerman, another political hardliner, came to the beleaguered Bolt's support.[15] Akerman made the political point that a Stolen Generation simply doesn't exist – instead, loving parents sent their children away voluntarily because they 'thought an education away from the persecution of camp life was in the best interests of their children'. To which Noyce countered: 'There is a simple, undeniable truth behind *Rabbit-Proof Fence*. Molly Craig, the 14-year-old heroine of our film, was determined to live her life in the way she wanted to, not in the way the government of the time had decreed she should.'[16] Full stop. But like Bolt before him, Akerman lashed out at Noyce personally when he said, '[T]here are some people determined to keep Australians divided by racist stereotyping of the sort perpetuated by misguided conspiracists spruiking the flawed Stolen Generation myth.' Doris Pilkington, who had been taken from her mother as a baby and was only reunited with her 21 years later, said simply: 'Recognise what happened to us, so that we can all be healed.'[17]

As Bolt and Akerman's attacks on the film hadn't been particularly successful – in fact, letters to the editors were overwhelmingly in favour of the film and strongly recommended that it be seen by all Australians – it was obviously time to bring fresh experts into the battle. This happened in a joint article by Peter Howson, Liberal minister for Aboriginal affairs in 1971 and 1972, and Des Moore, director of the Institute for Private Enterprise, an ultra-conservative think-tank. They argued that the film was attempting 'to give credibility to the now discredited Stolen Generation thesis . . . claims of forcible removal of half-caste children have been comprehensively rejected in three court cases.'[18] The authors' argument, they said, was based on 'facts' about the 'humane actions' of A.O. Neville. In relation to the authors' demand of factuality, Christine Olsen responded in the *Australian*: 'Peter Howson and Des Moore relate how, after Mr. Neville's death, his mother received about 500 letters from Aborigines praising his efforts. Mr. Neville died in 1954; his mother, Elizabeth Neville, died in 1895.'[19]

Why was the film – and its director – the target of such ferocious attacks? Noyce isn't necessarily a political flag bearer – though the subject matter of the film concerns him greatly. Foremost he is a film director and entertainer, not a politician or an academic. It might reasonably be argued that his approach to the topic made more people aware of this dark chapter in Australia's history than had any scholarly text. The film wasn't seen only by those people who were already aware of the events surrounding the story, but by a predominantly suburban, and even rural, audience who could by no means necessarily be labelled left-leaning liberals. By having the story taken from an abstract political level to a concrete personal level, each member of the audience was likely to at some point ask themselves: 'How would I feel if my child were taken away?' Robert Manne, associate professor of politics at Melbourne's La Trobe University and author of *In Denial: The Stolen Generation*, in a four-page newspaper article, concluded: '*Rabbit-Proof Fence* is not only a remarkably accurate account of a dark episode in our history. As it suggests, a simple story of seizure and the escape of three young "half-caste" girls can take us, if we are willing to open our eyes, to an understanding of the racial fantasies and phobias and to the genocidal thoughts that masqueraded as policies for the welfare of Aborigines in Australia's interwar years.'[20]

Was Noyce aware that the film would touch a very sensitive nerve in Australia's history and conscience?

I knew that the 1997 Royal Commission had recommended that an official apology be given to indigenous Australians, for the Stolen Generation policies. But I thought it was just the single-minded dickheadedness of the incumbent Liberal Party prime minister John Howard that prevented him from acknowledging the findings of a Royal Commission that had been instigated by a previous Labor government. Once the film came out I became well aware that, in fact, there were certain commentators in the country – who enjoyed a strong following – who were determined to convince Australians that the policies of forced separation were for the good of Aborigines, and that basically there is no such thing as the Stolen Generation because no one was really stolen. And that it all had been an invention of manipulative Aborigines and their left-leaning, guilt-ridden white supporters.

I was surprised at the vehemence with which these commentators attacked the film, seemingly determined – if they could – to prevent people from seeing the movie. And if they did see it, seemingly determined to prevent them taking its content seriously. This seemed to reveal a very deep fear about the issues, understandable in a way because for so long there has been very little academic investigation into any aspects of indigenous Australian history and culture. Except as an anthropological subject. The idea of genocide towards the original inhabitants was just too much of a challenge to the image we'd developed of ourselves and exported to the world. Like the deniers of the Holocaust, there are groups of conservative Australians who cannot confront the truth of our history.

I didn't feel personally hurt. But I did feel that the commentators were trying to destroy the movie and its message, and their attacks had nothing to do with art, nothing to do with history, nothing to do with truth – but everything to do with ideology. They were determined to infect as many other minds as possible with their own obsessions and denials. And it was interesting to realise there was a minority – or maybe not – in Australia who were in massive denial. And who would go to any length to encourage others in that blinkered view of ourselves. Once the movie became a success, Andrew Bolt and Piers Akerman, writing in the Murdoch press, tried to discredit me personally by attacking my credibility and motives, even suggesting that I was un-Australian for allowing the story to be exported. Publicist Emma Cooper tried to fuel the controversy to make up for our lack of advertising dollars [*laughs*]. So whenever one of these attacks appeared, she would immediately demand equal space to rebut it. And that seemed to work.

Following the old advertising saying that even bad publicity is good publicity, *Rabbit-Proof Fence* was a topic of general discussion by the time it opened around the country in late February/early March 2002. But this rather unexpected development was only the second step in the marketing, as Noyce had earlier embarked on 'information saturation':

Certainly I have tried to take some of the lessons I learned in Hollywood, particularly about marketing films, and apply them to selling an extremely independent-minded production like this. We used some of the Hollywood information-saturation techniques to try to sell the picture, so that when it opened almost everyone knew about the movie – even though it had a tiny budget and is in theory what normally might be considered art-house fare.

The Australian was the first to write about the project, in a lengthy article in June 2001. Then Noyce gave Channel Nine unlimited access to the various phases of pre-production and production. A crew headed by James Thomas consequently produced the five-part series that started airing on the *Today* show from 10 December 2001. This also resulted in the twenty-minute 'The Making of *Rabbit-Proof Fence*' program, broadcast on 10 February 2002, just eleven days prior to the premiere. By that time, Noyce was already busy travelling up and down the country, attending previews of the film, often accompanied by a member of the cast or crew. When the film eventually opened on 90 screens throughout Australia on 21 February, it had, in fact, become a cause célèbre.

'Bold in concept and inspirational in intent, . . . pic tells its tale of dogged courage and fortitude with a straightforward directness, and benefits immensely from the luminous presences of the children involved . . . Noyce is an accomplished story-teller, and while *Rabbit-Proof Fence* lacks the poetic vision of a film like *Walkabout*, it succeeds emotionally in the cause of what seems to be its primary aim, to advance an attitudinal change in Australians not normally sympathetic to the aboriginal cause,' *Variety* stated.[21] *The Age* claimed: 'Chris Doyle's cinematography shows us a bleached, harsh landscape, neither romanticised nor made strange.'[22]

Ironically, some of the papers that had carried attacks on the film in their opinion pages also published some of the most enthusiastic critical reviews, in part directly contradicting the papers' political stances. One was the *Herald Sun*: 'This is a landmark Australian film . . . marking a triumphant return to form for director Phillip Noyce after far too long on the schlockier end of the Hollywood assembly line . . . Without taking a tub-thumping stance, *Rabbit-Proof Fence* subtly shifts the Stolen Generation debate to where it should have been all along: as a tragic humanitarian riddle that still eludes fathomable answer.'[23]

The good reviews weren't confined to newspapers, though. 'It is one of the most finely crafted, most emotionally satisfying films ever made in this, or any other country' raved Peter Thompson on the Nine Network's *Sunday* program.[24] Frank Hatherley was equally enthusiastic: 'With its brilliantly managed performances and astonishing widescreen panoramas, *Rabbit-Proof Fence* vividly dramatises an aspect of colonial ignorance that continues to reverberate throughout the world . . . a testimony to [Noyce's] determination and sensitivity . . . something all Australians can be proud of.'[25]

Many rave reviews appear on the IMDb site and at Ain't It Cool News, and the reviewers' remarks are much less inhibited than those of the serious critics. 'This film does not achieve its end by slapping you in the face with strong, indigestible political comment. Instead, Noyce and his talented cast take hold of your heart and gently squeeze it until the pain is so intense your brain aches and tears roll down your cheeks.'[26] User ratings on the IMDb website even before the film had opened widely internationally showed the highest-ever appreciation of any Noyce film so far. Women in the 45-plus age group were its biggest fans, voting it a resounding 9.5 out of 10 on average. This correlates with its financial success at the Australian box office, where it made over A$7 million, making it almost the most popular Australian feature of the year.[27] But not only were the critics and movie-goers jubilant; the industry also recognised Noyce's achievement in making *Rabbit-Proof Fence* by awarding him 'Best Film' at the AFI Awards that year.[28]

This film has been most successful in the multiplexes all around the country in the outer belt of suburban Australia. I mean, there is almost no history of a film with indigenous characters working at the

Australian box office. The last time it happened was back in the 1950s with Charles Chauvel's *Jedda*.

It was gratifying to come back to Australia to make a project of historical and social relevance that would enter the nation's popular culture. I was attracted by a great and emotionally compelling story. But also by the idea of overturning conventions. The character that's portrayed on the film's poster is a strong, determined, loving, sensitive, attractive and intelligent Australian, who is also black. Where have you seen that before? Probably only once: Olympic 400 metres champion Cathy Freeman.

So the idea of making a film that celebrates Aboriginal family history as an important component of mainstream Australian history for me was an irresistible challenge – given the iconography that's being created. When I grew up we knew nothing about Aborigines, we didn't talk about them even though every large country town in my state of New South Wales had a reserve outside of town where indigenous people were forced to live. Aborigines weren't counted in the census until 1967 or given the vote until then. They weren't citizens. They were a second category of human beings. The idea of making a story where the heroine is the Aboriginal girl and you are presenting that as a normal, everyday part of popular culture and selling it aggressively in cinema multiplexes in the suburbs made the whole project worthwhile. Saddened as I was by Molly Craig's death at age 87 in early 2004, I was heartened that the London *Times*, *New York Times* and *Los Angeles Times* newspapers, and *Le Monde* in Paris, all felt it was important to record the passing of a genuine Australian heroine.

In 1977, Noyce had started his career as a director with *Backroads*, a road movie about a couple of black drifters (and one white one) on a car trip from the outback to the eastern seaboard, where all traces of Aboriginal culture have long since vanished. On the way, they receive help from some Aborigines. But no particular destination exists, and one by one the protagonists perish. It is a deeply pessimistic film.

Then, in 2001 Noyce returned to his homeland and again

embarked on a kind of road movie. But after 23 years much had changed: the three girls head inland from the west coast, to where there is still Aboriginal identity, in the deserts of Western Australia. They have a clear destination – Jigalong camp – and they undertake the journey in the traditional black man's way: by walking. Despite all the obstacles of climate, topography, and flora and fauna, they more or less proceed on their home turf. They are helped along their way and betrayed both by blacks and whites, and they finally make it home. It is a truly inspiring, optimistic film.

Backroads and *Rabbit-Proof Fence* clearly act as bookends around Noyce's work, and they are both recognisably Australian in several aspects. To start with, the underdog, the little Aussie battler, traditionally is a genuine icon in this country. He or she may eventually lose – but the triumph lies in having tried. Australian history is littered with examples – from the Eureka Stockade to Gallipoli, from Burke and Wills to Ned Kelly. Only two of the girls make it back to Jigalong and even they will be taken away again soon. The 2000-kilometre trek along the fence is a feat of epic proportions, no matter what the eventual outcome. This notion of being on the road, on the move – without necessarily arriving anywhere in the end – likewise is deeply enshrined in the Australian psyche.

Rabbit-Proof Fence is a story of any underdog who triumphs. It's a story of any outsider who exceeds their own expectations of themselves and the limitations other people place on them. It's about any underdog who overcomes the odds. And, essentially, it's not about the uniqueness of Aboriginal culture, but the ways in which we're all the same. It's about communality and the ties that bind, about love and interdependence between all parents and their children. Plus, it's about freedom. These are all elements that anybody can relate to.

And relate they did. Before it was even finished, *Rabbit-Proof Fence* was presold around the world to every major film-going country. By September 2003, it had made US$18 million world-wide. Part of the success was due to Noyce's unfaltering energy and enthusiasm, with which he initially promoted the film on an eighteen-stop festival tour around the world, 'which he did for free; he will get paid only if the picture does well enough to enrich 19 equity investors that include himself, Kenneth Branagh and composer Peter Gabriel'.[29] The film was 'acclaimed as marvellous, memorable and moving by most critics in Britain'.[30] Only the *Financial Times* panned *Rabbit-Proof Fence*, calling it 'a piece of ingratiating PC hooey, so steeped in political hindsight and liberal sentimentality that the lack of craft, artistry or originality can easily go unnoticed'.[31] Even though it was 'only' art-house fare, critical reaction was similarly positive in the United States, and had a strong emphasis on the 'human spirit' or 'humanity' of the film.

To make a long success story short, eventually the film and/or its makers made it on to several critics' list of top ten films of the year, and won the audience awards at the Aspen, Castellinaria, Denver, Leeds, São Paulo, Edinburgh and Valladolid film festivals. It received a Christopher Award in the Feature Film category at the 54th Annual Christopher Awards. The Christopher Awards salute media that 'affirm the highest values of the human spirit'. At the London Film Critics Circle Awards, Noyce won Best Director *ex aequo* for *Rabbit-Proof Fence* and *The Quiet American*. On top of that, an initial investment of A$10.5 million was approaching the A$18 million mark in box-office revenue in September 2003 – though these figures are somewhat misleading.[32]

It seems that foreign audiences had much less of a problem with the film's underlying politics than did the Australian Right. This is most apparent in the case of the US, with its poor history of race relations. Britain, of course, has the stain of wrongdoings committed against its colonial subjects. But it would appear that Australia is alone among such countries in refusing to acknowledge its historical transgressions. That English settlement of Australia took place without the Aborigines having been the victims of atrocities is not credible to most foreigners. At the end of the day, it wasn't Noyce who 'made us feel ashamed as Australians', as Andrew Bolt suggests,[33] but he and like-minded Australians who tried to discredit or even censor the film.

Once *Rabbit-Proof Fence* became unstoppable due to its domestic success, efforts were geared towards minimising the possible fall-out abroad. On 21 May 2002, Liberal MP Peter Slipper announced that he was opposed to the tagline that Miramax proposed to use on its posters: 'What if the government kidnapped your daughter? It happened every week in Australia from 1905–1971.' Noyce felt that Miramax was 'wrong to promote the film as a political expose'. But with all the media attention at hand, he cheekily added: 'Maybe we could strike a bargain. The Australian Government apologises to our nation's indigenous people and I make the Miramax people apologise for the poster.'[34] As could be expected, Miramax rejected Slipper's objection, saying they had 'conducted research which fully backs the words on the poster'.[35] Ten days later 'Australia's Special Minister of State Eric Abetz denounced Noyce and the film, declaring that he would publish brochures about its inaccuracies'.[36] As the *ABC News* reported, Abetz had 'spent government funds producing and distributing a brochure in his Tasmanian electorate, accusing the film of being dishonest and exaggerated'.[37]

There is no doubt that Noyce and his film had become tangled up in the domestic 'history wars', centring around the question of whether any, and if so, how many, Aborigines had died at the hands of white settlers – was it genocide or just a handful of unconnected tragic accidents? This war of the historians is being fought between what Henry Reynolds calls the 'three-cheers and the black-armband schools of history'[38] – the first of which 'holds that Australia's past is a succession of triumphs where white Europeans civilised a brown world . . . the [second] holds that white Australia has a dark past.'[39] The war erupted – at least in the public's perception – over the publication of Keith Windschuttle's *The Fabrication of Aboriginal History* in late 2002. The book not only refutes the hitherto generally acknowledged conclusion that genocide was inflicted on the Tasmanian Aborigines, but also accuses opponents of this idea of being engaged in a conspiracy of fraud and fabrication aimed at making Australians feel guilty.

As the attacks between the two camps increasingly turned personal, the spotlight was suddenly on Noyce again. This was possibly in response to his nomination for 'Australian of the Year' in *The Australian* newspaper,[40] but was almost certainly linked with his accusations, on humanitarian grounds, against the incumbent government in a press conference held after the AFI Awards.[41] Both Bolt and Akerman vehemently took up their attacks on Noyce again. Akerman labelled him 'notorious amongst purveyors of dubious revisionism', saying, 'If Australia's image does suffer abroad anywhere, except in the pages of the Left-wing media and among the theatrically politically-engaged (most of whom are of dubious intellect and originality), then the Noyces . . . are to blame.'[42] Bolt even turned the tables when he referred to Everlyn Sampi's frequent 'escapes' during the shoot: Noyce's 'attempt to give Everlyn a brighter future resembled Neville's bid to rescue Molly'.[43] In truth, Noyce has seen to it that once they reach the age of 21, 'each of the three young stars will find trust accounts derived from the film's profits, waiting to help them a little as they embrace life in 21st century Australia.'

The last one to take up his pen was Keith Windschuttle, in the *New Criterion*. Not only did he imply that Noyce was un-Australian by labelling him 'Australian born', but he also equated Noyce's treatment of the three girls – particularly the rebellious Sampi – with that of Neville.[44] In short, Noyce was singled out as a political contributor in a concerted effort by the Left to smear Australian history and Australia's reputation.

Fortunately, by 2002, Australian audiences were clearly too sophisticated and well educated to confuse a feature film with a political pamphlet. Instead, they flocked in droves to see a genuinely Australian film with huge popular appeal that has humanity pouring from almost every frame. To see a film that, worldwide, was clearly considered another artistic triumph for this country; and to see a film of which all Australians should be proud.

---

[1] *Rabbit-Proof Fence* press kit (Becker Entertainment).

[2] Ibid.

[3] Email from Kenneth Branagh to Phillip Noyce, dated 25 September 2000.

[4] Chris Doyle interviewed in *if* magazine (Sydney), no. 32, April 2001.

[5] *Rabbit Bulletin #5*.

[6] *Rabbit Bulletin #7*.

[7] Charisse Ede, 'An odyssey along the *Rabbit Proof Fence*', *The Age*, 6 December 2001.

[8] Ibid.

[9] Quoted in *Rabbit-Proof Fence* press kit, p. 13.

[10] Sarah Price, 'Mayor blast at indigenous film', *Northern Star*, 23 February 2002.

[11] Andrew Bolt, 'Rabbit-proof myths', *Herald Sun*, 14 February 2002.

[12] Phillip Noyce and Christine Olsen, 'Not myths, reality', *Herald Sun*, 27 February 2002.

[13] Andrew Bolt, 'It's still not true, Phillip', *Herald Sun*, 28 February 2002.

[14] Andrew Bolt, 'Andrew Bolt again defends his assertion that the film *Rabbit-Proof Fence* takes liberties with the truth', *Courier-Mail*, 2 March 2002.

[15] Piers Akerman, 'Artistic licence spoils this saga', *Sunday Telegraph*, 3 March 2002.

[16] Phillip Noyce, 'Rabbit-proof defence', *Sunday Telegraph*, 10 March 2002.

[17] Quoted in ibid.

[18] Peter Howson and Des Moore, 'A rabbit-proof fence full of holes', *The Australian*, 1 March 2002.

[19] Christine Olsen, 'Fence-follower's story: A true one', *The Australian*, 12 March 2002.

[20] Robert Manne, 'Fade into white – the plan to breed out Aboriginal colour', *Sydney Morning Herald*, 23 February 2002.

[21] David Stratton, '*Rabbit-Proof Fence*', *Variety*, 18 February 2002.

[22] Philippa Hawker, 'Simple yet powerful tale', *The Age*, 21 February 2002.

[23] Leigh Paatsch, 'Full proof', *Herald Sun*, 14 February 2002.

[24] Peter Thompson: *Rabbit-Proof Fence*. *Sunday* program, Nine Network Australia, review, 24 February 2002.

[25] Frank Hatherley: 'Rabbit-Proof Fence', 2 February 2002; cited at www.hanwayfilms.com/h–print–formats/print–films–rabbit.html

[26] Scott Abrahams, us.imdb.com

[27] It was beaten by *Crackerjack* by only a couple of thousand dollars.

[28] The film won two additional AFI awards: for Best Original Music Score and for Best Sound.

[29] Michael Fleming, 'Noyce on the "Fence" as he makes fest round', *Variety*, 18 October 2002.

30 'Rabbit-Proof Fence wows Britain', The Age, 9 November 2002.
31 Cited in The Age, 9 November 2002.
32 Noyce explains: 'The confusion comes from the difference between distribution guarantees (which is the money paid by distributors for the rights to the film) and the box-office grosses. The film has gross box-office earnings of A$30 million, which doesn't really mean anything, because of the large distribution guarantees paid in the various territories. Combining Australian box-office net earnings and foreign distribution guarantees, the film had returned A$18 million gross, which after advertising expenses and distribution costs has returned A$11 million net to investors. In other words: a small profit at this stage, which will steadily increase over the years. And then dramatically increase in ten years once the various distributors start to relicense the film in their territories.'
33 Andrew Bolt, 'You hypocrite, Phil', Herald Sun, 12 December 2002.
34 Quoted in 'Noyce no political poster boy', Daily Telegraph, 24 May 2002.
35 'Miramax stands by Rabbit slogan', Daily Telegraph, 4 June 2002.
36 Elaine Dutka, 'Aussies upset with Hollywood portrayal', LA Times Morning Report, 14 June 2002.
37 'Noyce defends film after Tasmanian MP's leaflet attack', ABC News, 12 June 2002.
38 Cited in Andrew Fraser, 'Black past was "covered in white"', The Australian, 3 October 2003.
39 Ibid.
40 Ian Gerard, 'A movie director of artistic integrity', The Australian, 28 December 2002.
41 Garry Maddox, 'Noyce Laments Nation's Loss of Humanity', Sydney Morning Herald, 9 December 2002.
42 Piers Akerman, 'Fenced in by his own revisionism', Sunday Telegraph, 29 December 2002.
43 Bolt, 'You hypocrite, Phil'.
44 Keith Windschuttle, 'Rabbit-proof fence: "A true story"?', New Criterion, March 2003.

Chapter 16

THE QUIET AMERICAN

The movie had collided with history in a most unfortunate manner.

Thomas Fowler (Michael Caine) enjoys his life as a foreign correspondent in Saigon during the last days of the French colonial rule. But when his beautiful Vietnamese mistress Phuong (Do Thi Hai Yen) becomes the object of affection of Alden Pyle (Brendan Fraser), a young American on a humanitarian mission, Fowler's life begins to unravel against the backdrop of war and the beginnings of the involvement of America in the conflict.

Like many Americans, we Australians had misgivings about the war in Vietnam. Australia became involved in a major way in 1965, when we committed troops to supposedly fight communism. We were then (as now) gripped by fear of the so-called yellow peril: billions of Asians waiting supposedly to steal our land, our women and our lifestyle. We committed to fight alongside the Americans and other allies in Vietnam because we accepted the domino theory that unless a stand was taken up in Southeast Asia against communism, then one by one the democracies of the region would fall. This was a particularly potent threat to Australia because we were supposedly the last and major domino. So, after Indonesia fell, the aggressive communist virus would be on our doorstep. Better to fight up in Vietnam to stop this cancer from spreading south to engulf us. As the later publication of government papers would show, Australia's involvement was also motivated by a desire to earn the gratitude of a United States who had saved us from invasion by Japan in 1942.

As a fourteen-year-old completing compulsory military training at high school I was taught how to avoid the bamboo spikes of a Vietcong booby trap, as the Vietnamese were seen as our principal enemy. Australians were subject to the draft, like many American teenagers, and in my family all three brothers were lucky not to have their birth date pulled from the barrel – an event that as a nation we witnessed for years on TV every few months as celebrities drew out dates to signify which teenagers would shortly be drafted. And so our neighbours and friends went to Vietnam, fought and came back full of disillusionment, and the disillusionment spread (as it did in America) to the whole nation, which by 1970 was wondering why we had been so easily duped just five years previously. Although I had escaped the war, like many of my generation I was filled with an unresolved sense of guilt towards Vietnam for all that had occurred.

In 1985 I became involved in a TV miniseries called *Saigon*, an adaptation of a part-documentary, part-fiction novel by Englishman Anthony Grey, which told the story of three generations of three families from three nations – French, American, Vietnamese – and their conflicts and intermarriages from the 1920s through to the 1970s with the fall of Saigon and the end of the Vietnam–American war. That project had been cancelled about four months before shooting was due to start, when the American network CBS, who were the principal sponsors, decided they had problems with the story line.

In 1995 I went to Vietnam for the first time to investigate the possibility of resurrecting *Saigon* but also because I had heard of an unusual reunion that was to take place in the north of the country to celebrate the arrival there in 1945 of the American Deer Team. This was a band of OSS operatives, forerunner of the CIA, who had parachuted into North Vietnam in the closing stages of the Second World War. Their mission was to link up with and arm a little-known Vietnamese rebel leader called Ho Chi Minh, so that Ho and his men could wage a rear-guard guerrilla action against the Japanese.

'But nine weeks later Japan capitulated. And armed with the [weapons] given by the Americans, and with the Americans trailing along beside him, Ho Chi Minh marched several hundred miles to Hanoi, [where], before the French had time to regroup and come back and claim the jewel that was their colony of Indochina, Ho Chi Minh, not for the last time, declared Vietnam to be independent. And the Americans who were with Ho, and who got to know him and his band of men, reported back to their superiors in the State Department and the army back in Washington, that Ho was first and foremost a nationalist, fighting for the independence of his country, and his communism was a means to an end, a way of organising, a way of arming, a way of carrying forward this fight for independence. And over the coming years, Ho sent seven letters to President Truman. Truman, of course, had replaced Roosevelt, the former president, who had a policy of decolonisation, who was dedicated towards freeing the former colonies of the European powers. But the seven letters that Ho Chi Minh wrote to Truman were all ignored even though in those seven letters he asked the Americans for assistance. He offered to cooperate with America. He offered to make Vietnam a protectorate of America. He asked for help on one condition, and he said in one amazing letter, "I don't care if a million American soldiers come to Vietnam so long as not one Frenchman sets foot in my country again." And of course the million soldiers did come . . . "[1]

The survivors of that Deer Team, as they were called, went back to North Vietnam 50 years later to meet up at Ho's former camp with their Vietnamese counterparts. Listening to those old soldiers and their stories, one couldn't help but be overwhelmed by their sense of regret. In the years since they were last there together in the jungle, several million people had died in a conflict between the two former allies. Having for the most part stood on the sidelines and watched as an enormous tragedy unfolded, these old soldiers were all naturally filled with regret.

Soon after that jungle reunion, back in Hanoi, I was sold a copy of a plain green-covered book. I had intended to buy Ho Chi Minh's prison poetry, but when I opened the book on a slow train from Hue to Hoi An in central Vietnam, I realised that before me was Graham Greene's novel *The Quiet American*. Surrounded by the Vietnamese ghosts of the independence wars, I was really struck by the ways in which Greene's thesis – composed from his observations made in the early and mid-fifties – answered so many questions that at the time of writing hadn't yet been asked. Particularly the fundamental question of the Vietnam–American war: why? Why did we fight? What possessed us? Why did we rain hell on the Vietnamese for so long and with such vehemence?

From Hoi An I arrived in Saigon, where for romantic reasons I had already booked into the Graham Greene Suite at the famous Continental Hotel. I phoned my office at Paramount Pictures in Los Angeles and asked them to find out who owned the rights to Greene's novel. About two days later they rang back and said the famed American director Sydney Pollack owned the rights. As it turned out, Sydney had been developing the film for six years with another acquaintance of mine, a Swedish producer called Staffan Ahrenberg, and had recently decided he no longer wanted to direct *Quiet* but was content to produce.

Pollack: 'No, no, no, no, no. I think when Staffan first brought it to me he had that idea, but I never said I would. I always said it was possible, that maybe I would. But I never got the kind of subjective, passionate, inside-of-it point of view. I always loved it, and always admired it, and always wanted it desperately to be a film, but I, I don't believe I ever saw it as a film for myself to direct.'[2] When Noyce eventually applied for the job of director, this came in very handy.

Pollack again: 'Initially in our very first screenplay, the melodrama of the piece wasn't utilised the way it should have been. The writer was a wonderful writer, and was so reverential to Graham Greene that he wanted to deal primarily with the philosophical aspects of it. And slowly it got worked on by other writers. And then when Phillip came on and began to work directly with the writers, it found its shape as a melodrama, but continued to be elusive in terms of a satisfying screenplay because of the difficulty of rounding out the American.'[3]

We developed the screenplay at Paramount, employing first Robert Schenkkan, an American writer who had won the Pulitzer Prize for his play *The Kentucky Cycle*. Robert and I returned to Vietnam in

1997 to survey potential locations and mapped out the adaptation. But once Paramount read that screenplay they decided to let it go, to put it in turnaround. Too costly, given its contentious subject matter.

Graham Greene's very personal connections to Indochina inspired him to write his novel. He visited Vietnam four times between 1951 and 1955, and his recollections of those visits are contained in his autobiographical works *Ways of Escape* and *Reflections*. After reading *Ways of Escape*, one could be forgiven for confusing Greene with the fictional character of Thomas Fowler. The novel was first published in 1955.

Soon after publication the American director and writer Joseph L. Mankiewicz purchased the rights. His version was shot in 1956 and 1957 in Saigon on the actual locations and also back at Cinecittá Studios in Rome. As was customary at the time, Mankiewicz chose a European actress to play the Vietnamese girl. Also – probably in response to the pressures of the just-concluded McCarthy era (but surprising because you wonder why he wanted to film the novel in the first place) – Mankiewicz agreed to the suggestion by the notorious CIA operative Edward Lonsdale that the ending of the book should be changed so that the English journalist Thomas Fowler is deceived by the communists into thinking that the innocent American is responsible for the bombing in the Saigon square. In Mankiewicz's version it's a communist plot, not a plot by a CIA-sponsored political splinter group. This suggestion from Lonsdale is documented in the Viking edition of *The Quiet American*, in a letter written by Lonsdale to Mankiewicz in 1956.

It should be added that 'Greene was furious, he called the 1958 film "a complete travesty", "incoherent" and "a real piece of political dishonesty." He also spoke of Mankiewicz's "treachery".'[4]

The project lay dormant while I went off to make *The Saint*. In the meantime, Sydney Pollack teamed up with a British–German company called Intermedia, headed by a Brit called Guy East and a Scotsman, Nigel Sinclair, who agreed to finance further development. Feeling that Schenkkan's version had lost some of the Greene elements that made the novel attractive in the first place, we brought on Christopher Hampton, the Academy Award–winning adaptor of *Dangerous Liaisons*, who finished his draft by the time I completed *The Bone Collector* in 1999.

When Noyce took over he revised the script, as Hampton was to discover much later. 'We had a frank exchange of views. We had tremendous disagreements. But at least Phillip kept me included in discussions right to the end. As a writer for hire, you can't ask for more.'[5] Though touched by many hands, the script 'ended up elegantly written and very much in the Greene spirit'.[6]

In fact, in the months before we started shooting, uncredited work on the screenplay was executed first by Paul Schrader and then Richard LaGravenese (*The Fisher King, The Horse Whisperer*).

In more than one way *The Quiet American* was an extremely difficult film to get made. Pollack: 'We couldn't get a studio in the world interested in making a film about Vietnam at this particular time in America. We were closely involved with a small company called Intermedia, and we had made a film with them called *Sliding Doors* when they were a small company. And as that film had a very high profit-to-cost ratio it made them kind of stars with the German Neuer Markt stock market, where they were able to raise a lot of money to enlarge the company. Bill Horberg, my colleague, and I pushed very hard at that particular time when they had just earned this money in the Neuer Markt. We had interest from Michael Caine, we had interest from Brendan Fraser, we had all of our ducks in a row, and this was the time to press. And to their credit, they went with it. To also give them credit for [their] reasonable amount of caution, they didn't particularly want to go with it as they had the same reservations that most businesspeople in Hollywood had, which was that this is a tough subject to do, that Americans had had it with Vietnam, we'd done our Vietnam War films. It wasn't a Vietnam story about American soldiers fighting in jungles. It was a very complicated, personal triangle where all the people were metaphors without being metaphors, where they had real melodramatic functions, but they each represented philosophical, and political and cultural, opposites and points of view. The energy and the innocence and the good intentions, but perhaps naïvety of America, the old-world wisdom but lack of resources and energy of Europe, and the Eastern inscrutable [sic] getting in between all of this, and being fought over and plied with by East and West. So you had this sort of ideal set-up, but to try to convince a financing company that this was a worthy thing to do was difficult.'⁷ In the end, it was 'an independent Australian–Vietnamese–German–English–American co-production. That's where the creative and financing elements come from – all of those.'⁸

The choice of lead actor wasn't an easy one and Noyce devoted much time to it over the years. The issues involved were complex. The Fowler character had to be well into middle age but still radiate sufficient sex appeal to believably attract and keep a beautiful mistress. And although the unlikely pairing of Fowler and Pyle would eventually slip into lethal sexual rivalry, this could not be obvious from the start. Sean Connery and Russell Crowe were among the possible choices. But either Noyce eventually dropped the idea of using one of them or the actors were not available.

In April 2000, Noyce approached Michael Caine, who immediately agreed to play the part. 'What attracted me to play Thomas Fowler was that it's one of the greatest parts you could get. There's every emotion from A to Z and back again, and he's not only a very deep character, he's a very wide character. When I got the script and re-read the book, I felt I knew how to do this. I was a certain age where I was experienced enough in life myself to be able to understand what drives a man like him, and I was experienced enough as an actor to think that I could play him. And it's a great part for any actor, a really great part. Plus, my criteria for making movies is the script, the script, the script – which of course was great – and who am I working with. I'm working with Phillip Noyce, a great director who I admired, and there is the package. You always go with the package in the end. It's no good me having this great script and going and working with bad actors and a rotten director.

'I did meet Graham Greene, I think, four times. I did a film of one of his books called *The Honorary Consul*, which he actually didn't like very much – the film. He didn't like any films that were made of his work, as a matter of fact, and he came up to me in a restaurant in London actually, and told me in no uncertain terms what he thought of the film. But he did say that he liked my performance. Now, I don't know whether he was telling the truth; he may have just tried to be nice when he'd just been so nasty. I always thought that there must have been something semi-autobiographical there because Graham Greene was a *Times* correspondent who was working in Saigon with a beautiful French mistress, and Thomas Fowler was a *Times* correspondent working in Saigon with a beautiful Vietnamese mistress. And just in observing Greene I got a first inkling of the sort of voice he would have used, the sort of man he would have been and – very important in English society – the class he came from, his education.'[9]

Caine, for various reasons, seems the perfect choice for the part. He belongs to a comparatively small group of actors who really like to travel – and as much of the filming was to be done in a Vietnam still suffering from the effects of the war with America and with only a basic infrastructure, this was an important consideration. Moreover, there probably aren't too many movie stars still alive who have actively been involved in a war on the front line and could draw from that experience. Maurice Joseph Micklewhite (Caine's real name) served with the Royal Fuseliers and had spent most of his two years of National Service in the trenches during the Korean War. Finally, Caine had proven himself as a seducer and lover in several films – even where there was a substantial difference in age between himself and his leading lady, as in *Blame it on Rio*.

'We feel that in this relationship, despite the age difference, he's going to be a reasonable man to the much younger girl; maybe he even has something genuine to offer her because of his age. But the main reason for wanting to cast Michael is because we, the audience, trust Michael Caine. We sort of identify with his basic humanity, we believe in him.'[10]

Or, as producer William Horberg put it, 'He brings such an immense warmth, vulnerability, credibility as a person, as an icon, to this role.'[11] Noyce's choice of Caine proved very lucky for the film's success.

But the Alden Pyle character had yet to be cast. At various stages Johnny Depp and Matt Damon were under consideration, but still no solution to the casting problem could be found.

I went off to Australia to start pre-production on *Rabbit-Proof Fence* and during that period, after some discussion by telephone, Brendan Fraser committed to make *The Quiet American* his next project.

Fraser: 'Initially, I didn't understand if Alden Pyle really was . . . capable of carrying out the actions which he does which cause such great calamity, or if . . . he really did. The specificity of that could only come from taking the best part of what the novel had to provide – which was a very intricate character study in describing virtues which led an audience to believe that he was a man of a duplicitous nature, a man who had a mission, and believed that he was doing what was right for a country in this time and place. And he believed so with such absolute certainty that his actions would justify the end. He truly believes that what he's doing is going to make the world a better place. He believes that he can uphold the virtues of democracy. He believes that the communists are going to take over the world, and that terrifies him to the very core of his being. But of course that gets thrown aside when he falls in love with a woman who he never expected to, and the love that he feels for her is really pure, and it's honest. It's something that's never happened to him before.'[12]

At that time the industry was preparing for a projected US actors' strike and Brendan decided to fit one more movie in before the strike. As he'd just done this big-budget special effects film, he wanted to try something more serious.

The Quiet American was a risky project at any time. But Intermedia felt more inclined to finance because Brendan Fraser had starred in one of the biggest-grossing films of that year – *The Mummy Returns* – and the projected strike would mean a potential product shortage. As it turned out, the strike didn't happen, but nobody knew that until a week before its anticipated start. But the prospect of industrial action very much contributed towards a project like *The Quiet American* being financed and properly budgeted so that it could be filmed on a reasonable scale. Obviously, it's not cheap to re-create a war in Vietnam in the early fifties.

Though we didn't finish shooting *Rabbit-Proof Fence* until mid-November 2001, I had to commit to a start date eight weeks later on *Quiet*, and that began a gruelling period of shooting and editing and then releasing two films simultaneously, which had started in July 2000 and continued to July 2003.

Do Thi Hai Yen, who played Phuong, was discovered after she came to a Saigon casting session with her boyfriend Quang Hai, who was eventually cast for the part of General Thé. Christine King, who had been responsible for casting the children for *Rabbit-Proof Fence*, noticed Hai Yen and asked her to audition. At the time she spoke very little English and had been in a couple of small films but certainly wasn't a highly experienced film actress. I continued to look in other parts of the Vietnamese diaspora world – in London, Paris, New York, Los Angeles and Sydney. But in many ways I was attracted by the same casting idea I had followed for *Rabbit-Proof Fence*, that sometimes the real thing is preferable to somebody that's acting. I found many overseas Vietnamese who looked right but whose body language and outlook on life had become overwhelmingly Westernised, and although, I suppose, the traditional task of an actor is to metamorphose into someone else, Hai Yen was the real thing – an old-fashioned Vietnamese woman of the early 1950s. She'd been cloistered in a Saigon ballet school for several years after growing up in a small northern village where her father was a singer, so she was imbued with traditional values and unpolluted by the homogenising forces of invading Western popular culture. She walked, talked and thought like a Vietnamese from the past. So I cast her.

Michael Caine remembers his first meeting with Do Thi Hai Yen very vividly. 'The first time I saw her in rehearsals, she came in the morning. She was very tiny, no make-up on, little sort of mousy girl, very nervous. And I said to Phillip, "I think we're going to have to find someone else." He said, "No, she can do it." I said, "You sure?" He said, "Yeah, she's got this Vietnamese thing. She's real." I said, "Come and get an American Vietnamese girl," or "There's lots of Vietnamese girls in France, or England – you know, much more, shall we say, worldly kind of girls." This girl looked very innocent. And he said, "No, don't you worry about it." And we rehearsed for four weeks, and Phillip worked so hard with this girl, and he eventually got this incredible performance out of her which quite stunned me. Towards the end of the picture I had long emotional scenes with her, and she went with me the whole way. I built up a relationship with her where she trusted me, and I would whisper to her all the time, "Let's do this. This is what we're going to do now." I never, ever let Phillip hear what I was saying, but I always whispered to her. I said, "I'm starting to get weak now, and now you're gonna be strong." And then Phillip would say "Action" and then we'd do it. And she did it. This girl works so hard and is extremely talented, and fortunately for us she had this extraordinary screen presence. She hardly spoke any English when we first met and she learned

English so fast and it was quite extraordinary to see her progress through the film.'[13]

Back in 1995 I had visited the Vietnam Feature Film Studio, the principal government filmmaking body in Hanoi, who produced films throughout the American war. And there I met a female film editor who trained at the Poona film school in India and was reasonably fluent in English. Tran Anh Hoa became a friend, adviser, translator and guide in the making of *The Quiet American*. And she introduced me to Soviet-trained director Dang Nhat Minh, whose work I would see as a judge at the 1997 Asia Pacific Film Festival in Sydney, where we awarded a jury prize to his film *The Return*. Dang Nhat Minh agreed to become second unit director on *The Quiet American*. Between the two of them they were very essential allies for the project, advising on the protocol of working with Vietnamese. And because of their excellent standing in the artistic community in Hanoi, the seat of power in Vietnam, each of them was a bridge between the old and the new guard – the old guard being those Vietnamese who took an active role in fighting the war against the French and the Americans, and the new guard who are post-revolutionary people born perhaps before reunification but who reached their maturity in the years after, in the post–American war years. Dang Nhat Minh had explained to me his own interpretation of 'the quiet american' of the title. To him, the quiet american was the pilot of the B-52 bomber who was flying silently above the clouds when he pressed the button that released the bomb that killed Minh's doctor father down below in the DMZ during the war. Minh's first-hand experience of the agony of war would later prove vital in bringing reality to the brutal post-bombing scene in the film, because he personally cast and prepared the Vietnamese actors featured as the victims of that bombing. In addition, Hoa introduced Vietnamese screenwriter Hong Ngat, who as a young woman had performed in a theatre troupe along the Ho Chi Minh Trail for Vietcong troops. Later she would be crucial in obtaining the necessary permits to allow shooting to proceed in Vietnam.

Still, the problems ahead for producer Bill Horberg were immense. 'I'd never been to Southeast Asia before, but from our first meeting in the planning of this project, Phil Noyce insisted, and quite correctly, that this film be shot on location where it was written, in Vietnam. It was going to be one of the first Western films of any size shot in that country. We went there in the fall of 2000, and started a scouting process of six or seven months looking for the locations of Greene's novel, many of which still exist today, but a great deal of the neighbourhoods he was describing, the central square of Saigon (now Ho Chi Minh City), just don't exist as they did 50 years ago. So we went through an incredibly extensive search of the country to try to find the locations that we could cobble together to re-create Greene's Saigon of the early 1950s.'[14]

Once again, Noyce chose Chris Doyle as his DoP. The choice immediately seems more appropriate this time than it did for *Rabbit-Proof Fence*.

Well, you know, Chris is in many ways Thomas Fowler, the part played by Michael Caine. Chris is an Australian who has run away from himself to Asia, reinvented himself there, and is absolutely and utterly addicted to the place. He feels at home in Asia but alienated in his home nation. Chris knows the smell, the quality of light, the psychology under the surface of this story.

'He's a man who couldn't really live anywhere else, and interestingly when we were shooting in Sydney on many weekends at wrap-up on a Friday night, Chris would catch a flight back to Hong Kong, Beijing or Taiwan, and then on Sunday night he'd catch a flight back to Sydney arriving at about 6 am just after the curfew was lifted on arrivals, and at 7.30 he'd be there on the set ready for work again, having buoyed himself with the sounds, the smells, the sights of his beloved Asia. And it's that sense of really understanding the rhythms of a place that Chris brings to the film in his lighting and his compositions.'[15]

After completing the *Rabbit* shoot, Chris and I flew from the outback of South Australia, stopped overnight in Sydney and then continued on to start pre-production in Ho Chi Minh City. Roger Ford, who production- and costume-designed *Rabbit*, had already started about a month earlier up in Vietnam, and line producer Antonia Barnard had been working for a few months on the production side. But it was going to be a helter-skelter preparation because I was already into post-production on *Rabbit* with no time for any rest. We weren't only racing the ticking clock of the impending actors' strike but also the necessity to complete filming during the cooler part of the year.

Immediately before the actual shoot, the principal actors rehearsed in Sydney for several weeks. Caine worked with Do Thi Hai Yen, while Fraser came to grips with his Pyle character: 'I think the rehearsal period before we shipped out to the location was invaluable for me. It not only allowed me to get to know the other cast members, but it allowed me to scour over the text to work with Christopher Hampton, our writer, to ask questions great and small, study the storyboards, and watch films of a similar genre. It was an intensive period of focus, really. And to tell you the truth, I probably did a little bit more research on Vietnam than I think Alden did. He seemed like he was book smart, straight out of Ivy League college. He'd been educated and he meant to do well, but at the same time we have to remember that he is on a mission, and we later learn that he's working for the office of the OSS, which is currently being called the CIA.'[16] Maybe Sydney Pollack comes closest to analysing Pyle when he says, 'Good intentions are often the most damaging and dangerous motives for terrible behaviour. It's always more dangerous when people think there is virtue in what they're doing. It gets close to religion.'[17] In that respect, the otherwise very different characters of Alden Pyle and A.O. Neville in *Rabbit-Proof Fence* are frighteningly similar.

The film shoot began in February 2001 and ended four months later in June.

There were the logistical problems you always have on a distant location, and particularly in a country with a relatively undeveloped road system, where it took a long time to change locations through crowded streets and narrow roads. In some parts of the country the accommodation wasn't of a high standard, although that's rapidly changing and mostly the crew stayed in five-star hotels.

Sydney Pollack, the executive producer with much experience in Western countries, eventually had to adapt to Eastern patience. 'Everything was an obstacle. The permits were a nightmare. Moving equipment was a nightmare. The censors were a nightmare. You just had to be patient.'[18] But Michael Caine harbours fond memories of the shoot. 'I had many pre-conceived notions about Vietnam, and every one of them was wrong. I thought it would be a war-torn country, very bitter people. Instead, I found a very beautiful country with few signs of war. I never encountered any animosity, just people who seemed genuinely pleased to see us.'[19]

Remembers producer Bill Horberg: 'We've heard a lot of stories about the challenges and difficulties of filming on location in Vietnam today. But because Phil Noyce had spent a lot of time on the ground here developing relationships with important people in the film industry, and had a spirit of wanting this film to be made in real partnership and collaboration with the Vietnamese, we were given access at high levels of the government and permission to shoot. We found ourselves delightfully working with almost 400 Vietnamese people employed on the crew of the film with Dang Nhat Minh, one of the most important Vietnamese directors, working hand in hand with Phillip as both the second unit director of the film, but also as a critical adviser to all the correct details of the place and of the people and of the story. I mean, there was a real determined effort to get it right, which couldn't have been achieved without the level of cooperation that we had, and the deep involvement of the people of Vietnam, who were anxious themselves to see this story re-created and done properly.'[20]

The Quiet American is a novel very close to the Vietnamese people, because just as Westerners find it illuminating about some of the reasons why we might have prosecuted that war, it helps the Vietnamese to understand why they were on the receiving end of hell for all that time. Our screenplay was read by their government censors who were on the set every day, but they never commented adversely on any content. The government assisted us to find and lock down all our locations, and facilitated the almost impossible task of staging huge explosions in the middle of Saigon in one of the busiest squares in Vietnam, which we were able to close for almost a week. We still had to negotiate with each individual shopkeeper and business in that square because, although Vietnam has a centralised Communist government, it's mostly a market economy. We had to pay each one of them and negotiate a contract with every single shop. In theory, it meant each little stall could have stopped us, and there were lots around . . . but they all cooperated. As I'd found working in Russia, there are some advantages for film crews trying to gain permissions in former totalitarian countries. Once the central government says yes, everyone follows.

We were assisted in all of this by the close relationship between Vietnam and Australia. About a year before shooting, America had finally gotten around to establishing an embassy in Vietnam and to officially recognising the Republic of Vietnam. But Australia did that back in December 1972. Within three weeks of the Whitlam Labor government coming to power, a four-man embassy was established at the Metropol Hotel in Hanoi, even while Nixon was delivering his Christmas surprise to the Vietnamese and bombing the city. So there's been this long political relationship from 1972 – 30 years of the Australians being in there. And Australia was one of the first Western nations to contribute towards reconstruction after the war. We had to cope with different cultural necessities in a country that has a unique history and different values, but at least our diplomats were well versed and well liked, particularly the ambassador at the time, Michael Mann (no relation to the film director).

Horberg: 'The Saigon that Greene wrote about no longer exists. So one of the real challenges we had as a production team in going to Vietnam was how to cobble together, from disparate locations around the country, the neighbourhoods and locations that were central to the telling of this story. The Cho Lan neighbourhood described extensively in the novel was mainly shot in a town called Hoi An, which is in the central coastal region about an hour outside of Da Nang. Other elements of Saigon were in fact shot in the north in the capital city of Hanoi, which is today much more intact in terms of the French colonial architecture of the period. It's a much more preserved place that has locations that were appropriate to the 50-year-old setting of this story. In fact, we shot the explosion in the square in the actual square that was written about, and where the historical event had actually taken place.'[21]

The explosion is the central sequence of the film, the key to our understanding of Pyle's character. It was shot on Rue Catinat outside Saigon's Continental Hotel, by the second unit under director Dang Nhat Minh. Extensive digital manipulation was necessary to re-create the ensemble look of the buildings surrounding the square. The real importance of the sequence, though, is on a different level, as Brendan Fraser would discover.

'It was an atrocious vision, all those mangled bodies on the street. And those are people who really have limbs missing: whether they've lost them or they were the result of birth defects, having stepped on a mine or a genetic disorder, having been affected by toxins or something like that. And to think that they would allow themselves to be dressed with special effects make-up to make it appear that they had just suffered these kinds of horrible injuries . . . Just looking at it as a human being standing there and seeing that, and hot weather with the smell of burning tyres and gasoline and just wreck [sic] everywhere, and knowing that underneath it all we're really just actors, we're people, we're hired here to do a job . . . But the commitment that the Vietnamese put into that was absolutely just stirring, and harrowing in a way that I never expected it to be, and there was absolutely no acting required at all to be a part of that. It affected me, it made me feel just awful to be that close to something that I pray I hope I never ever have to be in any measure of reality, but if that's as close as it gets I certainly have a clear understanding of what it means to be that terrified. And then to think that the person that I'm playing is in no small part responsible for it.'[22]

Though it is on a very different plane, there is another quite extraordinary scene in *The Quiet American*: its opening sequence. A river, rice fields, people on pushbikes, a warm tropical night; on the surface, the atmosphere is that of a tranquil small town. The viewer then notices, while the credits are rolling, that something – it's not clear what – is lurking in the background. It could be a big thunderstorm gathering, it could be a war raging in the far distance. When the camera slowly tilts down, all of a sudden the idyll is shattered as we notice a corpse floating in the water. Visually it is one of the strongest cinematic openings in a long time and absolutely coherent with the rest of the film.

That was my idea. It was a re-shoot of something that failed the first time. Originally it was to open with a Vietnamese fishing net rising to reveal the body of Alden Pyle in the net. But something went wrong and we had to come back and re-shoot that shot in a simpler manner. Most of the look of that sequence was achieved later by computer imagery. It was actually shot in the late afternoon and then the light was repainted in the computer. And all the tracer bullets and distant explosions were added in post-production.

While Noyce was feverishly working on his film about the origins of the single most important political event of the second half of the twentieth century, he couldn't possibly have imagined how much his work would soon become entangled in the military events brewing in the twenty-first century.

The first public test-screening of *The Quiet American* was held on 10 September 2001 in New Jersey, about half an hour outside Manhattan. It was a rainy night and the screening was delayed for three-quarters of an hour because Harvey Weinstein, the head of Miramax, had stopped to conclude the purchase of another film by an Australian director, Gregor Jordan's *Buffalo Soldiers*[23] – a caustic view of American soldiers set in Germany in the 1980s, which was screening that night at the Toronto Film Festival. That first-cut version of *Quiet* was 125 minutes long and the screening went reasonably well. We all agreed to meet next morning at Miramax headquarters on Greenwich Avenue in downtown New York, several blocks from the World Trade Center. Next night I was to test-screen *Rabbit-Proof Fence* in the Miramax theatre.

At 8.40 am on September 11, Kathleen McLaughlin and I found ourselves approaching Greenwich Avenue to deliver a video copy of *Rabbit* to Miramax and set up their theatre for the test-screening that night. As we neared the intersection I could see people running frantically along the street and pointing up into the air, and when we turned the corner there was what looked like a small commuter plane sticking out of the World Trade Center, having passed over us just 40 seconds earlier. And we stood there outside the Miramax building for the next two hours as the whole ugly tragedy unfolded before our eyes. We eventually met with Harvey Weinstein to discuss *The Quiet American* about two days later, at the offices of Talkbooks on the upper west side, where Miramax had set up an emergency office. A month later we returned to the New York area for the first of six additional previews and, as could be expected, the sequence of the aftermath of the bombing in the Saigon square reminded the audience of the carnage of that September day and was not at all well received. At a time when Americans were not in the mood for self-criticism or self-analysis, it seemed the whole movie had collided with history in a most unfortunate manner, because subsequent test-screenings kept sliding down in score. By late November we decided to give up screening and finish the film as best we could. But everyone with access to those scores was extremely pessimistic about the movie's prospects.

Noyce was still feeling pessimistic during a low-key internal pre-premiere for crew and cast on 24 March 2002 in Sydney at the Fox Studios cinemas in Moore Park. He addressed the audience very briefly, indicating that this screening might possibly be the first and only time the film would be seen. To those in attendance, *The Quiet American* immediately revealed its beauty and importance. Wonderful cinematography, superb acting, and artistic and political relevance merged in what was undoubtedly Noyce's most mature film. However, due to the nature of the screening, nothing of this was published in the media.

The film was eventually finished and delivered to Miramax in May of 2002, and Harvey Weinstein secretly screened the finished version to some friendly film critics, including former *New York Times* reviewer Janet Maslin. Janet severely criticised the movie in a private memo to Miramax, which was leaked to me.

In July 2002 I was told by Mark Gill, West Coast vice-president at Miramax who had brought the project into the company and later left to head up Warner Bros. Independent, that Harvey Weinstein wasn't inclined to release the film theatrically at all, given the negative reaction at the test-screenings. With Michael Caine and Sydney Pollack, I started to agitate to resurrect a film that looked like it had been confined to the vaults. Of course, in the lead-up to the actors' strike, all the studios had stockpiled product, and both *Quiet* and *Rabbit* were purchased by Miramax during a period when distribution companies were more adventurous because of the necessity to make sure that they had product available should production be disrupted.

We eventually cajoled Weinstein into entering the film in the Toronto Film Festival, and I contacted an old friend, Mickey Cottrell, a publicist I'd worked with when I was first in Hollywood and somebody who only tackles projects he really adores – which gives him enormous kudos as a publicist. Mickey saw *Quiet*, loved it, and agreed to try to raise awareness prior to Toronto, where the film was very well received by critics, film writers and the public, with many calling it Michael Caine's finest performance ever.

In fact, the reviews following the Toronto screening – where *The Quiet American* received standing ovations – and after the film's eventual limited release in November (to qualify for an Oscar run) were extremely enthusiastic. Caine's performance was universally acclaimed (*Time* magazine: Caine's 'career-capping performance guarantees him an aisle seat on Oscar Night';[24] the *New York Times*: 'a performance of astonishing understatement whose tone wavers delicately between irony and sadness'[25]). Equally, Chris Doyle's superb camerawork (*Los Angeles Times*: 'capturing both the chaos of Saigon street life and the country's parallel mystery and delicate beauty'[26]) and Do Thi Hai Yen's stunning acting debut were praised. As well, many critics acknowledged the film's superb direction. *Rolling Stone* stressed, 'It's a personal best for Aussie director Phillip Noyce, on a roll with his remarkable *Rabbit-Proof Fence*.'[27] Not least of the reasons for the film's success was Noyce having remained true to Greene's original story. To sum up: he had made a rewarding and intelligent feature with wide appeal, which was not just 'art-house fare'. In fact, the film seemed just about perfect, except for its stated un-American attitude.

Miramax honcho Harvey Weinstein claimed that after 9/11 he was told, 'You can't release this now: it's unpatriotic.'[28] But the blame lay not with Noyce, but with Graham Greene for the original novel's clear political statements. Noyce only exceeded Greene in this in the film's ending, which shows a series of newspaper headlines tracing the escalation of US involvement in Vietnam – something Greene naturally couldn't possibly have done in 1955. The *New York Times* said: 'The movie doesn't convey much strong political passion. Pyle may be buffoonish, but he's not evil.'[29] It was no wonder, then, that the media was starting to have second thoughts about Miramax's reluctance to release the film.

Some of the film writers were extremely hostile in their comments about Miramax, and in some ways the company was threatened with

media insurrection unless they could be seen to be treating with respect a film that many critics were acclaiming. Already in *Variety* there were rumblings from chief film critic Todd McCartney that Weinstein was suppressing the movie because he didn't want Michael Caine's performance to be in competition with Daniel Day-Lewis in *Gangs of New York*, a film in which Miramax had a US$35-million-plus investment. For our film, Miramax had paid just US$5.5 million for the US rights. In addition, a writer from the *New York Times* was actively pursuing the story that Harvey Weinstein was suppressing *Quiet* because of his own personal political ambitions in the New York area. Neither of those stories, to my mind, had any reality. But nevertheless, they were an indication of how the media latched on to *Quiet* and wanted to protect and defend it – particularly in an era where extreme conservatives held power in Washington and the nation was in the early stages of preparation for the 2003 war against Iraq. So what had been completely unpalatable just a year earlier when the film was shown in rough cut was now seen as part of a necessary pre-war debate. And in order to suppress the negative publicity, Harvey Weinstein immediately announced that *Quiet* would be released for a two-week season in New York and Los Angeles for Oscar consideration. But the Miramax Oscar campaign was always half-hearted, even after the National Board of Review named it fourth-best film of 2002. I do believe that both Harvey Weinstein and Sydney Pollack, as leading liberal intellectual lights, were disappointed and embarrassed by Brendan Fraser's version of Alden Pyle, both feeling that I had constructed a character that too easily made a bad guy out of the quiet American.

But as the old saying goes: even bad publicity is good publicity. As had happened in Australia some months earlier when Bolt and Akerman's attack on *Rabbit-Proof Fence* had bolstered its performance at the box office, Noyce's team took advantage of Miramax's reluctance to release the film.

Mickey Cottrell single-handedly revived the film by drawing attention to Miramax's negativity. Overnight the movie became controversial as people rushed to defend it, culminating with an article in the *Washington Times* with the headline 'Let the quiet American speak' (*laughs*). Exhibition became a cause célèbre, a rallying point for liberals across America, demanding the public be allowed to see this suppressed work of art. But even Harvey Weinstein realised the value of the media interest. At a New York meeting in early 2003 he first demanded a US$1000 payment for every time I had defamed him in the press, but then went on to say that we should keep it up as obviously we'd hit on a marvellous angle to publicise the film.

I had been attracted to the novel because it was a great murder mystery, a love story and a political thriller, all rolled into one. Also, its portrayal of Alden Pyle, the evangelical American political animal of the early fifties period, defined the basic tenets of American foreign policy at that time, and the icing on the cake that made it irresistible as a work of art was this portrait of American intervention into the sovereignty of a foreign country. In the fight against communism, the CIA devised a campaign of dirty tricks – destabilisation, misinformation, and so on, which have continued to underpin American foreign policy and precipitated numerous political catastrophes around the world. Of course, those policies were borne out of a very real belief that as the melting pot of all humanity, the social experiment that is the United States of America has a responsibility to the rest of the world to intervene, to take care.

In early 2003 I was in Hollywood at producer Mike Medavoy's house for a meeting addressed by ex–Australian foreign minister Gareth Evans, former US secretary of state Warren Christopher and ex–US president Bill Clinton. The theme of the meeting was 'Why do people dislike America?' The Australian spoke first, very gently, but coherently, laying out why some in the rest of the world may have lost patience with American foreign policy. The two Americans, including the former president, didn't answer any of his statements, but instead gave us a rundown of what was wrong with all the major non-US world leaders (*laughs*). That seemed like a perfect illustration of the problem.

Despite all this political arguing, Noyce never feared that the controversy might overshadow the film's merits.

'I don't think it was ever gonna overshadow the movie, just draw attention to a film that would otherwise be hard to promote.'[30]

Once it became clear that Miramax wasn't even prepared to treat crew and cast to the usual proper premiere festivities, other avenues were at hand. Fraser: 'When we left Vietnam, Phillip made a promise that he would thank the people who truly physically did the heavy lifting that allowed us to create this really important piece of cinema, and that's the Vietnamese people, and acknowledge the support that we got from the Ministry of Information and Culture, and also from members of the Communist Party. So in December 2002, just before Christmas, we flew to Hanoi and had a screening of the film for some 1400 people in one theatre, and then a couple other hundred in a theatre directly beneath it. We were received by Reuters, and CNN, and AP, and the BBC and many others. It was a big event for many reasons, but most importantly it was a big event because that's never happened before. A Hollywood film hasn't been shot in Vietnam, certainly not one with the subject matter such as this, and certainly not one that received the support that we have. I think it's poignant and poetic and telling that the place where we made this film received the honour of allowing us to give it back to them – a premiere of this film in Hanoi before a US premiere.'[31]

Unfortunately, the premiere wasn't all roses for Noyce.

'The film had been picked up for distribution across Vietnam by an independent local company. At first we thought that the film maybe wouldn't be accepted by the Vietnamese authorities, but after they viewed it they passed it for release across Vietnam. So I found myself with Tzi Ma and Brendan and Hai Yen on the stage in a downtown Saigon cinema before 1500 people for the film's premiere. And looking out towards the crowd, I saw all these little red dots on the top of

the video camcorders that were recording the festivities. When the movie started I stood up to leave because I'd seen the movie a couple of hundred times before, and I looked into the audience, and I saw again those little dots. And sure enough, by the time I got back to Australia, about a week later, the newspaper reports were already appearing: Vietnam had been flooded with tens of thousands of pirated copies of *The Quiet American*, copies that were made by the audience members at the premiere in Ho Chi Minh City. Within three weeks, the Vietnamese independent distributor's vision of opening up Vietnam to foreign movies in movie houses was destroyed by the pirate video sellers who set up outside each of the cinemas that were showing the film. For two dollars you could buy one ticket to see the movie, or for 50 cents you could buy a completely terrible copy with bad sound and bad image, but nevertheless, for a family that's earning just a few dollars a week, maybe it was worth it. All the publicity that the film had attracted – all the publicity that came from the first-ever Hollywood star premiere in Vietnam's history, with the real Hollywood actors, the director, and the local star – all of that work just went towards financing the pirates.'[32]

Despite the ongoing political trouble, 2002 ended, and 2003 started, on a high note artistically for Noyce. He had launched on the world markets two serious and successful films within one year, quite an extraordinary achievement. Having often been unfairly maligned in recent years, suddenly he was regarded with the utmost respect. During the Oscar campaign – with Michael Caine short-listed for Best Actor – a Noyce-style overkill sometimes seemed to be approaching.[33] But he sees only advantages in this situation.

In many ways the fact that two movies were out at the same time was a way of raising awareness for both. The *New York Times* ran an article about both films, as did the *Los Angeles Times*, and the *Times* and the *Guardian* in the UK, and so on. So many articles were initiated because one director had two films in distribution simultaneously. We even found that the awards for Best Director of the

Year from the US National Board of Review and the London Film Critics Circle came for both films.

I wouldn't have been able to make those two films if I hadn't served my time in Hollywood. *The Quiet American* wasn't a cheap movie at about US$25 million, and could never have been financed if I hadn't established a reputation as a director who made commercially viable movies. It's certainly interesting to see that the very reasons both films might be limited in their appeal was also the reason they found relative success. It's the trickiness of the subject matter and the themes tackled that made them attractive to audiences, at least in the comparatively limited releases they enjoyed worldwide. It's tremendously reassuring that you can make films from the heart and still find commercial as well as critical success.

One of a director's biggest fears, particularly as you grow older, is that you'll become out of touch with your audience and reach your 'use-by date' as a director. In some ways, I was beginning to feel too old to play the studio game of escapist entertainment.

It's also a matter of self-preservation, because if you continue to hunt with the pack chasing lowest-common-denominator commercial cinema, eventually you're no longer going to be obsessed with issues and ideas that your financiers are going to think are viable for such big-budget movies. Making smaller films which don't have to reach such a broad audience enables a director to keep making movies for longer.

It appears Noyce has now found a viable path for the future: with his immense experience and substantial Hollywood background, he is able to tackle subjects nearer his heart in films aimed at a more dedicated and slightly older age group. After his more limited Australian films and more popcorn-oriented Hollywood movies, he finally seems in touch with the world.

---

[1] Unpublished original DVD Phillip Noyce interview.
[2] Unpublished original DVD Sydney Pollack interview.
[3] Ibid.
[4] David Gritten, 'The film that scared a studio', *Daily Telegraph*, 26 November 2002.

[5] Quoted in Gritten, 'The film that scared a studio'.

[6] Kenneth Turan, 'An elegant story of corruptibility', *Los Angeles Times*, 22 November 2002.

[7] Unpublished original DVD Sydney Pollack interview.

[8] Unpublished original DVD Phillip Noyce interview.

[9] Unpublished original DVD Michael Caine interview.

[10] Unpublished original DVD Phillip Noyce interview.

[11] Unpublished original DVD Bill Horberg interview.

[12] Unpublished original DVD Brendan Fraser interview.

[13] Unpublished original DVD Michael Caine interview.

[14] Unpublished original DVD Bill Horberg interview.

[15] Unpublished original DVD Phillip Noyce interview.

[16] Unpublished original DVD Brendan Fraser interview.

[17] Unpublished original DVD Sydney Pollack interview.

[18] Quoted in Richard Corliss, 'A sigh for old Saigon', *Time Magazine Asia*, 22 October 2002.

[19] Quoted in ibid.

[20] Unpublished original DVD Bill Horberg interview.

[21] Ibid.

[22] Unpublished original DVD Brendan Fraser interview.

[23] Even this film was shelved for a long time. In a conversation held on 15 May 2003, Jordan was anxious not to blame Miramax for this, and points out that the later delays particularly were caused by his own concern for the film's chances at the box office. 'The audience have to be in the right mood', and with 9/11, Afghanistan and the war in Iraq, it seemed ill-advised to depict American soldiers shooting up heroin, and stealing and selling their own weapons. Although, on one hand, his film hits more of a 'raw nerve' than Noyce's, he was quick to label it as 'not damaging but satirical and almost philosophical', with *M*A*S*H* as its closest equivalent.

[24] Corliss, 'A sigh for old Saigon'.

[25] Stephen Holden, 'A jaded affair in a Vietnam already at war', *New York Times*, 22 November 2002.

[26] Turan, 'An elegant story of corruptibility'.

[27] Peter Travers, '*The Quiet American*', *Rolling Stone*, 20 November 2002.

[28] Quoted in Corliss, 'A sigh for old Saigon'.

[29] Holden, 'A jaded affair in a Vietnam already at war'.

[30] Unpublished original DVD Phillip Noyce interview.

[31] Unpublished original DVD Brendan Fraser interview.

[32] Unpublished original DVD Phillip Noyce interview.

[33] Caine missing out on an Oscar must have been a bitter pill, although Noyce had never really wanted to be in the race: 'You're just falling prey to a ridiculous competitiveness which we know is meaningless.' The Academy Awards in 2003 were irregular anyway, considering the build-up of anger over Weinstein's perceived pre-Oscar antics and tactics. But often whistleblowers are not popular either, and Caine might have been perceived as one of the more prominent ones.

Chapter 17
PHILLIP NOYCE – THE ESSENCE

I guess it's a funny obsession with spying on people.

So the triple feature that is Noyce's work comes to a preliminary end, or rather, to an interlude: to be continued. But before the credits roll and the curtain falls, it is time to ask what makes a Phillip Noyce film. Is there anything unifying in Noyce's work? Are there traits that make them typical Noyce films?

Noyce's body of work to date isn't easily classifiable, which pleases the director. In 1990 he was quoted as saying, 'If anyone ever writes a summary of my work, I hope they call me a chameleon, because they'd find it totally impossible to categorise me, at least stylistically.'[1] Indeed, they lack a common stylistic approach. Noyce is one of the few A-league Hollywood directors without a clear-cut artistic signature.

His first twenty years as a filmmaker were a constant search to find his own way to develop his very real talent. His early experimental films were followed by socially committed documentaries, low-budget features and TV miniseries, and then by Hollywood blockbusters requiring ever more people and ever bigger budgets. He has alternately been hailed as a non-mainstream director of 'worthy cause films' and branded a sell-out to commercialism. But Noyce has never been interested in simply imitating Hollywood. Instead, he has always been interested in manipulating an audience's emotions by providing gripping entertainment that has the widest possible general appeal.

'You have to be a megalomaniac to want to do this – and

I know it's hugely presumptuous – but I do gain a perverse pleasure in watching people in a theatre writhe en masse,' Noyce has freely admitted.[2] His wife, Jan Sharp, explains: 'Once Phillip was a big success making these films, people in Australia said to me, "Why doesn't he do the films he wants to do?" And I say, "These Clancy films absolutely *are* the films he wants to do. He loves that world." These films are very sincere expressions of his personality and temperament and mental life. They are absolutely his material.'[3]

Gillian Armstrong adds a slightly different perspective: 'Phil started with that grass-roots political conviction and that's still strongly there today. But on the practical side of actually getting a film made, they were the sort of films that he was offered and he had no choice. Still, at the same time, he does love action and he's the first to say so, and he loves doing his big action films. Over the years he sometimes said to me, "Gill, you wouldn't believe the money they [the studio] are giving me", saying, "Add another explosion." And of course no one ever says that to *me*. "You wouldn't believe it, they are giving me a storyboard artist four months beforehand" – the things I never would get. He was into the Hollywood game and politics. At the same time, I think that *Newsfront* is the film that he is most proud of.'[4]

But even in his American films he remains a wandering spirit, working in different genres and using different filmmaking styles depending on the stories, as he explained in the late 1990s:

'So given the limit on how many films you can make, and the fact that films are your life, and the fact that I want to continually be challenged as a life goal and as a film goal, I guess I want to keep making different kinds of movies. Each film I make – I hope – will be very different from the last one.'[5]

But even if no particular Noyce style exists, his feeling for actors certainly deserves a special mention. Nicole Kidman and Angelina Jolie had their breakthrough roles in his films, catapulting them into the pantheon of superstardom. This success may be partly due to Noyce's extraordinary skills in character development. Even those films of his that heavily rely on suspense all have characters that are extremely well developed and multi-dimensional. One needs only to compare his Tom Clancy adaptations with those of other directors for this to be apparent. In *The Quiet American* this has reached its peak so far: the film is a perfectly balanced combination of a story-driven political thriller with a character-driven emotional triangle. Possibly this film and *Clear and Present Danger* will eventually become his best-remembered works because both deal with issues that have become fundamentally important to the world's future. Noyce is generally best known, however, for his close affinity with all things surveillance-related, for the spying and high-tech gizmos which can be found en masse in his Hollywood films between 1990 and 2000.

I get my researchers to uncover the latest technology in any particular field and then push that technology a little bit further. Because you think to yourself, 'This is what's available or is now being used by the military or government agencies, so therefore what's being tested at the moment will be an advance on that and then we need to make another advance. Because the film will come out in eighteen months, so you need to project a little further ahead again.

The lure of Hollywood is always present, and many foreign directors who have succumbed have returned home disillusioned by their loss of artistic control over their projects. Phillip Noyce succeeded in the studio system, but his success came at a high price, sometimes hampering his artistic standing. 'Noyce remains proficient but is always at the mercy of his scripts,' wrote one commentator.[6] And in Hollywood, many 'producers and directors prefer to use multiple writers, hoping to bring in different points of view. It is not uncommon for a movie to have exhausted ten writers or more to complete the job.'[7] When you add to this the studios' infatuation with changing films at the last moment based on test-screenings or financial constraints, it is apparent that Noyce's success has been hard-earned on a personal level.

Unlike many of his fellow filmmakers, Noyce always worked loyally within the studio system and never tried to be an auteur filmmaker. But when he decided to drop *The Sum of All Fears*, a project that might have turned into another highlight of his Hollywood directing career, Noyce chose to return to Australia, where he has subsequently produced some of his most mature work to date. But even at that stage he was being dictated to by Hollywood, when Miramax delayed the release of *The Quiet American* despite its huge critical acclaim. Denouncing its 'lily-livered corporate entertainment executives', *The Australian* concluded: 'there are disturbing signs that Miramax is so rattled by the post-September 11 atmosphere that it is setting up the film to fail.'[8] Well, it didn't quite fail, but it's not hard to imagine how Harvey Weinstein's machinations might have further rattled Noyce's confidence in the studio system.

It seems that Noyce's sudden departure from the United States in 2000 was his way of taking time out, even though in this case it meant embarking on two new projects in just one year. With this move back to his roots across the Pacific, Noyce regained the artistic freedom that he had enjoyed a decade before, but now from a far superior position than when he had first left Australia. He now had the contacts to raise sufficient funds for his films without having to be at the mercy of government funding bodies run by bureaucrats, and he was now an accepted authority in the world of Australian film. (*Who Weekly* magazine ranked him the 13th most influential entertainer in Australia and the only film director on their list of the top 25.[9]) He was now self-assured enough to choose stories that were meaningful to him, and skilled in marketing his films and reaching his audience even in troubled times.

And Noyce also proved wrong those critics who had accused him of selling out. It immediately became apparent that his social and humanitarian concerns had remained intact despite the glitzy surface of his Hollywood output.

At this point, the repercussions of Noyce's return to Australia for his Hollywood career are unclear. Gillian Armstrong is optimistic: 'I think it should be the best point of Phil's career right now because he's proved that he's a commercial filmmaker and now with these last two films he's proved that there's also some artistic integrity. So he may now get the rare gems of the few times where the studios fund a film that actually has artistic integrity. I think that this return to Australia doing *Rabbit-Proof Fence* and doing *The Quiet American* – which has been his passion that he's wanted to do for many years – isn't that, in a sense, going back to more of the committed films?'[10]

Noyce himself claims that, of all his films, *Rabbit-Proof Fence* is both the best and the one closest to his heart because, he says, it portrayed Aborigines in a positive way not seen before in Australia. The film overturned conventions by celebrating Aboriginal family history as an important component of mainstream Australian history. A closer look at his body of work reveals that he has always had a deep concern with the plight of the Australian Aborigines.

And Noyce is determined to proceed further in that direction:

A project that I really would like to make is about Bennelong, the Aborigine who was befriended by Governor Phillip at the time of the establishment of the first colony at Sydney Cove. He so impressed Governor Phillip that he was sent to the court of the king in England, where he became a celebrity of sorts, impressing with his intelligence and wit, coinciding with a general interest 'in the Noble Savage'. This is really a story of the absolute first contact between the blacks and the whites in Australia, of the establishment of the European colony in Australia, but it's also a story of the origins of the extreme clash of cultures that goes to the heart of the Australian experience.

Such a project might again subject Noyce to the stinging barbs of the – political – critics. What makes him endure all these ups and downs? What ultimately leads him to make his films?

I first became interested in movies as a result of my fascination with the travelling tent shows that came to my small country town when I was a child. And my fascination with the tent shows was an attraction to the ability of the performer to engage the audience. So I've always seen myself as an entertainer of the public. Nothing gives me greater pleasure than to sit in a cinema where one of my films is screening and to feel the pleasure that I'm giving the audience. That's what makes it all worthwhile. I'd make films for nothing if they told me there was no other way of getting a film financed, just so that I could continue to feel the thrill of that contact with a satisfied public as you take them into the make-believe world that you've created for them.

Music slowly fades. Curtain.

---

[1] Michael Singer, *A Cut Above – 50 Film Directors Talk about their Craft* (Los Angeles: Lone Eagle, 1998), p. 204.
[2] Quoted in David Hay, 'Patriot missile takes on lethal weapon', *The Bulletin*, 23 June 1992, p. 98.
[3] Jan Sharp interview.
[4] Gillian Armstrong interview.
[5] Quoted in Singer, *A Cut Above*, p. 203.
[6] Mark Bould, 'Phillip Noyce', in *The Wallflower Critical Guide to Contemporary North American Directors* (London: 2001), p. 334.
[7] Art Linson, *What Just Happened? Bitter Hollywood Tales from the Front Line* (New York/London: Bloomsbury, 2002), p. 120.
[8] Lynden Barber, 'Out takes', *The Australian*, 29 November 2002.
[9] 'Australia's most influential entertainers', *Who Weekly* quoted in *Gold Coast Bulletin*, 13 December 2002.
[10] Gillian Armstrong interview.

Index